OXFORD STUDIES IN EUROPEAN LAW

Series Editors

PAUL CRAIG
Professor of English Law at St John's College, Oxford

GRÁINNE DE BÚRCA
Professor of Law at New York University School of Law

Compliance with European Consumer Law

OXFORD STUDIES IN EUROPEAN LAW

The aim of this series is to publish important and original research on EU law. The focus is on scholarly monographs, with a particular emphasis on those which are interdisciplinary in nature. Edited collections of essays will also be included where they are appropriate. The series is wide in scope and aims to cover studies of particular areas of substantive and of institutional law, historical works, theoretical studies, and analyses of current debates, as well as questions of perennial interest such as the relationship between national and EU law and the novel forms of governance emerging in and beyond Europe. The fact that many of the works are interdisciplinary will make the series of interest to all those concerned with the governance and operation of the EU.

OTHER TITLES IN THIS SERIES

Legislative Authority and Independence in the European Union
Martijn van den Brink

Secession and European Union Law
Núria González Campañá

Fiscal State Aid Law and Harmful Tax Competition in the European Union
Dimitrios Kyriazis

The Abuse of Constitutional Identity in the European Union
Julian Scholtes

Judging European Democracy
The Role and Legitimacy of National Constitutional Courts in the EU
Nik de Boer

EU Values Before the Court of Justice
Foundations, Potential, Risk
Luke Dimitrios Spieker

Postnational Constitutionalism
Europe and the Time of Law
Paul Linden-Retek

The Legislative Priority Rule and the EU Internal Market for Goods
A Constitutional Approach
Eadaoin Ní Chaoimh

The Jurisprudence of Constitutional Conflict in the European Union
Ana Bobić

Reflexive Governance in EU Equality Law
Emma Lantschner

Enhanced Cooperation and European Tax Law
Caroline Heber

Legal Pluralism in European Contract Law
Vanessa Mak

Europe's Passive Virtues
Deference to National Authorities in EU Free Movement
Jan Zglinski

Accountability in the Economic and Monetary Union
Foundations, Policy, and Governance
Menelaos Markakis

Official Secrets and Oversight in the EU
Law and Practices of Classified Information
Vigjilenca Abazi

Compliance with European Consumer Law

The Case of E-Commerce

FELIX PFLÜCKE

Postdoctoral Researcher, University of Luxembourg, Luxembourg

OXFORD
UNIVERSITY PRESS

OXFORD
UNIVERSITY PRESS

Great Clarendon Street, Oxford, OX2 6DP,
United Kingdom

Oxford University Press is a department of the University of Oxford.
It furthers the University's objective of excellence in research, scholarship, and education by publishing worldwide. Oxford is a registered trade mark of Oxford University Press in the UK and in certain other countries

Published in the United States of America by Oxford University Press
198 Madison Avenue, New York, NY 10016, United States of America

British Library Cataloguing in Publication Data
Data available

Library of Congress Control Number: 2024933329

ISBN 9780198906384

DOI: 10.1093/9780198906414.001.0001

The manufacturer's authorised representative in the EU for product safety is Oxford University Press España S.A. of El Parque Empresarial San Fernando de Henares, Avenida de Castilla, 2 – 28830 Madrid (www.oup.es/en or product.safety@oup.com). OUP España S.A. also acts as importer into Spain of products made by the manufacturer.

Series Editors' Preface

There are, as is well known, various approaches to legal analysis. Doctrinal analysis forms a core constituent element of legal study, so too do works that focus on the normative dimension of legal rules. Empirical analysis is also an essential component in this regard, more especially when the very raison d'etre of the specific branch of the law is to provide protection for a particular group of people, such as consumers.

The traditional approach to European consumer law concerning e-commerce has been to focus on the doctrinal and theoretical dimensions of the subject. There has been much valuable work in this regard. It should, however, be complemented by empirical work to test the efficacy of the legal status quo.

The present book fills this important gap. It is predicated on the assumption that compliance with consumer law is a critical issue for traders, consumers, and regulators alike, and that this can only be tested through rigorous empirical analysis. The study breaks new ground by furnishing empirically based evidence on trader compliance, investigating whether consumers are adequately protected, and identifying the factors that explain insufficient compliance.

The principal focus of the study is on legal duties of e-commerce traders in business-to-consumer transactions at the EU level and in 4 jurisdictions, these being France, Germany, the Netherlands, and the United Kingdom. The book highlights national divergences and scrutinizes the salient empirical evidence. The author develops an empirical approach to measure trader compliance, which thereby provides a firm foundation from which to assess the success and limitations of the existing regime. The substantive scope of the work is directed to e-commerce sales, including the national laws implementing the Unfair Contract Terms Directive, the E-Commerce Directive, and the Consumer Rights Directive. The territorial scope of the inquiry is bounded by the 4 states mentioned above.

The empirical findings are then used as the basis for policy recommendations directed to the relevant stakeholders: the EU institutions, the national legislators, e-commerce traders, and consumer organizations. There are, in addition, broader recommendations for the role that empirical legal evidence could play in European consumer law.

This book will be of interest to scholars of European consumer law, and also more broadly to all those who are concerned as to the effectiveness of EU law.

Paul Craig
Gráinne de Búrca

Acknowledgements

Originating as a doctoral research endeavour at the University of Oxford, this monograph underwent further development during my postdoctoral research at the University of Luxembourg and lectureship at Somerville College, Oxford. I profoundly appreciate the invaluable support I have received throughout my research journey. While I cannot acknowledge all contributors individually, I want to express my gratitude to a select few.

First and foremost, I thank my MPhil and DPhil supervisors, Dorota Leczykiewicz and Stephen Weatherill, for their intellectual guidance, kindness, and generosity of time I will never forget. My examiners at the MPhil and transfer, Birke Häcker and Christian Twigg-Flesner, and confirmation and viva voce, Birke Häcker and Vanessa Mak, provided robust checks on the project's direction and significantly shaped its content. The intellectual guidance of my postdoctoral supervisors, Herwig C. H. Hofmann and Dirk A. Zetzsche, supported me in taking the project to the next level. All of you are a source of inspiration and motivation to develop my ideas further.

In addition, I want to thank the convenors of the Institute of European and Comparative Law Lunchtime Seminar Series, the Comparative Law Discussion Group, and the Socio-Legal Studies Discussion Group for the invaluable co-events with the EU Law Discussion Group and the Empirical Legal Studies Discussion Group in Oxford. The Max Planck Institute for Comparative and International Private Law, The Queen's College, St Peter's College, and Somerville College provided a home outside Brasenose and the Law Faculty. I also gratefully acknowledge the financial and academic support of the Friedrich Naumann Foundation, Oxford Law Faculty, Brasenose College, and the NORFACE INDIGO project.

My project has also immensely benefited from the intellectual input, support, and guidance from several colleagues, teachers, and friends. In particular, I thank Jeremias Adams-Prassl, Nick Bamforth, Amelie Berz, Tom Boekestein, Hafsteinn Dan Kristjánsson, Giovanni De Gregorio, Riccardo De Giorgi, Julie Dickson, Max-Sebastian Dovi, Stefan Enchelmaier, Michel Erpelding, Adrian Foerster, Catalina Goanta, Cédric Hack Rollmann, Thierry Hirsch, Liane Huttner, Jan Könighaus, Gerd Lutz, Paolisa Nebbia, Julian Nowag, Giulia

Raimondo, Felix Tann, Melvin Tjon Akon, Johannes Ungerer, Jan Zglisnki, the Brasenose HCR, and my students. Thanks to all of you.

I am also grateful to Gráinne de Búrca and Paul Craig for their helpful feedback and for incorporating this monograph into the Oxford Studies in European Law series, the input of 3 anonymous peer reviewers, and to the dedicated team at Oxford University Press, particularly Charlotte Kershaw and Peter Daniell, for their unwavering editorial assistance.

The greatest thank you is to my parents, Annette and Wolfgang Pflücke, my grandparents, Roswitha and Günter Kittel, and my wife, Madeleine Mahoux, for their kind and loving support.

I am also extremely grateful for funding support by the NORFACE Joint Research programme on Democratic Governance in Turbulent Ages and co-funded by AEI, AKA, DFG, FNR, and the European Commission through Horizon 2020 under the Grant Agreement No 822166.

Contents

Detailed Contents

Tables

Cases Cited

European Union

France

Germany

The Netherlands

United Kingdom

Legislative Materials Cited

European Union

France

Germany

The Netherlands

United Kingdom

International and Soft Law Instruments

Abbreviations

AC	The Official Law Reports Appeal Cases
ADR	alternative dispute resolution
AfP	Zeitschrift für das gesamte Medienrecht: Archiv für Presserecht
AGB	Allgemeine Geschäftsbedingungen (terms and conditions)
AGB-Gesetz	Gesetz zur Regelung des Rechts der Allgemeinen Geschäftsbedingungen 1976 (German Law on Standard Business Terms)
AI	artificial intelligence
B2B	business-to-business
B2C	business-to-consumer
BGB	Bürgerliches Gesetzbuch (German Civil Code)
BGH	Bundesgerichtshof (German Federal Court of Justice)
BTW	Belasting over de toegevoegde waarde (value-added tax)
BW	Burgerlijk Wetboek (Dutch Civil Code)
CA	Cour d'appel (French Appeal Court)
Cass civ	Cour de cassation, civile (French Court of Cassation, civil chamber)
CCI	Chambre de commerce et d'industrie (French Chamber of Commerce)
CCS	Crown Commercial Services
CESL	Common European Sales Law
CISG	United Nations Convention on Contracts for the International Sale of Goods
CJEU	Court of Justice of the European Union
CMA	Competition and Markets Authority (UK)
COM	European Commission
CPAG	Consumer Policy Advisory Group
CPC	consumer protection cooperation
CRA 2015	Consumer Rights Act 2015 (UK)
CRD	Consumer Rights Directive
CUP	Cambridge University Press
DSD	Distance Selling Directive
EC	European Community
ECCG	European Consumer Consultative Group
ECD	E-Commerce Directive
ECHR	European Convention on Human Rights
ECLI	European Case Law Identifier
EEC	European Economic Community

EGBGB	Einführungsgesetz zum Bürgerlichen Gesetzbuche (Introductory Act to the German Civil Code)
EU	European Union
F4F	fit for future
HR	Hoge Raad (Dutch Supreme Court)
HRA	Handelsregister Abteilung A (German Company Register A)
HRB	Handelsregister Abteilung B (German Company Register B)
IHK	Industrie- und Handelskammer (German Chamber of Industry and Commerce)
Incoterms®	International Commercial Terms
KWK	Kamer van Koophandel (Dutch Chamber of Commerce)
NJW	Neue Juristische Wochenschrift
ODR	online dispute resolution
OECD	Organisation for Economic Co-operation and Development
OJ	Official Journal of the European Union
OLG	Oberlandesgericht (Higher Regional Court in Germany)
OLS	ordinary least squares test
OUP	Oxford University Press
PECL	principles of European contract law
PHR	Parket bij de Hoge Raad (Procurator General Office of the Dutch Supreme Court)
RCS	Registre du commerce et des sociétés (French Company Registry)
SME	small and medium-sized enterprises
TEU	Treaty on European Union
TFEU	Treaty on the Functioning of the European Union
TMG	Telemediengesetz (German Telemedia Act)
UCTA	Unfair Contract Terms Act 1977 (UK)
UCTD	Unfair Contract Terms Directive
UKHL	UK House of Lords
UKSC	United Kingdom Supreme Court
UPICC	principles of international commercial contracts
UWG	Gesetz gegen den unlauteren Wettbewerb (German Act against Unfair Competition)
VAT	value-added tax
VPN	virtual private network
WLR	Weekly Law Reports

1
Introduction

1 Setting the Scene

The debates surrounding European consumer law in e-commerce have traditionally centred on the theoretical and doctrinal aspects of consumer rights. Scholars and policy-makers have primarily neglected trader compliance and behaviour, resulting in little understanding of the effectiveness of European consumer contract law. The lack of empirical evidence and research methods has left a significant gap in the literature on this topic, which this book attempts to fill.

The book has drawn inspiration from the few existing empirical studies on trader compliance and the effectiveness of consumer law in e-commerce, which painted a grim picture of the situation. For example, a European Commission study on the levels of awareness of consumer rights among consumers and traders revealed that only 12.6 per cent of consumers and 53.5 per cent of traders were aware of fundamental statutory rights in e-commerce transactions.[1] This lack of awareness makes consumers particularly vulnerable to traders not complying with EU and national consumer protection standards. The European Commission has therefore carried out another study that measured compliance of e-commerce traders with regard to a handful of applicable consumer protection rules, detecting multiple compliance issues.[2] Only some academic studies have gone beyond the mainly doctrinal discussions and investigated how consumer law operates in practice.[3] Even these studies have multiple shortcomings, including that they have focused only on a limited number of consumer rights, did not consider national law, did not

[1] European Commission, 'Consumer Conditions Scoreboard: Consumers at home in the Single Market' (October 2017) 18–19, 22 http://ec.europa.eu/newsroom/just/document.cfm?action = display&doc_id = 45983 (accessed 12 January 2023). The fundamental statutory rights included in the study concerned 'unsolicited products, faulty product guarantees and cooling-off periods'.

[2] European Commission, 'Online shopping: Commission and consumer protection authorities urge traders to bring information policy in line with EU law' (31 January 2020) https://ec.europa.eu/commission/presscorner/detail/en/IP_20_156 (accessed 12 January 2023).

[3] Examples of doctrinal work which focused on the European Union's competence to enact consumer protection legislation or the benefits and shortcomings of further harmonization in EU consumer contract law include eg Stephen Weatherill, *EU Consumer Law and Policy* (2nd edn, Edward

Compliance with European Consumer Law. Felix Pflücke, Oxford University Press. © Oxford University Press 2024.
DOI: 10.1093/9780198906414.003.0001

focus on distance sale of goods contracts, or did not investigate reasons for non-compliance.[4]

Compliance with consumer law is a critical issue for traders, consumers, and regulators alike. This monograph aims to address this gap in the literature by investigating the compliance of e-commerce traders with EU and national consumer protection rules and identifying reasons for non-compliance. By examining the case of e-commerce, the monograph advocates for an evidence-based approach to the assessment of European consumer law. It highlights the potential for such an approach to develop proposals to increase trader compliance and detect and resolve future challenges.

Evidence-based policy-making is increasingly becoming the gold standard for legislative and regulatory interventions. In European consumer contract law, this shift occurred with the adoption of the REFIT (2012)[5] and Better Regulation (2019) agendas,[6] introducing mandatory impact assessments on the EU level.[7] The European Union has taken significant steps towards adopting evidence-based policies but still needs to improve in critical areas.

2 Objectives and Methodological Considerations

This monograph attempts to contribute to the debates on the effectiveness of EU consumer contract law by providing empirically-based evidence on

Elgar Publishing 2013) ch 1; Kathleen Gutman, *The Constitutional Foundations of European Contract Law: A Comparative Analysis* (OUP 2014) ch 9; Hein Kötz, *European Contract Law* (2nd edn, OUP 2017) ch 1. Other approaches have also been used, eg examining the law and economics of the harmonization process. See eg Ariel Porat, 'The Law and Economics of Mistake in European Sales Law' (2013) 50(Special Issue) Common Market Law Review 127; Alexander J Wulf, *Institutional Competition between Optional Codes in European Contract Law: A Theoretical and Empirical Analysis* (Springer Publishing 2014). Researchers have conducted only a few empirical studies on trader compliance. See eg Marco Loos and Joasia A Luzak, 'Wanted: A Bigger Stick. On Unfair Terms in Consumer Contracts with Online Service Providers' (2016) 39(1) Journal of Consumer Policy 63; Aashish Srivastava, 'The New EU Consumer Rights Directive: An Empirical Study on Compliance Issues by E-Tailers' (2017) 32(4) Journal of Business Law 282; Mary Donnelly and Fidelma Whit, 'Digital content and consumer protection: An empirical study of supplier compliance with consumer information obligations' (2019) 35(6) Computer Law & Security Review 1.

[4] Chapter 5.2 of this book examines relevant empirical studies in greater detail.

[5] European Commission, 'EU Regulatory Fitness' COM(2012) 746 final.

[6] European Commission, 'Better Regulation Guidelines' SWD(2021) 305 final.

[7] See eg Helen Xanthaki, 'Improving the Quality of EU Legislation: Limits and Opportunities?' in Sacha Garben and Inge Govaere (eds), *The EU Better Regulation Agenda: A Critical Assessment* (Hart Publishing 2018); Christine Riefa, 'The REFIT Process in the Area of Consumer Protection: Odds Stacked against Consumers' in Esther van Schagen and Stephen Weatherill (eds), *Better Regulation in EU Contract Law: The Fitness Check and the New Deal for Consumers* (Hart Publishing 2019).

trader compliance, investigating whether consumers are adequately protected, and identifying factors explaining insufficient compliance. It will argue that European consumer contract law should adopt an evidence-based approach to improve the effectiveness of the rules and enhance trader compliance. In particular, it will argue for a more prominent role for empirical legal studies in policy-making and enforcement, promoting an evidence-based approach. It will offer valuable lessons to all areas of law.

The first objective is to examine all legal duties of e-commerce traders in business-to-consumer transactions on the European Union level and in 4 jurisdictions (France, Germany, the Netherlands, and the United Kingdom). It will highlight national divergences and scrutinize (empirical) evidence as well as consumer and regulatory theories that underpin or reject the present rules. The second objective is to develop an empirical approach that measures trader compliance and factors affecting compliance and to apply it to an original hand-selected dataset (10,500 observations). This empirical investigation bridges the gap between studying norms and trader behaviour. The third and final objective is thus to develop and conceptualize a new approach to consumer law policy-making and enforcement, which seeks to challenge the status quo and improve effectiveness and quality systematically. The investigation will offer targeted policy recommendations based on empirical research into trader compliance.

The book begins with scrutinizing the development towards an evidence-based approach on the EU level, highlighting multiple shortcomings of the approaches taken so far. While legislators and regulators increasingly use empirical evidence, existing studies and guidelines need more scientific grounding. Therefore, at the heart of the book, the empirical research attempts to assess how e-commerce business-to-consumer transactions are regulated and determine trader compliance and the effectiveness of the rules. It also seeks to provide evidence on possible factors that affect trader compliance by referring to existing empirical studies and allowing for a more granular approach when regulating e-commerce transactions. Based on the existing evidence, Chapter 5 presents several hypotheses that the empirical dataset tests.

The book's empirical inquiry proposes measuring trader compliance with European consumer law by conducting 300 simulated e-commerce transactions in 4 countries (France, Germany, the Netherlands, and the United Kingdom). The data was collected by examining traders' websites and assessing them for compliance with a selected number of applicable rules using content analysis. Content analysis is a qualitative method[8] commonly used in the social sciences to gather data from texts, which has been successfully used, for instance, in respect of judgments[9] or interview transcripts.[10] This ties into the sharp increase in empirical projects using this approach to address law-in-action issues more widely.[11]

The method is particularly well suited for the objectives of this empirical inquiry: the traders' websites are the source to gather the data against which the study assesses trader compliance. As a result, it is necessary to examine the rules that apply to e-commerce transactions before formulating the empirical research design.[12]

3 Scope of Inquiry and Limitations

3 limitations in terms of scope are necessary to enable a concise analysis of the specific questions at hand. The first limitation narrows the book's content to e-commerce business-to-consumer sales contracts. Different rules, procedures, and regulatory theories apply to business-to-business and the provision of services contracts, making a limitation based on the nature of transactions of fundamental importance. The second limitation concerns the selection of consumer rights for the book's empirical study because it cannot include all of them. It confines the focus to the rules regulating e-commerce sales, including the national laws implementing the Unfair Contract Terms Directive,[13] the

[8] See generally Lisa Webley, 'Qualitative Approaches to Empirical Legal Research' in Peter Cane and Herbert Kritzer (eds), *The Oxford Handbook of Empirical Legal Research* (OUP 2010) 941–42.

[9] See eg Mark A Hall and Ronald F Wright, 'Systematic Content Analysis of Judicial Opinions' (2008) 96(1) California Law Review 63; James Goudkamp and Donal Nolan, 'Contributory Negligence in the Twenty-First Century: An Empirical Study of First Instance Decisions' (2016) 79(4) Modern Law Review 575; Gijs van Dijck, 'The Ordered Apology' (2016) 37(3) Oxford Journal of Legal Studies 562; Rowena Vasquez-Sosas, 'The Language of Agreement: A Content Analysis of Employment Contracts' (2017) 12(2) Journal of Humanities and Social Science 2279.

[10] See eg Urszula Jaremba and Elaine Mak, 'Interviewing Judges in the Transnational Context' (2014) 4(2) Law and Method 1.

[11] Research trends in empirical legal research have been examined in eg Frans Leeuw, 'Empirical Legal Research: The Gap between Facts and Values and Legal Academic Training' (2015) 11(2) Utrecht Law Review 19; Gijs van Dijck, Shahar Sverdlov, and Gabriela Buck, 'Empirical Legal Research in Europe: Prevalence, Obstacles, and Interventions' (2018) 12(2) Erasmus Law Review 105; Maryam Salehijam, 'The Value of Systematic Content Analysis in Legal Research' (2018) 23(1) Tilburg Law Review 34.

[12] Chapter 5 provides a detailed account of the empirical study's research design.

[13] Council Directive (EEC) 93/13 of 5 April 1993 on unfair terms in consumer contracts [1993] OJ L95/29 (Unfair Contract Terms Directive).

E-Commerce Directive,[14] and the Consumer Rights Directive.[15] The monograph excludes the Consumer Sales and Guarantees Directive as these deal with warranty issues and commercial guarantees,[16] but their implications are discussed as far as relevant. Furthermore, the empirical case study in the book solely assesses the compliance of e-commerce traders' websites without evaluating their adherence to consumer rules during interactions with consumers, which would necessitate actual purchases. The third and final limitation relates to the territorial scope of the inquiry. 3 current Member States and a former Member State have been selected for the book: France, Germany, the Netherlands, and the United Kingdom. The data collection for the empirical study of the book took place in September 2019, which means that, at the time of collecting the data, the United Kingdom was still part of the European Union.[17] The European Union's New Deal for Consumers is not part of the core inquiry since it was not in force at the time of data collection in 2019, but Chapter 7 addresses it.

4 Structure of the Book and Outline

The central argument of this monograph contends that European consumer law ought to embrace an evidence-based approach to enhance the effectiveness of the rules and foster trader compliance. The book first examines the rules for e-commerce transactions—from mandatory disclosures to unfair contract terms—as well as the evidence and theories underpinning or rejecting them. The book then provides an original empirical study investigating whether traders comply with the selected consumer rights. It also scrutinizes factors affecting compliance and how empirical evidence could shape the future of European consumer law. The underlying objective is to approach European consumer law in a novel way, advocating for a more evidence-based approach in the legislative and regulatory process. Consequently, the book also questions the limited role empirical legal evidence currently plays in European consumer

[14] Directive (EC) 2000/31 of 8 June 2000 on certain legal aspects of information society services, in particular electronic commerce, in the Internal Market [2000] OJ L178/1 (E-Commerce Directive).

[15] Directive (EU) 2011/83 of 25 October 2011 on consumer rights, amending Council Directive 93/13/EEC and Directive 1999/44/EC and repealing Council Directive 85/577/EEC and Directive 97/7/EC [2011] OJ L304/64 (Consumer Rights Directive).

[16] Directive (EC) 1999/44 of 25 May 1999 on certain aspects of the sale of consumer goods and associated guarantees [1999] OJ L171/12 (Consumer Sales and Guarantees Directive).

[17] Agreement on the withdrawal of the United Kingdom of Great Britain and Northern Ireland from the European Union and the European Atomic Energy Community [2019] OJ C384I/1; European Commission, 'A New Deal for Consumers' COM(2018) 183 final.

law and examines the potential of such studies. The following provides a roadmap of the book.

Chapter 2 reviews the existing (thin) empirical studies on trader compliance and examines their role in shaping European consumer contract law. It examines the Commission's REFIT exercise and Better Regulation agenda in consumer law. The REFIT assessments show that the Commission's guidelines are neither binding nor always aligned with scientific standards. Therefore, the chapter assesses whether empirical evidence has so far been able to underpin the legislative choices in EU consumer contract law and outlines how this process could be improved. This chapter also outlines how compliance should be measured so that empirical data can be translated into targeted and actionable policy recommendations, thus attempting to improve trader compliance with an evidence-based approach.

The underlying objectives of Chapter 3 are to provide doctrinal accounts of the consumer protection rights derived from the implementation of the 3 selected Directives, where relevant, examine its implementation into national law, and illuminate the evidence and consumer and regulatory theories underpinning it. The present study's empirical inquiry uses comparative observations to assess trader compliance, considering divergences between the 4 national jurisdictions. Therefore, it is fundamental to succinctly evaluate the relevant consumer rights before conducting compliance assessments. The discussion on existing (empirical) evidence and consumer theories is not limited to the ones used to justify the legislative choices. It also discusses theories and (empirical) evidence, such as behavioural studies on online trading, rejecting them. This combined approach bridges the gap between studying norms and online trader behaviour. The doctrinal account of the chapter focuses on the implementation of the Unfair Contract Terms Directive, the E-Commerce Directive, and the Consumer Rights Directive. The chapter depicts the change in European consumer contract law towards an evidence-based approach, such as the recent REFIT exercise and the Better Regulation agenda, and critically examines it. It shows the lack and need for law-in-action studies, setting the scene for the monograph's original empirical analysis.

Building on the 2 doctrinal chapters, Chapter 5 sets out the research design of the empirical case study, including how to define and measure compliance with EU and national consumer rules. In the first step, the chapter formulates the 4 hypotheses and presents arguments for why it tests them: the H_1 hypothesis claims that e-commerce traders fail to comply in full with their legal duties; the remaining hypotheses assess whether the company's size (H_2), the company's age (H_3), and the use of pre-drafted terms provided by public or semi-public authorities (H_4) affect compliance. The chapter also translates all the selected consumer rights examined in the previous 2 chapters into 35 dependent variables. It uses existing empirical evidence to determine possible factors of compliance, such as the company's size, which the study translates into independent variables. The chapter then presents the methods used to collect and analyse the data, including the inter-rater agreement, which ensures the reliability and validity of the empirical part of the study. The final section of the chapter reflects upon some of the methodological challenges.

Chapter 6 scrutinizes the collected empirical data and seeks to respond to the 4 hypotheses using descriptive statistics and regression models. This hypothesis testing is the focus of the first 2 subsections. The chapter then discusses the level of trader compliance with the consumers' substantive rights using descriptive statistics, providing exact numerical data on the levels of compliance with each right. The chapter concludes with a discussion section, which provides a qualitative account of how traders responded to consumer rights. It also links it with other studies and theories, such as economic studies, behavioural evidence, and consumer theories. All observations are placed within the context of online trading and the surrounding literature to explain trader behaviour. It also includes assessing whether the rules are workable and provide consumer protection in practice.

Chapter 7 aims to translate the empirical findings into targeted and actionable policy recommendations for the relevant stakeholders: the European Union institutions, the national legislators, e-commerce traders, and consumer organizations. Naturally, these recommendations focus on the study's empirical findings. They reside within the consumer law and policy debate in the European Union and the 4 national jurisdictions. The second part of the recommendations focuses on the future role empirical legal evidence could play in European consumer law. It argues for an evidence-based consumer law policy-making and enforcement approach to improve trader compliance and the quality of legislation. Based on the nuanced analysis in Chapter 2, this part outlines how policy-makers should turn research findings into policy.

The final chapter, Chapter 8, concludes the book. It summarizes the main arguments, outlines potential implications for European consumer contract law, provides unanswered questions, and makes some concluding remarks.

2

Evidence-based Consumer Law and Policy

1 Introduction

Evidence-based policy is a fundamental principle in public governance that emphasizes the importance of using evidence in the design and implementation of policies.[1] Evidence-based policy underscores the crucial role of research in shaping legislative frameworks, regulatory measures, and interventions, ultimately leading to more objective, informed, and impactful governance. In this context, evidence becomes the cornerstone of law and policy, guiding the path towards evidence-backed solutions that can better serve the needs and interests of societies and individuals. For over 2 decades, the European Union has embraced this principle, earning praise from the Organisation for Economic Co-operation and Development (OECD) for its persistent efforts to enhance the fit between regulatory frameworks and markets.[2] However, despite the European Union's commitment to improve, their approach has faced criticism, mainly in how they conduct assessments.

This chapter critically examines the current role and state of evidence-based law and policy in European consumer contract law. Focusing on the European Commission's Better Regulation agenda, this chapter reveals that the Commission's guidelines lack binding force and do not always adhere to robust scientific standards. Ultimately, the chapter advocates for a review of the current system to have a genuinely evidence-based approach, thus improving trader compliance, strengthening consumer protection, and advancing European consumer contract law.

[1] See eg Sandra Nutley and Jeff Webb, 'Evidence and the Policy Process' in Sandra Nutley, Huw TO Davies, and Peter Smith (eds), *What Works? Evidence-based Policy and Practice in Public Services* (Policy Press 2000) 25–26; Justin Parkhurst, *The Politics of Evidence: From Evidence-based Policy to the Good Governance of Evidence* (Routledge 2016) 14 ff.

[2] The Organisation for Economic Co-operation and Development (OECD), 'Better Regulation Practices across the European Union: Executive Summary' (19 March 2019) https://www.oecd-ilibrary.org/governance/better-regulation-practices-across-the-european-union_582c4ee9-en (accessed 16 April 2023).

Compliance with European Consumer Law. Felix Pflücke, Oxford University Press. © Oxford University Press 2024.
DOI: 10.1093/9780198906414.003.0002

2 The Commission's Better Regulation Agenda

Enacted in 2001,[3] the European Commission has continuously refined its Better Regulation agenda, significantly shaping the contours of European consumer contract law for more than 2 decades.[4] At its inception, the ambition of the initial agenda was to measure the real-world impact of legislation, for instance, on the Union's competitiveness and to simplify existing rules.[5] Before the agenda's adoption, evidence found application only in specific domains of law, exemplified by the requirement for scientific evidence in environmental policy.[6] This evolution marked a notable innovation in the realm of consumer law. The Better Regulation agenda was reformed in 2017 for the New Deal for Consumers,[7] focusing on 'effective application, implementation and enforcement'.[8] Its objectives now centre around evidence-based policy-making, simplifying and enhancing the effectiveness of EU laws while avoiding unnecessary burdens and involving citizens, businesses, and stakeholders in the decision-making process.[9]

The Commission's approach to Better Regulation reflects the principles of subsidiarity and proportionality,[10] which have governed EU law-making since the early days of the Union.[11] The 2 principles ensure that all legislative proposals undergo assessment based on them to achieve appropriate decision-making and avoid excessive actions. Guided by the principles of subsidiarity and proportionality, the Commission's Better Regulation approach fosters

[3] European Commission, 'European Governance: A White Paper' COM(2001) 428.

[4] See eg the contributions in Stephen Weatherill (ed), *Better Regulation* (Hart Publishing 2007); Sacha Garben and Inge Govaere (eds), *The EU Better Regulation Agenda: A Critical Assessment* (Hart Publishing 2018); Esther van Schagen and Stephen Weatherill (eds), *Better Regulation in EU Contract Law: The Fitness Check and the New Deal for Consumers* (Hart Publishing 2019). See also Hans-Wolfgang Micklitz, 'The Measuring of the Law through EU Politics' in Marja Bartl and Jessica C Lawrence (eds), *The Politics of European Legal Research* (Edward Elgar Publishing 2022) 224 ff.

[5] COM(2001) 428, 2; European Commission, 'Better Regulation for Growth and Jobs in the European Union' COM(2005) 97 final, 12.

[6] Single European Act (SEA) [1986] OJ L169/1, art 25.

[7] European Commission, 'A New Deal for EU Consumers' COM(2018) 183.

[8] European Commission, 'Better Regulation: why and how' (2023) https://commission.europa.eu/law/law-making-process/planning-and-proposing-law/better-regulation_en#:~:text=The%20Better%20Regulation%20agenda%20ensures,those%20that%20may%20be%20affected (accessed 25 March 2023). See eg Esther van Schagen, '"Better" Enforcement of EU Consumer Law: Exploring Responsive Enforcement' in Esther van Schagen and Stephen Weatherill (eds), *Better Regulation in EU Contract Law: The Fitness Check and the New Deal for Consumers* (Hart Publishing 2019) 144–46.

[9] European Commission (n 8).

[10] COM(2005) 97 final, 2, 4, and 9. cf Stephen Weatherill, *EU Consumer Law and Policy* (2nd edn, Edward Elgar Publishing 2013) 21–22.

[11] Before Maastricht, it only existed for environmental policy (Article 25 Single European Act 1987). It became a general principle in Maastricht (Article 5 of the Treaty establishing the European Community (TEC)). Nowadays, it is in Article 5(3) of the Treaty on European Union (TEU) and Protocol (No 2) on the application of the principles of subsidiarity and proportionality.

well-informed decision-making, which, as will be depicted in the following sections, has been continuously refined over the years.

3 Instruments for Generating Evidence

The concept of good governance encompasses both governmental effectiveness and regulatory quality.[12] Central to this notion is the presence of credible evidence, which intricately weaves data with hypotheses, i.e., using these data to substantiate or invalidate assumptions concerning regulated behaviour or the regulatory framework itself. This form of evidence necessitates upholding superior accuracy, quality, and impartiality benchmarks. Research on evidence-based consumer policy also emphasizes the importance of involving stakeholders from diverse disciplines to limit the tendency to analyse issues in isolation.[13]

The body of evidence concerning European consumer contract law, primarily sourced from the European Commission, has been experiencing an expansion in recent times. Advancements in data collection and analytical methodologies, along with the dynamic evolution of the regulatory landscape, have contributed to this expansion. Despite this rapid expansion, it remains imperative to recognize the existing limitations inherent to these tools, requiring a comprehensive and critical examination.

3.1 Stakeholder Consultations

Stakeholder consultations, being the oldest instrument, have played a pivotal role in the legislative process of the European Union, serving as a vital platform for engaging with relevant parties and gathering valuable insights and perspectives on European consumer law matters. These consultations have proven instrumental in shaping policies and regulations to protect and empower consumers.

[12] World Bank, 'The Worldwide Governance Indicators (WGI) project' (2023) http://info.worldbank.org/governance/wgi/#doc (accessed 23 April 2023). Discussed in Aurelia Colombi Ciacchi, 'Good Governance and the Fitness Check of EU Consumer Law' in Esther van Schagen and Stephen Weatherill (eds), *Better Regulation in EU Contract Law: The Fitness Check and the New Deal for Consumers* (Hart Publishing 2019) 192–93.

[13] Shmuel I Becher, 'Unintended Consequences and the Design of Consumer Protection Legislation' (2018) 93(1) Tulane Law Review 132.

In their early stages, stakeholder consultations faced a notable challenge due to the absence or scarcity of established standards for conducting them, despite the legal requirement in Article 11 of the Treaty on European Union to ensure coherency and transparency.[14] However, the European Union made significant improvements to address this limitation and enhance its effectiveness.[15] Stakeholder consultations have become mandatory in the present day, allowing feedback to 'call for evidence' documents and public consultation, either before legislation is accepted or in fitness checks.[16] The trend of regulating less while improving overall effectiveness prompted the decision to increase standards in the law-making stage.[17]

Despite drastic reforms, there is still a notable concern regarding consumer representation in stakeholder consultations, with Hans-Wolfgang Micklitz labelling the involvement of stakeholders as 'symbolic participation'.[18] Furthermore, Christine Riefa highlights that among the 19 stakeholders in the REFIT platform, which focused on regulatory fitness and performance, the only serious representative for consumers was BEUC.[19] Another criticism by Riefa was that the number of trade associations interviewed by the Commission was twice that of consumer representatives.[20] The REFIT platform's mandate concluded on 31 October 2019, and the Fit For Future (F4F) platform replaced it.[21] The Fit For Future platform is similar to

[14] Marxsen criticized the regime after conducting an empirical inquiry on stakeholder engagement in 2011 because the Commission failed to ensure transparency by not publishing all the findings of public consultations and having a consistent approach. Christian Marxsen, 'Open Stakeholder Consultations at the European Level: Voice of the Citizens?' (2015) 21(2) European Law Journal 272. For an overview of participation in the law-making process in the early days of EU consumer law, Ludwig Krämer, 'The Origins of Consumer Law and Policy at EU Level' Hans-Wolfgang Micklitz (ed), *The Making of Consumer Law and Policy in Europe* (Hart Publishing 2021) 19–21.

[15] See eg Rick Haythornthwaite, 'Better Regulation in Europe' in Stephen Weatherill (ed), *Better Regulation* (Hart Publishing 2007) 22–23. Haythornthwaite mostly praised the new approach by the European Commission but also discussed the criticism outlined by the Better Regulation Task Force.

[16] European Commission, 'Better Regulation Guidelines' SWD(2021) 305 final, s 3.2 and ch II; European Commission, '"Better Regulation" Toolbox: July 2023 Edition' (July 2023) ch 7 https://commission.europa.eu/system/files/2023-07/BR_toolbox_Jul_2023_en.pdf (accessed 25 July 2023). The stakeholder consultations were reformed in the Smart Regulation agenda: European Commission, 'Smart Regulation in the European Union' COM(2010) 543 final, 5, 10–11.

[17] Stephen Weatherill, 'The Challenge of Better Regulation' in Stephen Weatherill (ed), *Better Regulation* (Hart Publishing 2007) 3.

[18] Hans-Wolfgang Micklitz, 'The Targeted Full Harmonisation Approach: Looking behind the Curtain' in Geraint Howells and Reiner Schulze (eds), *Modernising and Harmonising Consumer Contract Law* (Sellier European Law Publisher 2009) 62.

[19] Christine Riefa, 'The REFIT Process in the Area of Consumer Protection: Odds Stacked Against Consumers' in Esther van Schagen and Stephen Weatherill (eds), *Better Regulation in EU Contract Law: The Fitness Check and the New Deal for Consumers* (Hart Publishing 2019) 29–30; BEUC, The European Consumer Organization, originally *Bureau Européen des Unions de Consommateurs*), is one of the oldest consumer organizations in the EU.

[20] Riefa (n 19) 30.

[21] European Commission, 'Suggest how to simplify and modernise existing laws and reduce regulatory burdens' (2023) https://ec.europa.eu/info/law/better-regulation/have-your-say-simplify_en (accessed 25 March 2023).

the REFIT platform, comprising a government[22] and stakeholder[23] group.[24] A recent public consultation on Digital Fairness in European consumer law attracted widespread participation, with 61.38 per cent of participants being consumers compared to 2.88 per cent of consumer organizations and 0.86 per cent of academics.[25] Nonetheless, it is still unclear whether and to what extent the Commission will consider the opinions submitted by consumers.[26]

Professional stakeholders such as non-governmental organizations and lobby firms probably carry more significant influence.[27] Since 1973, the European Consumer Consultative Group (ECCG) has aided the Commission by offering expert guidance on EU consumer-related matters.[28] The Consumer Policy Advisory Group (CPAG) replaced the ECCG as part of the New Consumer Agenda. The CPAG comprises 5 academics and 43 organizations, primarily representing business interests.[29] The lack of institutionalized effective consumer representation in stakeholder consultations is a critical issue that warrants attention. Consumer perspectives and concerns are crucial and should be given due consideration in policy-making processes. Consumers are the ultimate beneficiaries or victims of unworkable or ineffective consumer laws, and their involvement in shaping these laws is essential to ensure their effectiveness. To achieve a more comprehensive and balanced perspective, the Commission should include a diverse range of stakeholders and citizen narratives, as suggested by Sofia Ranchordás, who argues that they offer 'first-hand

[22] This includes representatives from national, regional, and local authorities, and the Committee of the Regions.

[23] This includes representatives from businesses, NGOs, and the European Economic and Social Committee.

[24] European Commission, 'Composition' (2023) https://commission.europa.eu/law/law-making-process/evaluating-and-improving-existing-laws/refit-making-eu-law-simpler-less-costly-and-future-proof/fit-future-platform-f4f/composition_en (accessed 25 March 2023).

[25] European Commission, 'Digital fairness: fitness check on EU consumer law: Public Consultation' (2023) https://ec.europa.eu/info/law/better-regulation/have-your-say/initiatives/13413-Digital-fairness-fitness-check-on-EU-consumer-law/public-consultation_en (accessed 28 July 2023).

[26] The literature also emphasizes the relevance of the policy area, as certain fields may necessitate detailed technical expertise. See Jan Beyers and Sarah Arras, 'Who feeds information to regulators? Stakeholder diversity in European Union regulatory agency consultations' (2020) 40(4) Journal of Public Policy 594.

[27] For a general overview of EU stakeholder engagement see eg Sarah Arras and Caelesta Braun, 'Stakeholders wanted! Why and how European Union agencies involve non-state stakeholders' (2018) 25(9) Journal of European Public Policy 1261.

[28] European Commission, 'The European Consumer Consultative Group' (2023) https://commission.europa.eu/strategy-and-policy/policies/consumers/consumer-protection-policy/our-partners-consumer-issues/consumer-policy-advisory-group-cpag/european-consumer-consultative-group-eccg_en (accessed 23 May 2023). cf Weatherill (n 10) 17–18.

[29] European Commission, 'Register of Commission Expert Groups and Other Similar Entities: Consumer Policy Advisory Group (E03750)' (2023) https://ec.europa.eu/transparency/expert-groups-register/screen/expert-groups/consult?lang=en&do=groupDetail.groupDetail&groupID=3750 (accessed 23 May 2023).

and diverse perspectives'.[30] Hence, consumers must sit at the table, and their opinions should wield significant influence.

European Union stakeholder consultations are crucial in shaping policies and legislation, aiming to incorporate diverse perspectives into decision-making.[31] Nonetheless, the extent of the impact of stakeholder consultations on EU policy- and law-making is still a topic of ongoing evaluation. On the national level, similar challenges and benefits arise with stakeholder consultations as Member States have their consultation mechanisms.[32] It is essential to acknowledge that opinions and evidence submitted during stakeholder consultations may not always be entirely objective, as political and business motivations from different stakeholders can influence them. Nonetheless, considering multiple perspectives allows for a more comprehensive understanding of the issues at hand, allowing policy-makers to see both sides of the coin and make more informed decisions.

3.2 Impact Assessments

Ex ante and ex post impact assessments in European consumer contract law emerged in light of the mandated review of the existing rules in 2001,[33] resulting in further harmonized measures. The first assessment outlined 4 options for the future of European contract law[34] and highlighted the need for further harmonization because minimum harmonization measures fail to achieve uniformity when addressing the same issues in the Internal Market.[35] The first impact assessments consequently faced widespread backlash, triggering a

[30] Sofia Ranchordás, 'Consultations, Citizen Narratives and Evidence-Based Regulation: The Strange Case of the Consultation on the Collaborative Economy' (2017) 19(1) European Journal of Law Reform 52.

[31] The EU has also experimented with a variety of different participation models. See eg Holly Jarman, 'Collaboration and Consultation: Functional Representation in EU Stakeholder Dialogues' (2011) 33(4) Journal of European Integration 385 https://doi.org/10.1080/07036337.2011.579748; Adriana Bunea, 'Designing stakeholder consultations: Reinforcing or alleviating bias in the European Union system of governance?' (2017) 56(1) European Journal of Political Research 46.

[32] The Organisation for Economic Co-operation and Development (OECD), 'Better Regulation Practices across the European Union' (19 March 2019) ch 2 https://www.oecd-ilibrary.org/sites/dd9b13ad-en/index.html?itemId=/content/component/dd9b13ad-en (accessed 16 April 2023).

[33] European Commission, 'Communication on European Contract Law' COM(2001) 398.

[34] ibid s 4.

[35] European Commission, 'A more coherent European contract law: An action plan' COM(2003) OJ C63/1 (paragraph 24). Jan Smits criticized the approach of the Commission and argued that they should instead adopt an optional contract code to establish 'what the market really wants'. Jan Smits, 'The Action Plan on a More Coherent European Contract Law' (2003) 10(2) Maastricht Journal of European and Comparative Law 115.

critical examination of their methods and findings.[36] Embracing the feedback and constructive criticism, a persistent commitment to improvement ensued, resulting in refinements to enhance the accuracy, comprehensiveness, and objectivity of subsequent impact assessments.[37] The impact assessment framework has matured significantly through a continuous learning process and a collaborative approach involving experts, stakeholders, and affected communities, culminating in a more robust and credible system that fosters informed decision-making.

According to the Better Regulation guidelines and toolbox,[38] ex ante impact assessments are currently mandatory 'for Commission initiatives that are likely to have significant economic, environmental or social impacts or which entail significant spending, and where the Commission has a choice of policy options.'[39] According to the Better Regulation guidelines, this requirement applies to all 'legislative and non-legislative initiatives and for delegated acts and implementing measures'.[40] The European Commission clarified in the Better Regulation guidelines that impact assessments aim to specify policy aims and examine whether and what kind of EU action is needed, outlining the pros and cons of each measure.[41]

According to the Commission guidelines, impact assessments can take various forms and are case-by-case assessments.[42] What is defined are the procedural steps and principles guiding it. Directorate generals that wish to adopt legislation are in charge of impact assessments, guided by 9 principles: comprehensive, proportionate, evidence-based, include stakeholders, unbiased, inclusion of respective Commission units, embedment in the European Union's policy cycle, transparent, and of high quality.[43] Impact assessments also need

[36] cf European Commission, 'European Contract Law and the revision of the acquis: the way forward' COM(2004) 651 final, Annex II; European Commission, 'Progress Report on the Commission Reform Beyond the Reform Mandate' COM(2005) 668 final, 13; European Commission, 'Green paper from the Commission on policy options for progress towards a European Contract Law for consumers and businesses' COM(2010) 348, 2. For an assessment of how the Commission's Barroso administration took the criticism to heart and improved Better Regulation from 2004 to 2006. See eg Ragnar E Lofstedt, 'The "Plateau-ing" of the European Better Regulation Agenda: An Analysis of Activities Carried out by the Barroso Commission' (2007) 10(4) Journal of Risk Research 423.

[37] See eg Giulia Listorti, Egle Basyte-Ferrari, Szvetlana Acs, and Paul Smits, 'Towards an Evidence-Based and Integrated Policy Cycle in the EU: A Review of the Debate on the Better Regulation Agenda' (2020) 58(6) Journal of Common Market Studies 1558.

[38] European Commission, 'Better Regulation Guidelines' SWD(2021) 305 final, s 3.4 and ch IV; European Commission, '"Better Regulation" Toolbox: July 2023 Edition' (July 2023) ch 8 https://commission.europa.eu/system/files/2023-07/BR_toolbox_Jul_2023_en.pdf (accessed 25 July 2023).

[39] European Commission, 'Better Regulation Guidelines' (n 38) 30; European Commission, '"Better Regulation" Toolbox: July 2023 Edition' (n 38) 42–43, 44–45.

[40] European Commission, 'Better Regulation Guidelines' (n 38) .

[41] ibid.

[42] ibid 9, 31.

[43] ibid.

to answer 7 specific questions[44] and are guided by 13 requirements, which are, on the contrary, rather vague. For instance, the guidelines do not prescribe a set methodology, but merely that interpreting and analysing the data should be appropriate.[45] Finally, the guidelines state that the Commission is not required to act on the preferred policy option, but such a decision would need justification.[46]

However, the quality of impact assessments still varies. Esther van Schagen rightly pointed out that impact assessments assume rather than analyse the impact of harmonization on European contract law.[47] Moreover, according to Christine Riefa, business representatives are given more weight in impact assessments.[48] From a normative point of view, the question also arises about the purpose of impact assessments. Esther van Schagen and Stephen Weatherill rightly point out that impact assessments should strengthen and not replace the political debate.[49] Another crucial question is who should carry out the impact assessments. Should this vital task be entrusted to the Commission, independent bodies without direct affiliation, or vested stakeholders directly affected by the outcomes? There is a notable challenge concerning potential biases in impact assessments conducted by the Commission and stakeholders, as their political or business preferences influence them. Conversely, while ostensibly impartial, independent bodies could face limitations imposed by Commission guidelines, compromising their autonomy, as is currently the case.[50] EU consumer law could overcome this issue by providing norms to which those guidelines for independent bodies should adhere to preserve impartiality. Furthermore, Dorota Leczykiewicz aptly contends that impact

[44] ibid 31–33: '1. What is the problem and why is it a problem?; 2. Why should the EU act?; 3. What should be achieved?; 4. What are the options for achieving the objectives?; 5. What are their economic, social and environmental impacts and who will be affected?; 6. How do the options compare (effectiveness, efficiency and coherence)?; 7. How will monitoring and subsequent evaluation be organised?'

[45] ibid 33.

[46] ibid 36.

[47] Esther van Schagen, 'The Hidden Potential of Regulatory Impact Assessments (RIAs) in the Private Law Acquis' (2014) 22(1) European Review of Private Law 82.

[48] Christine Riefa, 'The REFIT Process in the Area of Consumer Protection: Odds Stacked against Consumers' in Esther van Schagen and Stephen Weatherill (eds), *Better Regulation in EU Contract Law: The Fitness Check and the New Deal for Consumers* (Hart Publishing 2019) 26.

[49] Esther van Schagen and Stephen Weatherill, 'Impact Assessments in EU Contract Law' in Esther van Schagen and Stephen Weatherill (eds), *Better Regulation in EU Contract Law: The Fitness Check and the New Deal for Consumers* (Hart Publishing 2019) 5.

[50] Anne CM Meuwese, 'Inter-institutionalising EU Impact Assessment' in Stephen Weatherill (ed), *Better Regulation* (Hart Publishing 2007) 302–304; Esther van Schagen, 'The Fitness Check of EU Consumer Law and the Impact Assessment for the New Deal for Consumer' in Esther van Schagen and Stephen Weatherill (eds), *Better Regulation in EU Contract Law: The Fitness Check and the New Deal for Consumers* (Hart Publishing 2019) 109.

assessment reports have not earnestly addressed the matter of consumer financial burden, a lacuna that is also mirrored by the CJEU.[51]

In 2018,[52] the European Commission carried out an impact assessment on possible updates for the Unfair Contract Terms Directive,[53] the Unfair Commercial Practices Directive,[54] the Consumer Rights Directive,[55] and the Injunctions Directive.[56] The report built upon the Fitness Check in 2017, the evaluation of the Consumer Rights Directive in the same year, and the report on the implementation of the Recommendation on Collective Redress in 2018.[57] The 3 studies, for instance, deployed public consultations, including surveys and stakeholder panels, and the Consumer Conditions Scoreboard to generate data on how these instruments operate in practice. It brought to light that a notable need for trader compliance with EU consumer law persists within all economic sectors, both online and offline.[58] Furthermore, the assessment identified areas where ineffective consumer protection regulations cause unnecessary burdens and costs for traders following the rules.[59]

It attributed the lack of trader compliance to the findings of the Consumer Conditions Scoreboard. In this study, 20.1 per cent of consumers reported problems, and a survey among traders outlined that only 67 per cent of traders believe their competitors comply with consumer rules.[60] Despite the questionable methods, the 2018 impact assessment was built on these findings and concluded that compliance needs to improve.[61] Such an approach raises concerns

[51] Dorota Leczykiewicz, 'Regulatory Cost and the Consumer' in Dorota Leczykiewicz and Stephen Weatherill (eds), *Images of Consumers* (Hart Publishing 2016) 274–76.

[52] European Commission, 'Impact Assessment: Accompanying the document: Proposals for (1) amending Council Directive 93/13/EEC, Directive 98/6/EC of the European Parliament and of the Council, Directive 2005/29/EC of the European Parliament and of the Council and Directive 2011/83/EU of the European Parliament and of the Council as regards better enforcement and modernisation of EU consumer protection rules; and (2) on representative actions for the protection of the collective interests of consumers, and repealing Directive 2009/22/EC' SWD(2018) 96 final.

[53] Directive (EEC) 93/13 of 5 April 1993 on unfair terms in consumer contracts [1993] OJ L95/29 (Unfair Contract Terms Directive).

[54] Directive (EC) 2005/29 of 11 May 2005 concerning unfair business-to-consumer commercial practices in the internal market and amending Council Directive 84/450/EEC, Directives 97/7/EC, 98/27/EC and 2002/65/EC of the European Parliament and of the Council and Regulation (EC) No 2006/2004 of the European Parliament and of the Council [2005] OJ L149/22 (Unfair Commercial Practices Directive).

[55] Directive (EU) 2011/83 of 25 October 2011 on consumer rights, amending Council Directive 93/13/EEC and Directive 1999/44/EC and repealing Council Directive 85/577/EEC and Directive 97/7/EC [2011] OJ L304/64 (Consumer Rights Directive).

[56] Directive (EC) 2009/22 of 23 April 2009 on injunctions for the protection of consumers' interests[2009] OJ L110/30 (Injunctions Directive), no longer in force.

[57] Impact Assessment SWD(2018) 96 final, s 1.1.

[58] ibid.

[59] ibid.

[60] ibid s 2.3.1.

[61] ibid s 8.3.1.

about its adherence to rigorous academic standards, as the methodology and data collection methods employed may need to be more robust to draw definitive conclusions on the level of trader compliance with EU consumer law.[62]

Several academics have also criticized the approach in this impact assessment. Christine Riefa notes that the Commission labels the findings of the fitness checks as robust in the impact assessment despite the fitness check highlighting the limitations of the data.[63] Esther van Schagen also stresses that the impact assessment misrepresents part of the fitness check.[64] Van Schagen further highlights the lacuna of case law for certain issues despite national country reports including it.[65] Despite some concerns about the quality and potential biases, impact assessments are crucial in informing decision-making. However, it is essential to strengthen their purpose and reconsider the appropriate tools and entities responsible for generating good evidence.

Following the New Deal for Consumer announcement,[66] the Commission has called for another fitness check, including an impact assessment and evaluation, in light of the New Consumer Agenda in spring 2022.[67] The Commission is evaluating whether the Unfair Commercial Practices Directive,[68] the Consumer Rights Directive,[69] and the Unfair Contract Terms Directive[70] adequately protect consumers.[71] It will conclude in mid-2024, and whether the Commission will implement some feedback remains to be seen.

[62] A more detailed analysis follows in ch 5 of this book.

[63] Riefa (n 48) 24.

[64] Van Schagen (n 49) 119.

[65] ibid 117.

[66] European Commission, 'A New Deal for EU Consumers' COM(2017) 259 final; European Commission, 'Evaluation of the Consumer Rights Directive: Accompanying the document' SWD(2017) 169 final. European Commission, 'Report on the application of Directive 2011/83/EU of the European Parliament and of the Council of 25 October 2011 on consumer rights, amending Council Directive 93/13/EEC and Directive 1999/44/EC of the European Parliament and of the Council and repealing Council Directive 85/577/EEC and Directive 97/7/EC of the European Parliament and of the Council' COM(2017) 259 final.

[67] European Commission, 'New Consumer Agenda Strengthening consumer resilience for sustainable recovery' COM(2020) 696 final. Regarding sustainability issues in EU consumer law, see, eg, Felix Pflücke, 'The Limits of Consumer Law in Pursuing Sustainability' in Julian Nowag (ed), *Research Handbook on Sustainability and Competition Law* (Edward Elgar Publishing 2024).

[68] Directive (EC) 2005/29 of 11 May 2005 concerning unfair business-to-consumer commercial practices in the internal market and amending Council Directive 84/450/EEC, Directives 97/7/EC, 98/27/EC and 2002/65/EC of the European Parliament and of the Council and Regulation (EC) No 2006/2004 of the European Parliament and of the Council ('Unfair Commercial Practices Directive') [2005] OJ L149/22.

[69] Directive (EU) 2011/83 of the European Parliament and of the Council of 25 October 2011 on consumer rights, amending Council Directive 93/13/EEC and Directive 1999/44/EC of the European Parliament and of the Council and repealing Council Directive 85/577/EEC and Directive 97/7/EC of the European Parliament and of the Council [2011] OJ L304/64.

[70] Council Directive (EEC) 93/13 of 5 April 1993 on unfair terms in consumer contracts [1993] OJ L95/29.

[71] European Commission, 'Review of EU consumer law: Fitness Check of EU consumer law on digital fairness' (2023) <https://commission.europa.eu/law/law-topic/consumer-protection-law/review-eu-consumer-law_en> 28 July 2023.

3.3 Fitness Checks

Ex post fitness checks represent a relatively new instrument in European consumer law. These checks attempt to evaluate the effectiveness and coherence of existing legislation related to consumer law. Fitness checks effectively identify regulatory overlaps, inconsistencies, potential synergies, digitalization possibilities, and cumulative impacts within the policy area under examination.[72] They provide a comprehensive and holistic view of the effectiveness and coherence of the existing legislative framework, helping policy-makers make informed decisions and improve the overall regulatory landscape.

The REFIT exercise was the first formal fitness test in European consumer law.[73] With regard to consumer law,[74] it aimed to evaluate whether the Unfair Contract Terms Directive,[75] the Consumer Sales and Guarantees Directive,[76] the Price Indication Directive,[77] the Unfair Commercial Practices Directive,[78] and the Injunctions Directive[79] are effective, efficient, relevant, coherent, and have EU added values.[80] REFIT should also assess additional inefficiencies like

[72] Commission Guidelines (2021) 10. The Smart Regulation complemented the Better Regulation agenda in 2010, highlighting that a holistic approach throughout the policy cycle is necessary. European Commission, 'Smart Regulation in the European Union' COM(2010) 543 final, 4–5.

[73] European Commission, 'EU Regulatory Fitness' COM(2012) 746 final; European Commission, 'Digital contracts for Europe: Unleashing the potential of e-commerce' COM(2015) 633 final. For an overview see eg Alberto Alemanno, 'How Much Better Is Better Regulation? Assessing the Impact of the Better Regulation Package on the European Union: A Research Agenda' 2015) 6(3) European Journal of Risk Regulation 344; Francesco Sarpi, 'Better for Whom?' (2015) 6(3) European Journal of Risk Regulation 372.

[74] It also examined misleading and comparative advertising in B2B marketing. It falls outside the scope of inquiry of this book and is consequently not examined.

[75] Directive (EEC) 93/13 of 5 April 1993 on unfair terms in consumer contracts [1993] OJ L95/29 (Unfair Contract Terms Directive).

[76] Directive (EC) 1999/44 of 25 May 1999 on certain aspects of the sale of consumer goods and associated guarantees [1999] OJ L171/1 (Consumer Sales and Guarantees Directive), repealed and replaced by Directive (EU) 2019/771 of 20 May 2019 on certain aspects concerning contracts for the sale of goods, amending Regulation (EU) 2017/2394 and Directive 2009/22/EC, and repealing Directive 1999/44/EC [2019] OJ L136/28.

[77] Directive (EC) 98/6 of 16 February 1998 on consumer protection in the indication of the prices of products offered to consumers [1998] OJ L80/27 (Price Indication Directive).

[78] Directive (EC) 2005/29 of 11 May 2005 concerning unfair business-to-consumer commercial practices in the internal market and amending Council Directive 84/450/EEC, Directives 97/7/EC, 98/27/EC and 2002/65/EC of the European Parliament and of the Council and Regulation (EC) No 2006/2004 of the European Parliament and of the Council [2005] OJ L149/22 (Unfair Commercial Practices Directive).

[79] Directive (EC) 2009/22.

[80] European Commission, 'Report of the Fitness Check on Directive 2005/29/EC of the European Parliament and of the Council of 11 May 2005 concerning unfair business-to-consumer commercial practices in the internal market and amending Council Directive 84/450/EEC, Directives 97/7/EC, 98/27/EC and 2002/65/EC of the European Parliament and of the Council and Regulation (EC) No 2006/2004 of the European Parliament and of the Council (Unfair Commercial Practices Directive); Council Directive 93/13/EEC of 5 April 1993 on unfair terms in consumer contracts; Directive 98/6/EC of the European Parliament and of the Council of 16 February 1998 on consumer protection in the indication of the prices of products offered to consumers; Directive 1999/44/EC of the European Parliament and of the Council of 25 May 1999 on certain aspects of the sale of consumer goods and associated guarantees;

'excessive burdens overlaps, gaps, inconsistencies, implementation problems and/or obsolete measures' and synergies like 'improved performance, simplification, lower costs, reduced burdens'.[81]

The REFIT deployed various methods, focusing on 'analysis', 'consumer experience', and 'consultation'.[82] The analysis section contains a legal analysis of Member State legislation, case law, and literature. The consumer experience section includes consumer surveys, behavioural experiments, and mystery shopping exercises. The consultation stage featured targeted surveys, interviews and other case studies, workshops, and an online public consultation.

REFIT featured 3 external studies. The first study (Lot 1) examined the effectiveness of various consumer protection directives and regulations, involving interviews with 147 public authorities, 49 consumer associations, and 59 business associations across all EU Member States, along with a comprehensive business survey. The second study (Lot 2) focused on the Consumer Sales and Guarantees Directive,[83] aiming to explore the possibility of aligning legal rules for face-to-face and distance sales of goods. The results were presented in 2 separate reports and were instrumental in the legislative process on the proposal for a Directive on online and other distance sales.[84] Lastly, the Lot 3 study assessed consumer awareness and experiences exercising their rights, employing a large-scale consumer survey, mystery shopping exercises, and behavioural experiments. Moreover, the study benefited from the findings of various other studies performed by DG JUST, including investigations on consumer detriment measurement, consumer issues in the sharing economy, and evaluation of national procedural laws' impact on consumer protection under EU consumer law.

The Commission conducted several internal studies. First, an online public consultation was conducted in 2016, gathering 436 replies, with around 50 additional position papers submitted.[85] Secondly, a high-level conference named the 'Consumer Summit' was held in the autumn of 2016. Attended by

Directive 2009/22/EC of the European Parliament and of the Council of 23 April 2009 on injunctions for the protection of consumers' interests; Directive 2006/114/EC of the European Parliament and of the Council of 12 December 2006 concerning misleading and comparative advertising' SWD(2017) 209 final, ch 6. This was in light of the requirements in European Commission, 'Better Regulation Guidelines' SWD(2017) 350 final, 59–65.

[81] European Commission, 'Better Regulation Guidelines' (n 80) 54.

[82] SWD(2017) 209 final, s 4.

[83] Directive (EC) 1999/44 of 25 May 1999 on certain aspects of the sale of consumer goods and associated guarantees [1999] OJ L171/12.

[84] Proposal for a Directive on certain aspects concerning contracts for the online and other distance sales of goods COM/2015/0635 final, 2015/0288 (COD).

[85] SWD(2017) 209 final, s 4 and Annex 3 of. See also Lot 1 of the study integrated the findings.

approximately 450 representatives from national authorities, European institutions, consumer organizations, businesses, and academics, the summit facilitated discussions on critical issues and concluded with insights from thematic workshops.[86] Thirdly, DG JUST set up a dedicated stakeholder expert group through an open call for applications to ensure diverse perspectives and expertise. Comprising major EU-level consumer and civil society organizations, 5 significant national consumer associations, and the primary EU-level business associations, this stakeholder group played a vital role in shaping the evaluation process.[87] Fourthly, the REFIT exercise was presented and discussed at regular meetings of DG JUST networks of consumer protection organizations, namely the Consumer Protection Cooperation network, Consumer Policy Network, European Consumer Consultative Group, and European Consumer Centres network, starting from early 2016.[88] Finally, the findings of an evaluation by the European Economic and Social Committee (ECSC) enriched the Fitness Check. The Commission requested the ECSC to assess how civil society organizations across the European Union perceive and experience the implementation of EU consumer law at the national level.[89]

The Fitness Check's comprehensive analysis drew data from these external studies and consultation activities, combined with Eurobarometer data and other available evidence. However, the Commission admitted some limitations, particularly in obtaining precise cost estimates from business respondents. As highlighted in the discussion on stakeholder consultations, REFIT incorporated a consultation platform that critics heavily criticized for its inadequate inclusion of consumer groups.[90] Scholars such as Hans-Wolfgang Micklitz and Auélie A. Villanueva have expressed their perspective on REFIT, contending that it does not follow an evidence-based approach to policy-making but rather a policy-driven approach based on preconceived ideas. They argue that consumer law does not require REFIT but demands RETHINK.[91] Vanessa

[86] The Summit's details and conclusions are available on its official website. European Commission, 'European Consumer Summit 2016' (17 October 2016) https://ec.europa.eu/newsroom/just/items/34204 (accessed 25 July 2023).

[87] SWD(2017) 209 final, s 4.

[88] ibid s 4 and Annex 3

[89] ibid s 4.

[90] Riefa (n 4) 13 ff. The initial composition is provided in Commission Decision (2015/C 425/06) of 16 December 2015 on the appointment of members of the stakeholder group of the REFIT Platform [2015] OJ C425/8.

[91] Hans-Wolfgang Micklitz and Aurélie A Villanueva, 'REFIT or Rethink: The Politics of EU Research—A Grand Misunderstanding?' in Esther van Schagen and Stephen Weatherill (eds), *Better Regulation in EU Contract Law: The Fitness Check and the New Deal for Consumers* (Hart Publishing 2019) 38. Micklitz further notes that the Fitness Check fails the rationality test because it is driven by the full harmonization agenda. Hans-Wolfgang Micklitz, *The Politics of Justice in European Private Law: Social Justice, Access Justice, Societal Justice* (CUP 2018) 261.

Mak also rightly criticizes the Fitness Check for its failure to emphasize the absence of consumer rights as social rights, a right enshrined in EU law.[92]

It seems that the primary motivation behind REFIT was the previous unsuccessful attempt with the Common European Sales Law and the necessity to justify implementing more unified measures on the EU level.[93] It is thus vital to include consumers' voices and adhere to norms of generating good evidence.

Despite certain limitations, the fitness checks successfully integrated a wide range of inputs and perspectives to comprehensively evaluate the consumer protection instruments under consideration. Further fine-tuning would make this better. With further refinement, these checks have the potential to become even more comprehensive and effective.

4 Role and Impact of Evidence

Institutionalizing evidence collection for law and policy in the European Union is a significant development. As highlighted earlier in the chapter, the Commission carries out ex ante impact assessments and stakeholder consultations. Fitness checks play a crucial role in assessing the ex post situation by evaluating the correct implementation at the national level and the overall effectiveness of instruments. This part of the chapter examines whether a disparity exists between theory and practice, explicitly exploring whether the Commission consistently adheres to evidence-based approaches. Furthermore, the chapter will thoroughly scrutinize the process of translating empirical evidence into law and policy, aiming to shed light on the intricate dynamics between evidence and decision-making processes.

4.1 From Evidence to Impact

The European Commission's Better Regulation agenda has been pivotal in promoting evidence-based European consumer contract law and policy-making.

[92] Vanessa Mak, *Legal Pluralism in European Contract Law* (OUP 2020) 93.

[93] Roger Halson and David Campbell note that the European Commission should have already addressed additional evidence in the early harmonization debate. Roger Halson and David Campbell, 'Harmonisation and its discontents: a transaction costs critique of a European contract law' in James Devenney and Mel Kenny (eds), *The Transformation of European Private Law: Harmonisation, Consolidation, Codification or Chaos?* (CUP 2013) 116 ff. Other scholars have noted that this approach resembles the review a decade earlier, which attempted drastically to harmonize the EU consumer contract law acquis. See Geraint Howells, Christian Twigg-Flesner, and Thomas Wilhelmsson, *Rethinking EU Consumer Law* (Routledge 2017) 337–38.

As mentioned earlier in this chapter, the European Commission conducts impact assessments and engages in stakeholder consultations. Additionally, fitness checks are instrumental in assessing the ex post situation, evaluating the correct implementation at the national level and the overall effectiveness of legislative instruments. What has remained unanswered is whether a disparity exists between theory and practice, explicitly exploring whether the Commission consistently adheres to evidence-based approaches. Despite instruments like impact assessments, stakeholder consultations, and fitness checks, questions persist regarding how empirical evidence informs legislative choices and enforcement decisions. It is essential to evaluate whether the Commission's guidelines and procedures sufficiently ensure the application of robust scientific standards. Furthermore, it is fundamental to scrutinize the process of translating empirical evidence into law and policy thoroughly, shedding light on the intricate dynamics between evidence and real-term impact.

One significant aspect that needs addressing involves the representation and involvement of stakeholders, particularly consumers, in the policy-making process.[94] Stakeholder consultations serve as a critical avenue for gathering diverse perspectives and insights, yet concerns still need to be raised regarding the representation of consumer interests. To achieve a more comprehensive and balanced approach, ensuring adequate accounting for consumer perspectives and making their participation substantive and meaningful, such as through citizen narratives, is crucial rather than merely symbolic.[95]

Similarly, impact assessments provide a vital opportunity to assess the potential impact of legislative proposals before and after their implementation.[96] However, the methods and the consequent quality and objectivity of these assessments vary, and the Commission must enhance their accuracy, comprehensiveness, and objectivity. The choice of entities responsible for conducting impact assessments is also significant. Striking the right balance between Commission involvement, independent bodies, and vested stakeholders can help mitigate potential biases and ensure a more impartial evaluation process.

Evidence-based policy and law-making are about ensuring reliable data and empirical findings inform decisions. However, these assessments' methods and resulting quality and objectivity vary. Efforts should focus on improving accuracy, comprehensiveness, and objectivity.[97] Despite the availability of

[94] See section 3.1 of this chapter.
[95] See eg Ranchordás (n 30).
[96] See section 3.2 of this chapter.
[97] For instance, Christine Riefa cites and supports Van den Abeele, who argues that impact assessments are partly ignored or not carried out where they would be useful. Riefa (n 46) 27; Eric van den

evidence through impact assessments, stakeholder consultations, and other studies, the Commission is not legally obligated to act on the evidence presented. There have been concerns regarding the Commission's use of evidence, with some suggesting that they selectively choose which evidence to consider or even ignore certain evidence entirely. This approach could lead to policy decisions that lack genuine evidence-based support and contradict the available evidence. Consequently, there is a need for greater accountability and transparency in the policy-making process, ensuring that empirical data and research findings play a more decisive role in shaping policies and laws that best serve the interests of European consumers.

As the body of evidence on European consumer law expands, it becomes imperative to address its limitations and continuously enhance evidence-based law and policy. By establishing a more robust framework for evidence collection, analysis, and translation, the European Commission can strengthen consumer protection, improve trader compliance, and advance the overall effectiveness of European consumer contract law. By closing the gap between theory and practice and ensuring a more cohesive integration of empirical evidence into decision-making processes, the European Union can strive towards a more evidence-driven, transparent, and accountable approach to shaping consumer policies and rules.

4.2 The Role of Evidence in Legislation and Policy-Making

Beyond the scope of European consumer contract law, Member States' interests and stakeholders' perspectives significantly influence the policy-making process. The European Commission's Better Regulation agenda aims to balance the diverse national and stakeholder interests while ensuring effective consumer protection measures across the European Union.

The involvement of Member States is pivotal at various stages of the policy-making process. The European Parliament and Council engage in debates and discussions that allow for different viewpoints, reflecting the interests of their constituencies and respective national concerns. Additionally, the Council of the European Union, composed of national ministers representing each Member State, plays a crucial role in shaping EU consumer policies.

Abeele, '"Better Regulation": a bureaucratic simplification with a political agenda' Working paper 2015.4 (Etui) 62.

While the Better Regulation agenda emphasizes evidence-based policy-making, it is essential to acknowledge the intricate dynamics between evidence and policy formulation. Evidence, in the form of fitness checks, stakeholder assessments, and impact assessments, provides valuable insights into the potential consequences of proposed and existing policies. However, policy decisions may not always stem solely from empirical evidence but could also be influenced by political considerations, negotiations among Member States, and broader policy objectives, especially when the debate spans several policy cycles.[98]

Evidence should be viewed as a tool that enhances consumer contract law discourse. By providing factual information and empirical data, evidence contributes to a more informed and comprehensive understanding of the implications of various policy choices.[99] It can facilitate constructive debates, allowing stakeholders to consider the merits and drawbacks of different legislative options.

Stakeholder consultations, impact assessments, and fitness checks serve as mechanisms that incorporate evidence into the decision-making process. Stakeholder consultations allow consumers, businesses, and civil society organizations to provide their perspectives and feedback on proposed policies. Impact assessments assess the potential effects of legislative proposals, while fitness checks evaluate the effectiveness of existing legislation.

However, the effectiveness of evidence-based policy-making relies on the quality, transparency, and independence of the evidence presented. There is a need to ensure that evidence is free from biases, including those that may arise from lobby studies conducted by companies or on their behalf. Academic studies and independent research are critical in providing impartial and credible evidence to support policy decisions.

To strengthen evidence-based policy-making in European consumer contract law, it is essential to address the limitations of the existing evidence base, including promoting comprehensive studies investigating the practical implementation of consumer rights in different Member States. Establish robust metrics for measuring compliance with consumer protection measures, allowing the translation of empirical data into focused and actionable policy recommendations.

[98] Listorti, Basyte-Ferrari, Acs, and Smits (n 37) 1563.

[99] For example, in the form of behavioural insights. See eg Kai P. Purnhagen and Peter H. Feindt, 'Better Regulatory Impact Assessment: Making Behavioural Insights Work for the Commission's New Better Regulation Strategy' (2015) 6(3) European Journal of Risk Regulation 361.

In conclusion, while the Better Regulation agenda emphasizes evidence-based policy-making, the process remains influenced by Member State interests and political considerations. Nevertheless, evidence plays a crucial role in enhancing consumer contract law discourse and ensuring more informed decision-making. By addressing the limitations in the current evidence base and promoting the use of impartial research, the European Union can further advance its efforts to strengthen consumer protection and advance European consumer contract law in a well-informed and effective manner.

4.3 The Role of Evidence in Enforcement

The European consumer contract law landscape is undergoing a momentous transformation catalysed by the New Deal for Consumers and the new focus of the Better Regulation agenda. It is reshaping conventional practices, specifically focusing on effectively applying applicable rules. A cornerstone of this transformation is the elevation of evidence-based enforcement strategies and how experiences from enforcement actions can contribute to the consumer law and policy debate.

The shift towards mandated evidence collection regarding the enforcement of rules is crucial for several reasons. One of these reasons is the scheduled review of instruments. All legislative instruments include a date when authorities must review them, theoretically infusing dynamism into enforcement practices by ensuring their responsiveness and effectiveness.[100] Another reason is evidence-driven legislative changes, which emphasize the capacity of enforcement actions to scrutinize the real-world functioning of rules. The cyclical collection of evidence is a unique characteristic of this process, as enforcement actions metamorphose into evidence and elevate the status quo. These factors contribute to a more effective and efficient enforcement and law and policy regime.

When discussing review mechanisms, it is important to consider efficiency and efficacy. One key player in this area is the Consumer Protection Cooperation (CPC) Network, which is crucial in aggregating findings and collaboratively shaping enforcement actions. For instance, coordinated mystery shopping exercises can offer valuable insights into trader behaviour

[100] Van Schagen (n 8) 149.

and compliance levels.[101] However, empirical evidence is necessary to avoid 'hunches' in compliance reviews.[102] By scientifically examining the post-assessment actions taken, regulators and legislators can better understand the practical impacts of enforcement actions and how the rules operate in practice.

As an example of how enforcement can inform legislation: In the discourse on enforcement, an unexplored area emerges—exploring the factors that underlie non-compliance. The domain of Alternative Dispute Resolution (ADR) and Online Dispute Resolution (ODR) particularly stands out as there is limited empirical evidence.[103] The extent to which traders use or opt out of the EU Commission's ODR mechanism remains uncharted, calling for a more comprehensive exploration.[104]

The fusion of enforcement actions and evidence collection is a compelling catalyst for policy and legislative advancement. Member States predominantly execute enforcement actions and do not invariably align with an evidence-based approach. Nonetheless, these actions yield substantial influence in shaping law and policy, achieved by empirically assessing how laws manifest in real-world scenarios and fostering a continuous feedback loop between enforcement and law and policy development. This dynamic process takes on an innovative dimension. Initially designed to gauge the efficacy of laws, enforcement actions evolve into tangible evidence. This transformation could occur seamlessly, with the evidence thus generated as a guiding force in shaping future policies.

Furthermore, Stephen Weatherill aptly underscores the pivotal role of the Court of Justice.[105] According to Weatherill, the Court, at times, assumes the role of a 'jack in the box', i.e., the interpretations have 'a tendency to surprise, even shock.'[106] He emphasizes 2 key points to support his perspective. First, Weatherill contends that legislators should exercise greater diligence and precision during the drafting process, effectively restraining the Court within

[101] European Commission, 'Online shopping: Commission and Consumer Protection authorities urge traders to bring information policy in line with EU law' (31 January 2020) <https://ec.europa.eu/commission/presscorner/detail/en/IP_20_156> accessed 22 November 2022.

[102] Cary Coglianese, 'Building Better Compliance' (2022) 100 Texas Law Review 213.

[103] Directive (EU) 2013/11 on alternative dispute resolution for consumer disputes and amending Regulation (EC) No 2006/2004 and Directive 2009/22/EC [2013] OJ L165/63 (Directive on Consumer ADR); Regulation (EU) 524/2013 on online dispute resolution for consumer disputes and amending Regulation (EC) No 2006/2004 and Directive 2009/22/EC [2013] OJ L165/1 (Regulation on Consumer ODR).

[104] Further discussed in chs 6 and 7.

[105] Stephen Weatherill, 'The Court as a Jack-in-the-Box: An Old Story in a New Context' in Esther van Schagen and Stephen Weatherill (eds), *Better Regulation in EU Contract Law: The Fitness Check and the New Deal for Consumers* (Hart Publishing 2019).

[106] ibid 126.

stricter bounds.[107] Secondly, he advocates for a heightened recognition of CJEU case law in the context of fitness checks.[108] Weatherill's insights shed important light on the Court of Justice's influence and the need for a more refined approach to legislative processes and case law integration. Julian Nowag and Xavier Groussot take this point even further, arguing that judges should consider evidence like impact assessments, thereby creating better regulation and adjudication.[109]

In conclusion, the enforcement feedback loop cycle steers a new paradigm where evidence-based enforcement actions scrutinize existing laws and actively contribute to their refinement through generated evidence-backed insights. Institutionalizing data collection at the EU and national level could effectively harness this information to enhance compliance measures and ensure responsive enforcement and law-making.

5 Conclusion

This chapter has critically examined the role of empirical evidence in European consumer law and policy. The chapter focused on the European Commission's REFIT and Better Regulation agenda, underscoring the shortcomings of the Commission's guidelines and methods. It revealed a lack of binding force and adherence to scientific standards.

Building upon these observations, the chapter evaluated the extent to which empirical evidence supports policy choices in EU consumer contract law. Furthermore, the chapter emphasized the importance of establishing robust metrics for measuring compliance, enabling the translation of empirical data into targeted and actionable policy recommendations. Advocating for an evidence-based approach, the chapter highlighted the significance of enhancing trader compliance to strengthen consumer protection and advance European consumer contract law.

The chapter further explored the impact of the Better Regulation agenda on fundamental concepts and principles, such as subsidiarity and proportionality. It illustrated how these principles balance consumer protection and the needs of businesses operating in the European market. Additionally, the chapter provided an overview of the instruments employed by the Commission to

[107] ibid 139–40.
[108] ibid 137–39.
[109] Julian Nowag and Xavier Groussot, 'From Better Regulation to Better Adjudication? Impact Assessment and the Court of Justice's Review' in Garben and Govaere (n 4) 196.

foster effective consumer contract law, highlighting the multifaceted approach adopted by the Commission.

Moreover, the chapter delved into the process of transforming empirical evidence into meaningful policy recommendations, examining how the Commission navigates the complex interplay between evidence, policy formulation, and enforcement. It assessed the Commission's efforts to bridge the gap between evidence and policy in European consumer contract law. The chapter reviewed the evidence from the European Commission, acknowledging its limited depth. It discussed the importance of stakeholder consultations, impact assessments, fitness checks, and third-party studies in providing valuable insights and perspectives on consumer law matters. While the Commission is required to act on gathered evidence, practical implementation often deviates from this ideal.

This chapter underscored the need for an evidence-based approach to enhance consumer protection and advance European consumer contract law. By further integrating empirical evidence into consumer law and policy, the Commission can foster transparent, efficient, and effective regulatory practices that serve the interests of consumers and businesses operating within the Single Market. Nonetheless, evidence should only inform the political discourse rather than dictate it.

In light of the foundation laid by the present chapter, this monograph will assess in the following chapters whether the legislative choices in EU consumer contract law have evidence substantiating or rejecting them. It will critically examine the role of evidence in shaping EU consumer contract law and propose pathways for further improvement and refinement in Chapter 7.

3

Controlling Unfair Contract Terms

1 Introduction

Many scholars see the Unfair Contract Terms Directive as the first piece of EU consumer sales law that manifestly harmonized the substantive content of contracts.[1] One of the main functions of the Unfair Contract Terms Directive is the control of standard terms, that is, terms that are not individually negotiated. By prohibiting unfair terms in consumer standard form contracts, the Directive aims to remove 'frontiers' in the internal market,[2] thus strengthening the position of consumers[3] and increasing competition and choice for consumers.[4] According to the Court of Justice, controlling standard terms is required as 'the consumer is in a weak position vis-a-vis the seller or supplier, as regards both his bargaining power and his level of knowledge'.[5] In addition to the weak

[1] cf Hugh Collins, 'Good Faith in European Contract Law' (1994) 14(2) Oxford Journal of Legal Studies 229; Hugh Beale, 'Legislative Control of Fairness: The Directive on Unfair Terms in Consumer Contracts' in Jack Beatson and Daniel Friedmann (eds), *Good Faith and Fault in Contract Law* (Clarendon Press 1995) 231–33; Michael Schillig, 'Inequality of Bargaining Power Versus Market for Lemons: Legal Paradigm Change and the Court of Justice's Jurisprudence on Directive 93/13 on Unfair Contract Terms' (2009) 33(3) European Law Journal 336 ff; Paolisa Nebbia, 'Unfair Contract Terms' in Christian Twigg-Flesner (ed), *The Cambridge Companion to European Union Private Law* (CUP 2010) 216–17; Stephen Weatherill, *EU Consumer Law and Policy* (2nd edn, Edward Elgar Publishing 2013) 145–46; Norbert Reich and others, *European Consumer Law* (2nd edn, Intersentia 2014) 129–30; Jacobien W Rutgers, 'Unfair Terms in Consumer Contracts' in Louise Gullifer and Stefan Vogenauer (eds), *English and European Perspectives on Contract and Commercial Law: Essays in Honour of Hugh Beale* (Hart Publishing 2014) 279–80; Catalina Goanta, *Convergence in European Consumer Sales Law: A Comparative and Numerical Approach* (Intersentia 2016) 53–57.

[2] Directive 93/13/EEC, recital 1.

[3] ibid recital 6.

[4] ibid recital 7.

[5] Joined Cases C-240/98–C-244/98 *Océano Grupo Editorial SA v Roció Murciano Quintero; Salvat Editores SA v José M Sánchez Alcón Pradès, José Luis Copano Badillo, Mohammed Berroane, Emilio Viñas Feliú* ECLI:EU:C:2000:346, para 25. The Court of Justice has since then included this phrase in almost all cases concerning the fairness assessment of contract terms. See eg 2 recent cases: Case C-590/17 *Henri Pouvin, Marie Dijoux v Électricité de France (EDF)* ECLI:EU:C:2019:232; and Case C-266/18 *Aqua Med sp z oo v Irena Skóra* ECLI:EU:C:2019:282.

Compliance with European Consumer Law. Felix Pflücke, Oxford University Press. © Oxford University Press 2024.
DOI: 10.1093/9780198906414.003.0003

bargaining position, empirical legal evidence suggests that consumers do not read standard terms when they enter into B2C transactions.[6] Mindy Chen-Wishart notes that policing unfair terms ensures that the proffering party has no 'free hand to smuggle in highly subversive terms', increasing the likelihood of informed consent and protecting the institution of contract.[7]

Before and after its adoption, the Unfair Contract Terms Directive faced heavy criticism and was only accepted by the European Parliament and Council in 1993—after almost 2 decades of debate.[8] The discussion before adopting it centred on the content and the appropriate constitutional basis for introducing such a consumer protection instrument.[9] The problems caused by and after the Directive's adoption partly related to the fact that some Member States had already implemented earlier proposals from the Paris Summit in 1975.[10] The issue was that the Unfair Contract Terms Directive was partly redundant and conflicted with some existing national laws.[11] This tension

[6] Oren Bar-Gill and Omri Ben-Shahar, 'Regulatory Techniques in Consumer Protection: A Critique of European Consumer Contract Law' (2013) 50(Special Issue) Common Market Law Review 109; Yannis Bakos, Florencia Marotta-Wurgler, and David R Trossen, 'Does Anyone Read the Fine Print? Consumer Attention to Standard Form Contracts' (2014) 43(1) Journal of Legal Studies 31.

[7] Mindy Chen-Wishart, 'Regulating Unfair Terms' in Louise Gullifer and Stefan Vogenauer (eds), *English and European Perspectives on Contract and Commercial Law: Essays in Honour of Hugh Beale* (Hart Publishing 2014) 129–30.

[8] Paolisa Nebbia, *Unfair Contract Terms in European Law: A Study in Comparative and EC Law* (Hart Publishing 2007) 7–8.

[9] There was no explicit legislative basis for consumer protection prior to the adoption of the Maastricht Treaty, which introduced what is now art 169 of the Treaty on the Functioning of the European Union. The Unfair Contract Terms Directive relied not on this provision but on the predecessor to art 114 of the TFEU (harmonization of laws in order to improve the functioning of the internal market) and a debate on the EU's competence to legislate in consumer law in pursuit of the internal market project broke out. However, the importance of consumer protection in the EU's legal system gained momentum years later, in the Lisbon Treaty: art 38 of the Charter of Fundamental Rights was made formally binding, which explicitly refers to consumer protection as an objective of the Union's policies. See eg Stephen Weatherill, 'Competence and European Private Law' in Christian Twigg-Flesner (ed), *The Cambridge Companion to European Union Private Law* (CUP 2010) 58 ff; Stephen Weatherill, 'Consumer Policy' in Gráinne de Búrca and Paul Craig (eds), *Evolution of EU Law* (OUP 2011) 848–49; Weatherill (n 1) ch 1 and 145–46; Stephen Weatherill, 'Article 38 Consumer Protection' in Steve Peers and others (eds), *The EU Charter of Fundamental Rights: A Commentary* (Hart Publishing 2014) [38.01] ff; Dorota Leczykiewicz, 'Regulatory Cost, the Consumer, and the EU Constitutional Framework' in Dorota Leczykiewicz and Stephen Weatherill (eds), *The Images of the Consumer in EU Law: Legislation, Free Movement and Competition Law* (Hart Publishing 2016) pt III.

[10] Council Resolution of 14 April 1975 on a preliminary programme of the European Economic Community for a consumer protection and information policy [1975] OJ C92/1.

[11] cf Hugh Beale, 'Unfair Contracts in Britain and Europe' (1989) 42(1) Current Legal Problems 197; Edwoud H Hondius, 'The Reception of the Directive on Unfair Terms in Consumer Contracts by Member States' (1995) 3(2) European Review of Private Law 241; Mario Tenreiro, 'The Community Directive on Unfair Terms and National Legal Systems: The Principle of Good Faith and Remedies for Unfair Terms' (1995) 3(2) European Review of Private Law 273; Hugh Collins, 'The Directive on Unfair Contract Terms: Implementation, Effectiveness, and Harmonization' in Hugh Collings (ed), *Standard Contract Terms in Europe: A Basis for and a Challenge to European Contract Law* (Kluwer Law International 2008) 1 ff.

could be observed mainly in countries with rules that control unfair terms in standard form contracts, such as France,[12] Germany,[13] the Netherlands,[14] and the United Kingdom.[15] As the examination of the national implementing rules will show, in certain situations, these Member States provide a higher level of protection than that required by EU consumer law. The Unfair Contract Terms Directive introduced only minimum consumer protection standards, allowing for stricter national rules.[16]

The discussion in this chapter focuses on controlling unfair standard contract terms on the EU and national levels. Section 2.2 discusses the Unfair Contract Terms Directive's rules and EU case law. Section 2.3 examines the substantive control mechanisms in 4 Member States—France, Germany, the Netherlands, and the United Kingdom. The discussion in section 2.4 turns in more detail to the list of potentially unfair contract terms contained in the Annex to the Unfair Contract Terms Directive and explores how the Member States have transposed this list into national law. Whether the levels of protection differ between the 4 chosen Member States is of particular interest in this section, and the book must scrutinize the national divergences before the empirical examination of contracts. Otherwise, the study would fail to provide an accurate account of the levels of compliance.

2 Unfair Contract Terms Control on the EU Level

The Unfair Contract Terms Directive covers all kinds of sales and service contracts. The scope of the Directive limits its application to cross-border and domestic contracts that have not been individually negotiated (Article 3(2) of the Unfair Contract Terms Directive) between sellers or suppliers and consumers (Article 1(1) of the Unfair Contract Terms Directive).[17] The scope of application is further narrowed down in recitals 10 and 19, Articles 1(2) and 4(2),

[12] Loi no 78-23 of 10 January 1978 (*sur la protection et l'information des consommateurs de produits et de services*, also referred to as 'Loi Scrivener 1').

[13] Gesetz zur Regelung des Rechts der Allgemeinen Geschäftsbedingungen of 9 December 1976.

[14] BW (1992) arts 6:231–6:247.

[15] Unfair Contract Terms Act 1977.

[16] For instance, the adoption of the maximum harmonization Consumer Rights Directive forced Malta to lower the consumer protection standard concerning the right of withdrawal see Rebekah Tanti-Dougall, 'Implementation of the Consumer Rights Directive: Malta' (2014) 3(3) Journal of European Consumer and Market Law 187. For an examination of the implications of full harmonization see eg Vanessa Mak, 'Full Harmonization in European Private Law: A Two-Track Concept' (2012) 20(1) European Review of Private Law 213.

[17] Articles 2(b) and 2(c) of Directive 93/13/EEC define the terms 'consumer' and 'seller or supplier'.

and in Point 2 of the Annex to the Unfair Contract Terms Directive, but only Articles 1(2) and 4(2) affect the scope of the present study.[18] The 2 provisions exclude contract terms reflecting statutory rules (Article 1(2)) and the main subject matter and adequacy of the price from the fairness assessment 'in so far as these terms are in plain intelligible language' (Article 4(2)). Despite these limitations in the Directive's application, the scope of the instrument is reasonably broad; it even includes residential tenancy agreements.[19] There is also a temporal limit included in the Directive, and the rules only apply to contracts concluded after 31 December 1994 (Article 10(1) of the Unfair Contract Terms Directive).

The central element of the Unfair Terms Directive is the unfairness test under Articles 3 and 4, complemented by a list of terms which 'may be regarded as unfair' (Annex to the Directive). Article 3(1) of the Directive contains the so-called general clause, establishing a 4-limbed test to assess whether a contractual term is unfair: the contract clause must be (1) non-individually negotiated, (2) contrary to the requirement of good faith, (3) cause a significant imbalance in the parties rights and obligations, and (4) to the detriment of the consumer. The test contains 3 open-ended terms ('good faith', 'significant imbalance', and 'detriment') but does not further define them in the Directive.[20] Catalina Goanta suggests that the EU legislator most likely envisaged that the national courts would contribute to harmonizing such norms by referring unclear terms of the Directive to the Court of Justice via the preliminary reference procedure.[21]

[18] The Directive on Unfair Terms in Consumer Contracts does not apply to: 'contracts relating to employment, contracts relating to succession rights, contracts relating to rights under family law and contracts relating to the incorporation and organization of companies or partnership agreements' (recital 10); 'insurance contracts, the terms which clearly define or circumscribe the insured risk and insurer's liability' (recital 19); and 'contractual terms which reflect mandatory statutory or regulatory provisions and the provisions or principles of international conventions to which the Member State or the Community are party, particularly in the transport area' (art 1(2)). Furthermore, the '[a]ssessment of the unfair nature of the terms shall relate neither to the definition of the main subject matter of the contract nor to the adequacy of the price and remuneration, on the one hand, as against the services or goods supplies in exchange, on the other, in so far as these terms are in plain intelligible language' (art 4(2)). Point 2 of the Annex states that the potentially unfair clauses do not apply to financial service (a, b, and c), contracts of indeterminate duration (b), and price-indexation clauses (d). Nonetheless, Member States may enact stricter rules. cf Micklitz (n 1) 136–40.

[19] Case C-488/11 *Dirk Frederik Asbeek Brusse and Katarina de Man Garabito v Jahani BV* ECLI:EU:C:2013:341; Micklitz (n 1) 133.

[20] Recital 16 of the Directive provides some guidance on applying the good faith principle. In the assessment, 'an overall evaluation of the different interests involved' must take place, taking into account the bargaining power of the parties, 'whether the consumer had an inducement to agree to the term and whether the goods or services were sold or supplied to the special order of the consumer'. Furthermore, the good faith principle 'may be satisfied where [the trader] deals fairly and equitable with the other party whose legitimate interests [the trader] has to take into account'. For a detailed discussion on the good faith principle in European Contract Law see eg Collins (n 1); Reinhard Zimmermann and Simon Whittaker (eds), *Good Faith in European Contract Law* (CUP 2000).

[21] Goanta (n 1) 57.

A by-product of defining the test in more detail for particular circumstances is further harmonization of the law and further restrictions on national regulatory and judicial autonomy. Stephen Weatherill labels this form of harmonization 'the "Europeanisation" through case law'.[22]

According to the Court's case law, when assessing whether there is a 'significant imbalance', the national courts must take into account the nature of the goods and the surrounding circumstances, including all relevant contract terms and additional documents which form part of the contract (Article 4(1) of the Directive).[23] The CJEU confirmed in *Catalunyacaixa*[24] the definition of 'significant imbalance, to the detriment of consumers' provided in *Freiburger Kommunalbauten*[25] and *Pohotovosť*:[26]

> the concept of 'significant imbalance', to the detriment of the consumer, must be assessed in the light of an analysis of the rules of national law applicable in the absence of any agreement between the parties in order to determine whether, and if so to what extent, the contract places the consumer in a less favourable legal situation than that provided for by the national law in force. To that end, an assessment of the legal situation of that consumer having regard to the means at his disposal, under national law, to prevent continued use of unfair terms, should also be carried out.

The Court went on in *Catalunyacaixa* and defined the term 'contrary to the requirement of good faith':

> in order to assess whether the imbalance arises 'contrary to the requirement of good faith', it must be determined whether the seller or supplier, dealing fairly and equitably with the consumer, could reasonably assume that the

[22] Weatherill (n 1) 151–52, 156. For instance, Stephen Weatherill, Walter van Gerven, and Jan Smits predicted the harmonization through case law shortly after the adoption of the Unfair Contract Terms Directive. See Stephen Weatherill, 'Prospects for the Development of European Private Law through Europeanisation in the Court of Justice' (1995) 3(2) European Review of Private Law 307; Walter van Gerven, 'The Case-law of the European Court of Justice and National Courts as a Contribution to the Europeanisation of Private Law' (1995) 3(2) European Review of Private Law 367; Jan M Smits, 'A European Private Law as a Mixed Legal System: Towards a Ius Commune through the Free Movement of Legal Rules' (1998) 5(4) Maastricht Journal of European and Comparative Law 328.

[23] Case C-243/08 *Pannon GSM Zrt v Erzsébet Sustikné Győrfi* ECLI:EU:C:2009:350, para 39; Case C-137/08 *VB Pénzügyi Lízing Zrt v Ferenc Schneider* (n 19) para 42.

[24] Case C-415/11 *Mohamed Aziz v Caixa d'Estalvis de Catalunya, Tarragona i Manresa (Catalunyacaixa)* ECLI:EU:C:2013:164.

[25] Case C-237/02 *Freiburger Kommunalbauten GmbH Baugesellschaft & Co KG v Ludger Hofstetter and Ulrike Hofstetter* ECLI:EU:C:2004:209, para 21.

[26] Case C-76/10 *Pohotovosť sro v Iveta Korčkovská* ECLI:EU:C:2010:685, para 59.

consumer would have agreed to the term concerned in individual contract negotiations.[27]

The Court of Justice also confirmed its earlier ruling in *Invitel*, where it established that the Member States' courts had to take into account the guidelines provided by the CJEU when interpreting the good faith principle.[28] However, as pointed out above, the national courts must not consider the definition of the subject matter and the price/quality ratio as long as the terms are in plain, intelligible language (Article 4(2) of the Directive).[29] The Court of Justice laid down in *Kásler*[30] that plain, intelligible language not only means 'formally and grammatically intelligible'[31] but that the 'contract sets out transparently the reason for and the particularities' of the term.[32] The *contra proferentem* principle ensures compliance with the transparency requirement, establishing that ambiguous terms are interpreted in favour of the consumer (Article 5 of the Directive).[33]

In *Commission of the European Communities v Kingdom of Sweden* the Court of Justice found that the Directive does not require formal implementation of the list of potentially unfair terms contained in its Annex.[34] However, the Court explained that Member States must 'choose a form and method of implementation that offer a sufficient guarantee that the public can obtain knowledge of it'.[35] The Court concluded in paragraph 23 that it sufficed if Member States included the list contained in the Annex to the Directive in the 'preparatory work', which ensures that the public, so consumers and traders, can access the list (paragraph 24).[36] Contract terms corresponding to those in the list of

[27] Case C-415/11 *Catalunyacaixa* (n 24) para 76.
[28] Case C-472/10 *Nemzeti Fogyasztóvédelmi Hatóság v Invitel Távközlési Zrt* ECLI:EU:C:2012:242, para 22. Dorota Leczykiewicz, 'Private regulation, compliance and reviewability of contracts' in Roger Brownsword, Rob AJ van Gestel, and Hans-Wolfgang Micklitz (eds), *Contract and Regulation: A Handbook on New Methods of Law Making in Private Law* (Edward Elgar Publishing 2017) 353–54.
[29] The recitals to the Directive provide further details, in particular recital 19: 'whereas the main subject matter of the contract and the price/quality ratio may nevertheless be taken into account in assessing the fairness of other terms; whereas it follows, inter alia, that in insurance contracts, the terms which clearly define or circumscribe the insured risk and the insurer's liability shall not be subject to such assessment since these restrictions are taken into account in calculating the premium paid by the consumer'.
[30] Case C-26/13 *Árpád Kásler and Hajnalka Káslerné Rábai v OTP Jelzálogbank Zrt* ECLI:EU:C:2014:282.
[31] ibid para 71.
[32] ibid para 73.
[33] Stephen Weatherill, 'Empowerment is not the only fruit' in Leczykiewicz and Weatherill (n 9) 212–14; Stephen Weatherill, *The Internal Market as a Legal Concept* (OUP 2017) 160–61.
[34] Case C-478/99 *Commission of the European Communities v Kingdom of Sweden* ECLI:EU:C:2002:281.
[35] ibid para 22.
[36] cf Micklitz (n 1) 158; Weatherill (n 1) 149–50.

potentially unfair terms in the Directive's Annex were indirectly reviewed by the Court of Justice when it used the list of terms to interpret the general test of unfairness under Article 3. In addition to defining the general criteria of the unfairness test, the Court may also exceptionally declare a term unfair where the circumstances of the case leave no room for doubt.[37] The Court's treatment of these terms contained in the Annex to the Directive introduces de facto prohibitions of unfair contract terms on the EU level.[38] National courts must consider these CJEU cases when assessing the (un)fairness of terms in standard form consumer contracts.[39]

Article 6(1) of the Unfair Contract Terms Directive deals with the effects of recognizing terms as 'unfair', requiring the Member States to introduce provisions into their national laws which declare unfair terms non-binding upon consumers. The Court of Justice clarified that the provision 'must be interpreted as meaning that a contractual term held to be unfair must be regarded, in principle, as never having existed, so that it cannot have any effect on the consumer'.[40] Generally speaking, consumers do not need to contest such provision when they enter the contractual relationship; unfair terms are at no time binding upon them.[41] There are, however, exceptional circumstances in which the Court has accepted that a consumer may remain bound by such a clause. One instance is where a national procedural provision precludes the review of a potentially unfair contract term.[42] In the CJEU case *Asturcom Telecomunicaciones SL*,[43] a Spanish consumer contested neither an arbitration clause nor the consequent final arbitration award, and, under these circumstances, of unusual inattentiveness, the principle of *res judicata* operating in national law prevented the consumer from challenging the unfair term. The

[37] Joined Cases C-240/98–C-244/98 *Océano Grupo Editorial SA* (n 5); Case C-237/02 *Freiburger Kommunalbauten GmbH Baugesellschaft & Co KG v Ludger Hofstetter and Ulrike Hofstetter* ECLI:EU:C:2004:209.

[38] The book will examine some of the Court of Justice cases concerning the provisions in the Annex to the Directive in section 3.4.

[39] cf Weatherill (n 1) 156–58; Hans-Wolfgang Micklitz and Norbert Reich, 'The Court and Sleeping Beauty: The Revival of the Unfair Contract Terms Directive (UCTD)' (2014) 51(3) Common Market Law Review 771 ff; Peter Rott, 'Unfair Contract Terms' in Christian Twigg-Flesner (ed), *Research Handbook on EU Consumer and Contract Law* (Edward Elgar Publishing 2016) 292 ff.

[40] Joined Cases C-154/15, C-307/15 and C-308/15 *Francisco Gutiérrez Naranjo v Cajasur Banco SAU; Ana María Palacios Martínez v Banco Bilbao Vizcaya Argentaria SA (BBVA); Banco Popular Español, SA v Emilio Irles López, Teresa Torres Andreu* [2016] ECLI:EU:C:2016:980, para 61.

[41] Case C-243/08 *Pannon GSM Zrt v Erzsébet Sustikné Győrfi* (n 23).

[42] See generally Anthony Arnull, 'The Principle of Effective Judicial Protection in EU law: an Unruly Horse?' (2011) 36(1) European Law Review 51.

[43] Case C-40/08 *Asturcom Telecomunicaciones SL v Cristina Rodríguez Nogueira* ECLI:EU:C:2009:615. cf Martin Ebers, 'From *Océano* to *Asturcom*: Mandatory Consumer Law, Ex Officio Application of European Union Law and Res Judicata' (2010) 18(4) European Review of Private Law 823; Weatherill (n 1) 158.

case would have ended differently only if Spanish procedural law required a review in similar domestic situations, as this would trigger the application of the principle of equivalence.[44]

However, this is exceptional. Usually, the Court expects the consumer interest to prevail over obstacles caused by national procedural law. In the earlier CJEU case of *Mostaza Claro*,[45] where the consumer challenged the unfair term in the arbitral proceedings, the Court allowed the consumer to challenge the arbitral findings. Even though it was too late to challenge the arbitral findings under Spanish law, the Court took the side of the consumer, emphasizing that 'the aim of the Directive is to strengthen consumer protection'.[46] National courts must also evaluate out of their motion whether the contract contains potentially unfair terms.[47] The Court's commitment to safeguarding consumers is evident in another rule crafted by the CJEU, which is both creative and tailored to the specific context: national courts may set aside the unfair contract term and replace it with national provisions where the contract is otherwise not capable of continuing, but only where the invalidity of the unfair term would expose the consumer to particularly unfavourable consequences.[48]

The combination of open-ended norms and the non-binding and non-exhaustive list of potentially unfair terms might create a hotchpotch in the national contract laws, and the matter is made more complicated again as a result of the fact that the Directive is a minimum harmonization instrument (Article 8 of the Unfair Contract Terms Directive). Member States may opt for a higher level of protection and enact provisions which render certain clauses automatically unfair.[49] The initial proposal for the Unfair Contract Terms

[44] cf Arnull (n 42) 53–55, 65–66.

[45] Case C-168/05 *Elisa María Mostaza Claro v Centro Móvil Milenium SL* [2006] ECLI:EU:C:2006:675.

[46] ibid para 37. Stephen Weatherill, *Law and Values in the European Union* (OUP 2016) 180–81, 359–61.

[47] Case C-168/05 *Elisa María Mostaza Claro v Centro Móvil Milenium SL* [2006] ECLI:EU:C:2006:675, para 38; Case C-40/08 *Asturcom Telecomunicaciones SL v Cristina Rodríguez Nogueira* ECLI:EU:C:2009:615, para 59; Case C-243/08 *Pannon GSM Zrt v Erzsébet Sustikné Győrfi* (n 23) para 35; Vanessa Mak, 'Two levels, one standard? The multi-level regulation of consumer protection in Europe' in James Devenny and Mel Kenny (eds), *European Consumer Protection: Theory and Practice* (CUP 2012) 24–26.

[48] Case C-26/13 *Árpád Kásler and Hajnalka Káslerné Rábai v OTP Jelzálogbank Zrt* ECLI:EU:C:2014:282, paras 76–85; Vanessa Mak, *Legal Pluralism in European Contract Law* (OUP 2020) 162. See also 2 more recent judgments: Joined Cases C-70/17 and C-179/17 *Abanca Corporación Bancaria SA v Alberto García Salamanca Santos and Bankia SA v Alfonso Antonio Lau Mendoza and Verónica Yuliana Rodríguez Ramírez* ECLI:EU:C:2019:250, paras 56–64; and Case C-260/18 *Kamil Dziubak and Justyna Dziubak v Raiffeisen Bank International AG* ECLI:EU:C:2019:819, paras 46–56, 63–68.

[49] Article 9 of Directive 93/13/EEC obliges the Commission to report to the Council on the implementation of the Unfair Contract Terms Directive. cf Micklitz (n 1) 163.

Directive included a 'black list',[50] that is, a list of terms regarded as unfair in all circumstances, but the legislator did not adopt it due to the lack of political support.[51] Similarly, the 2008 proposal for the Consumer Rights Directive was not adopted. That proposal would have turned the Directive on Unfair Terms in Consumer Contracts into a maximum harmonization instrument,[52] but as a result of political opposition to this change, the finally adopted Consumer Rights Directive introduced only a requirement that the Member States report on the implementation of Directive 93/13 to the European Commission (now Article 8a the Unfair Contract Terms Directive).[53] Despite these failed attempts to enact further harmonized rules to control unfair terms, the Unfair Contract Terms Directive established a common mechanism to control unfair contract terms by introducing a general test of unfairness, the Directive introduced a common definition of standard terms, and contributed to the development of the transparency principle.

The nature of the Unfair Contract Terms Directive makes an examination of the national implementing rules indispensable. The chapter discusses how France, Germany, the Netherlands, and the United Kingdom have dealt with the obligation stemming from Articles 3 and 4 of the Directive and whether their approach is compatible with these duties and the Court of Justice case law.

[50] Proposal for a Council Directive on unfair terms in consumer contracts COM(1990) 322 final OJ C243/2, in particular art 2 of the Proposal and Annex to the Proposal. See generally Hans Erich Brandner and Peter Ulmer, 'The Community Directive on Unfair Terms in Consumer Contracts: Some Critical Remarks on the Proposal Submitted by the EC Commission' (1991) 28(3) Common Market Law Review 647.

[51] The Council was not in favour of introducing a 'black list'. See Official Journal of the European Communities, Volume 36, No C 21/97 (25 January 1992). There has also been an academic debate relating to the creation of a European-wide 'black list' of unfair contract terms see eg Hans-Wolfgang Micklitz, 'Reforming European Unfair Terms Legislation in Consumer Contracts' (2010) 6(4) European Review of Contract Law 347; Daniela Caruso, 'Black Lists and Private Autonomy in EU Contract Law' in Dorota Leczykiewicz and Stephen Weatherill (eds), *The Involvement of EU Law in Private Law Relationships* (Hart Publishing 2013).

[52] Proposal for a Directive of the European Parliament and of the Council on Consumer Rights COM(2008) 614. For a deeper discussion on the minimum versus maximum harmonization debate see eg Stephen Weatherill, *Contract Law of the Internal Market* (Intersentia 2016) ch 6; Simon Whittaker, 'Unfair Contract Terms and Consumer Guarantees: the Proposal for a Directive on Consumer Rights and the Significance of "Full Harmonisation"' (2009) 5(3) European Review of Contract Law 223.

[53] Consumer Rights Directive, art 32. cf Weatherill (n 1) 160. The Member State notifications can be accessed on the European Commission's website: European Commission, 'Notifications under Article 8a of Directive 93/13/EEC' (31 May 2019) https://ec.europa.eu/info/notifications-under-article-8a-directive-93-13-eec_en (accessed 4 July 2020). Chapter 3.3 will discuss the content of the notifications.

3 Unfair Contract Terms Control on the National Level

The discussion in this section focuses on controlling unfair standard contract terms in France, Germany, the Netherlands, and the United Kingdom. This section examines 3 key issues: (1) the national rules before the adoption of and subsequent changes made under the Unfair Terms in Consumer Contracts Directive (1993) in the Member States; (2) the current national legislative and judge-made rules; (3) comparative observations, highlighting convergences and divergences among the 4 countries.

As mentioned, Germany, the United Kingdom, and France implemented similar rules to those later introduced by the Directive, in 1976,[54] 1977,[55] and 1978[56] respectively. The Member States discussed these national consumer protection measures at the Paris Summit in 1972, where the EU Member States expressed their willingness to strengthen and coordinate consumer protection measures.[57] Despite the Member States' affirmations at the Summit and their efforts in enacting such rules at the national level, it took 2 decades to adopt the Directive on Unfair Terms in Consumer Contracts (1993). The sensitive nature of the Directive partly contributes to the length of the legislative debate.[58] After all, the Directive harmonized substantive consumer contract rules[59] and, according to Stephen Weatherill, also 'challenges contractual autonomy', which he argued was much more contested than existing EU consumer protection measures, such as the Doorstep Selling Directive.[60]

Although there were national rules concerning unfair terms in standard contracts dating back to the 1970s, most Member States had to amend the national rules that pre-dated the Unfair Contract Terms Directive. However, the Member States were slow to transpose the Directive into their national contract laws. For instance, France, Germany, the Netherlands, and the United Kingdom did not implement the Directive on Unfair Terms in Consumer Contracts on time. The Netherlands implemented the Directive only in 1999, the deadline being 31 December 1994.[61] The reasons for the delay in the

[54] Gesetz zur Regelung des Rechts der Allgemeinen Geschäftsbedingungen of 9 December 1976.

[55] Unfair Contract Terms Act 1977.

[56] Loi no 78-23 of 10 January 1978 (*sur la protection et l'information des consommateurs de produits et de services*; 'Loi Scrivener 1').

[57] Bulletin of the European Communities, 'Statement from the Paris Summit 19 to 21 October 1972' (October 1972, No 10) Luxembourg: Office for official publications of the European Communities, para 6 (Social Policy).

[58] cf Weatherill (n 1) 6, 145–46.

[59] As pointed out above in Weatherill (n 1); Beale (n 11); Hondius (n 11); Tenreiro (n 11); Collins (n 11).

[60] cf Weatherill (n 1) 144.

[61] Directive 93/13/EEC, art 10(1); Goanta (n 1) 224.

implementation vary between the Member States, but there are 3 possible explanations for the delay. First and foremost, the Member States believed that their national contract laws already contained the consumer rights enshrined in the Directive; the minimum harmonization character of the Directive allowed for more stringent rules,[62] and did not force the Member States to lower the level of protection.[63] Another explanation is that the Directive's open-ended norms, such as 'fairness' and 'good faith', were partly unknown in the national contract laws.[64] These 2 explanations are substantiated in the Dutch context by the omission to transpose the *contra proferentem* rule and the principle of transparency into the Dutch Civil Code.[65] The case ultimately ended up in the Court of Justice,[66] where the 'Netherlands Government has stated that the aims sought by the Directive could be attained through a schematic interpretation of the provisions of Netherlands law'.[67] The Court of Justice disagreed with that argument, holding that implementing the Directive in such a form 'cannot achieve the clarity and precision needed to meet the requirement of legal certainty'.[68] There is consequently an obligation to implement each provision of the Directive, except for the Annex, into national law.

The previous section of this chapter has highlighted several failed attempts to amend or replace the Unfair Contract Terms Directive. The Consumer Rights Directive only introduced minor changes: it inserted a provision into the Unfair Contract Terms Directive that obliges the Member States to report to the Commission national provisions that go further than the minimum harmonization rules of the Directive (Article 8a of the Unfair Contract Terms Directive).[69] France, Germany, the Netherlands, and the United Kingdom have notified the Commission under this provision that their national rules go beyond the required standard of the Directive. France has reported that its '[n]ational law also covers the unfairness of individually negotiated contract terms and contains a list of terms considered unfair in all circumstances (ie a black list) and a list of terms considered unfair unless it is proven that they are fair (*id est* a form of grey list)'. In the case of Germany, the Commission

[62] Directive 93/13/EEC, art 8.
[63] Hondius (n 11) 242. Hondius argued that most Member States had higher 'standards of consumer protection than the Directive'.
[64] Goanta (n 1) 55–57.
[65] Ewoud H Hondius, 'Unfair Contract Terms and the Consumer: ECJ Case Law, Foreign Literature, and Their Impact on Dutch Law' (2016) 24(3–4) European Review of Private Law 462.
[66] Case C-144/99 *Commission of the European Communities v Kingdom of the Netherlands* ECLI:EU:C:2001:257.
[67] ibid para 20.
[68] ibid para 21.
[69] Consumer Rights Directive, art 32.

website states that '[n]ational law contains 2 black lists of standard contract terms considered unfair'. The Dutch have notified the Commission that their '[n]ational law contains a list of contract terms considered unfair in all circumstances (*id est* black list) and a list of contract terms which may be considered unfair, *id est* a form of grey list. The list has been extended beyond that included in the UCTD'. Lastly, the United Kingdom has provided the following information: '[n]ational law does not go beyond the minimum standard of the UCTD. However, the indicative list in the Annex to the UCTD has been extended'.[70]

Before the chapter examines and compares the national rules concerning unfair contract terms, the terms 'indicative list', 'grey list', and 'black list' need to be clarified. EU law only defines 'indicative' and 'black' lists. The Annex to the Unfair Contract Terms Directive contains an 'indicative list'; that is, a list of terms that may be considered unfair. A 'black list' can be found in the Unfair Commercial Practices Directive 2005/29/EC: Annex 1 to the Directive lists 'commercial practices which are in all circumstances considered unfair'. There is no common definition of a 'grey list' on the EU level, and the use of this term is often misleading. For instance, Mindy Chen-Wishart labelled Schedule 2 Part 1 of the Consumer Rights Act 2015 as a 'grey list'.[71] One could argue that this is not entirely incorrect. The list in the 2015 Act is merely indicative, that is, there is a suspicion of unfairness, and also non-exhaustive like the list contained in the Annex to the Unfair Contract Terms Directive. Therefore, Schedule 2 Part 1 of the Consumer Rights Act 2015 falls within the category of an 'indicative list'. In addition, the United Kingdom's notification to the European Commission is imprecise since the Consumer Rights Act 2015 goes beyond the minimum standard of the Directive. In particular, the Act applies to individually negotiated terms (section 61) and contains 'black-listed' contract terms in sections 31 and 65; certain contract terms are also automatically invalid at common law. Equally, the notification of the German government to the European Commission that the BGB contains 2 'black lists' is incorrect. This chapter will reveal that the BGB has only 1 'black list' (see § 309 of the BGB), while § 308 of the BGB resembles in character the mechanism of a 'grey list' like Article R212-2 of the Code de la consommation and Article 6:237 of the BW. Terms contained in these 'grey lists' are presumed to be unfair with limited judicial discretion. Although § 308 BGB is slightly stricter than the French and Dutch 'grey lists', the German provision still grants some discretion

[70] European Commission (n 53).

[71] Mindy Chen-Wishart, *Contract Law* (6th edn, OUP 2018) 421. At page 421, Chen-Wishart refers to Schedule 2 Part 1 as a 'grey list', while at page 446, Chen-Wishart refers to Schedule 2 Part 1 as 'the list of indicatively unfair terms'.

to the courts. However, 'black lists' under the EU-wide Unfair Commercial Practices Directive definition allow no judicial discretion. Therefore, the chapter will refer to § 308 BGB as a 'grey list'.

The following sections in this chapter will look at all 4 jurisdictions and assess the extent to which the national laws go beyond the rules of the Directive. This examination will lay the foundation for the upcoming compliance assessments with the potentially unfair contract terms listed in the Annex to the Unfair Contract Terms Directive.

3.1 France

In the 1960s and 1970s, the French legislature introduced statutory provisions explicitly dealing with consumer-trader relations into the French Civil Code. The most far-reaching reforms were the enactments of the *Lois Scrivener* in 1978 and 1979,[72] where the loi no 78-23 prohibited certain clauses in consumer contracts.[73] The *Lois Scrivener* also installed the Commission on Unfair Clauses (*Commission des clauses abusives*) to compile a list of unfair clauses to be included in the regulatory provisions. Until the *Cour de cassation* judgment in 1991,[74] French courts could only declare contract terms unfair if the examples of unfair clauses in the regulatory provisions drafted by the administration listed them.[75] Several legislative reforms also shaped the French approach to policing unfair terms, especially in 1988,[76] 1993,[77] 1995,[78]

[72] Loi no 78-22 of 10 January 1978 (*relative à l'information et à la protection des consommateurs dans le domaine de certaines opérations de credit*); loi no 78-23 of 10 January 1978 (*sur la protection et l'information des consommateurs de produits et de services*); loi no 79-596 of 13 July 1979 (*relative à l'information et à la protection des emprunteurs dans le domaine immobilier*).

[73] See generally Hélène Bricks, *Les Clauses Abusives* (Librairie générale de droit et de jurisprudence 1982) ch 1; Nebbia (n 8) 6–9; Claire-Marie Péglion-Zika, *La notion de clause abusive* (Librairie générale de droit et de jurisprudence 2018) 4–7.

[74] Cass civ (1) 14 May 1991, no 89-20999.

[75] Simon Whittaker and Reinhard Zimmermann, 'Good faith in European contract law: surveying the legal landscape' in Reinhard Zimmermann and Simon Whittaker (eds), *Good Faith in European Contract Law* (CUP 2000) 36–37.

[76] Loi no 88-14 of 5 January 1988 (*relative aux actions en justice des associations agréées de consommateurs et à l'information des consommateurs*). See generally Geneviève Viney, 'Un pas vers l'assainissement des pratiques contractuelles: la loi du 5 janvier 1988 relative aux actions en justice des associations agréées de consommateurs' (1988) Juris-Classeur périodique, édition Entreprise 3355.

[77] Loi no 93-949 of 26 July 1993 (*relative au code de la consommation*). See generally Michel Trochu, 'Les clauses abusives dans les contrats conclus avec les consommateurs' (1993) Recueil Dalloz 316.

[78] Loi no 95-96 of 1 February 1995 (*concernant les clauses abusives et la présentation des contrats et régissant diverses activités d'ordre économique et commercial*). See generally Alain Bénabent, 'Clauses Abusives: le droit français et ses réactions à la directive européenne' (1995) 3(2) European Review of Private Law 211; Michel Testud, 'La transposition en droit interne de la directive communautaire sur les clauses abusives' (1996) 13 Dalloz Affaires 372; Hélène Davo, 'Clauses Abusives: loi du février 1995 transportant la directive 93/13/CCE en droit français' (1997) 5(2) European Review of Private Law

2008,[79] 2016,[80] and 2018.[81] In the most recent reforms in 2016 and 2018, the French legislator introduced 2 provisions which require that contract terms do not 'deprive a debtor's essential obligation of its substance' (Article 1170 of the Code civil) and that terms in standard form contracts 'which create a significant imbalance in the rights and obligations of the parties to the contract are deemed not written' (Article 1171 of the Code civil).[82] Article 1170 is of general application, including, for instance, individually negotiated terms, while Article 1171 states that it only covers standard contract terms (*contrats d'adhésion*) that do 'not concern either the main subject matter of the contract nor the adequacy of the price for the performance'.[83] Articles 1170 and 1171, therefore, fall within the scope of this book's empirical part, which assesses trader compliance in B2C e-commerce transactions. However, the general test under Article L212-1 of the Code de la consommation in connection with the regulatory provisions is more precise and stricter and thus serves as *lex specialis*.[84] It will thus be the focus of the present inquiry.

Article L212-1 of the Code de la consommation transposes almost word-for-word the content of the general test of the Unfair Contract Terms Directive (Articles 3(1) and 4(1) of the Directive). Like the Directive, Article L212-1 applies only to B2C contracts and to terms that do not define 'the main object of the contract or to the adequacy of the price or the remuneration for the good sold or the service offered, provided that the clauses are written in

157. Further details on this far-reaching reform and the surrounding academic debate are provided in Abbas Karimi, *Les clauses abusives et la théorie de l'abus de droit* (Librairie Generale de Droit et de Jurisprudence 2001); Anne-Marie De Matos, *Les contrats transfrontières conclus par les consommateurs au sein de l'Union européenne* (Presses Universitaires d'Aix-Marseille 2001); Elise Poillot, *Droit européen de la consommation et uniformisation du droit des contrats* (Librairie Generale de Droit et de Jurisprudence 2006).

[79] Loi no 2008-776 of 4 August 2008 (*modernisation de l'économie*). See generally Dalloz, *Commentaire Code de la consommation* (Dalloz 5 February 2020) ch 2.3.

[80] Décret no 2016-884 of 29 June 2016 (*relatif à la partie réglementaire du code de la consommation*). See generally Romain Loir, 'Les nouvelles définitions du professionnel, du consommateur et du non-professionnel' (2016) 27 Juris-Classeur périodique, édition Entreprise 1042; Philippe Stoffel-Munck, 'The Revolution in Unfair Terms' in John Cartwright and Simon Whittaker (eds), *The Code Napoléon Rewritten: French Contract Law after the 2016 Reforms* (Hart Publishing 2017) 150–52.

[81] Loi no 2018-287 of 20 April 2018 (*ratifiant l'ordonnance no 2016-131 du 10 février 2016 portant réforme du droit des contrats, du régime général et de la preuve des obligations*), in particular art 7. See generally Jean-Denis Pellier, 'L'ordonnance portant réforme du droit des contrats, du régime général et de la preuve des obligations enfin ratifiée!' (2018) Dalloz actualité 30 April 2018.

[82] Philippe Stoffel-Munck notes that the case law of the Cour de cassation shaped art 1170, while French consumer contract law influenced art 1171, in particular art L212-1 of the Code de la consommation. Stoffel-Munck (n 80) 147–48, 150–56.

[83] Stoffel-Munck (n 80) 148–49, 157–58.

[84] It is unclear whether this might change over time due to an increase in case law or further legislative changes.

a clear and understandable way'.[85] One significant difference between Article L212-1 and the Directive is that the French provision applies to individually negotiated contracts.[86] In addition, the French provision makes no explicit reference to good faith;[87] Article L212-1 of the Code de la consommation is also a legislative provision (*disposition législative*) and grants the administration the power to draft regulatory provisions which list unfair terms. Article L212-1 therefore provides the legal basis for the 2 regulatory provisions (*disposition réglementaire*, here *décret en Conseil d'État*) containing the *liste noire* and *liste grise*. The *list noire* (Article R212-1 of the Code de la consommation) contains examples of contract terms that are unfair under all circumstances. The *liste grise* (Article R212-2 of the Code de la consommation) operates under the presumption of unfairness, which does not impose an outright prohibition. However, it shifts the burden of proof that terms are not unfair onto traders.[88] The court assesses the trader's evidence that the clause is not unfair under the general test (Article L212-1 of the Code de la consommation). However, the court declares the contract term unfair when the trader fails to submit evidence.[89] The consequence of the extensive nature of the 2 lists is that it marginalizes the role of the general test of unfairness under Article L212-1. The fact that the Cour de Cassation has issued fewer than 50 rulings since enacting the general test further supports this assessment.[90]

Several exceptions apply to the 2 lists outlined in Article R212-3 and Article R212-4 of the Code de la consommation. Most of these exceptions fall outside of the scope of the present study: Article R212-3 no 1 and Article R212-4 paragraphs 1 and 2 apply to financial services; Article R212-3 no 2 applies to the purchase or sale of foreign currency, traveller's checks, or international money orders; Article R212-4 paragraph 3 applies to contracts of indefinite duration. Only Article R212-4 paragraph 4 is of interest. The provision allows traders to modify the contract terms unilaterally, contrary to Article R212-1 no

[85] Article L212-1(3) of the Code de la consommation resembles the content of arts 3(1) and 4(2) of the Unfair Contract Terms Directive 93/13/EEC.

[86] cf François Collart Dutilleul and Philippe Delebecque, 'Introduction: Le droit spécial des contrats' in François Collart Dutilleul and Philippe Delebecque, *Contrats civils et commerciaux* (11th edn, Dalloz 2019) [12].

[87] Formerly art L132-1 Code de la consommation (before the 2016 reform); Xavier Lagarde, 'Qu'est-ce qu'une clause abusive?' (2006) 80(6) Juris-Classeur périodique, édition générale 255; Simon Whittaker, 'Clauses abusives et garanties des consommateurs: la proposition de directive relative aux droits des consommateurs et la portée de l'"harmonisation complète"' (2009) Recueil Dalloz 1152; Stoffel-Munck (n 80) 150–52.

[88] It is not possible contractually to shift the burden of proof (*charge de la preuve*) onto consumers (art R212-1 no 12 of the Code de la consommation).

[89] Jérôme Julien, *Droit de la consommation* (2nd edn, Librairie générale de droit et de jurisprudence 2017) 296–99.

[90] Stoffel-Munck (n 80) 152.

3 and Article R212-2 no 6, where technical developments require such modifications. Nonetheless, Article R212-4 paragraph 4 provides that such a contract term should not affect the good's price, quality, or characteristics.

In addition to the 2 lists in the Code de la consommation, there are various lists of potentially unfair terms ('indicative lists'), separate for specific sectors, which the Commission draws up on Unfair Clauses (*Commission des clauses abusives*).[91] It illustrates the vital role of the administration in controlling contractual terms for fairness. However, the judiciary's role significantly increased by introducing the general test of unfairness (1993 and 1995 reforms).[92]

The French 'grey list' and 'black list' are not merely indicative like the Directive's Annex and go further than what the Unfair Contract Terms Directive requires. Consequently, unfair contract terms can be declared void under 3 mechanisms: the general test of unfairness, the *liste grise* ('grey list' character), and the *liste noire* ('black list' character).

3.2 Germany

In 1976, the German legislator introduced the Act Concerning the Regulation of the Law of Standard Business Terms (AGB-Gesetz)[93] to protect consumers from unfair standard contract terms.[94] Before adopting the AGB-Gesetz, unfair contract terms were controlled through the general duty to perform a contract in good faith (*Leistung nach Treu und Glauben*) contained in § 242 of the BGB and the related case law.[95] The AGB-Gesetz codified the judge-made rules, introducing a 'grey list' (*Klauselverbote mit Wertungsmöglichkeit*) and a 'black list' (*Klauselverbote ohne Wertungsmöglichkeit*) as well as a general test of

[91] The Commission on Unfair Clauses provides examples. See Commission des clauses abusives, 'Contrats de fourniture de gaz et d'électricité' (July 2020) http://www.clauses-abusives.fr/theme_recommandation/eau-electricite-gaz-gpl/ (accessed 20 July 2020).

[92] Stoffel-Munck (n 80) 151–52.

[93] Gesetz zur Regelung des Rechts der Allgemeinen Geschäftsbedingungen of 9 December 1976.

[94] For a detailed article-by-article commentary see eg Peter Ulmer, Hans Erich Brandner, and Horst-Diether Hensen (eds), *Kommentar zum Gesetz zur Regelung des Rechts der allgemeinen Geschäftsbedingungen* (Verlag Dr. Otto Schmidt KG 1982); Manfred Wolf, Norbert Horn, and Walter Lindacher (eds), *AGB-Gesetz* (C.H. Beck 1984).

[95] Also §§ 123 (voidability on the grounds of deceit or duress) and 138 (legal transactions contrary to public policy; usury) of the BGB; Entwurf eines Gesetzes zur Regelung des Rechts der Allgemeinen Geschäftsbedingungen (AGB-Gesetz) of 5 August 1975, page 10. For an account of the judge-made rules before the AGB-Gesetz see eg Jochen Neumann-Wedekindt, *Inhaltskontrolle allgemeiner Geschäftsbedingungen, dargestellt an Vertragsabschlussklauseln* (Dissertation at the Faculty of Law at the University of Münster 1968); Lorenz Fastrich, *Richterliche Inhaltskontrolle im Privatrecht* (CH Beck 1992).

unfairness (*Inhaltskontrolle*) into German law.[96] The 1976 reform constitutes the basis of the existing control mechanisms, and only reforms in 1996 and 2002 caused minor substantive changes.

2 additional provisions had to be introduced into the AGB-Gesetz in 1996 to ensure compliance with the Unfair Contract Terms Directive—the implementation deadline being 31 December 1994.[97] The first provision dealt with the conflict of law rule (§ 12 of the AGB-Gesetz), implementing Article 6(2) of the Directive. The second provision of the 1996 reform introduced a special regime for consumer contracts (§ 24a of the AGB-Gesetz), reflecting Article 3(2) of the Directive.[98]

6 years after the 1996 reform, in 2002, the German law of obligations was reformed (*Schuldrechtsreform*), and the BGB and the Unterlassungsklagengesetz (UKlaG) included the provisions from the AGB-Gesetz.[99] Since the 2002 reform, §§ 305–310 of the BGB—book 2 division 2 on 'drafting contractual obligations by means of standard business terms'—concern the regulation of standard contract terms; §§ 1 ff of the UKlaG accommodate the procedural rules.[100] The 2002 reform also implemented the Directive's transparency principle through § 307 No 1 of the BGB (*Transparenzkontrolle*).[101]

§§ 307 to 309 of the BGB are concerned with the substantive control of contractual terms which supplement or derogate from statutory provisions (§ 307 No 3). Standard contract terms falling within the scope of § 309 (*Klauselverbote*

[96] See eg Günther Stein, *Zum Spannungsverhältnis der Kontrollverfahren aufgrund des AGB-Gesetzes und § 242 BGB* (Duncker & Humblot 1982); Peter Josef Witte, *Inhaltskontrolle und deren Rechtsfolgen im System der Überprüfung allgemeiner Geschäftsbedingungen* (Dissertation at the Faculty of Law at the University of Münster 1983); Georg Kippels, *Die Inhaltskontrolle von allgemeinen Geschäftsbedingungen im kaufmännischen Geschäftsverkehr nach § 9 Abs 2 AGB-Gesetz unter besonderer Berücksichtigung der Klauselverbote der §§ 10 und 11 AGB-Gesetz* (Hundt Verlag 1990).

[97] Gesetz zur Änderung des AGB-Gesetzes und der Insolvenzverordnung of 19 July 1996.

[98] Norbert Reich, 'The implementation of Directive 93/13/EEC on unfair terms in consumer contracts in Germany' (1997) 5(2) European Review of Private Law 167; Georg Borges, *Die Inhaltskontrolle von Verbraucherverträgen* (Dunckler & Humblot 2000) 15–8; Irene Tilmann, *Die Klauselrichtlinie 93/13/EWG auf der Schnittstelle zwischen Privatrecht und öffentlichem Recht* (CH Beck 2003) 17–21.

[99] Gesetz zur Modernisierung des Schuldrechts of 26 November 2001. For further details on the legislative background see Reinhard Zimmermann, *The New German Law of Obligations: Historical and Comparative Perspectives* (OUP 2005) 30–35. Birke Häcker notes that the fear of some scholars that the reform might create new problems has not materialized and is an overall success. Birke Häcker, '*La Troisième Jeunesse du Code Civil*: A German Lawyer Looks at the Reform of French Contract Law' in John Cartwright and Simon Whittaker (eds), *The Code Napoléon Rewritten: French Contract Law after the 2016 Reforms* (Hart Publishing 2017) 390–91.

[100] For further details on the subsequent changes see Reiner Schulze and Hans Schulte-Nölke (eds), *Die Schuldrechtsreform vor dem Hintergrund des Gemeinschaftsrechts* (Mohr Siebeck 2001); Thomas M J Möllers, 'European Directives on Civil Law: The German Approach towards the Re-codification and New Foundation of Civil Law Principles' (2002) 10(6) European Review of Private Law 777; Jan Peter Teubel, *Rücktrittsrecht und AGB-Kontrolle nach der Schuldrechtsreform* (Duncker & Humblot 2018).

[101] Steffi Nobis, *Missbräuchliche Vertragsklauseln in Deutschland und Frankreich: Zur Umsetzung der Klauselrichtlinie 93/13/EWG des Rates* (Nomos 2005) 215–40; Tim Gero Joppich, *Die Kodifikation des Transparenzgebots in § 307 BGB* (Peter Lang 2008) 1–17.

ohne Wertungsmöglichkeit) are unfair and ineffective without the possibility of evaluation,[102] whereas contract terms falling within § 308 (*Klauselverbote mit Wertungsmöglichkeit*) are considered unfair and ineffective but are subject to judicial evaluation. Paolisa Nebbia points out that the German legislator still provides the judiciary with the necessary flexibility in its assessment, for instance, by including terms such as 'unreasonably high' (see § 308 No 7(a)).[103] Terms falling within § 308 of the BGB are presumed unfair, but undefined standards (*unbestimmte Rechtsbegriffe*) like 'unreasonably high' require context-specific, judicial evaluation (*umfassende Interessenabwägung*).[104] However, if a contract term is assessed under § 308, including an evaluation of undefined standards, but not considered unfair, no additional re-evaluation of such contract term occurs under the general test (§ 307).[105] The general test (*Inhaltskontrolle*) laid down by § 307 only assesses contract terms that fall outside the scope of §§ 308 and 309.[106] The general test of unfairness in § 307 provides that clauses become ineffective (*unwirksam*) 'if, contrary to the requirement of good faith, they unreasonably disadvantage the other party to the contract' (§ 307 No 1). A term is 'unreasonably to disadvantage' the consumer where it is unclear and incomprehensible (§ 307 No 1), is not compatible with other statutory provisions, (§ 307 No 2(1)), or limits essential contractual rights and duties jeopardizing the purpose of the contract (§ 307 No 2(2)). Consumers are also not bound by contract terms which are unusual and surprising in light of the circumstances (§ 305c).[107]

§ 310 provides exceptions for situations where §§ 307 to 309 do not apply, for instance, in contracts for the sale of energy or water (No 2). These exceptions fall outside the scope of the present study.[108]

[102] Wolfgang Wurmnest, '§§ 307-309' in Wolfgang Krüger (ed), *Münchner Kommentar zum Bürgerlichen Gesetzbuch Band 2 – Schuldrecht Allgemeiner Teil 1 §§ 241-310* (8th edn, CH Beck 2019) BGB § 309 [1 ff].

[103] Nebbia (n 8) 25.

[104] The test in § 307 of the BGB is used as the benchmark for the judicial evaluation of undefined standards contained in § 308.

[105] Mathias Wendland, 'Vorbemerkung zu §§ 307-309' in Gerald Mäsch and others (eds), *Staudinger BGB - Buch 2: Recht der Schuldverhältnisse: §§ 305-310; UKlaG (AGB-Recht 1 und Unterlassungsklagengesetz)* (18th edn, Sellier/de Gruyter 2019) BGB Vorbem zu §§ 307–309 [20–23].

[106] As pointed out above, § 242 of the BGB contains a general requirement to act according to the requirements of good faith. Concerning the control of standard terms, § 242 applies only where §§ 305-310 do not apply. Wurmnest (n 102) BGB Vor § 307 [11]. For a detailed account see generally Dirk Looschelders, Dirk Olzen, and Gottfried Schiemann, *Staudinger BGB - Buch 2: Recht der Schuldverhältnisse: §§ 241-243* (Sellier/de Gruyter 2019) BGB § 242.

[107] ibid 243; Wurmnest (n 102) BGB § 307 [1–7]; Phillip Hellwege and Lucinda Miller, 'Control of Standard Terms' in Gerhard Dannemann and Stefan Vogenauer (eds), *The Common European Sales Law in Context: Interactions with English and German Law* (OUP 2013) 441–42.

[108] § 310 No 2 of the BGB: 'Sections 308 and 309 do not apply to contracts of electricity, gas, district heating or water suppliers for the supply of electricity, gas, district heating or water from the supply grid to special customers to the extent that the conditions of supply do not derogate, to the disadvantage of

In conclusion, the German test to control contract terms under the lists in §§ 308 and 309 of the BGB goes beyond the level of protection envisaged by the Unfair Contract Terms Directive. Concerning the scope of the rules, the German provisions apply, like the Directive, only to non-negotiated contract terms (§ 305 No 1).[109]

3.3 The Netherlands

Unlike France, Germany, and the United Kingdom, the Netherlands only introduced provisions explicitly dealing with unfair contract terms in standard contracts in its new Civil Code (*Burgerlijk Wetboek*) in 1992.[110] After intense academic criticism of how the Dutch legislator had transposed the Directive into national law,[111] followed by an infringement proceeding brought by the European Commission, which ended up before the Court of Justice of the European Union,[112] the legislator amended the rules in November 1999 and

the customer, from orders on general conditions for the supply of standard-rate customers with electricity, gas, district heating and water. Sentence 1 applies with the necessary modifications to contracts for the disposal of sewage.'

§ 310 No 4 of the BGB: 'This division does not apply to contracts in the field of the law of succession, family law and company law or to collective agreements and private-sector works agreements or public-sector establishment agreements. When it is applied to employment contracts, reasonable account must be taken of the special features that apply in labour law; section 305 (2) and (3) must not be applied. Collective agreements and private-sector works agreements or public-sector establishment agreements are equivalent to legal provisions within the meaning of section 307 (3).'

[109] A different test applies for business-to-business transactions according to § 310 No 1 of the BGB, but most of the unfair terms listed in §§ 308-309 provide an indicative effect (*Indizwirkung*). See eg Harry Schmidt, 'Klauselverbote ohne Wertungsmöglichkeit' in Stefan Ernst and others (eds), *AGB-Recht: Kommentar* (12th edn, Otto Schmidt Verlag 2016) BGB § 308 No 1 [16], § 308 No 3 [18]; Matthias Lehmann and Johannes Ungerer, 'Save the "Mittelstand": How German Courts Protect Small and Medium-Sized Enterprises from Unfair Terms' (2017) 25(2) European Review of Private Law 313; Georg Maier-Reimer, 'AGB-Recht im unternehmerischen Rechtsverkehr: Der BGH überdreht die Schraube' (2017) 70(1) Neue Juristische Wochenschrift 1.

[110] For a critical examination of the rules prior and after the reform see Ewoud H Hondius, 'De rechtspositie van de consument naar nieuw burgerlijk recht' (1991) 5 Tijdschrift voor Consumentenrecht 325; Edwoud H Hondius, 'Non-implementation of the Directive on Unfair Contract Terms: the Dutch case' (1997) 5(2) European Review of Private Law 193.

[111] Hondius (1997) (n 110) 194–96.

[112] Case C-144/99 *Commission of the European Communities v Kingdom of the Netherlands* (n 66). See eg Marco Loos, 'Veroordeling Nederland wegens niet-omzetting Richtlijn oneerlijke bedingen' (2001) 2(9) Nederlands Tijdschrift voor Europees Recht 242; Jan M Smits, 'Nogmaals de richtlijn oneerlijke bedingen: Nederland veroordeeld wegens gebrekkige implementatie' (2001) Weekblad voor Privaatrecht, Notariaat en Registratie 853; Mark Wissink, 'Nederland veroordeeld wegens onvolledige omzetting van de richtlijn oneer-lijke bedingen: Noot bij HvJ EG 10 mei 2001, C-144-99, Commissie/ Nederland' (2002) 16(4) Nederlands Tijdschrift voor Burgerlijk Recht 152; Caroline Cauffman, Michael Faure, and Ton Hartlief, *Harmonisatie van het consumentencontractenrecht in Europa: consequenties voor Nederland* (Boom Juridische Uitgevers 2009).

June 2004.[113] The main points of concern were the non-implementation of the *contra proferentem* rule and the principle of transparency. The 1999 reform took both concerns into account.[114]

Articles 6:231 to 6:247 of the BW still contains the relevant provisions. The Dutch Civil Code contains a general test of unfairness in Article 6:233(a) of the BW, complemented by a 'black list' (*zwarte lijst*) in Article 6:236 of the BW and a 'grey list' (*grijze lijst*) in Article 6:237 of the BW. Terms that fall within the 'black list' are automatically unfair, while terms that fall within the 'grey list' are presumed to be unfair unless the trader can prove that they are not unfair. Whether the evidence submitted by traders is sufficient to prove that the term is not unfair must be assessed under the general clause (Article 6:233(a) of the BW).[115] If the contract term does not fall under either the 'grey' or the 'black' list, the term undergoes assessment under the general test (Article 6:233 of the BW):

(a) if, given the nature and other content of the contract, the manner in which the general conditions have come about, the mutually identifiable interest of the parties and the other circumstances of the case, it is unreasonably onerous for the other party;
(b) if the user has not offered the other party a reasonable opportunity to become acquainted with the general conditions.[116]

The Dutch Supreme Court (*Hoge Raad*) emphasized in *Bouwbedrijf Van Marrum/Wolff* that the courts always must assess the circumstances of the case before declaring a term voidable (*vernietigbaar*) under Article 6:233(a) of the BW.[117] In this case, the Dutch Supreme Court corrected an error of law by the

[113] Goanta (n 1) 63.
[114] Kamerstukken II, 1998/1999, 26 470, no 3 and no 5. cf Martijn W Hesselink, 'Codification and Europeanisation in the Netherlands' in Stefan Vogenauer and Stephen Weatherill (eds), *The Harmonisation of European Contract Law: Implications for European Private Laws, Business and Legal Practice* (Hart Publishing 2006) 43–45. Article 6:238(2) of the BW introduced the *contra proferentem* doctrine; the principle of transparency by arts 6:231 and 6:238 of the BW. cf Goanta (n 1) 63.
[115] Bart H Krans, Carel JJM Stolker, and Lodewijk W Valk (eds), *Tekst & Commentaar Burgerlijk Wetboek: Online Naslagwerk* (30 August 2021 edn, Wolters Kluwer 2021) BW Art 6:233 [2e]; Tjeerd GG Raijmakers, 'Art. 237: Burgerlijk Wetboek Boek 6' in Sjoerd P Bakker and others (eds), *Sdu Commentaar Vermogensrecht: Online Naslagwerk* (1 June 2021 edn, Sdu 2021) BW Art 6:237 [2]; Carla H Sieburgh, *Asser 6-III Algemeen overeenkomstenrecht* (15th edn, Wolters Kluwer 2018) [492]–[493].
[116] Translation by Sascha Hardt and Nicole Kornet (eds), *The Maastricht Collection: Selected National, European and International Provisions from Public and Private Law* (4th edn, Europa Law Publishing 2015) 348.
[117] HR 21 September 2012, ECLI:NL:HR:2012:BW6135 (*Bouwbedrijf Van Marrum/Wolff*) para 3.4. Krans, Stolker, and Lodewijk (n 115) BW Art 6:233 [2d]; Pieter TJ Wolters, 'Regels over de werking van de redelijkheid en billijkheid? Een analyse van de rechtspraak van de Hoge Raad' (2013) 8(9) Maandblad voor Vermogensrecht 251.

Court of Appeal because the court merely examined the circumstances present in all similar cases, de facto treating the clause as a 'black-listed' provision. It is worth mentioning that unlike in the case of Article 6:237, the burden of proof is on the consumer under the general test.[118]

The test in Article 6:233 of the BW does not refer to good faith. Instead, the Dutch Civil Code requires traders to act in good faith in Article 6:248 (*redelijkheid en billijkheid*). In 2002, the Dutch Supreme Court clarified that there is a 'two-track system', meaning that Article 6:248 applies alongside Article 6:233.[119] The difference between the 2 provisions is their scope, as Article 6:233 applies only to terms and conditions.[120] Article 6:231 specifically excludes individually negotiated contracts and contract terms governing the main subject matter that are formulated clearly and intelligibly from the scope of Article 6:233.[121] Articles 6:235, 6:245, and 6:247 of the BW provide further exceptions to the application of Article 6:233.[122] The judge can examine contract terms that fall outside of the scope of Article 6:233 under the general good faith provision (Article 6:248). Terms and conditions of B2C e-commerce transactions fall within the scope of Article 6:233 in connection with Articles 6:236 and 6:237, excluding Article 6:248 from the compliance assessments in the present book.

The general test under Article 6:233 and the duty to interpret national law in light of the Unfair Contract Terms Directive have provided sufficient consumer protection.[123] Furthermore, the Dutch 'grey list' and 'black list' go beyond what the Directive requires. Regarding the *ratione personae*, the Dutch rules, unlike

[118] ibid (HR); Krans, Stolker, and Lodewijk (n 115) BW Art 6:233 [2e]; Tjeerd GG Raijmakers, 'Art. 233: Burgerlijk Wetboek Boek 6' in Bakker (eds) (n 115) BW Art 6:233 [2.3].

[119] HR 14 June 2002, ECLI:NL:HR:2002:AE0659 (*Bramer/Colpro*), para 3.7. ibid (Raijmakers) BW Art 6:233 [2.1]; Sieburgh (n 115) BW Art 6:233 [485].

[120] BW, art 6:231(a).

[121] cf Sieburgh (n 115) [486]. Jans Smits noted in 2002 that art 6:248 is of general application and that art 6:233 of the BW serves as *lex specialis*. See Jan M Smits, 'Non-Performance and Remedies in General' in Danny Busch and others (eds), *The Principles of European Contract Law and Dutch Law: A Commentary* (Kluwer Law 2002) 345. As shown above, the Dutch Supreme Court further clarified the relationship of the provisions in the same year, *id est* that their application differs in scope and that art 6:233 is not stricter than art 6:248. Raijmakers (n 118) BW art 6:233 [1, 2.1]. Consequently, only art 6:233 of the BW is considered to assess trader compliance because the book focuses on terms and conditions.

[122] cf Sieburgh (n 115).

[123] See eg HR 13 September 2013, ECLI:NL:HR:2013:691; Hondius (n 105) 194; Charlotte Pavillon, 'Beter consumentenrecht: naar een scherpere consumentvriendelijke onredelijk bezwarend-norm' (2011) 63(8) Nederlands Tijdschrift voor Burgerlijk Recht 439; Marco Loos and RRM de Moor, 'Hoge Raad 13 september 2013, ECLI:NL:HR:2013:691' (2013) 11(6) Tijdschrift voor Consumentenrecht en Handelspraktijken 262; Ewoud H Hondius, 'Algemene voorwaarden' in *Monografieën BW: Consumentenrecht* (2nd edn, Kluwer 2013) 27 ff; Goanta (n 1) 63; Chantal Mak, 'Artikel 6:233 BW: Hoe de doorwerking van Europees consumentenrecht tornt aan het systeem van het Nederlandse privaatrecht' in Friso van de Pol and others (eds), *Vijftig weeffouten in het BW: Een ode aan het Burgerlijk Wetboek, ter ere van zijn 25-jarig bestaan* (Ars Aequi Libri 2017) 255ff.

the Directive, protect consumers and apply to companies with fewer than 50 employees (Article 6:235(b) of the BW).

3.4 The United Kingdom

The Unfair Contract Terms Act 1977 was the first statutory instrument in the United Kingdom that dealt directly with controlling unfair terms. The instrument provided a more coherent regime of controlling standard terms than the ones used by the common law, based on enforceability rules and contractual construction.[124] However, academics criticized the Act at a very early stage: Norman Palmer and David Yates criticized the Unfair Contract Terms Act 1977 because the rules can be circumvented by using duty-defining, rather than liability-excluding, clauses.[125] In addition, Hugh Beale criticized the reasonableness test in the Act as uncertain,[126] a deficiency addressed in subsequent years, for instance, by Schedule 2 (Guidelines for Application of Reasonableness Test) of the Unfair Contract Terms Act 1977.[127] Another point of criticism levelled against the Unfair Contract Terms Act 1977 was that the name of the Act is a 'misnomer' because it only covers certain contracts; at the same time, its scope goes beyond contract law, for instance, concerning 'business liability'.[128]

The Unfair Contract Terms Directive was implemented through the Unfair Terms in Consumer Contracts Regulations 1994, providing provisions explicitly dealing with consumer contracts and leading to a consumer-specific regime.[129] The legislator repealed the 1994 Regulation in

[124] For a critical examination of the rules prior and after the reform see Horton Rogers and Matthew Clarke, *The Unfair Contract Terms Act 1977* (Sweet & Maxwell 1978); Peter Thompson, *Unfair Contract Terms Act 1977* (Butterworths 1978); Hugh Beale, 'Unfair Contract Terms Act 1977' (1978) 5(1) British Journal of Law and Society 114.

[125] Norman Palmer and David Yates, 'The Future of the Unfair Contract Terms Act 1977' (1981) 40 Cambridge Law Journal 108.

[126] Hugh Beale, 'Unfair Contracts in Britain and Europe' (1989) 42(1) Current Legal Problems 197.

[127] See generally John Adams and Roger Brownsword, 'The Unfair Contract Terms Act: A Decade of Discretion' (1988) 104 Law Quarterly Review 94; Elizabeth MacDonald, 'Exclusion Clauses: the Ambit of s 13(1) of the Unfair Contract Terms Act 1977' (1992) 12 Legal Studies 277; Elizabeth MacDonald, 'UCTA Thirty Years On' in Andrew Burrows and Edwin Peel (eds), *Contract Terms* (OUP 2007) 154.

[128] Len S Sealy argued that the Act might create a 'separate body of "commercial law"'. One example he provided regarding the Act's scope was that the Act distinguishes between 'written standard-term' and 'international supply' contracts. Len S Sealy, 'Unfair Contract Terms Act 1977' (1978) 37(1) The Cambridge Law Journal 15.

[129] See generally Elizabeth MacDonald, 'Mapping the Unfair Contract Terms Act 1977 and the Directive on Unfair Terms in Consumer Contracts' (1994) Journal of Business Law 441; Anne de Moor, 'Common and Civil Law Conceptions of Contract and European Law of Contract: The Case of the Directive on Unfair Terms in Consumer Contracts' (1995) 3(2) European Review of Private Law 257; Chris Willett, 'The Directive on Unfair Terms in Consumer Contracts and its implementation

1999,[130] and the Consumer Rights Act 2015 replaced the Unfair Terms in Consumer Contracts Regulations 1999. Before adopting the Consumer Rights Act, the 1994/1999 Regulations applied in conjunction with the Unfair Contract Terms Act to consumer contracts, while B2B contracts were governed only by the Unfair Contract Terms Act.[131] Regarding consumer contracts, the significant difference between the instruments was that the Regulations applied only to not individually negotiated contract terms, while the Unfair Contract Terms Act was of general application.[132] Nowadays, the Unfair Contract Terms Act applies only to B2B contracts,[133] whereas the Consumer Rights Act applies to B2C contracts.[134]

Part 2 of the Consumer Rights Act 2015 regulates contractual terms. Under this regime, potentially unfair contract terms can be declared void under 2 mechanisms: the general test complemented by an indicative list and sections 31 and 65. The general test (section 62(4) and (5) of the CRA 2015, also section 64 of the CRA 2015) and the indicative and non-exhaustive list of potentially unfair terms (section 63(1) and (2) in conjunction with Schedule 2 of the CRA 2015) transposes the text of the Directive. Schedule 2 of the CRA provides additional examples of potentially unfair contract terms.[135] The general test of the CRA 2015 also provides the exact wording of the Unfair Terms in Consumer

in the United Kingdom' (1997) 2 European Review of Private Law 223; Gunther Teubner, 'Legal Irritants: Good Faith in British Law or How Unifying Law Ends Up in New Divergences' (1998) 61(1) Modern Law Review 11.

[130] Unfair Terms in Consumer Contracts Regulations 1999. For an overview see Elisabeth MacDonald, 'The Emperor's Old Clauses: Unincorporated Clauses, Misleading Terms and the Unfair Terms in Consumer Contracts Regulations' (1999) 58(2) Cambridge Law Journal 413; Susan Bright, 'Winning the Battle Against Unfair Contract Terms' (2000) 20(3) Legal Studies 331; Susan Bright, 'Unfairness and the Consumer Contract Regulations' in Andrew Burrows and Edwin Peel (eds), *Contract Terms* (OUP 2007); Chris Willett, 'General Clauses and the Competing Ethics of European Consumer Law in the UK' (2012) 71(2) The Cambridge Law Journal 412.

[131] The overlap between the instruments caused a discussion about further reform and unification. A summary of the academic and legislative debate is provided in Elizabeth Macdonald, 'Unifying Unfair Terms Legislation' (2004) 67(1) The Modern Law Review 69.

[132] Unfair Terms in Consumer Contracts Regulations 1994, reg 3; Unfair Terms in Consumer Contracts Regulations 1999, reg 5; Unfair Contract Terms Act 1977 (original version, as enacted) s 1(1). Macdonald (n 131) 71.

[133] See UCTA 1977, Sections 2(4), 3(3), and 7(4A).

[134] See CRA 2015, Section 61(4). cf Paula Giliker, 'The Consumer Rights Act 2015: a bastion of European Consumer Rights' (2017) 37(1) Legal Studies 78; Andrew Burrows, *A Casebook on Contracts* (6th edn, Hart Publishing 2018) ch 6; Nils Jansen, 'Unfair Contract Terms' in Nils Jansen and Reinhard Zimmermann (eds), *Commentaries on European Contract Laws* (OUP 2018) 920–22; Simon Whittaker, 'Distinctive Features of the New Consumer Contract Law' (2017) 133 Law Quarterly Review 47.

[135] See also the implementation of the transparency requirement (Directive 93/13, art 5) into UK law (CRA 2015, s 68), for instance, in Chris Willett and Martin Morgan-Taylor, 'Recognising the limits of transparency in EU consumer law' in James Devenney (ed), *European Consumer Protection: Theory and Practice* (CUP 2012).

Contracts Regulations 1999, so the case law interpreting the 1999 Regulation applies also to the Consumer Rights Act 2015.

The starting point of the unfairness assessment is section 62(5):

> Whether a term is fair is to be determined—
>
> (a) taking into account the nature of the subject matter of the contract, and
> (b) by reference to all the circumstances existing when the term was agreed and to all of the other terms of the contract or of any other contract on which it depends.

In the next step, the judge assesses whether the contract term is 'contrary to the requirement of good faith, it causes a significant imbalance in the parties' rights and obligations under the contract to the detriment of the consumer' (section 62(4)). In that assessment, the judge does not consider the 'main subject matter of the contract' or the 'appropriateness of the price payable under the contract' (section 64). As shown above in this chapter, the Court of Justice, and consequently, UK courts, further defined the general test of unfairness by considering these guidelines.[136]

Contract terms which fall within the scope of the list of potentially unfair terms provided in Schedule 2 Part 1 of the CRA 2015 must still be assessed under the general test (see section 63(2)). It is worth adding that the Competition and Markets Authority and other 'regulators' (listed in Schedule 3, subsection 8) review most unfair term cases and not the courts.[137] These

[136] According to *Anson's Law of Contract*, the 2 most important English cases concerning the meaning of 'fairness' have been *Director General of Fair Trading v First National Bank plc* [2001] UKHL 52, [2002] 1 AC 481 and *Cavendish Square Holding BV v Talal El Makdessi and ParkingEye Ltd v Beavis* [2015] UKSC 67, [2015] 3 WLR 1373. The 2 cases did not concern the CRA 2015, but the earlier examined 1994 and 1999 Regulations. Applying the fairness test in *ParkingEye*, the Court emphasized the context-specific nature of the assessment, in this case, the 'regulatory framework which determines how and in what circumstances it may be enforced' [111]. Jack Beatson, Andrew Burrows, and John Cartwright, *Anson's Law of Contract* (30th edn, OUP 2016) 224. The 2 cases followed the CJEU guidelines examined above. See ch 3.2. Concerning the UK's withdrawal from the European Union, Pavlos Eleftheriadis points out that the 'Supreme Court of the UK is not "bound" by any retained EU case law' according to Section 6(4) of the European Union (Withdrawal) Act 2018. He also notes that exceptions apply to Northern Ireland and that the current regime might change over time. Pavlos Eleftheriadis, 'Eleven Types of post-Brexit EU Law' *Oxford Business Law Blog* (8 January 2021) https://www.law.ox.ac.uk/business-law-blog/blog/2021/01/eleven-types-post-brexit-eu-law (accessed 30 January 2021).

[137] The Competition and Markets Authority provides a guidance document on the regulation of unfair contract terms. See Competition and Markets Authority, 'Unfair Contract Terms Guidance: Guidance on the unfair terms provisions in the Consumer Rights Act 2015' (31 July 2015) https://assets.publishing.service.gov.uk/government/uploads/system/uploads/attachment_data/file/450440/Unfair_Terms_Main_Guidance.pdf (accessed 26 July 2020).

'regulators' can, for instance, investigate complaints (Schedule 3, subsection 2) and apply for injunctions (Schedule 3, subsection 3).

Concerning the indicative list contained in Schedule 2 Part 1, the UK legislator has decided against 'gold-plating', that is, to not go beyond the rules of the Directive, for instance, by enacting a 'grey' or a 'black' list. However, in several instances, UK law goes beyond the standard of the Unfair Contract Terms Directive. Section 31 lists contractual obligations for which traders cannot limit liability under all circumstances. Equally, section 65 provides that any terms which limit trader liability in case of death or personal injury are invalid. Sections 31 and 65 originated in the Unfair Contract Terms Act 1977 and strongly resemble in character the mechanism of 'black lists' used in France, Germany, and the Netherlands.[138] Besides the 2 statutory provisions, some common law rules may equally provide consumers with a higher level of protection than under the Directive concerning penalty clauses and assignment. It is worth noting that these are the only contractual terms always unenforceable in the United Kingdom. Another instance where the UK rules go beyond the Directive's standard is the scope: the Consumer Rights Act 2015 also applies to individually negotiated terms (section 61).

3.5 Comparative Observations

Examining the national rules implementing the Unfair Contract Terms Directive has revealed that all 4 Member States have implemented the rules in the Directive, including the indicative and non-exhaustive list of potentially unfair terms contained in the Annex to the Directive. However, the method of implementation has varied. On the national level, 3 mechanisms of controlling standard consumer contracts for fairness were identified: (1) a term may be regarded unfair under the general test;[139] (2) a term is presumed unfair under a 'grey list' with limited judicial discretion;[140] (3) a term is considered unfair without the possibility of judicial (re-)evaluation (ie, 'black-listed').[141] There are minor but significant differences between the national 'grey lists'. Unlike the

[138] Section 2 of the UCTA 1977 replicates s 65 of the CRA 2015; ss 5 to 7 of the UCTA 1977 replicate s 31 of the CRA 2015.

[139] Code de la consommation, art L212-1; BGB, § 307; BW, art 6:233(a); Consumer Rights Act 2015, S 62 in connection with Schedule 2.

[140] Code de la consommation, art L212-1 in connection with art R212-2; BGB, § 308; BW, art 6:237 in connection with art 6:233(a).

[141] Code de la consommation, art L212-1 in connection with art R212-1; BGB, § 309; BW, art 6:236; Consumer Rights Act 2015, Ss 31 and 65 (penalty clause doctrine and assignment).

French and Dutch 'grey lists', which presume unfairness and shift the burden of proof that the terms are not unfair on traders, the German 'grey list' takes a more neutral approach. Terms falling within the 'grey list' of § 308 of the BGB are presumed unfair, but undefined standards like 'unreasonably high' require context-specific, judicial evaluation. The different consumer protection standards among the 4 jurisdictions also entail different levels of judicial control. In France, Germany, and the Netherlands, the adoption of 'grey' and 'black' lists marginalized the role of the general test, leaving little discretion for judges in assessing whether contract terms are unfair. Another observation is that some national rules are broader in scope. For instance, the French and Dutch rules apply to B2B contracts, and the UK and French rules apply to individually negotiated contracts. The following subsection will investigate the level of protection the 4 jurisdictions offer concerning the potentially unfair terms listed in the Directive's Annex, which the empirical part of the book will use to assess trader compliance.

4 The Annex to the Unfair Terms Directive as the Benchmark of Unfairness

As mentioned earlier in this chapter, the Annex to the Unfair Contract Terms Directive provides a list of terms that 'may be regarded unfair'.[142] Importantly, legislators designed the list to be an indicative and non-exhaustive list of unfair terms, which defines the general test of unfairness in the Directive. However, over time, the list has become an essential and integral part of the assessment process of unfair contract terms. It resembles the widely used technique of introducing lists, be they 'indicative', 'grey', or 'black', that define a general clause. The indicative list in the Unfair Contract Terms Directive's Annex guides national courts to carry out the unfairness test as envisaged by the European legislator. The previous section in this chapter established that the terms in the list become more than mere guidance when they are either implemented into national law as 'black' or 'grey' lists or rendered 'unfair' (not meeting the good faith standard) by the Court of Justice. All national codes now contain the general clause, and the Member States have implemented the indicative list entirely or partly into their national codes.[143]

[142] Directive 93/13/EEC, art 3(3).
[143] See ch 3.3.

Defining a general clause with a list of unfair terms brings certain advantages and will likely enhance legal certainty.[144] Consumers and traders would be aware of these terms due to these lists, which can lead to reduced litigation. However, a clause not contained in the list may still be considered unfair.[145] Thus, a contract free of terms in the lists is not necessarily free of 'unfair' contract terms. Moreover, many of the terms in the Directive's Annex are ambiguous, adding to the legal uncertainty. For instance, the use of terms such as 'inappropriately' (Point 1(b)), 'inadequate performance' (Point 1(b)), or 'disproportionally' (Point 1(e)).[146] It is thus of utmost importance to examine the CJEU's case law and whether and to what extent national law contains provisions addressing the unfair terms listed in the Directive's Annex. Such an assessment is indispensable before the empirical examination of consumer standard form contracts can occur.

This part of Chapter 3 examines the European Union and national provisions and cases relating to the potentially unfair clauses in the indicative list of the Annex to the Directive. The section examines not all the provisions but only the ones that apply to e-commerce consumer sales. Points 1(c),[147] (f),[148] (g),[149] (h),[150] (i),[151] and (n)[152] of the Annex to the Directive fall outside of the scope of the present study. The present section will also not consider the exceptions under Point 2 of the Directive's Annex because they are concerned with transferable securities or financial services. Chapter 3.3 reviewed the national rules implementing the Unfair Contract Terms Directive, including the national exceptions. Section 3 revealed that the German,[153] Dutch,[154] and UK[155] exceptions are irrelevant for this book because they do not apply to e-commerce consumer transactions. Only one of the French exceptions falls within the scope, which will be considered in this section.[156]

[144] Micklitz and Caruso (n 51).
[145] Case C-478/99 *Commission of the European Communities v Kingdom of Sweden* (n 34) para 20.
[146] cf Jansen and Zimmermann (n 134) 958.
[147] This point is concerned with providing services and not selling goods.
[148] ibid.
[149] This point is concerned with contracts of indeterminate duration.
[150] This point is concerned with contracts of fixed duration.
[151] This point is of a more practical nature: 'irrevocably binding the consumer to terms with which he had no real opportunity of becoming acquainted before the conclusion of the contract'.
[152] This point also falls outside the defined scope: 'limiting the seller's or supplier's obligation to respect commitments undertaken by his agents or making his commitments subject to compliance with a particular formality'.
[153] BGB, §§ 309 No 7 and 310 No 1, 2, and 4.
[154] BW, arts 6:236, 6:237.
[155] Consumer Rights Act 2015, Sch 2 Pt 2.
[156] Code de la consommation, arts R212-3 and R212-4. Only art R212-4 applies to the present study.

4.1 Limitation of Liability in Case of Death or Personal Injury

Article 3 of the Unfair Contract Terms Directive, in connection with Point 1(a) of the Annex to the Directive, lists clauses as potentially unfair which exclude or limit the liability of traders or their suppliers in case of death or personal injury of the consumer, resulting from the trader's or the supplier's act or omission. The provision's wording suggests that any form of exclusion or limitation of liability in case of death or personal injury may be regarded as unfair if the liability results from an act or omission of the trader or supplier. The national courts have not referred such a scenario under the preliminary reference procedure to the Court of Justice of the European Union. The provision remains indicative since there is no interpretation on the EU level of Point 1(a) of the Directive's Annex.

4.1.1 France

Article L212-1, in connection with Article R212-1 no 6 of the Code de la consommation, renders clauses automatically unfair ('black list') which limit or exclude liability to compensate the consumer where the trader does not fulfil its contractual obligation (*limitation de responsabilité*). It means a contractual term restricting the trader's liability will be deemed unfair under all circumstances, leaving no discretion to the courts.[157] A recent case of the Court of Cassation (*Cour de cassation*) confirmed that traders cannot limit the amount of compensation, that is, they cannot impose a cap on the amount of damages that consumers can claim.[158] In addition, traders may not reduce the amount of damages owed to consumers below the value of the actual damage.[159]

The French provision is stricter and provides a higher level of protection for consumers than Point 1(a) Annex of the Unfair Contract Terms Directive because there is no need to assess the general test when Article R212-1 no 6 of the Code de la consommation applies: the term is automatically unfair and ineffective.[160] The French provision is also wider, as, unlike the Directive, Article R212-1 no 6 encompasses liability for death or personal injury and covers damage consumers suffer if traders fail to fulfil any of their obligations. The

[157] Julien (n 89) 313–14; Jean-Denis Pellier, *Droit de la consommation* (2nd edn, Dalloz 2018) 126–29.

[158] Cass civ (1) 11 December 2019, no 18-21164; Jean-Denis Pellier, 'Retour sur les clauses noires' (2019) Dalloz actualité (24 December 2019).

[159] Recently applied and confirmed in CA Rennes 8 March 2019, RG no 15-09167.

[160] Julien (n 89) 299, 314; Alain Bénabent, *Droit des Obligations* (17th edn, Librairie générale de droit et de jurisprudence 2018) 160–61.

French legislator formulated the regulatory provision so broadly that it also covers Point 1(b) of the Annex to the Unfair Contract Terms Directive, which Chapter 3.4.2 will discuss.

4.1.2 Germany

The Directive's scenario where a contract term limits trader liability in case of death or personal injury of the consumer falls within § 309 No 7 lit. a of the BGB. According to this provision, terms which aim to limit or exclude liability for negligent or intentional fault which cause injury to life, body or health are automatically unfair.[161] German courts do not need to evaluate terms falling within the scope of § 309 of the BGB (*Klauselverbote ohne Wertungsmöglichkeit*), and, as in all unfair terms cases, unfair clauses do not bind consumers.[162]

While the scope of § 309 No 7 lit. a and Point 1(a) of the Unfair Contract Terms Directive's Annex is the same, the German provision is stricter as it renders clauses allowing traders to limit their liability always unfair. This means that the German legislator opted for a higher level of consumer protection than envisaged by the Directive. Assuming that the Directive's Annex sets an EU-wide standard, this has not always been the case. Before adopting the Unfair Contract Terms Directive in 1993, German law contained a provision on the limitation of liability (*Freizeichnung von der Haftung*) in case of death or personal injury (§ 11 No 7 of the AGBG). The AGBG provision had a more limited scope than the subsequently adopted Point 1(a) of the Directive's Annex because it covered only cases of *culpa lata*, so gross negligence (*grobe Fahrlässigkeit*), or *dolus*, so intent (*Vorsatz*), and not of *cupla levis*, that is slight negligence (*einfache Fahrlässigkeit*).[163] Nonetheless, the German courts concluded that a clause limiting trader liability in cases of slight negligence should also be considered unfair and consequently ineffective (*unwirksam*).[164] § 309 No 7 lit. a of the BGB has codified this development.[165]

[161] The liability of suppliers of traders can equally not be limited (see also § 278 of the BGB). Mark-Oliver Mackenrodt, *Technologie statt Vertrag? Sachmangelbegriff, negative Beschaffenheitsvereinbarungen und AGB beim Kauf digitaler Güter* (Mohr Siebeck 2015) 144, 274.

[162] BGB, § 306.

[163] In addition to the exceptions mentioned above in this section, § 309 No 7 lit. a of the BGB does not apply to 'transport and tariff rules, authorised in accordance with the Passenger Transport Act [Personenbeförderungsgesetz], of trams, trolley buses and motor vehicles in regular public transport services' (§ 309 No 7 of the BGB).

[164] Wurmnest (n 102) BGB § 309 No 7 [2–4].

[165] See eg BGH NJW-RR 2015, 738. Christensen in Stefan Ernst and others (eds), *AGB-Recht: Kommentar* (12th edn, Otto Schmidt Verlag 2016) BGB § 309 No 7 [5–8].

4.1.3 The Netherlands

A provision covering the content of Point 1(a) Annex of the Unfair Contract Terms Directive can be found in letter (f) of the *grijze lijst* ('grey list') contained in Article 6:237 of the Burgerlijk Wetboek. Article 6:237(f) provides that any contract term which limits or excludes the trader's obligation to pay statutory damages (*wettelijke verplichting tot schadevergoeding*) is presumed unfair when the term is unreasonably onerous (*vermoed onredelijk*).[166] Whether the term is unreasonably onerous must be assessed under the general test of unfairness (Article 6:233(a)).[167] In a recent case, a Dutch lower court deemed a clause limiting liability unreasonably onerous because the party offering it had insurance coverage for such risks.[168] It is worth noting again that Article 6:237 provides that the burden of proof (*bewijslast*) lies with the trader.

Another observation is that the Dutch legislator does not explicitly provide that the clause must limit the liability of an act or omission causing death or personal injury. The provision is of a more general nature, that is, it provides a broader scope, encompassing the protection envisaged by Point 1(a) of the Directive's Annex.[169] Consequently, the provision in the Dutch Civil Code provides a higher level of protection for consumers—the Dutch provision is wider and stricter—than Point 1(a). However, the level of protection is not as high as in countries where such terms are unfair under all circumstances, that is, 'black-listed'.

4.1.4 The United Kingdom

Section 65 of the Consumer Rights Act 2015 declares clauses where traders exclude or restrict negligence liability in cases of death or personal injury of consumers unenforceable.[170] Personal injury encompasses 'any disease and any impairment of physical or mental condition' (section 65(3)). Section 65(4) also defines negligence as a breach of:

[166] Krans, Stolker, and Valk (n 115) BW Art 6:237 [4(c)]; Raijmakers (n 115) BW Art 6:237 [3.1].

[167] The operation of the general test and the 'grey list' were examined in ch 3.3 *The Netherlands*. An example where a lower court applied the test cornering art 6:237(f) is Rechtbank Rotterdam (14 March 2018) ECLI:NL:RBROT:2018:2779, para 2.5.

[168] Rechtbank Rotterdam (3 June 2020) ECLI:NL:RBROT:2020:5566, para 4.17.

[169] Jacob Hijma, 'Validity: Art. 4:110-4:119' in Danny Busch and others (eds), *The Principles of European Contract Law and Dutch Law: A Commentary* (Kluwer Law 2002) 216.

[170] cf John Cartwright, 'Information Obligations and Disinformation of Consumers: English Law Report' in Gert Straetmans (ed), *Information Obligations and Disinformation of Consumers* (Springer Publishing 2019) 120.

(a) any obligation to take reasonable care or exercise reasonable skill in the performance of a contract where the obligation arises from an express or implied term of the contract,
(b) a common law duty to take reasonable care or exercise reasonable skill,
(c) the common duty of care imposed by the Occupiers' Liability Act 1957 or the Occupiers' Liability Act (Northern Ireland) 1957, or
(d) the duty of reasonable care imposed by section 2(1) of the Occupiers' Liability (Scotland) Act 1960.

In addition, subsection (5) states that it is irrelevant:

(a) whether a breach of duty or obligation was inadvertent or intentional, or
(b) whether liability for it arises directly or vicariously.

The effect of section 65 is that such contract terms are unenforceable, making it de facto a 'black-listed' term. Section 66 contains several exceptions where section 65 does not apply, such as those concerning insurance (section 66 (1)(a)), creation or transfer of an interest in land (section 66 (1)(b)), discharge or indemnity (section 66(2)), Damages Scotland Act 2011 (section 66(3)), and liability of an occupier of premises, in some circumstances (section 66(4)). These exceptions do not apply to e-commerce consumer sales transactions.

Section 65 is a *lex specialis* provision and operates independently from the general test under section 62.[171] In case the trader's clause falls outside the scope of section 65, Schedule 2 of the 2015 Act contains a more general rule. However, unlike section 65, Schedule 2 Part 1(1) covers strict liability, an act or omission of the trader.[172]

In terms of the standard of consumer protection, because section 65 of the Consumer Rights Act 2015 renders such limitation clauses unenforceable, it should be regarded as going beyond the envisaged standard of the Unfair Contract Terms Directive. Schedule 2 Part 1(1) uses the exact wording as the Directive and keeps the indicative nature of the list of terms. Consequently, whether a contract term resembling Schedule 2 Part 1(1) is unfair must be assessed under the general test (section 62).[173]

[171] Consumer Rights Act 2015, ss 62(8)(d), 63(2).
[172] Ewan McKendrick, *Contract Law* (8th edn, OUP 2018) 474.
[173] Chapter 3.3 (*The United Kingdom*) examined the operation of the general test and indicative list.

4.1.5 Comparative Observations

All 4 legal systems protect consumers from terms limiting trader liability as provided in the Annex to the Directive, demonstrated by their banning of such clauses. Such clauses are automatically unfair in France, Germany, and the United Kingdom (under section 65 of the Consumer Rights Act 2015). In the Netherlands, traders must prove that such terms are not unfair in light of the surrounding circumstances. The examination revealed that it is doubtful that Dutch courts would accept such clauses as fair. In the case of the United Kingdom, one must distinguish between terms falling under section 65 and those to which the general test in section 62 in connection with Schedule 2 Part 1(1) of the Consumer Rights Act 2015 will apply. In the former case, the terms will be unenforceable, whereas, in the latter, it will be within the courts' discretion to render them unenforceable. The examination of the national laws has revealed that all 4 legal systems provide either the same or more generous protection than Article 3 in connection with Point 1(a) of the Directive's Annex.

4.2 Exclusion or Limitation of Compensation in Case of Total or Partial Non-performance

Article 3, in connection with Point 1(b) of the Annex to the Unfair Contract Terms Directive, provides that contractual clauses may be unfair where:

> [a clause is] inappropriately excluding or limiting the legal rights of the consumer vis-a-vis the seller or supplier or another party in the event of total or partial non-performance or inadequate performance by the seller or supplier of any of the contractual obligations, including the option of offsetting a debt owed to the seller or supplier against any claim which the consumer may have against him.

The national courts have not yet asked the Court of Justice to interpret the general test of unfairness in light of Point 1(b) of the Directive's Annex. Consequently, no interpretation is available on the EU level, granting more discretion to the Member States.

4.2.1 France

As mentioned and examined in the previous section of the present chapter (see Chapter 3.4.1), the duties of traders contained in Article L212-1 in connection with Article R212-1 no 6 of the Code de la consommation (*limitation de responsabilité*) covers the issue of consumer compensation in the case of total or partial non-performance.[174] In addition, French law prohibits contractual clauses which allow traders to restrict consumers' right to terminate the contract in the case of trader non-performance (Article R212-1 no 7). The provisions are consequently wider and stricter than Point 1(b) of the Directive's Annex.

4.2.2 Germany

Contractual clauses excluding or limiting compensation in case of total or partial non-performance of traders are always unfair according to § 309 No 8 of the BGB in conjunction with §§ 309 No 3 and No 7 lit. b of the BGB. §§ 309 No 3, No 7 lit. b, and No 8 deal with various forms of contractual duties: the right to set off a claim (No 3); the exclusion or limitation of liability for damages (No 7 lit. b); and other exclusions of liability for breaches of contractual duties (No 8). All 3 provisions are stricter, that is, contained in the 'black list' (*Klauselverbote ohne Wertungsmöglichkeit*), and are also more precise than the provision in the Directive's Annex.

Point 1(b) Annex of the Directive lists the possibility of setting off a debt as an example of a right which cannot be limited. A German provision transposing this is § 309 No 3 of the BGB (*Aufrechnungsverbot*), but the German provision is more precise than the Directive. The Directive provides that the consumer can set off 'any claim', whereas the BGB requires that the claim 'is uncontested or has been finally and non-appealably established'.[175] Another provision which transposes parts of Point 1(b) is No 7 lit. b, prohibiting clauses which allow traders to limit or exclude liability for damages caused by gross negligence (*grobes Verschulden*) breach of statutory duties.[176] The third provision transposing parts of Point 1(b) of the Directive's Annex is § 309 No 8, which contains other rights that the trader's terms and conditions cannot limit. No 8 lit. a, protects consumers from clauses which exclude the right to free oneself from the contract (*Ausschluss des Rechts, sich vom Vertrag zu lösen*).[177] No 8 lit. b provides further prohibited clauses: exclusion and referral to third

[174] Julien (n 89) 313–14; Pellier (n 157) 126–29.

[175] Wurmnest (n 102) BGB § 309 No 3 [3–4]; Schäfer in Stefan Ernst and others (eds), *AGB-Recht: Kommentar* (12th edn, Otto Schmidt Verlag 2016) BGB § 309 No 3 [2a–2c].

[176] Wurmnest (n 102) BGB § 309 No 7 [3–4]; Christensen in Stefan Ernst and others (eds), *AGB-Recht: Kommentar* (12th edn, Otto Schmidt Verlag 2016) BGB § 309 No 7 [6–7].

[177] Wurmnest (n 102) BGB § 309 No 8 [4]; Christensen in Stefan Ernst and others (eds), *AGB-Recht: Kommentar* (12th edn, Otto Schmidt Verlag 2016) BGB § 309 No 8 [1–3].

parties (aa); limitation to cure (bb); expenses for cure (cc); withholding cure (dd); cut-off period for notice of defects (ee); and making limitation easier (ff).

It is unlikely that one of the 3 provisions would not cover a clause falling within the scope of Point 1(b) Annex of the Unfair Contract Terms Directive.[178] However, in such a scenario, consumers could rely on the general clause contained in § 307 of the BGB.[179] Considering the broad scope of the provisions, it is doubtful that consumers have to rely on this default option.[180] The German provisions go beyond the Directive: the scope is broader, and the terms covered by Point 1(b) would be rendered 'unfair' by the BGB.[181]

4.2.3 The Netherlands

The Dutch Civil Code does not provide one specific provision regulating clauses that aim to exclude or limit the compensation in case of total or partial non-performance of traders. Several particular provisions regulate this scenario. The *zwarte lijst* ('black list') of Article 6:236 of the BW contains 3 out of the 7 relevant provisions; the *grijze lijst* ('grey list') of Article 6:237 of the BW includes the remaining 4 provisions.

The first provision examined in the *zwarte lijst* is Article 6:236(a). This provision prohibits terms which deprive consumers entirely and unconditionally of the right to demand the performance of traders.[182] Under Article 6:236(b), clauses which exclude or restrict consumers' right to dissolve (*bevoegdheid tot ontbinding*) the contract are always unfair.[183] The third provision, Article 6:236(c), prohibits contractual terms which exclude or restrict the consumer's statutory rights, including allowing traders fully or partially to suspend performance.[184]

The *grijze lijst* provides a more general provision. Article 6:237(b) lists clauses as presumably unfair, allowing traders to deviate from consumers' reasonable expectations (*redelijke verwachting*).[185] The provision states that it uses the statutory obligations of traders as the benchmark for assessing whether it meets

[178] Wurmnest (n 102) BGB § 309 No 3 [3–4].
[179] BGH NJW 2018, 2042.
[180] Christensen in Stefan Ernst and others (eds), *AGB-Recht: Kommentar* (12th edn, Otto Schmidt Verlag 2016) BGB § 309 No 8 [3]; Wurmnest (n 102) BGB § 309 No 3 [3–4], § 309 No 7 [3–4], § 309 No 8 [4].
[181] ibid.
[182] Krans, Stolker, and Valk (n 115) BW Art 6:236 [4(a)]; Tjeerd GG Raijmakers, 'Art. 236 – Burgerlijk Wetboek Boek 6' in Bakker (n 115) BW art 6:236 [4.1].
[183] Krans, Stolker, and Valk (n 115) BW art 6:236 [4(a)]; Raijmakers (n 182) BW art 6:236 [4.1]. cf Ruth Sefton-Green, 'Case Studies' in Ruth Sefton-Green (ed), *Mistake, Fraud and Duties to Inform in European Contract Law* (CUP 2009) 300–301.
[184] Krans, Stolker, and Valk (n 115) BW art 6:236 [4(a)]; Raijmakers (n 182) BW art 6:236 [4.1].
[185] Krans, Stolker, and Valk (n 115) BW art 6:237 [4(b)]; Raijmakers (n 115) BW art 6:237 [3.1].

consumers' reasonable expectations. Another provision covering the content of Point 1(b) is Article 6:237(c), which requires traders to prove that a clause allowing traders to provide a performance deviating essentially from the promised performance is not unfair; traders must also allow consumers to dissolve the contract.[186] As discussed in Chapter 3.4.1, Article 6:236(f) prohibits traders from limiting their obligation to pay statutory damages. The last provision presumes that terms that exclude or limit the right to offset a debt or grant traders more far-reaching rights to settle are unfair (Article 6:237(g)).[187] The evidence put forward by traders to prove that such terms are not unfair according to the Dutch 'grey list' needs to be assessed under the general test (Article 6:233(a)).

The provisions of the *Burgerlijk Wetboek* address both the right to demand performance and the right to damages in case of total or partial non-performance. Overall, the Dutch provisions are wider and surpass the indicative nature of the Directive's list. Contractual clauses caught by Point 1(b) are either automatically unfair and ineffective ('black-listed') or require traders to prove that such clauses are not unfair ('grey-listed').

4.2.4 The United Kingdom

According to section 31(1) of the Consumer Rights Act 2015, contractual clauses are invalid and not binding on consumers when traders limit or restrict their liability concerning:

(a) section 9 (goods to be of satisfactory quality);
(b) section 10 (goods to be fit for particular purpose);
(c) section 11 (goods to be as described);
(d) section 12 (other pre-contract information included in contract);
(e) section 13 (goods to match a sample);
(f) section 14 (goods to match a model seen or examined);
(g) section 15 (installation as part of conformity of the goods with the contract);
(h) section 16 (goods not conforming to contract if digital content does not conform);
(i) section 17 (trader to have right to supply the goods etc.);
(j) section 28 (delivery of goods);
(k) section 29 (passing of risk).[188]

[186] Krans, Stolker, and Valk (n 115) BW art 6:237 [4(b)]; Raijmakers (n 115) BW art 6:237 [3.1]. Chapter 3.4.5 will examine the provision and respective case law.

[187] Krans, Stolker, and Valk (n 115) BW art 6:237 [4(d)]; Raijmakers (n 115) BW art 6:237 [3.1].

[188] Section 31(3) provides that s 31(1) includes any exclusion or restriction of liability which prevents an obligation or duty to arise or limit its extent.

Furthermore, section 31(2) states that contract terms are not binding on consumers when these terms:

(a) exclude or restrict a right or remedy in respect of a liability under a provision listed in subsection (1),
(b) make such a right or remedy or its enforcement subject to a restrictive or onerous condition,
(c) allow a trader to put a person at a disadvantage as a result of pursuing such a right or remedy, or
(d) exclude or restrict rules of evidence or procedure.[189]

In addition, exemption clauses which may fall outside the scope of section 31 'may be regarded as unfair' according to the general test complemented by the list of potentially unfair terms in Schedule 2 Part 1(2) of the Consumer Rights Act 2015. This provision transposes almost word-for-word Point 1(b) of the Annex to the Unfair Contract Terms Directive.[190] Consequently, terms containing exemption clauses outside section 31 are not automatically unfair. Like all other potentially unfair terms listed in Schedule 2, courts must examine such clauses under the general unfairness test (section 62 of the Consumer Rights Act 2015).

4.2.5 Comparative Observations

All 4 jurisdictions have enacted provisions which prohibit terms excluding or limiting compensation in the event of total or partial non-performance of traders. Such clauses are always unfair in France and Germany. It depends on whether the contract clause falls within the scope of the 'black-listed' provisions in the Netherlands and the United Kingdom. Otherwise, courts presume such clauses as unfair under the 'grey list' in the Netherlands or assess them in light of the general test of unfairness in the United Kingdom. Another observation is that the German and Dutch provisions are, on their own, much narrower than the provision contained in the Directive's Annex. However, the combined coverage of the provisions is the same.

[189] However, s 31(1i) and s 31(2) 'so far as it relates to liability under section 17, do not apply to a term of a contract for the hire of goods' (s 31(5)). cf Cartwright (n 170) 119–20.

[190] Ewan McKendrick notes that the term 'inappropriately' has not been defined by the UK courts. See McKendrick (n 172).

4.3 One-sided Compensation for Cancellation

According to Article 3, in connection with Point 1(d) of the Annex to the Unfair Contract Terms Directive, traders may not:

> [r]etain sums paid by the consumer where the latter decides not to conclude or perform the contract, without providing for the consumer to receive compensation of an equivalent amount from the seller or supplier where the latter is the party cancelling the contract.

The Court of Justice has yet to be asked by the national courts to rule on any issues relating to one-sided compensation clauses in light of Point 1(d).

4.3.1 France

One-sided compensation clauses (*dédit*) fall within the scope of Article L212-1 in connection with Article R212-2 no 2 of the Code de la consommation. The French regulatory provision provides the same content as Point 1(d) of the Directive's Annex, but unlike the Directive, the French rule contains a specific provision on deposits.[191] In addition, Article R212-2 no 2 is in the *liste grise* ('grey list'). The list operates under the presumption of unfairness, which does not impose an outright prohibition, but shifts the burden of proof on traders. Consequently, Article R212-2 no 2 is broader and stricter than the Directive.[192]

4.3.2 Germany

§ 308 No 7 of the BGB and §§ 309 No 5 and No 6 of the BGB reflect the content of Point 1(d) of the Directive's Annex. The 'grey list' (*Klauselverbote mit Wertungsmöglichkeit*) contains the first provision: § 308 No 7 of the BGB deals with the reversal of contracts (*Abwicklung von Verträgen*). While § 309 No 5 deals with lump-sum claims for damages (*Pauschalierung von Schadensersatzansprüchen*) and § 309 No 6 with penalty clauses (*Vertragsstrafen*).[193] Whether a clause will be deemed unfair with or without evaluation depends on which category a claim falls under.

[191] Julien (n 89) 313–16; Pellier (n 157) 126–29.

[192] Such terms are always unfair ('black list') if traders secretly cancel the contract and withhold sums paid by consumers (art R212-1 no 9 of the Code de la consommation). The provision is of a more practical nature and is consequently not taken into account for assessing trader compliance in the present study.

[193] Fuchs in Stefan Ernst and others (eds), *AGB-Recht: Kommentar* (12th edn, Otto Schmidt Verlag 2016) BGB § 309 No 6 [5–10].

§ 309 No 5 of the BGB regulates contractually agreed lump sums. A lump sum is unfair where it exceeds the damages expected to be paid by the consumer under normal circumstances (*gewöhnlichen Lauf der Dinge*) or the customarily occurring reduction in the value of the product (*gewöhnlich eintretende Wertminderung*) (No 5 lit. a). Moreover, No 5 lit. b prohibits lump-sums where the consumer is not expressly permitted to demonstrate that damage or reduction in value has taken place (*Schaden oder eine Wertminderung*) or that the damage or reduction is significantly less than the lump-sum claim (*wesentlich niedriger als die Pauschale*).[194]

Another provision that consumers might invoke is § 309 No 6 of the BGB. According to this provision, contractual penalties in the case of non-acceptance (*Nichtabnahme der Leistung*) or late acceptance of the performance (*verspätete Abnahme der Leistung*), payment default (*Zahlungsverzug*) or consumers freeing themselves from the contract (*Lösung vom Vertrag*) are prohibited.[195]

If the contractual term does not fall within the scope of §§ 309 No 5 and No 6 of the BGB, courts can assess the term under § 308 No 7 of the BGB.[196] The provision requires that contract terms must not contain a clause, which in the case of the reversal or termination of the contract, requires the consumer to pay an 'unreasonably high remuneration for enjoyment or use of a thing or a right or for performance rendered' (No 7a) or 'unreasonably high reimbursement of expenses' (No 7b). As discussed in Chapter 3.3, the courts have the power to evaluate whether the sum is 'unreasonably high' (*unangemessen hoch*) in the circumstances of the case, weighing the overall interests of the parties (*Gesamtabwägung der Interessen der Vertragspartner*). According to the German Federal Court of Justice, the benchmark for assessing whether a compensation clause is unreasonable depends on the amount of compensation a trader could claim under applicable statutory provisions (for instance, § 649 of the BGB).[197] The provision in the Directive's Annex only requires that the sum be equivalent to what consumers could claim when the trader breaches the contract.

It follows that the provisions in the BGB are stricter and broader than the indicative provision in Point 1(d) of the Annex to the Unfair Contract Terms Directive.

194 ibid BGB § 309 No 5 [5–9]; Wurmnest (n 102) BGB § 309 No 5 [1–3].

195 Fuchs in Stefan Ernst and others (eds), *AGB-Recht: Kommentar* (12th edn, Otto Schmidt Verlag 2016) BGB § 309 No 6 [5–10]; Wurmnest (n 102) BGB § 309 No 6 [1–3].

196 Schmidt in Stefan Ernst and others (eds), *AGB-Recht: Kommentar* (12th edn, Otto Schmidt Verlag 2016) BGB § 308 No 7 [4–5c]; Wurmnest (n 102) BGB § 308 No 7 [2–3].

197 BGH NJW 2011, 1954.

4.3.3 The Netherlands

Dutch law does not contain a specific provision regulating one-sided compensation for cancellation clauses. However, 2 provisions in the grijze lijst ('grey list') fulfil a similar function. Article 6:237(f) of the BW declares clauses unfair when a contract term frees traders wholly or partly of a statutory obligation to pay damages.[198] Article 6:237(i) governs situations where a penalty is imposed on the consumer in case the contract is terminated for any other reason than the consumer failing to fulfil his obligations, for example, the cancellation of the contract.[199] Such clauses are only regarded as fair if the compensation is a reasonable sum (*redelijke vergoeding*) for the loss suffered by traders or profit of which traders were deprived; there must also be a legitimate interest to impose such a fee.[200]

The Dutch provisions consequently cover the content of Point 1(d) of the Directive's Annex, but the 'grey list' contains Article 6:237(f) and (i), making the standard stricter. If they fall within the 'grey list', traders must prove that such a clause is not unfair; in the light of Article 6:237(i), traders must provide the amount of actual damage suffered. The traders' evidence is then subject to the test of the general clause under Article 6:233(a).

4.3.4 The United Kingdom

The Consumer Rights Act also contains a provision that deals with one-sided compensation clauses. Schedule 2 Part 1(4) of the Consumer Rights Act 2015 transposes Point 1(d) of the Annex to the Unfair Contract Terms Directive: the standard does not differ from the one provided under the Directive. One-sided compensation clauses are likely unfair, but courts must assess them under the general test contained in section 62.

4.3.5 Comparative Observations

Examining the national rules has revealed that the French, German, and Dutch provisions are stricter and more precise than Point 1(d) of the Annex to the

198 Chapter 3.4.1 has already examined this provision.

199 Krans, Stolker, and Valk (n 115) BW art 6:237 [5(a)]; Raijmakers (n 115) BW art 6:237 [3.2].

200 See eg a recent case by a Dutch lower court, Rechtbank Amsterdam 29 June 2020, ECLI:NL:RBAMS:2020:3087. In this case, the court emphasized that the most favourable estimation for loss or lost profits prevailed and found that the trader could not provide sufficient evidence that they sustained a third per cent loss. However, in an earlier case at the Court of Appeal in Arnhem-Leeuwarden, the proffering party could successfully prove that it suffered a 30 per cent loss. The trader provided evidence of its loss, in this case, the annual return statements. Before inserting such a clause into its terms and conditions, the trader contacted a consumer organization to assess whether such a clause was unfair. Based on all the evidence of the proffering party, the court found the clause is not unreasonably onerous. See Gerechtshof Arnhem-Leeuwarden (25 August 2015) ECLI:NL:GHARL:2015:6249.

Unfair Contract Terms Directive. The United Kingdom's provision provides the same standard as the Directive, that is, the general test of unfairness assesses it in light of the indicative provision. All 4 jurisdictions, therefore, protect consumers from one-sided compensation clauses.

4.4 Excessive Compensation

Contractual terms requiring consumers who fail to fulfil their obligations to pay a 'disproportionately high sum in compensation' may be regarded unfair according to Article 3 in connection with Point 1(e) of the Annex to the Unfair Contract Terms Directive. The Court of Justice faced an excessive compensation clause in *Pohotovost*.[201] The contractual clause concerned late payment in a credit agreement and provided an annual interest rate of 91.25 per cent. In light of Article 3 in connection with Point 1(e), the Court held: '[a] disproportionately high sum in compensation, is to be regarded as unfair in the light of all the circumstances attending the conclusion of the contract'.[202] Therefore, whether the contract can continue without the unfair term is a matter for the national courts;[203] the Court of Justice reaffirmed *Freiburger Kommunalbauten*.[204] The Court delivered a more substantive ruling in *Banco Santander*, where the Court defined a disproportionately high compensation as 'a rate exceed[ing] by more than 2 percentage points the ordinary interest rate provided for in that agreement'.[205] The rulings on excessive compensation clauses by the Court of Justice ultimately limit the national judicial and regulatory autonomy.

4.4.1 France

Article L212-1, in connection with Article R212-2 no 3 of the Code de la consommation, deals with penalty clauses (*clause pénale*) like Point 1(e) of the Annex to the Directive.[206] There is only one minor difference: the French provision requires the penalty payment to be manifestly disproportionate

[201] Case C-76/10 *Pohotovosť sro v Iveta Korčkovská* (n 26).
[202] ibid para 60.
[203] ibid para 61. The court reached the same conclusion regarding excessive compensation clauses in 2 additional cases concerning late payment interests and in cases on cumulative effects of contractual sanctions. For late payment see Case C-415/11 *Catalunyacaixa* (n 24); Joined Cases C-96/16 and C-94/17 *Banco Santander v Mahamadou Demba, Mercedes Godoy Bonet and Rafael Ramón Escobedo Cortés v Banco de Sabadell SA* ECLI:EU:C:2018:643. Concerning cumulative effects see Case C-377/14 *Radlinger Radlingerová Ernst Georg Radlinger and Helena Radlingerová v Finway as* ECLI:EU:C:2016:283.
[204] Case C-237/02 *Freiburger Kommunalbauten GmbH Baugesellschaft & Co KG* (n 25).
[205] Joined Cases C-96/16 and C-94/17 *Banco Santander* (n 203) para 71.
[206] Julien (n 89) 313–16; Pellier (n 157) 126–29.

(*manifestement disproportionné*) and not just disproportionate. In practice, there appears not to be a difference.[207] However, unlike in the Directive, excessive compensation clauses are presumed unfair ('grey list'), and the burden is on traders to prove that the clause is not unfair.[208] The court will then assess whether such a term is unfair by considering the surrounding circumstances.

4.4.2 Germany

In Germany, excessive compensation claims (§ 309 No 6 of the BGB) and lump-sum agreements (§ 309 No 5 of the BGB) are unfair under all circumstances. This chapter has examined both provisions.[209] The 2 German provisions are more context-specific and together also broader than Point 1(e) of the Directive's Annex. Furthermore, terms falling within their scope are always unfair without the possibility of a different judicial assessment. Consumers can have the sum reduced under § 343 of the BGB, while traders can claim compensation for their reasonable expenses.[210]

4.4.3 The Netherlands

Article 6:237(i) and Articles 6:91-6:94 of the BW reflect the content of Point 1(e).[211] The former covers contractual penalties concerning the termination of the contract other than for consumers failing to fulfil their obligations.[212] The chapter established that compensation clauses are only regarded as fair when consumers fail to fulfil their obligations, and the compensation is a reasonable sum (*redelijke vergoeding*) for the loss or profit suffered. Articles 6:91-6:94 of the BW cover contractual penalties imposed in other situations. These provisions presume that penalty clauses are unfair that go beyond statutory damages (Articles 6:92(2) and 6:94 of the BW). Therefore, Articles 6:237(i) and 6:91-6:94 are broader and stricter than Point 1(e) of the Directive's Annex.

4.4.4 The United Kingdom

Penalty clauses are not enforceable at common law.[213] At first glance, this offers more robust protection for the consumer than the Consumer Rights Act 2015 provides, as it always prevents the consumer from being bound by such a

[207] See eg Cass civ (1) 1 February 2005, no 01-16.733.
[208] Julien (n 89) 313–16; Pellier (n 157) 126–29.
[209] See ch 3.4.3.
[210] Wurmnest (n 102) BGB § 309 No 6 [2–3].
[211] Krans, Stolker, and Valk (n 115) BW art 6:237 [5(a)]; Raijmakers (n 115) BW art 6:237 [3.2].
[212] Chapter 3.4.3 examined this provision.
[213] See the most recent judgment of the UK Supreme Court on this point: *Cavendish Square Holding BV* (n 136). cf Hans-Wolfgang Micklitz, *The Politics of Justice in European Private Law: Social Justice, Access Justice, Societal Justice* (CUP 2018) 64–66.

clause. However, consumers face difficulty proving that the contract term is a penalty clause because a contract term is only a penalty clause where there is no legitimate interest in deterring the contractual breach. In such circumstances, reliance on such a term is considered an 'exorbitant' or 'unconscionable' alternative to common law damages.[214] About what constitutes an exorbitant sum, Chen-Wishart argues that, in the light of *ParkingEye Ltd*, it must be 'very substantially more than necessary to deter the breach' so the 'parties have a generous margin of error'.[215] There is plenty of room for a trader to seek to show a legitimate interest in relying on the clause to deter the breach rather than claim damages, in which case the clause stands.[216] Under the Consumer Rights Act, by contrast, the starting point is the protection of the consumer as a weaker party. As Lord Neuberger pointed out, the general test, now section 62 of the Consumer Rights Act 2015,[217] 'is significantly more favourable to the consumer than would be applied by a court in this country under the penalty doctrine'.[218]

In addition to the penalty clause doctrine, penalty clauses may be considered unfair under Schedule 2 Part 1(6) of the Consumer Rights Act 2015. The provision transposes, once again, almost word-for-word, the Directive into UK law. In addition, Part 1(5) of Schedule 2 prohibits terms which require a disproportionally high sum in compensation 'where the consumer decides not to conclude or perform the contract'. Courts must assess contract clauses which

[214] Chen-Wishart (n 71) 564–67; Jonathan Morgan, 'The Penalty Clause Doctrine: Unlovable but Untouchable' (2016) 75(1) The Cambridge Law Journal 12.

[215] Chen-Wishart (n 71) 566.

[216] The case amended the 4 tests outlined in *Dunlop Pneumatic Tyre Co Ltd v New Garage and Motor Co Ltd* [1915] AC 79 and labelled as one of the most essential English cases of the last century. According to Roger Halson, the most significant change to the common law rule on penalty clauses has been that it 'now places emphasis upon the justifying interest of the party seeking to enforce the clause' and whether it is proportionate in the circumstances of the case. He also suggests that it will be sufficient to apply the 'genuine pre-estimate of loss' test, *id est* whether the sum is a genuine pre-estimate of the loss in case the breach occurs, in less complex cases, for example, simple damage clauses in standard form contracts. Roger Halson, *Liquidated Damages and Penalty Clauses* (OUP 2018) 32, 71–72.

[217] *Cavendish Square Holding BV v Talal El Makdessi and ParkingEye Ltd v Beavis* [2015] UKSC 67, para 303 (Lord Neuberger): 'Article 3(1) of the Directive is the counterpart to regulation 5(1) and is identically worded.' The Consumer Rights Act 2015 (s 62(4)) now includes the provision of the Unfair Terms in Consumer Contracts Regulations 1999.

[218] *Cavendish Square Holding BV* (n 217) para 309 (Lord Neuberger): 'That test is significantly more favourable to the consumer than would be applied by a court in this country under the penalty doctrine. Whereas the starting point at common law is that parties should be kept to their bargains, and it is for those objecting that a clause is penal to establish its exorbitant nature, the starting point of the Directive is that the consumer needs special protection, and it is for the supplier to show that a non-core term which is significantly disadvantageous to the consumer, as compared with the ordinary operation of the law without that term, is one which the supplier can fairly assume that the consumer would have agreed in individual negotiations on level terms. The burden is on the supplier to adduce the evidence necessary to justify that conclusion.' The harmonization of European private law also impacts the wider common law world. See Birke Häcker, 'Divergence and Convergence in the Common Law: Lessons from the Ius Commune' (2015) 131 Law Quarterly Review 424.

fall within Schedule 2 Part 1(5) and (6) under the general test of section 62 of the Consumer Rights Act 2015.

4.4.5 Comparative Observations

The Court of Justice has interpreted Article 3 in the light of Point 1(e) of the Directive's Annex, and, as a result, there is an EU-wide standard regulating penalty clauses. However, examining the Court of Justice cases has revealed that the rules do not apply to e-commerce sales but only to financial services. Member States protect consumers from penalty clauses: in the United Kingdom, through the indicative list of potentially unfair terms or as part of the penalty clause doctrine; in France and the Netherlands, through 'grey lists'; and in Germany, through a 'black list'. All 4 jurisdictions have rules that are stricter than the Directive.

4.5 One-sided Changes to the Contract

Contractual clauses which allow traders to change terms unilaterally and without a valid reason mentioned in the contract may be considered unfair in light of Article 3 in connection with Point 1(j) of the Annex to the Unfair Contract Terms Directive. National courts have submitted several preliminary references concerning price variation clauses to the Court of Justice.[219] In *Nemzeti Fogyasztóvédelmi Hatóság*, the Court established that for price variation clauses to be effective, such clauses must be 'set out in plain, intelligible language and, as the case may be, whether consumers have a right to terminate the contract'.[220] The Court went further in *RWE Vertrieb AG*[221] establishing a 4-limb test for price variation clauses in gas contracts: (1) price variation clauses must meet the requirements of good faith, balance, and transparency;[222] (2) it must be assessed whether such a term is unfair in the circumstances of the case;[223] (3) such a clause must be included for a valid reason, and, in particular, consumers must be able to foresee such a clause, based on clear, intelligible criteria, before the conclusion of the contract;[224] (4) and that consumers must

[219] Case C-472/10 *Nemzeti Fogyasztóvédelmi Hatóság v Invitel Távközlési Zrt* [2012] ECLI:EU:C:2012:242; Case C-92/11 *RWE Vertrieb AG v Verbraucherzentrale Nordrhein-Westfalen eV* ECLI:EU:C:2013:180; Case C-348/14 *Maria Bucura v SC Bancpost SA* ECLI:EU:C:2015:447.
[220] Case C-472/10 *Nemzeti Fogyasztóvédelmi Hatóság v Invitel Távközlési Zrt* (n 219) para 31.
[221] Case C-92/11 *RWE Vertrieb AG v Verbraucherzentrale Nordrhein-Westfalen eV* (n 219).
[222] ibid para 47.
[223] ibid para 48.
[224] ibid para 55.

have an effective right to terminate the contract.[225] Point 3 and 4 of the CJEU's test further defines Point 1(j), that is, a price variation clause requires a valid and foreseeable reason and allow consumers to free themselves from the contract. The universal nature of this test stems from the fact that the CJEU has also applied it in other situations, for example, in cases concerning price variation clauses in exchange rate conversions for mortgage loans[226] and unilateral changes of interest rates.[227] Thus, the Court has restricted the discretion of the national legislators and courts.

4.5.1 France

The French Consumer Code prohibits unilateral contract changes (*modifications unilatérales*) by traders.[228] According to Article L212-1 in connection with Article R212-2 no 6 of the Code de la consommation, clauses allowing for one-sided changes to the contract are presumed unfair.[229] A more specific regulatory provision is Article R212-1 no 3 of the Code de la consommation, which prohibits ('black list') traders from modifying the clauses of the contract relating to its duration, the characteristics, and the price of the goods.[230] The 2 regulatory provisions are not only more precise than Point 1(j) of the Annex to the Directive but also provide a higher level of protection: (1) a clause allowing for one-sided changes (*modifications unilatérales*) is either presumed unfair ('grey list') or automatically unfair ('black list'); (2) a clause allowing for one-sided changes can never be justified under French law unless the clause falls within the exception listed in the following paragraph.[231]

Several exceptions apply to Articles R212-1 no 3 and R212-2 no 6. The only exception to the provisions in this context permits contractual modifications linked to technical developments (Article R212-4 no 4). The provision provides the reasons for this exception: such changes do not result in an increase in price, deterioration in quality, or a change of characteristics. Thus, Article R212-4 no 4 allows for changes when the contract terms envisage such justifications. While the other exceptions listed in Article R212-3 and Article

[225] ibid.
[226] Case C-26/13 *Árpád Kásler and Hajnalka Káslerné Rábai v OTP Jelzálogbank Zrt* (n 30).
[227] Case C-143/13 *Bogdan Matei and Ioana Ofelia Matei v SC Volksbank România SA* ECLI:EU:C:2015:127.
[228] Julien (n 89) 325–26; Dalloz, *Code de la consommation – annote & commenté* (24th edn, Dalloz 2020) 215.
[229] CA Douai 28 February 2019, RG no 16-05841.
[230] Julien (n 89) 313–14; Bénabent (n 160) 160–63.
[231] Pellier (n 157) 127. Jacques Mestre, 'Clause de modification unilateral' in Frédéric Buy and others (eds), *Les principales clauses des contrats d'affaires* (2nd edn, Librairie générale de droit et de jurisprudence 2018) 515-520.

R212-4 cover Point 2 of the Annex to the Directive, the exception created by Article R212-4 no 4 is not. An exception that considers technical developments is a forward-looking response to the growing influence of digitization in e-commerce sales and the expansion of digital services more broadly. A software update could be an example of technical development in light of Article R212-4 no 4.[232]

4.5.2 Germany

§ 308 No 4 of the BGB deals with the unilateral reservation to modify the contract terms (*Änderungsvorbehalt*).[233] The German provision is very similar to Point 1(j) of the Annex to the Unfair Contract Terms Directive. On the substantive level, there is, however, one very minor difference. Point 1(j) provides that traders may alter the contract terms if they offer a valid reason previously specified. § 308 No 4 prohibits traders from altering the contract 'unless the agreement of the modification or deviation can reasonably be expected of the other party to the contract when the interests of the user are taken into account'. Whether it is 'reasonable' (*zumutbar*) in the circumstances of the case is subject to judicial assessment (*umfassenden Interessenabwägung*).[234] The German Federal Court of Justice held that clauses allowing for a deviation are unfair where traders could have indicated that there might be a need for modification already at the time of the conclusion of the contract.[235]

Consequently, traders must demonstrate that modifying the contract terms is of considerable interest (*erhebliches Interesse*), for instance, if such a modification is unavoidable (*unvermeidbar*). The German Federal Court of Justice has also held that modification clauses are fair if they benefit consumers.[236] § 308 No 4 of the BGB covers the content of Point 1(j), but, due to the characteristics of the German 'grey list', it is stricter than the Directive's Annex.

4.5.3 The Netherlands

As discussed in Chapter 3.4.2, clauses which allow traders to offer a performance that deviates essentially from the contract (*wezenlijk van de toegezegde prestatie afwijkt*) are unfair unless consumers are entitled to free themselves from the contract Article 6:237(c) of the BW. There is also a *lex specialis*

[232] ibid Mestre; Dalloz (n 228) 217.
[233] Wurmnest (n 102) BGB § 308 No 4 [1–3].
[234] Schmidt in Stefan Ernst and others (eds), *AGB-Recht: Kommentar* (12th edn, Otto Schmidt Verlag 2016) BGB § 308 No 4 [1, 3a–3c].
[235] BGH NJW-RR 2009, 1641. ibid (Schmidt) BGB § 308 No 4 [9].
[236] ibid.

provision in Article 6:236(i) of the BW concerning a unilateral price modification, which this chapter will examine later.[237] Both provisions go beyond the indicative nature of the Directive's Annex: clauses which fall within the scope of Article 6:236(i) are automatically unfair and ineffective, while clauses falling within the scope of Article 6:237(c) are presumed to be unfair, the trader retaining the possibility of proving that the clause is not unfair in the circumstances of the case (Article 6:233(a)).[238] It follows that the Dutch provisions are narrower than Point 1(j), and in rare cases, there may be a need to assess terms in the light of the general test.[239]

4.5.4 The United Kingdom

Schedule 2 Part 1(11) of the Consumer Rights Act 2015 uses the exact wording as the Directive's Annex. In addition, Schedule 2 Part 1(12) lists clauses which allow for unilateral changes in the characteristics of the subject matter as potentially unfair. Contract terms falling within the scope of either provision must pass the general test of section 62. There is no apparent divergence between Schedule 2 Part 1(11) of the CRA 2015 and the provision in the Directive's Annex.

4.5.5 Comparative Observations

The national courts have submitted multiple preliminary references to the Court of Justice concerning contract clauses allowing for a unilateral contract modification. The Court has interpreted the general test of unfairness in light of Point 1(j) of the Annex to the Unfair Contract Terms Directive on several instances. For instance, traders must comply with the requirements of the 4-limb test of *RWE Vertrieb AG*[240] when they include price variation clauses in their terms. The chapter established that the threshold to meet these requirements is high. The national level also addresses clauses allowing for one-sided changes to the contract, but it is worth noting again that the national courts must consider the Court of Justice case law. While all 4 jurisdictions have provisions explicitly dealing with clauses allowing for unilateral changes of the

[237] See ch 3.4.7.

[238] AC van Schaick, 'Contents and Effects' in Danny Busch and others (eds), *The Principles of European Contract Law and Dutch Law: A Commentary* (Kluwer Law 2002) 270.

[239] An Attorney General of the Dutch Supreme Court confirmed this observation, clarifying that the Dutch 'grey list' and 'black list' do not cover all of point 1(j) of the Annex to Directive 93/13/EEC. If a provision falls outside the scope of the 2 lists, courts must assess it under the general test. PHR 23 May 2014, ECLI:NL:PHR:2014:1900, para 3.26.

[240] Case C-92/11 *RWE Vertrieb AG v Verbraucherzentrale Nordrhein-Westfalen eV* (n 219).

contract terms, the level of protection on the national level differs: the United Kingdom has a general test of unfairness used in conjunction with the indicative list; Germany uses a 'grey list'; and France and the Netherlands use a mixture of a 'grey list' and a 'black list'. The French exception allowing traders to unilaterally change the contract terms in light of technological advancement, as long as it does not affect the quality and price of the goods, is likely to be accepted as a valid reason for a unilateral change of the contract in the other jurisdictions. It is in line with the Court of Justice case *RWE Vertrieb AG*, where the Court of Justice held that a one-sided change to the contract terms could be justified by transparently including a valid and foreseeable reason in the contract and allowing consumers to terminate it.[241]

4.6 One-sided Changes to the Product

Point 1(k) of the Annex to the Unfair Contract Terms Directive states that a contract term may be unfair where traders 'alter unilaterally without a valid reason any characteristics of the product or service to be provided'. Point 1(j) is the general provision (one-sided changes to the contract), while Point 1(k) serves as *lex specialis*. There are several judgments of the Court of Justice on Point 1(j) but none on Point 1(k).

4.6.1 France

Article L212-1, in connection with Article R212-1 no 3 of the Code de la consommation, covers contractual clauses allowing for changes to the product's characteristics. The French legislator opted for a higher level of protection and included such clauses in the *liste noire* ('black list').[242] This leaves no discretion to the courts and renders such clauses invalid. Traders can, however, invoke Article R212-4 no 3, which allows traders to modify the contract terms linked to technical developments, but only where it does not lead to an increase in the price, a deterioration in quality, or a change of the product's characteristics.[243] It is unlikely that a clause allowing for one-sided changes to the product fulfils the requirements of Article R212-4 no 3, since such a clause affects the product's characteristics.

[241] ibid para 55.
[242] Julien (n 89) 313–16; Pellier (n 157) 126–29.
[243] Dalloz (n 228); Bénabent (n 160) 160–63.

4.6.2 Germany

The 'grey list' (*Klauselverbote mit Wertungsmöglichkeit*) of the German Civil Code entails a provision dealing with unilateral changes to the product's characteristics. § 308 No 4 of the BGB is broader, as it encompasses both Point 1(j) and Point 1(k), and also stricter ('grey list' character) than Point 1(k) of the Annex to the Directive.[244] § 308 No 4 has already been examined in the previous section of this chapter, dealing with one-sided changes to the contract.[245]

4.6.3 The Netherlands

Article 6:237(c) of the BW presumes that contractual clauses are unfair in case terms allow traders to deviate from the performance agreed with consumers unless consumers have the right to free themselves from the contract.[246] The Dutch provision is stricter as it does not allow for a justification, and such clauses allowing for unilateral changes of the characteristics of the goods are always presumed to be unfair ('grey list'). Article 6:237(c) is also broader than Point 1(k) since it not only encompasses the unilateral alteration of the characteristics of the goods but a deviation from the entire contractually agreed performance.

4.6.4 The United Kingdom

Schedule 2 Part 1(13) of the Consumer Rights Act 2015 transposes almost word-for-word the text of the provision in the Directive's Annex. Contract terms falling within the scope of this provision need to be assessed under the general test (section 62), particularly the term 'valid reason', which neither the Act nor case law defines.

4.6.5 Comparative Observations

Member States have yet to submit a preliminary reference to the Court of Justice concerning the interpretation of Article 3 in connection with Point 1(k) of the Annex to Directive. On the national level, France prohibits ('black list') clauses allowing for unilateral product changes. Germany and the Netherlands have included these terms in their 'grey lists'; in the United Kingdom, such clauses are assessed under the general test in connection with the indicative

[244] Schmidt in Stefan Ernst and others (eds), *AGB-Recht: Kommentar* (12th edn, Otto Schmidt Verlag 2016) BGB § 308 No 4 [3a–3c]; Wurmnest (n 102) BGB § 308 No 4 [2–3].

[245] See ch 3.4.5.

[246] Chapter 3.4.5 examined this provision.

Annex to the CRA. The previous section of this chapter already mentioned that the French exception, allowing for unilateral changes due to technological developments, not affecting the price and quality of the good, would most likely be accepted in the other 3 jurisdictions as well.[247]

4.7 Price Variations

Courts may consider a contract term unfair where traders determine the price of the goods at delivery or increase the price without allowing consumers to withdraw from the contract (Article 3 in connection with Point 1(l) of the Annex to the Unfair Contract Terms Directive). The national courts have actively referred cases dealing with price variation clauses to the CJEU. These cases have been explored earlier in this chapter, and the examination has revealed that these CJEU decisions establish an EU-wide prohibition ('black list' character). As a result, courts declare contract clauses which allow traders to set the price at the time of delivery or a later stage without granting consumers the possibility to withdraw as unfair unless these clauses pass the 4-limb test of *RWE Vertrieb AG*.[248]

4.7.1 France

The French Consumer Code regulates price variation clauses through Article L212-1 in connection with Article R212-1 no 3 of the Code de la consommation.[249] The regulatory provision is broader, prohibiting all price changes, and is also stricter, as clauses attempting to increase the price are always unfair under the *liste noire* ('black list').[250] However, one of the exceptions above applies to Article R212-1 no 3. According to Article R212-4 no 3, traders are allowed to modify the contract terms linked to technical developments, but only where it does not increase the price, leads to a deterioration in quality, or changes in the characteristics. The consequence is that traders can modify some parts of the contract, but, among other things, traders are not allowed to increase the price. It is, therefore, doubtful that traders could rely on the exception in Article R212-4 no 3.

[247] See ch 3.4.5. In particular see Case C-92/11 *RWE Vertrieb AG v Verbraucherzentrale Nordrhein-Westfalen eV* (n 219).
[248] ibid (*RWE Vertrieb AG*) paras 47, 48, 55.
[249] Julien (n 89) 313–16; Pellier (n 157) 126–29.
[250] Dalloz (n 228) 216; Bénabent (n 160) 160–63.

4.7.2 Germany

Price increases at short notice (*kurzfristige Preiserhöhung*) are prohibited by § 309 No 1 of the BGB. Any clauses leading to an increase in price within 4 months of the conclusion of the contract are considered unfair. It includes *Tagespreisklauseln*, so prices that depend on the current value but not in case of continuing obligations (*Dauerschuldverhältnisse*).[251] § 309 No 1 of the BGB is more precise than Point 1(l) Annex of the Unfair Contract Terms Directive and provides better protection for consumers. Under the German provision, such clauses are automatically unfair, regardless of whether traders provide for a right to withdraw or whether the price is not excessive.[252] Furthermore, unlike in the Directive, a prohibition to increase the price within 4-month is provided in § 309 No 1, up to 3 months longer than the provision contained in the Consumer Rights Directive 2011/83.[253]

4.7.3 The Netherlands

Price variation clauses are also always unfair in the Netherlands. Article 6:236(i) of the BW prohibits clauses ('black list') which allow traders to increase the agreed price within 3 months after the conclusion of the contract.[254] Similar to the provision in the Directive's Annex, traders may only include such a clause in case they provide that consumers are entitled to free themselves from the contract when traders rely on this term.[255] Therefore, Article 6:236(i) is more precise and stricter than Point 1(l) of the Directive's Annex.

4.7.4 The United Kingdom

In the United Kingdom, Schedule 2 Part 1(14) and Part 1(15) of the Consumer Rights Act 2015 list price variations clauses as potentially unfair. Under Schedule 2 Part 1(14), clauses 'may be considered unfair' when the terms give traders the discretion to determine the 'price payable under the contract after the consumer has become bound by it, where no price or method of determining the price is agreed when the consumer becomes bound'. Schedule 2

[251] BGB, § 309 No 1(2). See for instance, BGH NJW 1985, 621.

[252] Fuchs in Stefan Ernst and others (eds), *AGB-Recht: Kommentar* (12th edn, Otto Schmidt Verlag 2016) BGB § 309 No 1 [4-10]; Wurmnest (n 102) BGB § 309 No 1 [2–6].

[253] Traders must deliver the goods within 30 days. Otherwise, according to art 18(1) of the Consumer Rights Directive 2011/83/EU, consumers can free themselves from the contract. See ch 4.3.1.5 of this book for further details.

[254] Krans, Stolker, and Valk (n 115) BW art 6:236 [5(b)]; Raijmakers (n 182) BW art 6:236 [4.4]. Both commentaries note that price changes after 3 months are still subject to review under the general test (art 6:233(a)).

[255] This observation was also emphasized by the Attorney General at the Dutch Supreme Court in PHR 5 April 2019, ECLI:NL:PHR:2019:346, especially para 6.11.1.

Part 1(15) provides that a clause 'may be unfair' where a contractual term allows traders to increase the price without giving consumers the right to cancel the contract 'if the final price is too high in relation to the price agreed when the contract was concluded'. The courts can determine whether such clauses are unfair under the general test (section 62). The examination showed that the 2 provisions in Schedule 2 transpose Point 1(l); thus, the level of consumer protection under the CRA and the Directive is the same.

4.7.5 Comparative Observations

The CJEU case law and national statutory provisions regulate price variation clauses. The French, German, and Dutch provisions are all stricter ('black list'); the German and Dutch rules are also more precise, only allowing for an increase in the price, respectively, 4 months and 3 months after the conclusion of the contract. National judges must also consider the case law of the Court of Justice, particularly the 4-limb test of *RWE Vertrieb AG*.[256]

4.8 One-sided Interpretation of the Contract

Article 3, in connection with Point 1(m) of the Annex to the Unfair Contract Terms Directive, lists terms as potentially unfair that are:

> [g]iving the seller or supplier the right to determine whether the goods or services supplied are in conformity with the contract, or giving him the exclusive right to interpret any term of the contract'

Otherwise, traders would have complete discretion in deciding whether the goods conform with the contract. This provision is another example of a one-sided term that is to the detriment of consumers and may be considered unfair. The national courts have not asked the Court of Justice to interpret the general test of unfairness in light of Point 1(m) of the Directive's Annex. However, the Consumer Rights Directive, a maximum harmonization instrument, requires that traders inform consumers about 'the existence of a legal guarantee of conformity of goods'.[257] This provision falls within the category of mandatory disclosures and creates a positive obligation for traders.

[256] Case C-92/11 *RWE Vertrieb AG v Verbraucherzentrale Nordrhein-Westfalen eV* (n 219) paras 47, 48, 55. See ch 3.4.5.

[257] Consumer Rights Directive, art 6(1)(l). Chapter 4.3.1.1 examines this provision further.

4.8.1 France

Article 3 and Point 1(m) of the Directive's Annex are replicated in French law by Article L212-1 in connection with Article R212-1 no 4 of the Code de la consommation.[258] The wordings used in the Directive and the provision in the French Consumer Code are the same. The only difference is that clauses allowing one-sided interpretation (*pouvoir d'interprétation*) of contractual terms are automatically unfair (included in the 'black list') under the French provisions.

4.8.2 Germany

Several provisions in the BGB prohibit contractual clauses which allow traders to determine the conformity of goods or grant them the exclusive right to interpret the contract. Unlike the Directive, the BGB lays down a series of more precise traders' obligations prohibiting traders from limiting the legal guarantees consumers could rely on §§ 309 No 7 and No 8 of the BGB in case of a dispute, and, by default, on the general clause in § 307 of the BGB.[259] No 7 concerns clauses that exclude or limit liability for injury to life, body, or health and in case of gross fault, which the chapter already explored.[260] The chapter already examined No 8 concerning clauses which exclude or limit liability for breaches of other obligations (*sonstige Haftungsausschlüsse bei Pflichtverletzung*), in particular defects (lit. b).[261] The German provisions are more precise than Point 1(m), and consumers enjoy a higher level of protection when such clauses fall within § 309 No 7 or No 8 BGB. In any event, consumers will not be subject to a lower standard, as the general test (§ 307 of the BGB) ensures that the level of protection is the same as the one envisaged by the Directive.[262]

4.8.3 The Netherlands

Article 6:236(d) of the BW prohibits clauses allowing traders to assess whether they have fulfilled all their obligations.[263] As a result, Article 6:236(d) is much broader than Point 1(m) since the Dutch provisions cover the interpretation of all trader obligations and not merely the interpretation of the conformity of

[258] Julien (n 89) 313–16; Pellier (n 157) 126–29.

[259] Christensen in Stefan Ernst and others (eds), *AGB-Recht: Kommentar* (12th edn, Otto Schmidt Verlag 2016) BGB § 309 No 7 [6–8], § 309 No 8 [3].

[260] See ch 3.4.1 and ch 3.4.2.

[261] Christensen in Stefan Ernst and others (eds), *AGB-Recht: Kommentar* (12th edn, Otto Schmidt Verlag 2016) BGB § 309 No 8 [1–3]; Wurmnest (n 102) BGB § 309 No 8 [4–5].

[262] Christensen in Stefan Ernst and others (eds), *AGB-Recht: Kommentar* (12th edn, Otto Schmidt Verlag 2016) BGB § 309 No 8 [33ff]; Wurmnest (n 102) BGB § 309 No 8 [4].

[263] Krans, Stolker, and Valk (n 115) BW art 6:236 [4(a)]; Raijmakers (n 182) BW art 6:236 [4.1].

goods or the terms of the contract. In Dutch law, such terms are included in the 'black list' rather than an indicative list, as in the Directive.

4.8.4 The United Kingdom

Schedule 2 Part 1(16) of the Consumer Rights Act 2015 transposes word-for-word the text of Point 1(m) of the Annex to the Directive. As mentioned above, all terms listed in Schedule 2 are only 'potentially' unfair and need to be assessed, in each case, under the general test of unfairness (section 62).

4.8.5 Comparative Observations

Contractual terms allowing traders to exclusively interpret the contract or determine whether the goods supplied conform with the contract are always unfair in France, Germany, and the Netherlands. In the United Kingdom, courts assess such clauses under the general test in connection with Schedule 2 Part 1(16).

4.9 One-sided Compliance with Obligations

Contract clauses allowing for one-sided compliance with obligations by traders may be regarded as unfair according to Article 3 in connection with Point 1(o) of the Annex to the Unfair Contract Terms Directive. It is the case where the trader obliges the consumer to fulfil his obligation even though the trader is not performing its own obligation. The national courts have yet to ask the Court of Justice to interpret the general test of unfairness in light of Point 1(o).

4.9.1 France

In France, Article L212-1, in connection with Article R212-1 no 5 of the Code de la consommation (*exception d'inexécution*), transposes Point 1(o) of the Annex to the Directive. While the wording of the French provision is the same as in the Annex, it provides a higher level of protection because the *liste noire* ('black list') contains it.[264] This provision leaves no discretion to the judge, which means that clauses allowing for one-sided compliance with the contract are deemed unfair under all circumstances.

[264] Julien (n 89) 313–16; Pellier (n 157) 126–29.

4.9.2 Germany

§ 309 No 2 and § 309 No 8 of the BGB regulate contract clauses concerning one-sided compliance with obligations. § 309 No 2 provides that the consumer's right to refuse performance (*Leistungsverweigerungsrecht*) cannot be excluded or limited (No 2 lit. a), nor can the right to retention of the consumer be excluded or limited (No 2 lit. b).[265] § 309 No 8 lit. a prohibits clauses which exclude the right of consumers to free themselves from the contract if the trader breaches one of its duties, except for defective goods. No 8 lit. b further lists consumers' rights concerning defective goods.[266] The German provisions are consequently broader and stricter than Point 1(o) of the Annex to the Directive.

4.9.3 The Netherlands

One-sided compliance with obligations clauses falls within Article 6:236(b) and Article 6:236(c) of the BW.[267] Article 6:236(b) prohibits clauses that exclude or restrict consumers' right to dissolve the contract. In contrast, Article 6:236(c) prohibits clauses which exclude or limit the trader's obligation to perform the contract according to the statutory provisions in the BW. The Dutch provisions are wider and stricter than Article 3 in connection with Point 1(o).

4.9.4 The United Kingdom

Schedule 2 Part 1(18) of the Consumer Rights Act 2015 transposes word-for-word the text of Point 1(o) of the Annex to the Directive. Courts must assess terms included in Schedule 2 under the general test of unfairness (section 62).

4.9.5 Comparative Observations

Contractual terms allowing for one-sided compliance with obligations are considered unfair under all circumstances in France, Germany, and the Netherlands. The United Kingdom only goes up to the standard of the Directive, and such terms must be assessed under the general test and Schedule 2 Part 1(18).

[265] Schäfer in Stefan Ernst and others (eds), *AGB-Recht: Kommentar* (12th edn, Otto Schmidt Verlag 2016) BGB § 309 No 2 [3–5]; Wurmnest (n 102) BGB § 309 No 2 [2].

[266] Christensen in Stefan Ernst and others (eds), *AGB-Recht: Kommentar* (12th edn, Otto Schmidt Verlag 2016) BGB § 309 No 8 [3]; Wurmnest (n 102) BGB § 309 No 8 [4]. See ch 3.4.2 in this volume.

[267] See ch 3.4.5.

4.10 Transfers of Contracts to other Traders under Less Favourable Conditions

According to Article 3 in connection with Point 1(p) of the Directive's Annex, clauses allowing traders to transfer their rights and duties in cases where this reduces the guarantees for consumers without their consent may be considered unfair. The national courts have not yet asked the Court of Justice to consider such a scenario.[268]

4.10.1 France

Article L212-1, in connection with Article R212-2 no 5 of the Code de la consommation, reproduces almost word-for-word Point 1(p) of the Annex to the Directive.[269] Nonetheless, consumers enjoy even higher protection under French law due to the reversed burden of proof ('grey list'). To show that the term is not unfair, traders need to prove that the assignment of the contract (*cession de contrat*) is not likely to lead to a reduction in consumer rights and that the consumer has willingly and knowingly consented to it.[270]

4.10.2 Germany

§ 309 No 10 of the BGB deals with changing the other party to the contract (*Wechsel des Vertragspartners*). The provision provides that the change is allowed in case the trader provides the name of the third party to the consumer (§ 309 No 10 lit. a) and where the consumer has the right to withdraw from the contract (§ 309 No 10 lit. b).[271] The German provisions are not only stricter, as clauses falling within the scope of § 309 are always unfair ('black list'), but also more precise than the provision in the Annex, which merely requires that the change of the other party to the contract does not lower without the consumer's consent the legal guarantees.[272]

4.10.3 The Netherlands

Article 6:236(e) of the BW prohibits clauses which allow traders to transfer their obligations under less favourable conditions for consumers to other traders unless consumers have the right to free themselves from the contract at

[268] cf Jansen in Jansen and Zimmermann (n 134) 961.

[269] Julien (n 89) 313–16; Pellier (n 157) 126–29; Bénabent (n 160) 160–63.

[270] See eg a recent judgment of the *Cour de Cassation* on the assignment of contracts: Cass civ (1) 6 December 2017, no 16-14974. Dalloz (n 228) 216.

[271] cf Dominik Klimke, *Die Vertragsübernahme* (Mohr Siebeck 2010) 243–44.

[272] Habersack in Stefan Ernst and others (eds), *AGB-Recht: Kommentar* (12th edn, Otto Schmidt Verlag 2016) BGB § 309 No 10 [3–4]; Wurmnest (n 102) BGB § 309 No 10 [2–4].

any time or the clause provides for mergers and acquisitions of companies.[273] The Dutch provision provides the exact legal requirements as Point 1(p) of the Directive's Annex but is stricter ('black list' character).

4.10.4 The United Kingdom

Schedule 2 Part 1(19) of the Consumer Rights Act 2015 transposes Point 1(p) of the Directive's Annex. It needs to be assessed in court whether a clause allowing traders to transfer their obligations to other traders under less favourable conditions would pass the unfairness test under section 62 of the Consumer Rights Act 2015. Hugh Beale, Wolf-Georg Ringe, and Ewan McKendrick point out that such an assessment under the general test is not required. Under the law of assignment, it is impossible to transfer contractual obligations to another party without the consent of the other contracting party.[274] Such terms would thus be ineffective unless the consumer consents to the transfer.

4.10.5 Comparative Observations

Clauses which allow for the transfer of contracts to other traders under less favourable conditions for consumers are ineffective in Germany, the Netherlands, and the United Kingdom, while in France, traders must prove that it is not unfair to include such a clause in the contract. All jurisdictions mandate that consumers must be able to free themselves from the contract in case of a transfer of the contract to a third party.

4.11 Limitation of Rights to Legal Action

Article 3, in connection with Point 1(q) of the Annex to the Unfair Contract Terms Directive, provides that consumers must have a right to redress. Contract terms 'may be considered unfair' when such terms exclude or hinder consumers from taking legal action or exercising legal remedies, primarily by:

[1] requiring the consumer to take disputes exclusively to arbitration not covered by legal provisions,

[273] Krans, Stolker, and Valk (n 115) BW art 6:236 [4(b)]; Raijmakers (n 182) BW art 6:236 [4.2]. cf also Steven Bartels, 'Substitution of New Debtor: Transfer of Contract' in Danny Busch and others (eds), *The Principles of European Contract Law and Dutch Law: A Commentary II* (Kluwer Law International 2006) 135–36.

[274] Hugh Beale and Wolf-Georg Ringe, 'Transfer of Rights and Obligations' in Gerhard Dannemann and Stefan Vogenauer (eds), *The Common European Sales Law in Context: Interactions with English and German Law* (OUP 2013) 523-526; McKendrick (n 172) 477.

[2] unduly restricting the evidence available to [consumers] or
[3] imposing on [consumers] a burden of proof which, according to the applicable law, should lie with another party to the contract.

The Court of Justice indicated that jurisdiction clauses are unfair when they require the consumer to appear in front of a court situated a long way from the consumer's domicile, making it difficult for the consumer to participate in the proceedings.[275] In *Océano*, the CJEU ruled that the general test of unfairness interpreted in light of Point 1(q) also covers domestic jurisdiction clauses, where it 'may make it difficult for [consumers] to enter an appearance',[276] emphasizing the relevance of costs and distance about the price of the goods in assessing the term's fairness.[277] Such an evaluation also applies to contract terms that refer to national statutory provisions concerning the jurisdiction in consumer disputes.[278]

The CJEU has had a chance to look at arbitration clauses and remedies. One of the relevant cases is *Asturcom Telecomunicaciones SL*,[279] examined earlier in Chapter 3.3. In *Asturcom* a consumer contested neither an arbitration clause nor the consequent final arbitration award, and, under these circumstances, of unusual inattentiveness, *res judicata* under national law prevented the consumer from challenging the unfair term. The chapter has already emphasized that this is rather exceptional and, under normal circumstances, the Court expects the consumer interest to prevail over obstacles created by national procedural law. In another case, the Court ruled that a contract clause which required consumers exclusively to submit their claims to a permanent arbitration tribunal and against whose decisions no judicial remedy under domestic law needed to be assessed for unfairness, taking into account 'all of the circumstances surrounding the conclusion of that contract'.[280] National courts must especially:

> verify whether the clause at issue has the object or effect of excluding or hindering the consumer's right to take legal action or exercise any other legal

[275] Joined Cases C-240/98–C-244/98 *Océano Grupo Editorial SA* (n 5); Case C-243/08 *Pannon GSM Zrt v Erzsébet Sustikné Győrfi* (n 23); Case C-137/08 *VB Pénzügyi Lízing Zrt v Ferenc Schneider* ECLI:EU:C:2010:659. cf Leczykiewicz (n 28) 354.
[276] ibid (*Océano*) para 22.
[277] ibid para 24.
[278] Case C-266/18 *Aqua Med sp z oo v Irena Skóra* ECLI:EU:C:2019:282.
[279] Case C-40/08 *Asturcom Telecomunicaciones SL v Cristina Rodríguez Nogueira* ECLI:EU:C:2009:615.
[280] Case C-342/13 *Katalin Sebestyén v Zsolt Csaba Kővári, OTP Bank, OTP Faktoring Követeléskezelő Zrt, Raiffeisen Bank Zrt* ECLI:EU:C:2014:1857.

> remedy; and take account of the fact that the communication to the consumer, before the conclusion of the contract at issue, of general information on the differences between the arbitration procedure and ordinary legal proceedings cannot alone rule out the unfairness of that clause.[281]

Similarly, contract clauses restricting available remedies may be considered unfair. National courts must assess 'to what extent, the term in question derogates from the rules applicable in the absence of agreement between the parties to make it more difficult for the consumer, given the procedural means at his disposal, to take legal action and exercise rights of the defence'.[282]

In addition to the CJEU-made rules outlined above, consumers are protected from 'unfair' jurisdiction clauses also by Regulation (EU) 1215/2012 on the jurisdiction and the recognition and enforcement of judgments in civil and commercial matters ('Brussels I Regulation (Recast)').[283] Section 4 of the Brussels I Regulation (Recast) regulates jurisdiction over consumer contracts. The Regulation applies to business-to-consumer contracts (Article 17(2)(c) of the Regulation) where consumers act outside of their trade or profession (Article 17(1) of the Regulation). Traders may not bring a claim against the consumer outside their domicile (Article 18(2) of the Regulation). According to Article 19, the parties can depart from these rules by an agreement:

(1) which is entered into after the dispute has arisen;
(2) which allows the consumer to bring proceedings in courts other than those indicated in this Section; or
(3) which is entered into by the consumer and the other party to the contract, both of whom are at the time of conclusion of the contract domiciled or habitually resident in the same Member State, and which confers jurisdiction on the courts of that Member State, provided that such an agreement is not contrary to the law of that Member State.

Another European Union instrument is Regulation (EC) 593/2008 ('Rome I'), which regulates the choice of law clauses. Article 6 of the Rome I Regulation provides that the law of the consumer's habitual residence applies to B2C

[281] ibid para 36.
[282] Case C-415/11 *Catalunyacaixa*, para 75.
[283] Regulation (EU) 1215/2012 of 12 December 2012 on jurisdiction and the recognition and enforcement of judgments in civil and commercial matters [2012] OJ L351/1. For example, Lorna E Gillies, 'Recent developments in the approximation of EU private international laws: towards mutual trust, mutual recognition and enhancing social justice in civil and commercial matters' in Christian Twigg-Flesner (ed), *Research Handbook on EU Consumer and Contract Law* (Edward Elgar Publishing 2016).

contracts.[284] Consequently, through Regulation (EC) 593/2008 and Regulation (EU) 1215/2012, as well as the case law relating to the Unfair Contract Terms Directive,[285] there are de facto prohibitions on the EU level concerning contract terms which restrict the consumer's right to redress.

4.11.1 France

The French Consumer Code (*Code de la consommation*) prohibits limiting the consumer's right to redress. The Code contains 3 provisions corresponding to Point 1(q) of the Directive's Annex. The first provision prohibits ('black list') clauses which impose the burden of proof on consumers (*charge de la prevue*), even though it is legally on traders (Article L212-1 in connection with Article R212-1 no 12 of the Code de la consommation).[286] Article L212-1, in connection with Article R212-2 no 10, states that clauses are presumed unfair ('grey list') when they eliminate or hinder the consumer's right to take legal action or access remedies, including by demanding from them to enter a non-regulated ADR or offer ADR exclusively. Furthermore, contractual clauses allowing for the restriction of evidence (*modes de preuve*) are presumed unfair ('grey list) under Article L212-1 in connection with Article R212-2 no 9. The French provisions transpose the rights enshrined in Article 3 in connection with Point 1(q) of the Annex to the Directive. However, unlike the Directive, the French provisions are not merely indicative. Instead, French law either presumes that such clauses are unfair according to the *liste grise* ('grey list') or considers them always unfair under the *liste noire* ('black list').

4.11.2 Germany

The German Civil Code prohibits contract clauses which limit access to justice. § 309 No 14 of the BGB deals with the waiver to enter into litigation (*Klageverzicht*). No 14 prohibits a clause requiring consumers to submit their claims to arbitration before they can legally challenge it, which is much stricter than the Directive Point 1(q) of the Directive's Annex only covers clauses forcing consumers to enter exclusively into 'arbitration not covered by legal provisions'.[287] Furthermore, § 309 No 12 of the BGB deals with the second part of Point 1(q) of the Annex, the one relating to terms restricting evidence

[284] See eg Laura Maria van Bochove, 'Overriding Mandatory Rules as a Vehicle for Weaker Party Protection in European Private International Law' (2014) 7(3) Erasmus Law Review 147.

[285] Regulation (EC) 593/2008 of 17 June 2008 on the law applicable to contractual obligations (Rome I) [2008] OJ L177/6.

[286] Julien (n 89) 313–16; Pellier (n 157) 126–29; Bénabent (n 160) 160–63.

[287] Fuchs in Stefan Ernst and others (eds), *AGB-Recht: Kommentar* (12th edn, Otto Schmidt Verlag 2016) BGB § 309 No 14 [7]; Wurmnest (n 102) BGB § 309 No 14 [4-5].

available to consumers and placing the burden of proof (*Beweislast*) on consumers.[288] No 12 lit. b further states that the reversed burden of proof includes asking consumers to confirm certain facts unless this concerns the receipt of goods.

§§ 309 No 12 and No 14 are stricter than the provision in the Directive's Annex, as terms falling within these provisions are automatically unfair.

4.11.3 The Netherlands

Dutch law equally prohibits terms that restrict the right of redress. Article 6:236(n) of the BW declares clauses unfair when traders ask consumers to attend arbitration unless consumers have 1 month after traders invoke such a term to bring a claim with the competent national court.[289] Article 6:236(k) of the BW treats clauses as unfair which exclude or limit the right of the other party to provide evidence or change the burden of proof (*bewijslast*) to the consumer's disadvantage. Particularly, when such clauses require consumers to confirm the quality of the performance owed to them or placing the burden of proof on consumers.[290] The Dutch rules are consequently much more precise than the one in the Directive's Annex, and these provisions are not merely indicative.

4.11.4 The United Kingdom

In the United Kingdom, clauses restricting remedies available to consumers may be regarded as unfair in the light of the general test in conjunction with Schedule 2 Part 1(20) of the Consumer Rights Act 2015. The 2015 Act transposes, once again, word-for-word, the Directive into UK law. Contractual clauses are, however, invalid according to section 31(2) in case such clauses:

> (a) exclude or restrict a right or remedy in respect of a liability under a provision listed in [Section 31] subsection (1),
> (b) make such a right or remedy or its enforcement subject to a restrictive or onerous condition,

[288] Habersack in Stefan Ernst and others (eds), *AGB-Recht: Kommentar* (12th edn, Otto Schmidt Verlag 2016) BGB § 309 No 12 [5–6]; Wurmnest (n 102) BGB § 309 No 12 [2–3].

[289] Krans, Stolker, and Valk (n 115) BW art 6:236 [7(d)]; Raijmakers (n 182) BW art 6:236 [4.6]. Furthermore, Raijmakers notes that the provision only covers arbitration clauses since the reform in 2015. Whether to include arbitration clauses in letter (n) was discussed in Vesna Lazic, 'Arbitration Law Reform in the Netherlands: Formal and Substantive Validity of an Arbitration Agreement' in Sjef van Erp and Lars van Vliet (eds), *Netherlands Reports to the Seventeenth International Congress of Comparative Law* (Intersentia 2006) 136–38.

[290] Krans, Stolker, and Valk (n 115) BW art 6:236 [7(a)]; Raijmakers (n 182) BW art 6:236 [4.6].

(c) allow a trader to put a person at a disadvantage as a result of pursuing such a right or remedy, or
(d) exclude or restrict rules of evidence or procedure.

Lit. (a) refers to section 31(1), which bans traders from excluding or limiting their liability concerning: the goods to be of satisfactory quality (a), to be fit for a particular purpose (b), to be as described (c), to match a sample (e), to match a model seen or examined (f), not conforming to contract if digital content does not conform (h); other pre-contract information included in contract (d); installation as part of conformity of the goods with the contract (g); trader to have right to supply the goods etc. (i); delivery of goods (j); and passing of risk (k). Traders are consequently prohibited from including terms which limit the availability of a remedy or restrict enforcement of the above rights (section 31(2)(a)) or impose a restrictive or onerous condition (section 31(2)(b)), put consumers at a disadvantage when they pursue such a right or remedy (section 31(2)(c)) or exclude or restrict rules of evidence or procedure (section 31(2)(d)). The rules contained in section 31 of the Consumer Rights Act 2015 are stricter and more precise than Point 1(q) of the Directive's Annex. Courts assess clauses that fall outside the scope of section 31 under the general test (section 62 of the Consumer Rights Act 2015 in connection with Schedule 2 Part 1(20)).[291]

4.11.5 Comparative Observations

All 4 Member States provide context-specific and precise provisions beyond the Directive and the CJEU case law. The French provisions replicate Point 1(q) of the Annex but offer a higher level of protection because the relevant terms are either automatically unfair and ineffective ('black list') or presumed to be unfair ('grey list'). In the United Kingdom, such clauses are not binding the consumer if they restrict the consumer rights in section 31 of the CRA 2015. Courts assess clauses relating to the right to take legal action under the general test. The German and Dutch legislators have also enacted stricter rules, rendering clauses restricting the right of redress unfair and ineffective under all circumstances.

[291] The rules on jurisdiction and choice of law clauses remain valid in the UK after Brexit. Rome I is retained EU Law under the European Union (Withdrawal) Act 2018. Sections 15A and 15B of the Civil Jurisdiction and Judgments (Amendment) (EU Exit) Regulations 2019 (amended in 2020) transpose the rules on consumer disputes from the Brussels I Recast Regulation into the Civil Jurisdiction and Judgments Act 1982. Johannes Ungerer, 'No Sunset of Retained EU Conflict of Laws in the UK, but Increased Risk of Sunburn' *Conflict of Laws* (26 July 2023) https://conflictoflaws.net/2023/no-sunset-of-retained-eu-conflict-of-laws-in-the-uk-but-increased-risk-of-sunburn/ (accessed 11 August 2023).

5 Evidence and Theory in Unfair Contract Terms Legislation

Upon a comprehensive analysis of the rules governing unfair contract terms, it becomes evident that the legislative framework supporting these regulations does not find its basis in scientifically grounded evidence. Instead, it draws upon a diverse array of alternative foundations and principles. Legislators initially conceived these rules on the foundational premise of consumer rationality. This foundation, derived from the neo-classical economic theory, asserts consumers as rational actors capable of making informed decisions.[292]

Underpinning this legislative framework is the notion that consumers, in their role as rational actors, are endowed with the ability to make decisions that maximize their utility and welfare.[293] This presumption, often associated with the neo-classical economic perspective, informs the regulatory approach by empowering consumers with information rights.[294] These rights serve as instruments of consumer protection, ensuring that individuals have access to relevant information necessary for making informed choices in contractual relationships.[295] The legislator designed the framework to enable consumers to exercise their rights to information, thereby enhancing their bargaining power and mitigating the risk of exploitative contract terms.

However, it is imperative to recognize that the formation of the legislative framework governing unfair contract terms did not solely rely on theoretical constructs. As depicted in this chapter, law-makers also developed the Unfair Contract Terms Directive from national practices, including legislation and case law. By incorporating these insights into the legislative foundation, policymakers sought to balance theory and real-world applicability. National practices, reflective of cultural, economic, and societal nuances, played a pivotal role in shaping the contours of the Directive.

[292] Vanessa Mak, *Legal Pluralism in European Contract Law* (OUP 2020) 88. For an overview on the image of the consumer see Leczykiewicz and Weatherill (n 9) chs 2, 5, and 8.

[293] See eg Fabrizio Esposito, *The Consumer Welfare Hypothesis in Law and Economics: Towards a Synthesis for the 21st Century* (Edward Elgar Publishing) ch 6.

[294] See eg Iain Ramsay, *Consumer Law and Policy: Text and Materials on Regulating Consumer Markets* (Hart Publishing 2012) ch 6; Mak (n 291) 88. For an overview of the pro and cons of this theory, Geraint Howells, 'The Potential and Limits of Consumer Empowerment by Information' (2005) 32(2) Journal of Law and Society 349.

[295] Brander and Ulmer criticized the earlier version of the Directive. They argue that if the proposed Directive were to apply to all types of consumer contracts, not just standard ones, it would significantly restrict individual autonomy and the economic functions of freedom of contract, potentially diluting the principle of a free market economy. Hans Erich Brandner and Peter Ulmer 'The Community Directive on Unfair Terms in Consumer Contracts: some critical remarks on the proposal submitted by the EC Commission' (1991) 28(3) Common Market Law Review 647.

Nonetheless, the Commission attempted to remedy the lack of scientifically grounded evidence with a fitness check and guidelines, but they have several areas for improvement. Evidence in the *ex post* Fitness Check on the Directive needs to be more extensive, although it does include parts of national practices, literature reviews, and a cost-benefit analysis.[296]

One part of the Fitness Check consisted of consumer surveys. Merely 6 per cent of consumers stated that they enormously benefitted through the protection on unfair terms;[297] in the consumer rights awareness index, only 40 per cent of respondents knew that unfair terms do not bind them.[298] The Commission also conducted an online public consultation, during which most respondents expressed that implementing an EU-wide 'black list' or adopting a uniform model for terms and conditions would enhance consumer protection.[299] It was merely a survey and not supported by further evidence.

Furthermore, the Commission presented doctrinal research indicating that national courts do not consistently apply CJEU case law.[300] However, the European Commission's guidance on the Directive completely neglects national case law and statutory provisions, even though the instrument is a minimum harmonization instrument and the Member States can enact stricter rules.[301] The guidance merely provides the notification of Member States to the Commission on national peculiarities, but some of the statements are as short as one sentence.[302] Additional evidence is necessary to depict how traders implement the rules on unfair terms in business-to-consumer transactions.

The rules on unfair contract terms exhibit a complex interplay between theoretical frameworks and practical experiences. While they may have originated from the premise of consumer rationality within neo-classical economic theory, they have evolved to encompass a broader spectrum of influences. This multifaceted approach underscores the dynamic nature of legislative development, where theory and practice converge to create a framework that seeks to protect consumers while maintaining the integrity of contractual relationships in a diverse and ever-evolving digital marketplace.

[296] Commission, 'Report of the Fitness Check' SWD(2017) 209 final 134–39; European Commission, 'Study for the Fitness Check of EU consumer and marketing law: Final report Part 1—Main report' (2017) 441–43.

[297] ibid 34 (Figure 14).

[298] ibid 32 (Figure 12).

[299] ibid 95–97. Matthias Lehmann and Danny Busch suggested to turn the Directive into a Regulation: Matthias Lehmann and Danny Busch, 'Make It Stringent: A Plea for an Unfair Terms Regulation' (2023) 31(6) European Review of Private Law 1175.

[300] Commission (n 296) 97.

[301] European Commission, 'Guidance on the interpretation and application of Council Directive 93/13/EEC on unfair terms in consumer contracts' [2019] OJ C323/4.

[302] ibid Annex II.

6 Conclusion

This chapter first examined the implementing obligations arising from the Unfair Contract Terms Directive. The inquiry has then focused almost entirely on assessing whether the terms included in the non-exhaustive and indicative list in the Annex to the Unfair Terms Directive can be considered unfair on the EU and national levels. The chapter revealed that the Court of Justice has interpreted the general test under Article 3 of the Directive in a way which has harmonized the national judicial practice.[303]

The Member States' laws frequently also go beyond the envisaged indicative nature of the Directive's Annex. All 4 jurisdictions have enacted statutory provisions which render some of the terms listed in the Annex 'unfair', excluding the application of the general test of unfairness.[304] France, Germany, the Netherlands, and the United Kingdom follow a relatively similar pattern. Each jurisdiction, as Article 3 of the Directive requires, has a general test under which clauses can be rendered unfair. Furthermore, these jurisdictions included lists in their statutory provisions, which may be 'indicative', 'grey', or 'black'. As a result of the extensive use of 'grey lists' and 'black lists' in France, Germany, and the Netherlands, courts have little discretion in rendering (or not rendering) certain contract terms unfair. The Commission regularly updates the unfair terms lists in France on Unfair Clauses (*Commission des clauses abusives*). On the contrary, only a handful of contract terms are always unfair in the United Kingdom, allowing for a high degree of judicial discretion. However, like in the other 3 jurisdictions, the courts' discretion in the United Kingdom is limited by statutory provisions (section 62 of the Consumer Rights Act 2015) and domestic and EU case law. Another UK peculiarity is that there have been few cases concerning unfair terms in court because the Competition and Markets Authority and other regulators can investigate such cases.[305] Administrative enforcement of consumer contract law also exists in France[306] and the

[303] With regard to the selected potentially unfair terms see points 1(e), (j), (l), and (q) of the Annex to the Unfair Contract Terms Directive.

[304] This also supports the argument of Hondius, who claimed that the Member States mostly provided for stricter rules before enacting the Directive. Hondius (n 11) 242.

[305] McKendrick (n 172) 477–80. For a more detailed account of the enforcement practices in the United Kingdom see Christine Riefa and Chris Willett, 'Enforcement and Effectiveness of Consumer Law in the UK' in Hans-Wolfgang Micklitz and Geneviève Saumier (eds), *Enforcement and Effectiveness of Consumer Law* (Springer Publishing 2018).

[306] Sabine Bernheim-Desvaux and Patricia Foucher, 'L'effectivité du droit français de la consommation' in Hans-Wolfgang Micklitz and Geneviève Saumier (eds), *Enforcement and Effectiveness of Consumer Law* (Springer Publishing 2018) 289–91, 293–97. Hans-Wolfgang Micklitz notes that the French Unfair Terms Commission (*Commission des clauses abusives*) is the key actor in policing unfair contract terms in France. See Micklitz (n 213) 132–34.

Netherlands,[307] but not in Germany.[308] In practice, most unfair terms are challenged and then removed by traders before they end up in court or resolved in the lower courts. Consequently, as shown in the previous sections, there is only little case law in the 4 jurisdictions. Nonetheless, examining the rules implementing the Unfair Contract Terms Directive offers sufficient detail to measure trader compliance with these rules.

Examining the rules on unfair contract terms also highlighted that the legislative framework relied not on scientifically grounded evidence but instead on alternative foundations. Initially, legislators formulated these rules upon the presumption of consumer rationality, empowering consumers through information rights emanating from the neo-classical economic theory. Subsequently, legislators created the framework by incorporating national practices into its foundation.

[307] In the Netherlands, the Authority for Consumers and Markets (*Autoriteit Consument & Markt*) or other sector-specific regulators can investigate whether traders use unfair terms. According to Vanessa Mak, the regulators closely collaborate with the Dutch Consumer Organization (*Consumentenbond*). They can bring a claim on behalf of consumers in the form of collective redress under art 3:305a of the BW. Vanessa Mak, 'Enforcement and Effectiveness of Consumer Law: The Netherlands' in Hans-Wolfgang Micklitz and Geneviève Saumier (eds), *Enforcement and Effectiveness of Consumer Law* (Springer Publishing 2018) 394–99, 402–405.

[308] Consumer and trader organizations and private parties can challenge unfair contract terms and, if necessary, take traders to court. Further details are provided in Maurice Nürnberg, *Die Durchsetzung von Verbraucherrechten: Eine rechtsvergleichende Analyse der Verbraucherrechtsdurchsetzung in Frankreich, den Niederlanden und Deutschland* (Nomos 2020), who compares the German approach with the French and Dutch approaches. The German Federal Ministry for Economic Affairs and Energy published a report in 2018 on the potential benefits of administrative enforcement of consumer (contract) law. See Rupprecht Podszun, Christoph Busch, and Frauke Henning-Bodewig, 'Behördliche Durchsetzung des Verbraucherrechts? Darstellung und Systematisierung von Möglichkeiten und Defiziten der privaten Durchsetzung des Verbraucherschutzes sowie Einbeziehung der Kartellbehörden zu dessen Durchsetzung' Bundesministerium für Wirtschaft und Energie (February 2018) https://www.bmwi.de/Redaktion/DE/Publikationen/Studien/behoerdliche-durchsetzung-des-verbraucherrechts.pdf?__blob=publicationFile&v=13 (accessed 12 December 2020). An English summary of the report is provided in Ruprecht Podszun, Christoph Busch, and Frauke Henning-Bodeweig, 'Consumer Law in Germany: A Shift to Public Enforcement?' (2019) 8(2) Journal of European Consumer and Market Law 75.

4

Mandatory Disclosures and Substantive Consumer Rights

1 Introduction

This chapter illuminates the legal obligations the Member States impose on e-commerce traders through the implementation of the E-Commerce Directive and the Consumer Rights Directive As was the case in Chapter 3, it goes beyond a mere analysis of the legislation and delves into the evidence and consumer theories that influenced or contradicted the rules. Section 4.2 focuses on the implementation of the information and formal requirements of the minimum harmonization E-Commerce Directive in France, Germany, the Netherlands, and the United Kingdom. The discussion in section 4.3 centres around the mandatory disclosures and substantive consumer rights contained in the Consumer Rights Directive. The primary focus of this section is on the rules enshrined in the Directive, as it is a maximum harmonization instrument and Member States cannot deviate from the Directive's standard. The chapter concludes the doctrinal part of the thesis, setting out the rights consumers enjoy in e-commerce transactions, which the following chapters will use to assess trader compliance.

2 The E-Commerce Directive

The E-Commerce Directive signified a crucial milestone in adapting legal frameworks to the digital age, shaping how online businesses conduct their work and protect consumer rights. It deals with a variety of legal issues: section 1 sets out the establishment and information requirements (Articles 4 to 5); section 2 governs commercial communications (Articles 6 to 8); section 3 deals with contracts concluded by electronic means (Articles 9 to 11); section 4 concerns liability of intermediary service providers (Articles 12

Compliance with European Consumer Law. Felix Pflücke, Oxford University Press. © Oxford University Press 2024.
DOI: 10.1093/9780198906414.003.0004

to 15). Only sections 1 and 3 apply to e-commerce consumer sales transactions. For instance, it states that electronic contracts must be equivalent to contracts concluded on paper.[1] In addition to redefining the treatment of online contracts, the Directive also introduced new information and formal requirements. These new disclosure requirements complemented existing rules in Articles 4 and 5 of the Distance Selling Directive.[2] The minimum harmonization Distance Selling Directive has since been repealed and replaced by the maximum harmonization Consumer Rights Directive. Mandatory disclosures covered by the Consumer Rights Directive are subsequently not examined in this section of Chapter 4 but in the one that follows. It also does not deal with information and formal requirements outside the study's scope.[3]

Nowadays, the Consumer Rights Directive covers most of the mandatory disclosures in the E-Commerce Directive except for 4 information and formal requirements. The 2 information requirements place a duty on traders permanently and visibly to display their public trade or register number and VAT number on their websites.[4] The 2 formal requirements place a duty on traders to guide consumers on how to conclude the contract and the languages available for the contract conclusion.[5] The E-Commerce Directive is a minimum harmonization instrument, making an examination of the rules on the national levels indispensable, as Member States can introduce stricter rules.[6]

Another noteworthy characteristic of the Directive is its broad and far-reaching scope. As a framework directive, it applies to all information service providers,[7] including e-commerce traders, as their service is remunerated, carried out from a distance electronically, and provided on individual request.[8] Selling goods online is explicitly listed as a potential activity of an information

[1] E-Commerce Directive, art 9.

[2] Directive (EC) 97/7 of 20 May 1997 on the protection of consumers in respect of distance contracts [1997] OJ L144/19 (Distance Selling Directive). Aurelio Lopez-Tarruella, 'A European Community Regulatory Framework for Electronic Commerce' (2001) 38(6) Common Market Law Review 1356.

[3] For instance, e-commerce traders do not fall within activities that 'are subject to an authorization scheme' (E-Commerce Directive, art 5(1)(e)) nor regulated professions (E-Commerce Directive, art 5(1)(f)).

[4] ibid arts 5(1)(d) and 5(1)(g).

[5] ibid arts 10(1)(a) and 10(1)(d).

[6] ibid art 3; Arno R Lodder, 'Directive 2000/31/EC on Certain Legal Aspects of Information Society Services, in Particular Electronic Commerce, in the Internal Market' in Arno R Lodder and Andrew Murray (eds), *EU Regulation of E-Commerce* (Edward Elgar Publishing 2017) 30–32.

[7] Article 1 of the E-Commerce Directive outlines the objectives and scope of the instrument. Andrej Savin, *EU Internet Law* (2nd edn, Edward Elgar Publishing 2017) 45–49.

[8] The E-Commerce Directive does not define 'information society services', but recital 17 of the Directive refers to art 1(2) of Directive 98/34/EC as amended by Directive 98/48/EC (now Directive 2015/1535/EU, art 1(1)(b)). The limitations in Annex I to Directive 2015/1535/EU do not affect e-commerce traders.

service provider.[9] The E-Commerce Directive furthermore applies to both business-to-consumer and business-to-business transactions,[10] reflecting the ambition of the Directive to 'lay down a clear and general framework to cover certain legal aspects of electronic commerce in the internal market'[11] and to 'ensure that electronic commerce could fully benefit from the internal market'.[12] This approach means that it applies horizontally, that is, beyond e-commerce sales, as it provides a legal framework for almost all online transactions.[13]

The Directive laid the foundation for various other legal instruments, for instance, regulating electronic signatures or copyrights.[14] Andrej Savin notes that this 'flexible structure' allows the instrument to adapt to future challenges.[15] The mandated reviews of the E-Commerce Directive by the European Commission[16] and independent bodies, such as the Copenhagen Economics Institute,[17] have also been positive. These studies confirmed the Commission's ex ante assessment that the Directive would save legal costs for traders and increase consumer trust, although the breadth, depth, and quality were not scientifically rigorous.[18]

[9] E-Commerce Directive, recital 18.

[10] ibid art 2(d). Article 1(4)–(6) define further limitations, but they do not fall within the scope of the present study.

[11] ibid recital 7.

[12] ibid recital 4.

[13] The European Commission presented its first framework proposal for a directive in 1997, responding to the increase in online transactions and the subsequent need to regulate e-commerce. One year later, the European Commission presented the first legislative proposal for the Directive. After a Parliament-Council navette, they approved the final draft on 8 June 2000 (art 24 of the E-Commerce Directive). European Commission, 'A European Initiative in the sector of Electronic Commerce' COM(1997) 157 final (not published in the *Official Journal* of the European Union); European Commission, 'Proposal for a European Parliament and Council Directive on certain legal aspects of electronic commerce in the internal' COM(1998) 586 final OJ C30/4.

[14] Lopez-Tarruella (n 2) 1339–40; Stephen Weatherill, 'The Regulation of E-Commerce under EC Law: The Distribution of Competence between Home States and Host States as a Basis for Managing the Internal Market' in Henk Snijders and Stephen Weatherill (eds), *E-commerce Law: National and Transnational Topics and Perspectives* (Kluwer Law International 2003) 14–16; Lodder (n 6) 16–17.

[15] Savin (n 7) 71–72.

[16] Article 21 of the E-Commerce Directive requires that the Commission reviews the instrument regularly. See European Commission, 'First Report on the application of Directive 2000/31/EC of the European Parliament and of the Council of 8 June 2000 on certain legal aspects of information society services, in particular electronic commerce, in the Internal Market (Directive on electronic commerce)' COM(2003) 702 final.

[17] Copenhagen Economics, 'Study on the economic impact of the electronic commerce Directive' (September 2007); ULYS Consortium, 'Study on Liability of Internet Intermediaries' (2007). Both studies are available via the European Commission website: European Commission, 'Studies: 2007' (24 March 2017) https://ec.europa.eu/digital-single-market/en/news/archive-e-commerce-directive-what-happened-and-its-adoption (accessed 4 November 2019).

[18] European Commission, 'Proposal for a European Parliament and Council Directive on certain legal aspects of electronic commerce in the internal market' COM(1998) 586 final OJ C30/4, 98/0325 (COD) 7–9.

The time limit of the Directive required implementation into national law by 17 January 2002.[19] However, Germany is the only jurisdiction included in the present study that implemented the Directive on time.[20] Although France, the Netherlands, and the United Kingdom failed to implement the Directive within the time limit provided, the 3 countries eventually implemented the Directive.[21] Despite the slight delay, the implementation of the E-Commerce Directive was carried out relatively smoothly compared to the Unfair Contract Terms Directive.

2.1 Information and Formal Requirements

One centrally important distinction in the Directive lies between the information requirements (Article 5) and the formal requirements (Article 10). Under Article 5, traders must display the prescribed information permanently and visibly on their websites,[22] while traders need only comply with the formal requirements under Article 10 before the contract's conclusion.[23] Furthermore, while Article 5 is of general application, Article 10 does not apply to 'contracts concluded exclusively by exchange of electronic mail or by equivalent individual communications'.[24] E-commerce traders typically do not individually communicate with consumers, making this limitation irrelevant to the present study.

The Commission's ex ante assessment stated that most disclosure requirements did not exist at the time or complement those of the Distance Selling Directive, which, according to the Commission, would increase transparency and trust.[25] While the discussion in Chapter 3 showed that consumer theories

[19] E-Commerce Directive, art 22.

[20] Only Austria, Germany, and Luxemburg implemented the Directive on time. See European Commission, 'National transposition measures communicated by the Member States concerning: Directive 2000/31/EC of the European Parliament and of the Council of 8 June 2000 on certain legal aspects of information society services, in particular electronic commerce, in the Internal Market' (2019) https://eur-lex.europa.eu/legal-content/EN/NIM/?uri=CELEX:32000L0031 (accessed 10 October 2019).

[21] ibid. According to the European Commission's database, Germany implemented the E-Commerce Directive in November and December of 2001, the United Kingdom in August 2002, the Netherlands in 2004, and France only in 2004 and 2005.

[22] E-Commerce Directive, art 5(1). Lodder (n 6) 33; Dominik Lubasz and Monika Namysłowska, 'Directive 2000/31/EC: Article 5 General information to be provided' in Reiner Schulze and Dirk Staudenmayer (eds), *EU Digital Law: Article-by-Article Commentary* (Bloomsbury 2020) E-Commerce Directive, art 5[1].

[23] E-Commerce Directive, art 10(1); Lodder (n 6) 43–45.

[24] E-Commerce Directive, art 10(4); Lodder (n 6) 45.

[25] COM(1998) 586 final OJ C30/4, 98/0325 (COD) 10, 12, 22–23, 26.

support information duties, the discussion on the Consumer Rights Directive below shows that too much information might overwhelm consumers.

The following paragraphs examine how France, Germany, the Netherlands, and the United Kingdom implemented the 4 pre-contractual information and formal requirements. As pointed out above, Member States can deviate from the minimum harmonization E-Commerce Directive; it is, therefore, crucial to assess whether national laws hold traders to different standards.

2.1.1 Public Trade or Register Number

E-commerce traders must display their trade or public register identification number on their website, where it must be 'easily, directly and permanently accessible'.[26]

French law requires traders to provide either their company (*registre du commerce et des sociétés*) or trade register number (*répertoire des métiers*) on their website.[27] Traders can obtain the company registration number from the registrar (*greffe*) of the local commercial court.[28] In contrast, the Chamber of Skilled Trades and Crafts (*Chambres de Métiers et de l'Artisanat*) assigns the trade registration number to enterprises operating in one of the regulated professions.[29] According to the French regulatory provision, e-commerce traders need to obtain a company registration number, 'RCS' for short, and display it on their website to identify themselves, which includes the name of the authorizing commercial court.

Like the French approach, Germany has separate registers for industry and commerce (*Industrie- und Handelskammer*) and skilled crafts (*Handwerkskammer*). However, § 5(1) No 4 of the Telemediengesetz outlines that traders must display their official registration number on their websites. Different registers exist for trades, clubs, partnerships, and cooperatives.[30]

[26] E-Commerce Directive, art 5(1) and 5(1)(d); Lodder (n 6) 33, 36; Lubasz and Namysłowska (n 22) E-Commerce Directive, art 5 [36, 51–54].

[27] See Code de la consommation, art L111-2 in connection with art R111-2 no 1(c); Jérôme Julien, *Droit de la Consommation* (2nd edn, Librairie générale de droit et de jurisprudence 2017) 116; Thomas Piazzon, 'L'information et la désinformation des consommateurs: Rapport français' in Gert Straetmans (ed), *Information Obligations and Disinformation of Consumers* (Springer Publishing 2019) 166–68.

[28] Direction de l'information légale et administrative, 'Recherche sur les entreprises immatriculées au registre du commerce et des sociétés (RCS)' (2019) https://www.service-public.fr/professionnels-entreprises/vosdroits/R19859 (accessed 4 October 2019).

[29] Chambres de Métiers et de l'Artisanat, 'Le portail des Chambres de Métiers et de l'Artisanat: Immatriculation au Répertoire des métiers' (2020) https://www.artisanat.fr/porteur-de-projet/lancer-mon-activite/immatriculation-au-repertoire-des-metiers (accessed 5 October 2020).

[30] Matthias Hartmann, 'Telemedienrecht' in Artur-Axel Wandtke (ed), *IT-Recht und Medienstraftrecht* (2nd edn, De Gruyter 2011) 56–58; Jan Müller-Broich, *Telemediengesetz* (Nomos 2012) TMG § 5 [11]; Markus Messinger, *Rechtsunsicherheiten bei internationalen elektronischen Handelsgeschäften* (Mohr Siebeck 2014) 293.

Typically, e-commerce traders need a trade registration number (*Handelsreg isternummer*).[31] Depending on their legal form, German law abbreviates it as HRA or HRB.[32] The latter HRB register contains companies with limited liability (*Gesellschaft mit beschränkter Haftung*).[33] Traders must acquire such a number at their local district court (*Amtsgericht*).[34] The only exceptions are micro companies (*Kleingewerbebetriebe*) and private corporations (*Gesellschaft bürgerlichen Rechts*), which do not necessarily need to be registered.[35] All other traders need to display the trade registration number, including the name of the registry, on their website.[36] The German Federal Court of Justice (*Bundesgerichtshof*) clarified that providing the information in the contact details or legal notice of the trader's website is sufficient.[37]

The Dutch implementing provision also requires traders to display their public register number on their website (*Kamer van Koophandel Nummer*).[38] This number is automatically allocated to registered traders by the Dutch Chamber of Commerce (Article 9(a) of the Handelsregisterwet 2007) as they manage the commercial register (*Handelsregister*).[39]

The United Kingdom transposed the Directive's requirement that traders need to display their registration number on their websites through Regulation 6(1)(d) of the Electronic Commerce (EC Directive) Regulations 2002.[40] As in

[31] Portal of the Justice Authorities of the Federal and State Governments, 'Gemeinsames Registerportal der Länder' (2019) https://www.handelsregister.de/rp_web/mask.do (accessed 4 October 2019).

[32] Handelsregisterverordnung, § 3.

[33] ibid § 3(3).

[34] § 14 of the Handelsgesetzbuch; § 1 of the Handelsregisterverordnung.

[35] Handelsregisterverordnung, § 3.

[36] OLG Hamburg AfP 2008, 511, where the trader failed to provide its trade registration number and the details of the relevant supervisory authority (as selling real estate is subject to an authorization scheme) on its website. The Court found that the TMG applies to all commercial information service providers (*sämtliche kommerziellen Telemediendienste*), but failing to comply with the 2 information requirements is not an automatic breach of the Act against Unfair Competition (Gesetz gegen den unlauteren Wettbewerb, UWG). cf Dirk Wüstenberg, 'Immer wieder Online-Impressum: Die Rechtsprechung seit der UGP-Richtlinie bis und die Rechtslage insbesondere ab Juni 2013' (2013) 9(11) Verbraucher und Recht 407.

[37] BGH NJW 2006, 3633. cf Sandra V Wagner, *Verbraucherschutz bei Vertragsschluss im Internet: ein Vergleich zwischen englischem und deutschem Recht* (De Gruyter 2010) 118–19.

[38] Burgerlijk Wetboek, art 6:230b No 2. Arno R Lodder, Mark GA Egeler, and Wanda EL van Kerkvoorden, *Cyber Law in the Netherlands* (Kluwer Law International 2016) [251].

[39] Kamer van Koophandel, 'KVK-nummer: alles wat je moet weten' (2020) https://www.kvk.nl/informatiebank/kvk-nummer-alles-wat-je-moet-weten/ (accessed 5 October 2019).

[40] Mark Turner, Mary Traynor, and Herbert Smith, 'E-Commerce Directive: UK Implementation' (2002) 18(6) Computer Law & Security Report 399. The requirement to display the registration number has been replicated in s 7(1) and (2) of the Companies (Trading Disclosures) Regulations 2008, and s 25(1) and (2) of the Company, Limited Liability Partnership and Business (Names and Trading Disclosures) Regulations 2015.

the Netherlands, the register automatically allocates every incorporated company a registration number.[41]

This examination shows that only minor divergences reflecting technical differences exist in the 4 jurisdictions. All jurisdictions require traders to display their public register or trade number on their website, including the name of the issuing authority. French and German traders must provide the name of the local court where their company is registered. On the contrary, UK traders only need to give the nation where they registered their business: England and Wales, Scotland, or Northern Ireland. As there is only one central company register in the Netherlands, these distinctions do not exist.

2.1.2 VAT Number

Traders must also display their value-added tax (VAT) identification number on their website.[42] Like the requirement to display the trade register number, the VAT number must be 'easily, directly and permanently accessible'.[43] Authorities allocate VAT identification numbers to all legal persons in the European Union who carry out an economic activity,[44] including the supply of goods.[45] Authorities provide e-commerce traders with a VAT number consisting of a country code, for instance, NL for the Netherlands, and an individually allocated number.[46]

All 4 jurisdictions have transposed this information requirement for traders, and no substantive differences exist: French traders need to provide the *N° TVA intracommunataire*;[47] German traders need to provide either the VAT registration number (*Umsatzsteueridentifikationsnummer*) or business identification number (*Wirtschafts-identifikationsnummer*);[48] Dutch traders must provide their *belasting over de toegevoegde waarde* (BTW) number;[49] and traders in the United Kingdom must display their value-added tax number on their website.[50]

[41] Companies Act 2006, s 106.

[42] E-Commerce Directive, art 5(1)(g); Lodder (n 6) 36; Lubasz and Namysłowska (n 22) E-Commerce Directive, art 5 [44–45].

[43] E-Commerce Directive, art 5(1); Lodder (n 6) 33; Lubasz and Namysłowska (n 22) E-Commerce Directive, art 5 [51–54].

[44] Directive 2006/112, art 9(1).

[45] ibid art 14.

[46] ibid art 215.

[47] See Code de la consommation, art L111-2 in connection with art R111-2 no 1(e). See also Julien (n 27) 116.

[48] TMG § 5(1) No 6 and Umsatzsteuergesetz, § 27a; Hartmann (n 30); Müller-Broich (n 30) TMG § 5 [15]; Messinger (n 30) 293; Stefan Kolb, *Die Übergangsregelung der Richtlinie über unlautere Geschäftspraktiken* (Mohr Siebeck 2015) 121, 293.

[49] BW, art 6:230b No 4; Lodder, Egeler, and Wanda (n 38) [251].

[50] Electronic Commerce (EC Directive) Regulations 2002, reg 6(1)(g); Turner, Traynor, and Smith (n 40) 399.

2.1.3 Guidance on Contract Conclusion

Article 10(1)(a) of the E-Commerce Directive introduces a duty for traders to provide guidance on how consumers conclude a contract on their website.[51] Traders must do so before consumers place their orders.[52] In practice, traders need to provide this information to consumers once they have expressed their intention to purchase something on the website, for example, by placing an item in their 'basket'.[53] At this stage, the website must outline the following steps, for instance, delivery and payment options or the possibility of reviewing the order. The French,[54] German,[55] Dutch,[56] and UK[57] implementing rules do not go beyond the level of protection of the Directive.

2.1.4 Language Requirement

Another requirement under the Directive is that traders must offer all information required by both the E-Commerce Directive and the Consumer Rights Directive in the languages in which consumers can conclude contracts (Article 10(1)(d) of the E-Commerce Directive).[58] Otherwise, consumers would find it difficult to enter into the contractual relationship or seek redress, for instance, where the description of the goods is in another language than the terms and conditions. However, Article 10(1)(d) of the E-Commerce Directive does not impose a duty on traders to offer the possibility of concluding a contract in more than one language.[59]

[51] Christian Twigg-Flesner, Reiner Schulze, and Jonathon Watson, 'Protecting rational choice: information and the right of withdrawal' in Geraint Howells, Iain Ramsay, and Thomas Wilhelmsson (eds), *Handbook of Research on International Consumer Law* (2nd edn, Edward Elgar Publishing 2018) 115; Esther Arroyo Amayuelas, 'Directive 2000/31/EC: Article 10 Information to be provided' in Reiner Schulze and Dirk Staudenmayer (eds), *EU Digital Law: Article-by-Article Commentary* (Bloomsbury 2020) E-Commerce Directive, art 10 [3, 5].

[52] E-Commerce Directive, art 10(1).

[53] Lodder (n 6) 43–44.

[54] According to art 1127-1 no 1 of the Code Civil, this requirement applies to B2B and B2C transactions. See Geoffray Brunaux, 'La protection dépendante du contexte contractuel' in Natacha Sauphanor-Brouillaud and others, *Les contrats de consommation: Règles communes* (2nd edn, Librairie générale de droit et de jurisprudence 2018) [734].

[55] BGB, § 312i(1) No 2 in connection with EGBGB, art 246c No 1. See also Messinger (n 30) 294; Christiane Wendehorst, '§ 312i Allgemeine Pflichten im elektronischen Geschäftsverkehr' in Franz Jürgen Säcker and others (eds), *Münchener Kommentar zum Bürgerlichen Gesetzbuch* (8th edn, CH Beck 2019) BGB § 312i [69–70].

[56] BW, art 6:227b No 1(a); Lodder, Egeler, and Wanda (n 38) [253].

[57] Electronic Commerce (EC Directive) Regulations 2002, reg 9(1)(a); Turner, Traynor, and Smith (n 40) 400–401; Donal Nolan, 'Offer and Acceptance in the Digital Age' in Andrew Burrows and Edwin Peel (eds), *Contract Formation and Parties* (OUP 2010) 84–86.

[58] Twigg-Flesner, Schulze, and Watson (n 51) 5, 11; Savin (n 7) 55–56; Lodder (n 6) 44; Esther Arroyo Amayuelas, 'Directive 2000/31/EC: Article 10 Information to be provided' in Reiner Schulze and Dirk Staudenmayer (eds), *EU Digital Law: Article-by-Article Commentary* (Bloomsbury 2020) E-Commerce Directive, art 10 [8–11].

[59] Wendehorst (n 55) [78].

France,[60] Germany,[61] the Netherlands,[62] and the United Kingdom[63] implemented the language requirement into their national laws. France is the only country that goes beyond the minimum standard of the Directive, explicitly requiring traders operating in France to provide the contract terms in the state's official language.[64]

2.2 Comparative Notes on the Implementation

The examination of the national rules implementing the E-Commerce Directive revealed that the 4 Member States generally only go up to the standard of the Directive. Only France decided to enact stricter rules concerning the language requirement contained in Article 10(1)(d), obliging traders to provide the contract terms in French as a minimum. There is also no case law to date by the Court of Justice of the European Union (CJEU) concerning the 4 trader duties found in Articles 5 and 10. Nonetheless, the laws of the 4 jurisdictions offer sufficient detail for the empirical assessment of how traders need to implement the pre-contractual information and formal requirements. Regarding empirical evidence and consumer theories, the E-Commerce Directive lacks robust scientific grounding, but the information and formal requirements fit within the theory of consumer empowerment through information rights, which the following section critically discusses in detail.

3 The Consumer Rights Directive

The Consumer Rights Directive is a maximum harmonization directive with fully aligned specific rules concerning the provision of goods and services in

[60] Code de la consommation, art L224-76. The French legislator has decided to extend the scope of the provision to B2B contracts. See Code Civil, art 1127-1 no 3. See also Mustapha Mekki, 'France: The French Reform of Contract Law: The Art of Redoing Without Undoing' (2017) 10(1) Journal of Civil Law Studies 233; Brunaux (n 54).

[61] BGB, § 312i(1) No 2 in connection with EGBGB, art 246c No 4; Messinger (n 30) 294; Wendehorst (n 55) [75–78].

[62] BW, art 6:227b No 1(d); Lodder, Egeler, and Wanda (n 38) [253].

[63] Regulation 9(1)(d) of the Electronic Commerce (EC Directive) Regulations 2002; Turner, Traynor, and Smith (n 40) 400–401.

[64] See the provisions and literature in n 60. For a general discussion on language requirements in consumer contracts see Simon Whittaker, 'The Language or Languages of Consumer Contracts' (2006) 8 Cambridge Yearbook of European Law 229; Geraint Howells, Bevan Marten, and Wolfgang Wurmnest, 'Language of Information, Contract, and Communication' in Gerhard Dannemann and Stefan Vogenauer (eds), *The Common European Sales Law in Context: Interactions with English and German Law* (OUP 2013).

distance and off-premises consumer contracts, such as the right of withdrawal or information and formal requirements. The Directive repealed and replaced the Doorstep Selling Directive[65] and the Distance Selling Directive[66] and added new substantive rules to the European Consumer Acquis. The Consumer Rights Directive also slightly amended the Unfair Terms Directive[67] and the Consumer Sales and Guarantees Directive.[68] In the original proposal of the European Commission, the Directive was also supposed to replace the Unfair Terms Directive and the Consumer Sales and Guarantees Directive and thus replace the minimum harmonization directives with a maximum harmonization instrument. This ambitious proposal would have further unified the consumer laws of the EU Member States,[69] but the initiative failed due to political objections in the European Parliament and Council.[70] The Common European Sales Law met the same fate,[71] the proposal for which was withdrawn in 2015.[72]

The Directive's scope is vertical and non-sectoral, which means that the implementing rules must apply to all B2C distance[73] and off-premises[74] contracts concerning the provision of goods and services.[75] The *lex specialis* rule

[65] Council Directive (EEC) 85/577 to protect the consumer in respect of contracts negotiated away from business premises [1985] OJ L372/31 (Doorstep Selling Directive).

[66] Directive (EC) 97/7 on the protection of consumers in respect of distance contracts [1997] OJ L144/19 (Distance Selling Directive).

[67] Council Directive (EEC) 93/13 on unfair terms in consumer contracts [1993] OJ L95/29 (Unfair Terms Directive).

[68] Directive (EEC) 99/44 on certain aspects of the sale of consumer goods and associated guarantees [1999] OJ L171/12 (Consumer and Guarantees Sales Directive).

[69] Hans-Wolfgang Micklitz and Norbert Reich, 'Crónica de una muerte anunciada: The Commission proposal for a "Directive on consumer rights"' (2009) 46(2) Common Market Law Review 471 ff; Kathleen Gutman, *The Constitutional Foundations of European Contract Law: A Comparative Analysis* (OUP 2014) 32–36; Klaus Tonner, 'From the Kennedy Message to Full Harmonising Consumer Law Directives: A Retrospect' in Kai Purnhagen and Peter Rott (eds), *Varieties of European Economic Law and Regulation: Liber Amicorum for Hans Micklitz* (Springer Publishing 2014) 703–705; Joasia A Luzak and Vanessa Mak, 'The Consumer Rights Directive' in Arthur S Hartkamp and others (eds), *De invloed van het Europese recht op het Nederlandse privaatrecht* (Kluwer 2014) 70–72.

[70] For an overview of the debates in the legislative process see Stephen Weatherill, 'The Consumer Rights Directive: How and why a quest for "coherence" has (largely) failed' (2012) 49(4) Common Market Law Review 1286–.

[71] European Commission, 'Proposal for a Regulation of the European Parliament and of the Council on a Common European Sales Law (CESL)' COM(2011) 635 final.

[72] See eg Hugh Beale, 'Art. 66-68: The Sources of Contract Terms Under the CESL' in Aurelia Colombi Ciacchi (ed), *Contents and Effects of Contracts-Lessons to Learn from the Common European Sales Law* (Springer Publishing 2016) 75–81.

[73] Consumer Rights Directive, art 2(7): '"distance contract" means any contract concluded between the trader and the consumer under an organised distance sales or service-provision scheme without the simultaneous physical presence of the trader and the consumer, with the exclusive use of one or more means of distance communication up to and including the time at which the contract is concluded'. According to recital 20 of the Directive, the instrument applies to contracts concluded through traditional and electronic means.

[74] ibid art 2(8).

[75] Martijn Hesselink notes that the scope of the Directive 'paved the way toward relatively autonomous consumer contract law'. See Martijn W Hesselink, 'Toward a Sharp Distinction between b2b

for specific sectors further limits the applicability of the Directive (Article 3(2)), with the effect that any provision of sectoral EU instruments prevails over the Directive. In addition, specific sectors, such as healthcare and social services, are entirely excluded from the scope of the Directive.[76] There are, however, no limitations concerning e-commerce sales. Regarding the Directive's definition of traders and consumers, the instrument has adopted similar definitions to the ones contained in the Distance Selling Directive.[77] According to Stefan Grundman and Klaus Tonner, the EU legislator has addressed the dual-use problem, that is to say, whether a consumer acts in a private or commercial capacity, by adopting an even broader definition than the one offered by the CJEU in the *Gruber*[78] case.[79]

and b2c? On Consumer, Commercial and General Contract Law after the Consumer Rights Directive' (2010) 18(1) European Review of Private Law 77.

[76] Consumer Rights Directive, art 3(3). Although outside the scope of the present study, the material scope of the Consumer Rights Directive also covers the supply of goods that are of public interest: water, electricity, gas, and district heating (recitals 11, 19, and 21 and arts 2(3) and 3(1)). However, the Directive's rules on delivery (art 18) and passing of risk (art 20) do not apply 'to contracts for the supply of water, gas or electricity, where they are not put up for sale in a limited volume or set quantity, of district heating or the supply of digital content which is not supplied on a tangible medium' (Consumer Rights Directive, art 17(1)).

[77] The Distance Selling Directive did not use the term traders. Instead, the Directive used the term supplier (Distance Selling Directive, art 2(3)). The definitions in the Consumer Rights Directive are more precise. Recital 16 of the Consumer Rights Directive explicitly provides that the definition of trader does not affect the laws on legal representation of the EU Member States. Its definitions will apply only within the Consumer Rights Directive regime since the Directive does not introduce general consumer law principles. The Consumer Rights Directive, art 2(1) states: '"consumer" means any natural person who, in contracts covered by this Directive, is acting for purposes which are outside his trade, business, craft or profession'. See also recital 17 of the Directive. Article 2(2) of the Directive states: '"trader" means any natural person or any legal person, irrespective of whether privately or publicly owned, who is acting, including through any other person acting in his name or on his behalf, for purposes relating to his trade, business, craft or profession in relation to contracts covered by this Directive'.

[78] Case C-464/01 *Johann Gruber v BayWa AG* ECLI:EU:C:2005:32, para 54: 'A person who concludes a contract for goods intended for purposes which are in part within and in part outside his trade or profession may not rely on the special rules of jurisdiction laid down in Articles 13 to 15 of the Convention, unless the trade or professional purpose is so limited as to be negligible in the overall context of the supply, the fact that the private element is predominant being irrelevant in that respect.'

[79] Stefan Grundmann, 'The EU Consumer Rights Directive: optimizing, creating alternatives, or a dead end?' (2013) 18(1) Uniform Law Review 103; Klaus Tonner, 'The Consumer Rights Directive and Its Impact on Internet and other Distance Consumer Contracts' in Norbert Reich and others (eds), *European Consumer Law* (2nd edn, Intersentia 2014) 397. Stefan Grundmann voices his concerns about the uncertainty around the new consumer/trader distinction, especially regarding the term 'predominant' trade purpose contained in recital 17 of the Consumer Rights Directive: 'The definition of consumer should cover natural persons who are acting outside their trade, business, craft or profession. However, in the case of dual purpose contracts, where the contract is concluded for purposes partly within and partly outside the person's trade and the trade purpose is so limited as not to be predominant in the overall context of the contract, that person should also be considered as a consumer.' Consumers, however, fall outside the scope of the Directive in cases where the purpose of the transaction becomes predominantly professional after concluding the (here service) contract. See Case C-498/16 *Maximilian Schrems v Facebook Ireland Limited* ECLI:EU:C:2018:37, paras 36–38.

The most important feature of the Directive is its imperative nature. Consumers cannot waive rights they derive from the national rules which implement the Directive: contractual clauses that directly or indirectly restrict the statutory rights of consumers are at no time binding.[80] This provision of the Consumer Rights Directive demonstrates the protective nature of the legal instrument, where the European legislator tried to close every possible loophole.[81] Like all EU consumer contract law instruments, Directive leaves the enforcement[82] and imposition of penalties for non-compliance to national authorities.[83] However, the rules under which they operate at the domestic level remain subject to EU law principles including effectiveness, proportionality, and dissuasive effect.

The chapter has already highlighted that the Consumer Rights Directive provides for a targeted full harmonization standard, which does not allow the Member States to opt for a lower or higher level of protection. The Directive, however, contains several options which allow the Member States to deviate from the rules of the Consumer Rights Directive.[84] The options concern off-premise sale of goods and service contracts,[85] contracts concluded by telephone,[86] and other scenarios,[87] which all fall outside the scope of the empirical enquiry of the present study and are thus not examined further.[88] Despite these regulatory choices, the common-place practice of opting for a higher level of protection—known as gold-plating, which EU minimum harmonization

[80] Consumer Rights Directive, art 25.
[81] Weatherill (n 70) 1306.
[82] Consumer Rights Directive, art 23.
[83] ibid art 24.
[84] ibid art 4.
[85] ibid arts 3(4), 7(4), and 9(3).
[86] ibid art 8(6).
[87] ibid arts 6(7), 6(8), and 5(3). Article 6(7) allows Member States to maintain or introduce language requirements concerning the contractual information duties. The possibility of introducing a language requirement examined the previous section regarding the E-Commerce Directive (E-Commerce Directive, art 10(1)(d)). Article 6(8) grants Member States the option to impose additional information requirements to the extent that such a possibility exists under Directive 2000/31/EC on electronic commerce and Directive 2006/123/EC on the services in the internal market. National information requirements introduced in addition to the ones contained in the E-Commerce Directive fall outside the scope of the study because it would not allow for a comparison of the levels of compliance between the 4 Member States. Article 5(3) allows Member States to exclude the information and formal requirements in art 5(1) from day-to-day transactions immediately performed by traders and consumers.
[88] France is the only jurisdiction included in the present study which adopted all of the options in the Directive in the most favourable way for consumers. Guillaume Busseuil, 'Implementation of the Consumer Rights Directive: France' (2014) 3(4) Journal of European Consumer and Market Law 271; Christoph Busch, 'Implementation of the Consumer Rights Directive Germany' (2014) 3(2) Journal of European Consumer and Market Law 119; Joasia A Luzak and Vanessa Mak, 'Implementation of the Consumer Rights Directive: The Netherlands' (2014) 3(2) Journal of European Consumer and Market Law 127; Christian Twigg-Flesner, 'Consumer Sales in the United Kingdom after the Implementation of the Consumer Rights Directive' in Giovanni de Cristofaro and Alberto de Franceschi (eds), *Consumer Sales in Europe: After the Implementation of the Consumer Rights Directive* (Intersentia 2016) 195–96.

directives permit—is restricted by the Directive's maximum harmonization nature.[89] Nonetheless, Member States can enact (stricter) rules if they fall outside the material scope of the Directive. For instance, Member States can extend the scope of the Directive to B2B scenarios.[90] For the present study, all information and formal requirements and substantive rights of consumers are only examined on the EU level, as the Member States are not allowed to deviate from these rules in the context on which this book focuses.

Before adopting the Consumer Rights Directive, the European Union only adopted minimum harmonization instruments to regulate e-commerce distance sales.[91] Some Member States had used the option of adopting stricter rules.[92] However, the European Commission clarified in its strategy papers that it would continue to issue proposals for maximum harmonization instruments to govern at-distance and off-premises contracts to facilitate cross-border trade.[93] This shift towards using maximum instead of minimum harmonization Directives has been highly controversial. Stephen Weatherill observes that creating one standard of consumer protection leaves no room for national regulatory innovation, which, in his view, subsequently limits local autonomy and choice.[94] More general criticism against the Directive and the current approach in European contract law concerns their failure to consider empirical evidence, such as the findings of behavioural law and economics.[95] Several academics have questioned the approach taken concerning mandatory disclosures.[96] In the view of Christoph Busch, divided evidence exists on

[89] Article 29 of the Consumer Rights Directive requires that Member States report the 'use of any of the regulatory choices referred to in Article 3(4), Article 6(7), Article 6(8), Article 7(4), Article 8(6) and Article 9(3)' to the European Commission. For additional deviations and inconsistencies in the implementation of the Directive's options in other Member States see Giovanni de Cristofaro, 'After Implementing Directive 2011/83/EU in the Member States: Are the National Provisions on Consumer Contracts Really Harmonised? Some Critical Remarks' (2014) 3(4) Journal of European Consumer and Market Law 217.

[90] Consumer Rights Directive, recitals 13 and 14; Tonner (n 79) 400–401.

[91] Catalina Goanta conducted an empirical study on the converging effects of the EU's harmonization policies, for instance, concerning the national implementation of the Distance Selling Directive. See Catalina Goanta, *Convergence in European Consumer Sales Law: A Comparative and Numerical Approach* (Intersentia 2016) 271.

[92] This part of the chapter provides further details on the level of consumer protection before adopting the Consumer Rights Directive.

[93] European Commission, 'Consumer Policy Strategy 2002-2006' COM(2002) 208 final; European Commission, 'EU Consumer Policy Strategy 2007-2013' COM(2007) 99 final.

[94] Weatherill (n 70) 1316–17.

[95] See eg Horst Eidenmüller, 'Why Withdrawal Rights?' (2011) 7(1) European Review of Contract Law 18; Joasia A Luzak, 'To Withdraw or Not to Withdraw? Evaluation of the Mandatory Right of Withdrawal in Consumer Distance Selling Contracts Taking into Account Its Behavioural Effects on Consumers' (2011) 37(1) Journal of Consumer Policy 91; Elizabeth Hall, Geraint Howells, and Jonathon Watson, 'The Consumer Rights Directive: An Assessment of Its Contribution to the Development of European Consumer Contract Law' (2012) 8(2) European Review of Contract Law 164.

[96] See eg Christoph Busch, 'The future of pre-contractual information duties: from behavioural insights to big data' in Christian Twigg-Flesner (ed), *Research Handbook on EU Consumer and Contract*

how consumers process information and whether mandatory disclosures lead to more informed decisions. Busch also questions whether the current pre-contractual information system is fit for purpose in light of a 'trend towards more personalisation'.[97]

The European Union adopted the final proposal of the Directive on 25 October 2011, with a deadline for implementation into national law by 13 June 2014.[98] France,[99] Germany,[100] the Netherlands,[101] and the United Kingdom[102] implemented the Consumer Rights Directive into national law on time.[103] The European Union revised the Consumer Rights Directive as part of the Commission's New Deal for Consumers,[104] and the Member States had to transpose the new Directive 2019/2161/EU by 28 May 2022.[105] Only Chapter 7 addresses the New Deal for Consumers because these rules did not bind traders at the time of writing and mostly fell outside the book's scope.

Law (Edward Elgar Publishing 2016) 239–40; Geneviève Helleringer and Anne-Lise Sibony, 'European Consumer Protection Through the Behavioral Lense' (2017) 23(3) The Columbia Journal of European Law 617.

[97] Busch (n 96).

[98] Consumer Rights Directive, art 28(1).

[99] Loi no 2014-344 of 17 March 2014 (*relative à la consommation*); Décret no 2014-1061 of 17 September 2014 (*relatif aux obligations d'information précontractuelle et contractuelle des consommateurs et au droit de retractation*); Ordonnance no 2016-301 of 14 March 2016 (*relative à la partie législative du code de la consommation*); Décret no 2016-884 of 29 June 2016 (*relatif à la partie réglementaire du code de la consommation*); Carole Aubert de Vincelles, 'Consumer Sales in France after the Implementation of the Consumer Rights Directive' in Giovanni de Cristofaro and Alberto de Franceschi (eds), *Consumer Sales in Europe: After the Implementation of the Consumer Rights Directive* (Intersentia 2016) 59–60; Busseuil (n 88) 270–74.

[100] Gesetz zur Umsetzung der Verbraucherrechterichtlinie und zur Änderung des Gesetzes zur Regelung der Wohnungsvermittlung vom 20 September 2013 (27 September 2013) Bundesgesetzblatt Teil 1, 3642–70. Martin Schmidt-Kessel, 'Consumer Sales in Germany after the Implementation of the Consumer Rights Directive' in Giovanni de Cristofaro and Alberto de Franceschi (eds), *Consumer Sales in Europe: After the Implementation of the Consumer Rights Directive* (Intersentia 2016) 74–77, 83; Busch (n 88) 119–22.

[101] Kamerstukken II, 2012/2013, 33 520, no 3; Marco Loos, 'Consumer Sales in the Netherlands after the Implementation of the Consumer Rights Directive' in Giovanni de Cristofaro and Alberto de Franceschi (eds), *Consumer Sales in Europe: After the Implementation of the Consumer Rights Directive* (Intersentia 2016) 110–12; Luzak and Mak (n 88) 127–29.

[102] Consumer Contracts (Information, Cancellation and Additional Charges) Regulations 2013; The Consumer Rights (Payment Surcharges) Regulations 2012; Legal Notice No 175 of 2013: Contract and Tort Act (Amendment) Regulations 2013; Legal Notice No 176 of 2013: Consumer Protection (Unfair Trading) Act 2008 (Amendment) Regulations 2013; Legal Notice No 177 of 2013: Consumer Rights on Contract Regulations 2013; The Consumer Rights Act 2015; Twigg-Flesner (n 88) 196–98, 204–205; Paula Giliker, 'The Transposition of the Consumer Rights Directive into UK Law: Implementing a Maximum Harmonization Directive' (2015) 23(1) European Review of Private Law 9; Christian Twigg-Flesner, 'Consolidation rather than codification—or just complication? The UK's Consumer Rights Act 2015' (2019) 27(1) Zeitschrift für Europäisches Privatrecht 170 ff.

[103] European Commission, 'National transpositions by Member State' (2020) https://eur-lex.europa.eu/legal-content/EN/NIM/?uri=celex:32011L0083 (accessed 20 October 2020).

[104] European Commission, 'A New Deal for Consumers' (Communication) COM(2018) 183 final.

[105] Directive 2019/2161/EU, art 7.

3.1 Mandatory Disclosures and Substantive Rights

The Consumer Rights Directive further harmonized existing and introduced new mandatory disclosures and substantive consumer rights. Traders must comply with the national rules implementing the Directive's information and formal requirements in the pre-contractual phase. In contrast, consumers can only rely on the substantive rules after the conclusion of the contract. This section examines how the Consumer Rights Directive's consumer contract rules operate and determines whether these rules fall within the scope of the present study.

3.1.1 Information Requirements

The Directive requires traders to make certain information available to consumers in distance contracts. Article 6 of the Consumer Rights Directive includes an exhaustive list of specific information that must be set out in a 'clear and comprehensible manner' on traders' websites. In an e-commerce distance contract, traders must provide consumers with the main characteristics of the goods,[106] the identity of the trader,[107] the geographical address,[108] the total price of the goods or services inclusive of taxes,[109] the costs for the use of distance communication,[110] the payment arrangements, delivery and performance,[111] the conditions of the rights of withdrawal (including a model withdrawal form),[112] the costs for returning the goods,[113] and the existence of a legal guarantee of conformity of goods.[114] Several information

[106] Consumer Rights Directive, art 6(1)(a).

[107] ibid art 6(1)(b).

[108] ibid art 6(1)(c) and (d). Article 6(1)(c) states that traders must provide their 'telephone number, fax number and e-mail address, where available'. The CJEU recently clarified that traders can provide any form of 'communication capable of satisfying the criteria of direct and effective communication', so not only the 3 options provided in the Directive. See Case C-649/17 *Bundesverband der Verbraucherzentralen und Verbraucherverbände: Verbraucherzentrale Bundesverband eV v Amazon EU Sàrl* ECLI:EU:C:2019:576, para 53.

[109] Consumer Rights Directive, art 6(1)(e).

[110] ibid art 6(1)(f).

[111] ibid art 6(1)(g).

[112] ibid art 6(1)(h), (j), and (k).

[113] ibid art 6(1)(i).

[114] ibid art 6(1)(l). See Evelyne Terryn and Joyce Vandenbulcke, 'Directive 2011/81/EU: Article 6 Information requirements for distance or off-premises contracts' in Reiner Schulze and Dirk Staudenmayer (eds), *EU Digital Law: Article-by-Article Commentary* (Bloomsbury 2020) Consumer Rights Directive, art 6 [24] ff; David Kästle-Lamparter, 'Art 2:403: Information Requirements for Distance and Off-premises Consumer Contracts' in Nils Jansen and Reinhard Zimmermann (eds), *Commentaries on European Contract Laws* (OUP 2018) art 2:403 [12–20], who contrasts the information requirements of the Distance Selling Directive and the E-Commerce Directive with the ones in the Consumer Rights Directive, and notes that the obligations for traders are almost identical.

requirements apply only to contractual situations not covered by the present study.[115]

Consumers have a remedy in cases where traders fail to provide some of the information required under Article 6. For instance, consumers do not bear any additional costs should a trader fail to indicate the total price of the goods, as required by Article 6(1)(e), or the costs of returning the goods, as required by Article 6(1)(i).[116] The Directive also places the burden of proof on traders.[117]

Other instruments, such as the E-Commerce Directive, take precedence when it comes to the regulation of information and formal requirements (*lex specialis*).[118] Nonetheless, Member States must refrain from adopting any additional pre-contractual information and formal requirements when implementing the Consumer Rights Directive into national law (Article 8(10) of the Directive).[119] The compliance assessments will, therefore, only consider the above-mentioned provisions.

While the information and formal requirements did not build on a scientific foundation in the Directive's ex ante impact assessment, the ex post fitness check outlined the importance of these requirements. The fitness check's consumer survey showed that the most important information online is the display of the goods' price (80 per cent), closely followed by the products' details (75 per cent), additional delivery charges (74 per cent), and the sellers' name (70 per cent).[120] However, the discussion below on the right of withdrawal will illustrate the divided evidence regarding how consumers process information.

3.1.2 Formal Requirements

The Directive's formal requirements in Article 8 place a duty on traders to display the information under Article 6(1) in a particular manner to consumers. The first legal requirement is that traders must provide the information to consumers 'in a way appropriate to the means of distance communication used in plain and intelligible language', *id est* a durable medium.[121] Traders must provide consumers with certain information before the conclusion of

[115] Consumer Rights Directive, art 6(1)(p–s). Article 6(1)(t) of the Directive falls within the book's scope, and section 4.3.1.6 of this chapter discusses it in detail. Failing to comply with certain information duties may also breach art 7(4) of the Unfair Commercial Practices Directive (EC) 2005/29.

[116] Consumer Rights Directive, art 6(6).

[117] ibid art 6(9); Weatherill (n 70) 1292–95; Grundmann (n 79) 108–11.

[118] Consumer Rights Directive, arts 6(8) and 8(9).

[119] Weatherill (n 70) 1295; Grundmann (n 79) 111–12.

[120] SWD(2017) 209 final 61 (Figure 28). The price of the goods was also the most important factor in the decision-making (87 per cent); 68 (Figure 29).

[121] See Consumer Rights Directive, art 8(1) in connection with art 2(10). See also Terryn and Vandenbulcke (n 114) Consumer Rights Directive, art 6 [22].

the contract,[122] that is the characteristics of the goods,[123] the identity of the trader,[124] the total price of the goods or services inclusive of taxes,[125] and the conditions of the rights of withdrawal.[126] Moreover, traders must make consumers 'aware in a clear and prominent manner, directly before the consumer places his order, of'[127] the characteristics of the goods,[128] and the total price of the goods or services, including taxes.[129] Additional information requirements contained in the Directive but falling outside the parameters of the present study are those relating to the duration of the contract[130] and 'the minimum duration of the consumer's obligations under the contract'.[131] In addition, traders must inform consumers of any applicable delivery restrictions and all possible forms of payment at the beginning of the purchase process.[132] A further formal requirement mandates that traders must send the confirmation of the conclusion of the contract to consumers on a durable medium within a reasonable period, which the Directive defines as any time before the delivery of the goods.[133] Compliance with delivery and contract confirmation requirements will not be assessed in the present study, as to do so would necessitate the purchase of the goods in question.

3.1.3 Right of Withdrawal

Assessing trader compliance with the right of withdrawal involves the investigation of fulfilment by them with a series of independent legal duties. First and foremost, consumers enjoy a 14-day 'cooling off' period to decide whether to keep the goods.[134] The withdrawal period begins on the day when 'the consumer or a third party other than the carrier and indicated by

[122] Consumer Rights Directive, art 8(4).
[123] ibid art 6(1)(a).
[124] ibid art 6(1)(b).
[125] ibid art 6(1)(e).
[126] ibid art 6(1)(h); Terryn and Vandenbulcke (n 114) Consumer Rights Directive, art 6 [24] ff.
[127] Consumer Rights Directive, art 8(2).
[128] ibid art 6(1)(a).
[129] ibid art 6(1)(e); David Kästle-Lamparter, 'Art 2:405: Formal and Additional Requirements for Distance Consumer Contracts' in Nils Jansen and Reinhard Zimmermann (eds), *Commentaries on European Contract Laws* (OUP 2018) art 2:405 [2–6], who examines the formal requirements in distance consumer contracts, including a comparison between the former rules of the Distance Selling Directive and the new ones contained in the Consumer Rights Directive.
[130] Consumer Rights Directive, art 6(1)(o).
[131] ibid art 6(1)(p).
[132] ibid art 8(3).
[133] ibid art 8(7). That confirmation should include all information required by art 6(1) of the Directive unless it was provided to the consumer in advance (ibid art 8(7)(a)). See also Weatherill (n 70) 1295; Tonner (n 79) 404–406. Special rules apply to the sale of digital content under arts 8(7)(b) and 16(m) of the Consumer Rights Directive.
[134] Consumer Rights Directive, art 9.

the consumer acquires physical possession of the good'.[135] However, in cases where the consumer has ordered multiple goods together, the cooling-off period starts with the date of delivery of the last item.[136] The same applies where purchased goods consist of multiple lots or pieces.[137]

Consumers also do not have to justify their decision or be required to bear any withdrawal costs.[138] Traders are, however, allowed to charge consumers where they have opted for 'a type of delivery other than the least expensive type of standard delivery offered by the trader',[139] where the trader has stipulated in its terms that the consumer will bear the costs of returning the goods,[140] and additionally 'for any diminished value of the goods resulting from the handling of the goods other than what is necessary to establish the nature, characteristics and functioning of the goods'.[141] The Directive prohibits Member States from extending the scope of the statutory right of withdrawal to situations where: (1) the price of the goods is dependent on fluctuations in the financial market;[142] (2) the goods are specified or personalized for the consumer's needs;[143] (3) the goods are liable to deteriorate or expire rapidly;[144] (4) the goods are sealed and not suitable for return;[145] (5) the goods are due to their nature inseparably mixed with other items;[146] (6) the goods are alcoholic beverages;[147] (7) the goods have been specifically requested and installed;[148] (8) audio or video recordings and computer software have been unsealed by the consumer;[149] (9) the goods are newspapers, periodicals, or magazines except the supply of subscription contracts;[150] and (10) goods purchased at public auctions.[151] These situations do not affect the scope of the present study.

Traders are furthermore required to inform consumers about the right of withdrawal before or at the time of purchase, and they also must provide a

[135] ibid art 9(2)(b).
[136] ibid art 9(2)(b)(i).
[137] ibid art 9(2)(b)(ii). However, the rules differ for regular deliveries. In this case, the clock starts ticking as soon as the first of the good arrives. See ibid art 9(2)(b)(iii).
[138] ibid art 9(1).
[139] ibid art 13(2).
[140] ibid art 14(1).
[141] ibid art 14(2). See Caroline Cauffman, 'The Consumer Rights Directive Adopted' (2012) 19(1) Maastricht Journal of European and Comparative Law 215.
[142] Consumer Rights Directive, art 16(b).
[143] ibid art 16(c).
[144] ibid art 16(d).
[145] ibid art 16(e).
[146] ibid art 16(f).
[147] ibid art 16(g).
[148] ibid art 16(h).
[149] ibid art 16(i).
[150] ibid art 16(j).
[151] ibid art 16(k).

withdrawal form.[152] Annex I to the Consumer Rights Directive contains an example of how such a withdrawal form should look, but traders can provide their own form or an electronic option on their website.[153] Consumers, in turn, must use the withdrawal form[154] or 'make any other unequivocal statement setting out [their] decision to withdraw from the contract'.[155] In case of a dispute, consumers must prove that they have exercised their right of withdrawal by Article 11 of the Directive.[156] Traders' failure to inform consumers about the right has several far-reaching consequences. Most importantly, the Directive extends the 'cooling-off' period to 12 months from the end of the statutory withdrawal period.[157] However, should traders inform consumers of their right to withdraw within 12 months, the withdrawal period expires within 14 days.[158] Another consequence of failing to provide the information is that the trader must bear the risk of the goods diminishing value [159] and cover the costs of returning the goods to them if they failed to stipulate that consumers were liable for the cost of returning the goods.[160]

The consumer's withdrawal from the contract has 3 far-reaching effects. First, the cancellation terminates the obligations of the parties to perform the contract,[161] including any ancillary contracts.[162] Secondly, the consumer must send back the goods within 14 days after the consumer has communicated the decision to withdraw to the trader.[163] The third effect is that the Directive requires that the trader reimburse the consumer within 14 days from the date of withdrawal, using the same method as for the payment.[164] The Directive stipulates that the trader only has to reimburse the consumer once

[152] ibid art 6(1)(h). The Directive does not require that traders display the model withdrawal form in case the 'means of distance communication . . . allows limited space or time to display the information', eg contracts concluded by telephone. See Case C-430/17 *Walbusch Walter Busch GmbH & Co KG v Zentrale zur Bekämpfung unlauteren Wettbewerbs Frankfurt am Main eV* ECLI:EU:C:2019:47, para 46. See also Terryn and Vandenbulcke (n 114) Consumer Rights Directive, art 8 [21].

[153] Consumer Rights Directive, art 11(3).

[154] ibid art 11(1)(a).

[155] ibid art 11(1)(b).

[156] ibid art 11(4).

[157] ibid art 10(1).

[158] ibid art 10(2). This idea of providing a remedy in case of a failure on the trader's part to notify the consumer is not novel. The Distance Selling Directive already provided for such a remedy but limited the maximum withdrawal period to 3 months (Directive 97/7/EC, art 6(1)).

[159] Consumer Rights Directive, art 14(2).

[160] ibid art 14(1).

[161] ibid art 12(a).

[162] ibid art 15. Like the withdrawal rules governing the main contract, the termination of ancillary contracts may not incur any costs for consumers unless one of the previously discussed exceptions in arts 13(2) or 14 of the Directive apply. Member States can provide more detailed rules on the termination of ancillary contracts. See ibid art 15(2). Weatherill (n 70) 1300–301.

[163] Consumer Rights Directive, art 14(1).

[164] ibid art 13(1). Traders may only opt for a different method in case consumers have agreed to it and are not liable to a fee.

it has received the returned goods or proof of their return unless the trader states in its terms that it will collect the goods itself.[165] As mentioned above, the trader is not obliged to reimburse the consumer fully in all circumstances.[166]

Before adopting the Consumer Rights Directive, different withdrawal periods existed nationally. Under the minimum harmonization Distance Selling Directive, the Member States were allowed to enact withdrawal periods of more than 7 days.[167] The maximum harmonization nature of the Consumer Rights Directive does not allow for more stringent rules on the national level.[168] One consequence of the new rules under the Consumer Rights Directive is that it forced Malta and Slovenia to reduce their statutory withdrawal period from15 to 14 days.[169] However, the withdrawal period did increase in most of the European Union Member States, including France (previously 7 calendar days),[170] the Netherlands (previously 7 working days),[171] and the United Kingdom (previously seven working days).[172] German law already provided a 2-week withdrawal period, which increased to 1 month, where the information on withdrawal rights had been provided to consumers only after the contract's conclusion.[173] The Consumer Rights Directive harmonized all technical rules surrounding the withdrawal right,[174] which means that Member States may not provide for any other requirements.

[165] ibid art 13(3).
[166] ibid arts 13(2), 14.
[167] Directive 97/7/EC, art 6(1).
[168] See Weatherill (n 70) 1317, who notes that the 'pursuit of "coherence" in Europe must be weighed against the virtue of local autonomy and the value of regulatory experimentation.' For an assessment of the advantages and disadvantages of full harmonization in EU consumer law see Stephen Weatherill, 'Maximum versus Minimum Harmonization: Choosing between Unity and Diversity in the Search for the Soul of the Internal Market' in Niamh Nic Shuibhne and Laurence W Gormley (eds), *From Single Market to Economic Union: Essays in Memory of John A. Usher* (OUP 2012) 185–89.
[169] Hans Schulte-Nölke and Andreas Börger, 'Distance Selling Directive (97/7)' in Hans Schulte-Nölke, Christian Twigg-Flesner, and Martin Ebers (eds), *EC Consumer Law Compendium: The Consumer Acquis and its transposition in the Member States* (Sellier European Law Publishers 2009) 346–47; Rebekah Tanti-Dougall, 'Implementation of the Consumer Rights Directive: Malta' (2014) 3(3) Journal of European Consumer and Market Law 187.
[170] Code de la consommation (version of 26 July 2005) art L121-20. Schulte-Nölke and Börger argued that the old French rules were in breach of the rules of the Directive because 7 '*jours francs*' equal 7 calendar days, excluding Sundays and public holidays. See Schulte-Nölke and Börger (n 169) 346–47.
[171] BW, art 7:46d (version of 31 October 2007). Jan M Smits, 'Epistemology and Methodology of Comparative Law' in Mark van Hoecke (ed), *Epistemology and Methodology of Comparative Law* (Hart Publishing 2004) 237; Schulte-Nölke and Börger (n 169) 346–47.
[172] Regulation 11 of the Consumer Protection (Distance Selling) Regulations 2000; Schulte-Nölke and Börger (n 169) 346–47.
[173] See § 355 of the BGB (version of 8 December 2004); Boris Schinkels, 'Der Kommissionsentwurf einer Verbraucherrechte-Richtlinie und seine Sprengkraft für § 355 BGB' (2009) 64(15/16) Juristen Zeitung 774.
[174] Schulte-Nölke and Börger (n 169) 347–51.

The Directive is designed to simplify the withdrawal process (Article 11(1)) and offer legal certainty to both traders and consumers (recital 44).[175]

The ex ante impact assessment of the Commission cited the cost of fragmentation and inconsistencies as one of the justifications for the harmonized right of withdrawal, citing a Eurobarometer trader survey on cross-border trade.[176] Daniel Krähmer and Roland Strausz argue that mandatory withdrawal rights provide a level-playing field between e-commerce traders and traditional stores.[177] However, whether the statutory withdrawal right corrects the information asymmetry in business-to-consumer distance contracts remains unanswered, as some behavioural evidence questions whether consumers benefit from a cooling-off period.[178] Despite the evidence and theories, the Commission revealed in the ex post fitness check that 67 per cent of consumers perceive the information on the right of withdrawal in online commerce as very important or important in online commerce.[179] However, the Commission's investigation into e-commerce traders revealed significant non-compliance, with over a quarter of traders failing to give details on withdrawal methods and almost half omitting information on return timelines.[180]

It follows that the new rules governing the statutory right of withdrawal provide consumers with more generous and harmonized rules. As pointed out by Stephen Weatherill, the Directive also codified some of the case law on the Distance Selling Directive and Doorstep Selling Directive, thereby increasing legal certainty.[181] The Consumer Rights Directive's also contributed to harmonizing all technical rules of the right of withdrawal.[182] All these rules are aligned and provide a strong remedy for consumers. Traders nonetheless have the option to give consumers more extended withdrawal periods. From a business standpoint, withdrawal rights make 'economic sense when the buyer most efficiently learns of a product through use or inspection at home and the product either does not depreciate rapidly or depreciate but in a fashion

[175] Cauffman (n 141) 215–16.
[176] European Commission, 'Impact Assessment Report' SEC(2008) 2544, 11–12.
[177] Daniel Krähmer and Roland Strausz, 'Optimal Sales Contracts with Withdrawal Rights' (2015) 82(2) The Review of Economic Studies 784.
[178] Eidenmüller (n 95) 7–9; Luzak (n 95) 108–109.
[179] SWD(2017) 209 final 61 (Figure 28).
[180] European Commission, 'Online shopping: Commission and Consumer Protection authorities urge traders to bring information policy in line with EU law' (31 January 2020) https://ec.europa.eu/commission/presscorner/detail/en/IP_20_156 (accessed 22 November 2022).
[181] Weatherill (n 70) 1295–98.
[182] Schulte-Nölke and Börger (n 169) 345–47, 349–51.

that can be easily measured and compensated for'.[183] The dataset of the present study might reflect such differences between products.

3.1.4 Passing of Risk

Another substantive consumer right places the risk of loss or damage to goods before delivery on traders.[184] According to the Directive, the risk passes to consumers when they, or a third party indicated by them other than the carrier, have acquired physical possession of the ordered goods. If the consumer commissioned the carrier, the risk passes to the consumer as soon as their commissioned carrier takes possession of the goods.[185] However, traders are not legally obliged to inform consumers about their rights concerning the passing of risk.[186]

Rules on the passing of risk only existed on the European Union level after the adoption of the Directive, as consumers only had a right to have the goods delivered without any faults.[187] The Directive has thus added further harmonized rules to the European Consumer Contract Acquis,[188] which, according to the Commission's ex post impact assessment, 'may affect consumer confidence'.[189] However, traders are not required to include the information contained in Article 20 in their terms and conditions. However, they must do it faithfully in case they include a provision governing the passing of risk.

3.1.5 Delivery

Another substantive part of the contract which the Directive regulates is the delivery time. This chapter has established that traders are not only required to provide consumers with an estimated delivery date[190] but are, by default, also required to transfer the 'physical possession or control of the goods' to consumers within 30 days of the conclusion of the distance contracts.[191] Nonetheless, this is not a legal requirement because consumers and traders

[183] Omri Ben-Shahar and Eric A Posner, 'The Right to Withdraw in Contract Law' (2011) 40(1) Journal of Legal Studies 145.
[184] Consumer Rights Directive, art 20.
[185] Weatherill (n 70) 1305; Grundmann (n 79) 118–19; Luzak and Mak (n 69) 90.
[186] See the Directive's information and formal requirements in sections 4.3.1.1 and 4.3.1.2 of this chapter.
[187] Thomas Rüfner, 'Art 18:307: Passing of Risk in a Consumer Sales Contract' in Nils Jansen and Reinhard Zimmermann (eds), *Commentaries on European Contract Laws* (OUP 2018) art 18:307 [3–11], who provides an historical and comparative account concerning the rules on passing of risk in consumer sales contracts. See Directive 1999/44/EC, art 5(3).
[188] Stefan Wrbka, *European Consumer Access to Justice Revisited* (CUP 2015) 181.
[189] SEC(2008) 2544, 14. The European Commission presented several alternatives to the participating stakeholder groups (19–20).
[190] Consumer Rights Directive, art 6(1)(g).
[191] ibid art 18(1).

may agree on a more extended delivery period. Consumers can only terminate the contract if the trader fails to deliver the goods within an additional period. In any case, consumers may terminate the contract immediately if the trader refuses to deliver the goods, the agreed delivery date is essential in the circumstances, or the consumer informs the trader of a specific date before ordering the goods.[192] Traders failing to comply with the above rules are obliged to reimburse consumers upon the termination of the contract.[193] In this situation, national recourse remedies may apply, in accordance with Article 18(2) of the Consumer Rights Directive.[194]

The fitness check confirms the relevance of the delivery rules: 22 per cent of complaints with the Commission's ODR system concerned the delivery of goods, with 71 per cent of consumers finding the information on the delivery important in the decision-making process.[195]

Article 18 provides consumers with a strong remedy, but one would have to order the goods to verify trader compliance. This consumer right is consequently not taken into account in the empirical examination. Nonetheless, further observations on delivery times are provided in the discussion section of Chapter 6.

3.1.6 Alternative and Online Dispute Resolution

Traders may offer consumers the possibility of resolving a dispute via alternative dispute resolution (ADR) or online dispute resolution (ODR). However, traders must inform consumers of the existence of these dispute resolution mechanisms and the method of accessing them.[196] The Directive on Consumer Alternative Dispute Resolution[197] and the Regulation on Consumer Online Dispute

[192] ibid art 18(2); Grundmann (n 79) 119; Christina Markou, 'Directive 2011/83/EU on Consumer Rights' in Lodder and Murray (n 6) 226–27.

[193] Consumer Rights Directive, art 18(3).

[194] ibid art 18(4); Weatherill (n 70) 1305.

[195] SWD(2017) 209 final 28, 68 (Figure 29).

[196] Concerning ADR see art 6(1)(t) of the Consumer Rights Directive in connection with art 13 of the Consumer ADR Directive. As for ODR see art 6(1)(t) of the Consumer Rights Directive in connection with art 14 of Regulation (EU) 524/2013 (ODR Regulation).

[197] Directive (EU) 2013/11 on alternative dispute resolution for consumer disputes and amending Regulation (EC) No 2006/2004 and Directive 2009/22/EC [2013] OJ L165/63 (Consumer ADR Directive). The Directive on Consumer ADR came into force in July 2013, and Member States had to set up an ADR infrastructure by July 2015. The Directive requires the ADR institution to hear and decide on the complaint within 90 days (Consumer ADR Directive, art 8(e)). To be recognized as ADR institutions, the ADR providers need to fulfil 6 requirements: (1) must have expertise, be independent, and impartial (art 6 of the Consumer ADR Directive); (2) must be transparent (art 7 of the Consumer ADR Directive); (3) work effectively, resolving consumer disputes within 90 days (art 8 of the Consumer ADR Directive); (4) the proceedings should be fair (art 9 of the Consumer ADR Directive); (5) respect the principles of liberty, meaning that consumers are only bound by the decision if they consented to it (art 10 of the Consumer ADR Directive); and (6) legality, meaning that consumers cannot waive their mandatory rights under European Union and national law (art 11 of the Consumer ADR Directive). See generally

Resolution[198] provide further details on consumer ADR and ODR. According to the Consumer Rights Directive, providing for ADR or ODR is not a pre-contractual requirement.[199] Instead, Regulation (EU) 524/2013 mandates that traders display an electronic link to the European Commission's Online Dispute Resolution platform on their website.[200] It allows traders and consumers to submit their claims to a certified institution that provides ADR or ODR. Both ADR and ODR co-exist with regular redress mechanisms and are an accessible, fast, and cost-efficient mechanisms compared to legal proceedings in court.[201] Taking part in ADR or ODR is optional, so neither traders nor consumers can be forced to participate in out-of-court proceedings.[202] The optional nature of the dispute resolution mechanism is the Achilles' heel of the current system, and consumers might consequently not be offered access to them in a dispute. The Commission's investigation into trader compliance neglected this because it only revealed that 45 per cent of traders failed to provide the link.[203] The empirical part of the book thus not only examines compliance with the trader's duty to display the link to the Commission's ODR platform in their terms and conditions[204] but also measures whether traders are willing to participate in ODR.[205]

Naomi Creutzfeldt, 'Alternative Dispute Resolution for Consumers' in Michael Stürner, Fernando Gascón Inchausti, and Remo Caponi (eds), *The Role of Consumer ADR in the Administration of Justice: New Trends in Access to Justice under EU Directive 2013/11* (Sellier European Law Publishers 2015) 3 ff.

198 Regulation (EU) 524/2013 on online dispute resolution for consumer disputes and amending Regulation (EC) No 2006/2004 and Directive 2009/22/EC [2013] OJ L165/1 (Regulation on Consumer ODR). The Regulation on Consumer ODR placed an obligation on the European Commission to set-up an ODR mechanism through which traders and consumers can solve their dispute online (ODR Regulation, art 5). The European Commission has implemented this requirement by launching the ODR online platform. See European Commission, 'Online Dispute Resolution: Resolve your online consumer problem fairly and efficiently' (2020) https://ec.europa.eu/consumers/odr/main/?event=main.home.show (accessed 6 December 2020); Creutzfeld (n 197).

199 Consumer Rights Directive, art 6(1)(t).

200 ODR Regulation, art 14(1); Pablo Cortés, *The Law of Consumer Redress in an Evolving Digital Market: Upgrading from Alternative to Online Dispute Resolution* (CUP 2017) 132–37.

201 For a general overview of the ODR and ADR regime on the EU and national level see eg Pablo Cortés, 'The New Landscape of Consumer Redress: The European Directive on Consumer Alternative Dispute Resolution and the Regulation on Online Dispute Resolution' in Pablo Cortés (ed), *The New Regulatory Framework for Consumer Dispute Resolution* (OUP 2016) 17 ff.

202 Consumer ADR Directive, art 10(2). Furthermore, the fitness check highlighted that the European Commission does not record outcomes of disputes, eg consumer satisfaction. See SWD(2017) 209 final 28.

203 European Commission (n 180).

204 Case C-380/19 *Bundesverband der Verbraucherzentralen und Verbraucherverbände: Verbraucherzentrale Bundesverband eV v Deutsche Apotheker- und Ärztebank eG* ECLI:EU:C:2020:498, where the Court of Justice confirmed that traders are required to display the hyperlink to the ODR platform in their general terms and conditions (according to art 13 of the Consumer ADR Directive), and that it 'is not sufficient in that respect that the trader either provides that information in other documents accessible on his website, or under other tabs thereof, or provides that information to the consumer in a separate document from the general terms and conditions, upon conclusion of the contract subject to those general terms and conditions' (para 36).

205 The present study will also track instances where traders referred to other ODR platforms. Another development has been that some e-commerce traders introduced their platform Online Dispute Resolution schemes. For example, eBay, one of the largest e-commerce platforms and most

3.2 Comparative Notes on the Implementation

The previous subsection revealed that the Consumer Rights Directive introduced new substantive rules and increased the level of protection for consumers. For instance, the right of withdrawal has been expanded from seven days to 14 days in France, the Netherlands, and the United Kingdom. The Directive thus harmonized several rules on the EU level.[206] Furthermore, in line with the Better Regulation agenda, the Directive was backed with evidence, but not all consumer theories or studies confirmed the legislative choices. It is, however, a significant improvement, especially compared to the process regarding the Unfair Contract Terms Directive.

4 Conclusion

In conclusion, this chapter delved into the legal obligations imposed upon traders through national regulations implementing the E-Commerce Directive and the Consumer Rights Directive. These rules serve as the yardstick against which trader compliance will be measured. The chapter first scrutinized the E-Commerce Directive's intricacies, examining how the Member States adopted it and whether they deviated from its minimum harmonization standard. The investigation revealed only minor technical disparities and one noteworthy divergence between national implementing laws and the Directive. France stands out as the sole jurisdiction among those examined, surpassing the E-Commerce Directive's standard by mandating the provision of terms and conditions in the French language as a minimum requirement.[207] The examination of the Consumer Rights Directive remained limited to the European Union context because it is a maximum harmonization instrument, leaving no room for Member States to deviate from its standard. Any options allowing such divergence, falling beyond the scope of this study, were not examined.

established ODR provider, allows traders and consumers to resolve their disputes on their platform without going to court or paying a fee. Louis F Del Duca, Colin Rule, and Kathryn Rimpfel, 'eBay's De Facto Low Value High Volume Resolution Process: Lessons and Best Practices for ODR Systems Designers' (2014) 6 Yearbook on Arbitration and Mediation 204.

[206] The CJEU's case law also interpreted specific provisions and principles, further harmonizing the European Consumer Contract Law Acquis. The European Commission has compiled the most relevant developments in a guidance document. See European Commission, 'Guidance on the interpretation and application of Directive 2011/83/EU of the European Parliament and of the Council on consumer rights' [2021] OJ C525/1.

[207] Code de la consommation, art L224-76.

The overarching objective of this inquiry was also to ascertain whether empirical evidence informed the legislative decisions underpinning these 2 Directives. By doing so, the book seeks to shed light on the rationale behind these legal frameworks and their implications for stakeholders. The chapter depicted increased utilization and enhancement of evidence from the E-Commerce Directive to the Consumer Rights Directive. The E-Commerce Directive lacked a real scientific grounding, while the Consumer Rights Directive showcased sophistication with some caveats.

This chapter marks the conclusion of the book's first part, carefully examining the regulatory landscape governing e-commerce transactions. The following empirical inquiry will assess trader compliance against these legal provisions.

5
Research Design

1 Introduction

At the heart of this book lies the empirical investigation into the levels of compliance of e-commerce traders with consumer protection rules and the reasons underlying it. Earlier chapters have provided the foundation for the empirical case study of the book. Chapter 1 addressed the objectives and methods used, including the use of content analysis and its limitations. The second chapter outlined how the European Commission gathers evidence and its role in the political discourse. The third and fourth chapters explored the European Union and national rules that apply to e-commerce sales transactions and whether evidence and consumer theories support the legislative choices. The present chapter is concerned with the book's research design, specifically how the following empirical inquiry defines, measures, and analyses levels of compliance. It focuses on the choice of specific definitions and interpretations, how the study confirms or rejects the hypotheses, and how it attempts to translate the empirical findings into policy recommendations. Setting out the research design is indispensable. It not only concretizes the scope of the empirical part of the book but also reveals some of its methodological challenges. There is another reason why an in-depth engagement with the methodology is necessary, which has to do with the nature of this study. Empirical legal research requires full transparency on why and how data is collected and analysed.

This chapter begins by introducing the hypotheses and expected findings of the case study and critically examines previous studies. It then discusses how it translates consumer rights and the objective characteristics of the simulated purchases into dependent and independent variables. The chapter also deals with how it generated the data for the case study. Because there was no existing dataset available when the research started, it was necessary to create a dataset by simulating 300 e-commerce consumer purchases in 4 jurisdictions: France, Germany, the Netherlands, and the United Kingdom. In the next step, the chapter outlines the techniques for the data analysis, including

Compliance with European Consumer Law. Felix Pflücke, Oxford University Press. © Oxford University Press 2024.
DOI: 10.1093/9780198906414.003.0005

the measurement of the levels of compliance, the statistical tools used, and the visualization of the findings. Finally, the chapter concludes by reflecting upon some of the methodological challenges of the empirical inquiry.

2 Hypotheses

This section outlines several hypotheses and expectations derived from the broader debate on compliance with European consumer contract law. The present study collected data to determine the levels of compliance in the sampled contracts (H_1) and to investigate the subsequent correlation between the compliance levels and such factors as the size of the trader's company (H_2), the incorporation date of the trader's enterprise (H_3), and the use of standard contract terms that are drafted and provided by public or semi-public organizations (H_4). The following subsections define the hypotheses.

2.1 Non-compliance Hypothesis

Research on compliance has shown that contract terms are biased to the advantage of e-commerce traders.[1] All 3 studies examining compliance with European Union rules used content analysis to gather the data; all 3 studies have also referred to consumer rights on the EU level and not the national level. For instance, Loos and Luzak scrutinized the terms and conditions of 4 online service providers and assessed whether these providers complied with 7 consumer rights under the Unfair Contract Terms Directive. The scope of that study differs from the one carried out in the present inquiry because on the one hand, Loos and Luzak focused on service contracts rather than on the sale of goods. Another substantial difference is that the authors did not evaluate the terms and conditions against all consumer rights under the Directive and did not consider national law, which is crucial because it is a minimum harmonization Directive. Srivastava, as well as Donnelly and Whit, on the other

[1] See Marco Loos and Joasia A Luzak, 'Wanted: A Bigger Stick. On Unfair Terms in Consumer Contracts with Online Service Providers' (2016) 39(1) Journal of Consumer Policy 63; Aashish Srivastava, 'The New EU Consumer Rights Directive: An Empirical Study on Compliance Issues by E-Tailers' (2017) 32(4) Journal of Business Law 282; Mary Donnelly and Fidelma Whit, 'Digital content and consumer protection: An empirical study of supplier compliance with consumer information obligations' (2019) 35(6) Computer Law & Security Review 1. Similar evidence emerged in the United States. See Florencia Marotta-Wurgler, 'Competition and the Quality of Standard Form Contracts: The Case of Software License Agreements' (2008) 5(3) Journal of Empirical Legal Studies 447.

hand, scrutinized compliance of online sales in light of the Consumer Rights Directive, a maximum harmonization instrument, but included only a subset of the rights taken into account by the present book. In addition to the above-mentioned academic studies, the European Commission carried out an EU-wide study to determine trader compliance with the right of withdrawal, the minimum 2-year legal guarantee, the duty to disclose the full purchase price on the website, to refer to online dispute resolution (ODR), and to comply with the Geo-blocking Regulation.[2]

All studies were much smaller in sample size; that is, the number of traders but, most importantly, these studies neither investigated the causes of non-compliance nor covered the rights consumers have under national law. It is of interest to establish whether e-commerce traders comply in full with the national rules stemming from the 3 selected European Union instruments. In light of the surrounding academic literature and examined empirical evidence, the first hypothesis (H_1) that the inquiry will verify is: 'E-commerce consumer contracts do not comply in full with the selected legal duties stemming from the national rules implementing the Unfair Contract Terms Directive, the E-Commerce Directive, and the Consumer Rights Directive.'

2.2 Company Size Hypothesis

A recent study by the Competition and Markets Authority (CMA) on the familiarity of businesses in the United Kingdom (where the number of businesses asked was 1,250) with the Consumer Rights Act 2015 (CRA 2015) revealed that company size had an overall positive influence on awareness of their legal duties: the larger a company, the more aware the members were of the consumer rights contained in the CRA 2015.[3] Nonetheless, only 19 per cent of large businesses were familiar with the CRA 2015. Loos and Luzak provided

[2] European Commission, 'Online shopping: Commission and Consumer Protection authorities urge traders to bring information policy in line with EU law' (31 January 2020) https://ec.europa.eu/commission/presscorner/detail/en/IP_20_156 (accessed 12 August 2020). Chapter 2.3 of the present book examines further studies of the European Commission, but they fail to provide academically significant results and are thus not included again.

[3] Competition and Markets Authority/IFF Research, 'Unfair Contract Terms Research' Competition and Markets Authority (19 October 2016) 40 https://assets.publishing.service.gov.uk/government/uploads/system/uploads/attachment_data/file/561518/UK_businesses__understanding_of_unfair_terms_in_consumer_contracts__IFF_Research_.pdf (accessed 29 April 2020). A smaller study on rights awareness was also conducted by the European Commission. See European Commission, 'Consumer Conditions Scoreboard: Consumers at home in the Single Market' (October 2017) http://ec.europa.eu/newsroom/just/document.cfm?action=display&doc_id=45983 (accessed 3 September 2020).

additional evidence concerning the compliance of large enterprises with the Unfair Contract Terms Directive, whereas Facebook, twitter, Google, and Dropbox used service terms that '[would be] unlikely to pass the Directive's unfairness test'.[4] However, their sample consisted only of these 4 large enterprises. According to a policy paper of the European Commission, larger companies are 'more likely to receive complaints'.[5] However, their study failed to determine whether that is due to more instances of non-compliance or merely due to higher sales. Adding to the debate about trader compliance within the European Union, Marotta-Wurgler investigated whether, in the United States, there was a correlation between the trader's market share and the quality of its terms and conditions, establishing no significant correlation.[6]

The empirical evidence seems divided on this issue but suggests that larger traders are more aware of their legal duties. Further research is necessary to determine whether company size affects compliance, hence the second hypothesis (H_2): 'Large e-commerce traders are more likely to comply with the selected consumer protection rights than small and medium-sized enterprises.'

2.3 Incorporation Date Hypothesis

Traders that have been in business for longer should have fewer violations than recently incorporated enterprises because they have more experience and expertise in their trade. However, one could argue that traders who have been in business for longer use outdated terms and conditions because they fail to update them. Existing research has attempted to explore whether company age affects compliance. For instance, the UK CMA included company age as an independent variable in their Unfair Contract Terms Study from October 2016.[7] However, the CMA researchers capped the age variable only at 999 years. It might explain why they did not receive statistically robust results for the report's final discussion section.[8]

[4] Loos and Luzak (n 1) 88.

[5] European Commission (n 3) 57.

[6] Florencia Marotta-Wurgler, 'Competition and the Quality of Standard Form Contracts: The Case of Software License Agreements' (2008) 5(3) Journal of Empirical Legal Studies 471, 474–75.

[7] Competition and Markets Authority/IFF Research (n 3) 20–21. Nonetheless, it is worth noting that, in addition to the size of the enterprise, reviewing the terms and conditions frequently increased familiarity with the CRA 2015; Competition and Markets Authority/IFF Research (n 3) 55–56.

[8] Florencia Marotta-Wurgler has provided statistical evidence that company age might influence compliance in standard terms. She capped the company age variable at 25 years; see Marotta-Wurgler (n 6) 458. In addition, see Florencia Marotta-Wurgler, 'Are "Pay Now, Terms Later" Contracts Worse for Buyers? Evidence from Software License Agreements' (2009) 38(2) The Journal of Legal Studies 334.

The analysis carried out in this study will attempt to verify the claim that company age affects compliance. To carry out this verification effectively, the incorporation date will be capped at 30 years, as it is unlikely that traders were involved in online sales before 1989.[9] Nonetheless, the study will carry out the same test without capping the company age. Therefore, the third hypothesis (H_3) of the empirical examination is: 'E-commerce traders that have operated on the market for a longer time are more likely to comply with the selected consumer rights selected compared to companies that were incorporated more recently.'

2.4 Pre-drafted Terms Hypothesis

Public or semi-public bodies sometimes provide pre-drafted standard terms and conditions, as recommended by the European Commission in 2001[10] and reinforced in 2003[11] and 2004.[12] Traders that use these pre-drafted standard terms should, in theory, comply with all applicable consumer protection rules.[13] It is interesting whether empirical data can confirm this claim. However, it is impossible to determine how many traders based their terms on pre-drafted terms before the data collection. Equally, traders who used the pre-drafted terms may not have done it faithfully or incorrectly. For example, they may have changed them to some degree to provide a higher level of protection. Thus, the first stage of the evaluation will establish whether a trader has used pre-drafted standard terms. The study will establish it by comparing the sampled set of terms to pre-drafted standard terms available online. In this way, the study will determine the number of traders using pre-drafted standard

[9] See generally European Commission, 'The European Digital Single Market: Its Role in Economic Activity in the EU' (2015) 6ff https://ec.europa.eu/jrc/sites/jrcsh/files/JRC98723.pdf (accessed 22 November 2020). John Fernie, Leigh Sparks, and Alan McKinnon, 'Retail logistics in the UK: past, present and future' (2010) 38(11) International Journal of Retail & Distribution Management 894.

[10] European Commission, 'European Contract Law' (Communication) COM(2001) 398 final, para 56.

[11] European Commission, 'A more coherent European contract law: An action plan' (Communication) COM(2003) OJ C63/1.

[12] Commission, 'European Contract Law and the revision of the acquis: the way forward' (Communication) COM(2004) 651 final, para 2.2.3.

[13] See generally Jens Karsten and Ali R Sinai, 'The Action Plan on European Contract Law: Perspectives for the Future of European Contract Law and EC Consumer Law' (2003) 26(2) Journal of Consumer Policy 168; Ulf Bernitz, 'The Commission's Communications and Standard Contract Terms' in Stefan Vogenauer and Stephen Weatherill (eds), *The Harmonisation of European Contract Law: Implication for European Private Laws, Business and Legal Practice* (Hart Publishing 2006) 189–90; Giuditta Cordero-Moss, 'Standard contract terms as an alternative to legislation' in Christian Twigg-Flesner (ed), *Research Handbook on EU Consumer and Contract Law* (Edward Elgar Publishing 2016).

terms and the scale of the changes. When a trader bases even small parts of its terms and conditions on pre-drafted ones, such as the structure, the trader's terms will count as being based on pre-drafted terms. Chapter 7.2 will include additional observations on the terms used by traders who relied on pre-drafted terms. This approach allows for a more case-by-case approach, and it will be interesting to see where traders depart from terms pre-drafted by public or semi-public organizations. Section 5 of this chapter outlines further details concerning the data collection process. The 4th and final hypothesis (H_4) is: 'E-commerce traders that base their terms and conditions on pre-drafted standard contract terms are more likely to comply with the selected consumer rights.'

3 Defining and Measuring Compliance

The present study will use dependent variables to investigate whether the sampled consumer contracts comply with the selected consumer rights. It will divide the legal duties stemming from the national rules implementing the 3 Directives into 35 dependent variables. Each variable represents one consumer right in a business-to-consumer online purchase. The present study groups the variables into several categories: unfair contract terms; information and formal requirements, including the rules governing access to alternative or online dispute resolution; right of withdrawal; and the passing of risk.

The book developed a compliance scale to measure the contracts' compliance levels with the rules selected in this study (Table 5.1 below). Determining the

Table 5.1 Compliance Scale

Compliance Scale	Implications for Dependent Variable	Exceptions
1	The trader does not comply with this rule	1.4 in case of omissions. Finer distinctions in case of unfair contract terms (Table 5.2 below)
2	The trader does not provide information concerning this rule	In case of a positive duty to inform, a score of 1.4
3	The trader complies with this rule	
4	The trader provides a higher standard than required by this rule	Sometimes not possible

levels of compliance is critical for the statistical analysis. The compliance scale ranges from 1 to 4. A score of 1 means that the provision in the contract has a lower standard than the applicable rules. A score of 2 implies that the contract is silent and does not address the consumer right at stake. A score of 3 stands for the same standard as in the applicable rules. A score of 4 means the contract provides a higher standard. It is worth noting that the numbers are only used as value-neutral variables to make the compliance levels visible.

The compliance scale has to reflect the nature of the legal duties, as traders' duties are both positive and negative. On the one hand, positive duties require that traders act, for example, to provide certain information. Negative duties, on the other hand, require that traders refrain from doing something, such as inserting an unfair contract term into their terms and conditions. As a result, not including a specific term in a contract might result in a score of 1 (non-compliance) in case of a positive duty but a score of 2 (silence) in the case of a negative duty.

The research design adapts the compliance scale to each legal scenario (Tables 5.3 to 5.6). A good example is mandatory disclosures, where traders have a positive duty to provide certain information: it is, for instance, not possible to provide a higher level of protection, while at the same time, an omission counts as non-compliance. It is worth adding that this scale does not measure how far traders deviate from the particular rule. It is impossible to obtain a lower compliance score because of 2 violations of the same consumer right. There is also no further subdivision of the levels of compliance: one non-compliance is enough for a score of 1. Traders may also provide contract terms that go beyond the statutory rules, which justifies the need for an additional variable: a score of 4.

However, the research design draws finer distinctions concerning the rules prohibiting unfair contract terms. Chapter 3 established that the nature of the national rules requires such a differentiation because 3 levels of unfairness exist: (1) a term may be unfair under the general test; (2) a term is presumed unfair under a 'grey list' with limited judicial discretion; (3) a term is considered unfair without the possibility of judicial (re-)evaluation (ie 'black-listed'). The empirical analysis must reflect the diverging rules. Otherwise, the study would ignore the intentions of the national legislators, who provided for a hierarchy of norms, ie they gave each legal scenario a different weight. The compliance scale considers these differences and introduces further subcategories, namely scores of 1.1 to 1.3 (Table 5.2).

The following tables will present the selected consumer rights (dependent variables) and their corresponding scores. As mentioned above, the compliance scale (or scoring system) will adapt to every dependent variable.

Table 5.2 Levels of Non-Compliance Unfair Contract Terms

Category	Definition	Jurisdictions
1.1	'General test': the court must assess the contract terms. Contract terms falling within the scope of the Directive's Annex are suspected to be unfair	France (Article L212-1); Germany (§ 307); the Netherlands (Article 6:233(a)); the United Kingdom (section 62 in connection with Schedule 2)
1.2	'Grey list': terms are presumed to be unfair with limited judicial discretion	France (Article L212-1 in connection with Article R212-2); Germany § 308); the Netherlands (Article 6:237 in connection with Article 6:233(a))
1.3	'Black list': such terms are always unfair with no judicial discretion	France (Article L212-1 in connection with Article R212-1); Germany (§ 309); the Netherlands (Article 6:236); the United Kingdom (sections 31 and 65; penalty clause doctrine and assignment) EU (invalid jurisdiction and choice of law clauses)

Notes: The Code de la consommation contains the French rules; the BGB the German rules; the BW the Dutch provisions; and the CRA 2015 the UK rules. See Chapter 3.3 and Chapter 3.4 for a detailed examination of the national differences.

3.1 Unfair Contract Terms Directive

In Table 5.3 below, a trader needs to score 22 points to align with the underlying rules fully and, in addition, must never attain a score of 1. The rules governing unfair terms do not confer a positive duty upon traders but a negative one, which means that traders must not include an unfair term in their standard terms. Silence is tracked separately from compliance but, for the empirical examination, it falls within the compliance category (a score of 3). As mentioned, violations are further subcategorized into 3 categories (Table 5.2 above). Table 5.4 will provide how each Member State addresses the unfair terms scenarios selected for the study to track lower standards (a score of 1) and compliance (a score of 3).

3.2 E-Commerce Directive

To align with the underlying rules, a trader must achieve 12 points in the information and formal requirements section (Table 5.5 below). In addition, a trader must never receive a score of 1. The information and formal requirements

Table 5.3 Dependent Variables and Compliance Scale Unfair Contract Terms Directive

Dependent Variables	Article (Annex 1)	Text of the Directive	Compliance Scale
Unfair Contract Terms			
X1	(a)	[E]xcluding or limiting the legal liability of a seller or supplier in the event of the death of a consumer or personal injury to the latter resulting from an act or omission of that seller or supplier	1 = lower 2 = silence 3 = same
X2	(b)	[I]nappropriately excluding or limiting the legal rights of the consumer vis-à-vis the seller or supplier or another party in the event of total or partial non-performance or inadequate performance by the seller or supplier of any of the contractual obligations, including the option of offsetting a debt owed to the seller or supplier against any claim which the consumer may have against him	1 = lower 2 = silence 3 = same
X3	(d)	[P]ermitting the seller or supplier to retain sums paid by the consumer where the latter decides not to conclude or perform the contract, without providing for the consumer to receive compensation of an equivalent amount from the seller or supplier where the latter is the party cancelling the contract	1 = lower 2 = silence 3 = same
X4	(e)	[R]equiring any consumer who fails to fulfil his obligation to pay a disproportionately high sum in compensation	1 = lower 2 = silence 3 = same
X5	(j)	[E]nabling the seller or supplier to alter the terms of the contract unilaterally without a valid reason which is specified in the contract	1 = lower 2 = silence 3 = same
X6	(k)	[E]nabling the seller or supplier to alter unilaterally without a valid reason any characteristics of the product or service to be provided	1 = lower 2 = silence 3 = same

X7	(l)	[P]roviding for the price of goods to be determined at the time of delivery or allowing a seller of goods or supplier of services to increase their price without in both cases giving the consumer the corresponding right to cancel the contract if the final price is too high in relation to the price agreed when the contract was concluded	1 = lower 2 = silence 3 = same
X8	(m)	[G]iving the seller or supplier the right to determine whether the goods or services supplied are in conformity with the contract, or giving him the exclusive right to interpret any term of the contract	1 = lower 2 = silence 3 = same
X9	(o)	[O]bliging the consumer to fulfil all his obligations where the seller or supplier does not perform his	1 = lower 2 = silence 3 = same
X10	(p)	[G]iving the seller or supplier the possibility of transferring his rights and obligations under the contract, where this may serve to reduce the guarantees for the consumer, without the latter's agreement	1 = lower 2 = silence 3 = same
X11	(q)	[E]xcluding or hindering the consumer's right to take legal action or exercise any other legal remedy, particularly by requiring the consumer to take disputes exclusively to arbitration not covered by legal provisions, unduly restricting the evidence available to him or imposing on him a burden of proof which, according to the applicable law, should lie with another party to the contract	1 = lower 2 = silence 3 = same

Notes: The study adapted the text of the Directive. Chapter 3 provides further details.

Table 5.4 Dependent Variables of the National Rules Implementing the UCTD

Dependent Variables	CJEU Case Law	France	Germany	The Netherlands	The United Kingdom
X1	No	Article R212-1 no 6	§ 309 No 7 lit. a	Article 6:237(f)	Section 65 Schedule 2 Part 1(1)
X2	No	Article R212-1 no 6 and no 7	§ 309 No 8 of the BGB in connection with §§ 309 No 3 and No 7 lit. b	Articles 6:236(a), (b), and (c) Articles 6:237(b), (c), (f), and (g)	Section 31 Schedule 2 Part 1(2)
X3	No	Article R212-2 no 2	§ 308 No 7 §§ 309 No 5 and No 6	Articles 6:237(f) and (i)	Schedule 2 Part 1(4)
X4	Yes	Article R212-2 no 3	§§ 309 No 5 and No 6	Article 6:237(i) Articles 6:91-6:94 of the BW	Penalty clause doctrine Schedule 2 Part 1(5) and (6)
X5	Yes	Article R212-1 no 3 Article R212-2 no 6	§ 308 No 4	Article 6:236(i) Article 6:237(c)	Schedule 2 Part 1(11) and (12)
X6	No	Article R212-1 no 3	§ 308 No 4	Article 6:237(c)	Schedule 2 Part 1(13)
X7	Yes	Article R212-1 no 3	§ 309 No 1	Article 6:236(i)	Schedule 2 Part 1(14) and (15)
X8	No	Article R212-1 no 4	§§ 309 No 7 and No 8	Article 6:236(d)	Schedule 2 Part 1(16)
X9	No	Article R212-1 no 5	§§ 309 No 2 and No 8	Article 6:236(b) and (c)	Schedule 2 Part 1(18)
X10	No	Article R212-2 no 5	§ 309 No 10	Article 6:236(e)	Assignment Schedule 2 Part 1(19)
X11	Yes	Article R212-1 no 12 Articles R212-2 no 9 and no 10	§§ 309 No 12 and No 14	Article 6:236(n) and (k)	Section 31 Schedule 2 Part 1(20)

Notes: The Code de la consommation contains the French rules; the BGB the German rules; the BW the Dutch provisions; and the CRA 2015 the UK rules. Article R212-1 and Article R212-2, § 308, Article 6:237, and Schedule 2 must be read in connection with the national general test of unfairness, see Table 5.2. For a detailed examination of the national differences see Chapter 3.3 and Chapter 3.4.

Table 5.5 Dependent Variables and Compliance Scale E-Commerce Directive

Dependent Variable	Article	Text of the Directive	Compliance Scale
Information and Formal Requirements			
Y1	5(1)(d)	[W]here the service provider is registered in a trade or similar public register, the trade register in which the service provider is entered and his registration number, or equivalent means of identification in that register	1 = lower 3 = same
Y2	5(1)(g)	[W]here the service provider undertakes an activity that is subject to VAT, the identification number referred to in Article 22(1) of the sixth Council Directive 77/388/EEC of 17 May 1977 on the harmonisation of the laws of the Member States relating to turnover taxes—Common system of value added tax: uniform basis of assessment (2)	1 = lower 3 = same
Y3	10(1)(a)	[T]he different technical steps to follow to conclude the contract	1 = lower 3 = same
Y4	10(1)(d)	[T]he languages offered for the conclusion of the contract	1 = lower 3 = same

Notes: The study adapted the text of the Directive. Chapter 4.2 provides further details.

place a positive duty upon traders. An omission of such a disclosure automatically breaches the consumer protection rules, so it receives a score of 1. Under these circumstances, traders cannot obtain a higher score, as the traders either provide all the required information or fail to do so. Chapter 4 examined all rules implementing the outlined standard in Table 5.5. The chapter has established that the national rules implementing the Directive differ only on a technical level. Only France has decided to enact stricter rules concerning the language requirement,[14] obliging traders to provide the contract terms in French.[15] Consequently, an additional table pointing out the national divergences is unnecessary.

3.3 Consumer Rights Directive

To align fully with the underlying rules, a trader must achieve 33 points in the information and formal requirements section, including the alternative dispute resolution (ADR)/ODR section (Table 5.6). Traders also need to

[14] E-Commerce Directive, art 10(1)(d).

[15] For B2C contracts see art L224-76 of the Code de la consommation. For B2B contracts see art 1127-1 no 3 of the Code Civil. Chapter 4.2.1 (Language Requirement) provides further details.

Table 5.6 Dependent Variables and Compliance Scale Consumer Rights Directive

Dependent Variable	Article	Text of the Directive	Compliance Scale
Information and Formal Requirements			
Z1a	6(1)(a)	The main characteristics of the goods or services, to the extent appropriate to the medium and to the goods or services. [displayed before consumers place their order (Article 8(2))]	1 = lower 3 = same
Z1b	6(1)(b)	The identity of the trader, such as his trading name.	1 = lower 3 = same
Z1c	6(1)(c)	The geographical address at which the trader is established or the geographical address and identity of the trader on whose behalf he is acting.	1 = lower 3 = same
Z1d	6(1)(e)	The total price of the goods or services inclusive of taxes. [displayed before consumers place their order (Article 8(2))]	1 = lower 3 = same
Z1e	6(1)(g)	The arrangements for payment [. . .]	1 = lower 3 = same
Z1f	6(1)(g)	[. . .] the time by which the trader undertakes to deliver the goods [. . .]	1 = lower 3 = same
Z1g(i)	6(1)(h)	Where a right of withdrawal exists, the conditions, time limit and procedures for exercising that right in accordance with Article 11(1) [CRD] [. . .]	1 = lower 3 = same
Z1g(ii)	6(1)(h)	[. . .] as well as the model withdrawal form set out in Annex I (B) [CRD].	1 = lower 3 = same
Z1h	6(1)(l)	A reminder of the existence of a legal guarantee of conformity for goods. [i.e. with national rules]	1 = lower 3 = same
Z1i	8(1)	With respect to distance contracts, the trader shall give the information provided for in Article 6 (1) [CRD] or make that information available to the consumer in a way appropriate to the means of distance communication used in plain and intelligible language. In so far as that information is provided on a durable medium, it shall be legible.	1 = lower 3 = same

Right of Withdrawal			
Z2a(i)	9(1)	The consumer has a 14 days period to withdraw from distance [. . .] contract [. . .]	1 = lower 2 = silence 3 = same 4 = higher
Z2a(ii)	9(1)	[. . .] without giving any reason.	1 = lower 2 = silence 3 = same
Z2b	9(2)b	[I]n the case of sales contracts, the day on which the consumer or a third party other than the carrier and indicated by the consumer acquires physical possession of the goods.	1 = lower 2 = silence 3 = same 4 = higher
Z2c	9(2)b(i)	[I]n the case of multiple goods ordered by the consumer in one order and delivered separately, the day on which the consumer or a third party other than the carrier and indicated by the consumer acquires physical possession of the last good.	1 = lower 2 = silence 3 = same 4 = higher
Z2d	9, 13(2), 14(1)	**The right of withdrawal** may not incur any costs unless **the consumer has expressly opted for a type of delivery other than the least expensive type of standard delivery offered by the trader.** The consumer shall only bear the direct cost of returning the goods unless the trader has agreed to bear them or the trader failed to inform the consumer that the consumer has to bear them.	1 = lower 2 = silence 3 = same 4 = higher
Z2e	14(1)	Unless the trader has offered to collect the goods himself, the consumer shall send back the goods or hand them over to the trader or to a person authorised by the trader to receive the goods, without undue delay and in any event not later than 14 days from the day on which he has communicated his decision to withdraw from the contract to the trader.	1 = lower 2 = silence 3 = same 4 = higher
Z2f	13(1)	The trader shall reimburse all payments received from the consumer, including, if applicable, the costs of delivery without undue delay and in any event not later than 14 days from the day on which he is informed of the consumer's decision to withdraw from the contract in accordance with Article 11. The trader shall carry out the reimbursement referred to in the first subparagraph using the same means of payment as the consumer used for the initial transaction, unless the consumer has expressly agreed otherwise and provided that the consumer does not incur any fees as a result of such reimbursement.	1 = lower 2 = silence 3 = same 4 = higher

(*continued*)

Table 5.6 Continued

Dependent Variable	Article	Text of the Directive	Compliance Scale
Passing of Risk			
Z3a	20	In contracts where the trader dispatches the goods to the consumer, the risk of loss of or damage to the goods shall pass to the consumer when he or a third party indicated by the consumer and other than the carrier has acquired the physical possession of the goods. [. . .]	1 = lower 2 = silence 3 = same 4 = higher
Z3b	20	[. . .] However, the risk shall pass to the consumer upon delivery to the carrier if the carrier was commissioned by the consumer to carry the goods and that choice was not offered by the trader, without prejudice to the rights of the consumer against the carrier.	1 = lower 2 = silence 3 = same 4 = higher
ADR or ODR			
Z4	6(1)(t)	Where applicable, the possibility of having recourse to an out-of-court complaint and redress mechanism, to which the trader is subject, and the methods for having access to it. [i.e. the link to the ODR platform of the European Commission]	1 = lower 3 = same

Notes: The study adapted the text of the Directive. Chapter 4.3 provides further details.

earn 18 points in the remaining categories. Additionally, a trader must never receive a score of 1. Similarly to the consumer rights examined in the previous table, the information and formal requirements must be complied with, and an omission of disclosure automatically violates these requirements. The remaining provisions are optional because there is no positive duty to include a term that deals with a given issue, but the traders who choose to do so must comply.

4 Possible Compliance Factors

The independent variables are the objective characteristics of the contractual relationship, namely the size and age of the trader's enterprise and whether the trader based their terms and conditions on standard contract terms drafted and provided by public or semi-public organizations. Factors such as these may have an impact on compliance. From a statistical viewpoint, the independent variables will also serve as control variables in the statistical analysis in Chapter 6. The following subsection of the present chapter provides details of the data collection and analysis conducted to determine these 3 variables for each trader.

The study categorized traders into small and medium-sized enterprises (SMEs) and large enterprises. The European Commission considers traders a large enterprise when the annual turnover is over €50 million or the yearly balance sheet total exceeds €43 million.[16] In addition, the Commission identified the number of employees as another indicator of large enterprises, namely companies with more than 250 employees. The present study uses the 3 categories because each trader's market share and annual turnover only concerning online sales is unknown. Therefore, using the rough company size of a trader is a good indicator of the financial means of an enterprise. A trader falls within the category of SMEs by default if no company data is available since large traders' company data are publicly available. Large enterprises must register with national authorities and can potentially appear on stock exchanges. In contrast, smaller traders may not need to register their companies or reveal their annual turnovers publicly. The study covers 182 SMEs and 118 large enterprises (Table 5.7). The distribution of the company size seems similar in France, Germany, and the

[16] Commission Recommendation (EC) 2003/361 of 6 May 2003 concerning the definition of micro, small and medium-sized enterprises [2003] OJ L124/36, Annex art 2. When the data was collected for the study in September 2019, the conversion rate for euros into GBP was approximately 1.13.

Table 5.7 Overview Independent Variables

	Large Enterprises	SMEs	Average Age	Average Age (Capped at 30 Years)	Use of Pre-Drafted Terms
Country					
France	33	42	20.17	17.12	0
Germany	34	41	18.29	15.09	0
The Netherlands	16	59	19.64	15.56	56
The United Kingdom	35	40	21.22	16.75	0
Industry					
Electronics	33	27	19.35	16.42	13
Fashion	29	31	21.68	17.88	8
Sports equipment	11	49	13.93	13.57	9
Home decor	24	36	20.49	15.60	13
Print media	21	39	24.82	17.32	13
Company size					
Large			26.09	20.11	14
SME			15.44	13.35	42
Total	**118**	**182**	**19.89**	**16.18**	**56**

Notes: Number of SMEs by default: overall (45); France (2); Germany (22); the Netherlands (13); the United Kingdom (8). Number of businesses without identifiable age: overall (18); France (0); Germany (13); the Netherlands (3); the United Kingdom (2). Average age in years and until 2019. The study rounds all numbers to the nearest two decimal places.

United Kingdom. In contrast, the Netherlands has around half the number of large enterprises compared to the other 3 jurisdictions. Similarly, fewer large companies sell sports equipment than the other 4 products.

Moreover, the study recorded the traders' date of incorporation (age), and, additionally, the age has been capped at 30 years since it is unlikely that any enterprise had a strategy for online sales in the 1980s.[17] Without capping the age, the average age is around 20 years. The average age capped at 30 years is lower, around 16 years. Traders selling sports equipment are significantly younger than those selling the other 4 products. Another observation is that the traders selling print media have been trading the longest when looking at the average age. However, when the study caps the age at 30 years, booksellers come only second (Table 5.7).

[17] See eg Fernie (n 9). Florencia Marotta-Wurgler also capped the company age around the year 1990; see Marotta-Wurgler (n 1) 458.

Dutch traders were the only ones who used pre-drafted terms and conditions. Several German traders included similar provisions on the statutory notice concerning the right of withdrawal (*Widerrufsbelehrung*). However, more is needed to include them in the pre-drafted terms category, as this is a legal requirement. The 56 Dutch traders based their contract terms on pre-drafted terms and conditions are 14 large enterprises and 42 SMEs. The statistical model has to take into account the fact that only Dutch traders are using pre-drafted terms. Otherwise, the model would provide data on the 56 Dutch traders versus French traders, German traders, UK traders, and the remaining 19 Dutch traders.

5 Data Collection

The brief survey of the academic literature on trader compliance revealed that there are no empirical studies on whether consumer contracts used in online transactions conform with all the EU and national rules regulating e-commerce sales. Consequently, there are no pre-existing datasets on the levels of compliance for e-commerce consumer contracts. The raw data in the form of actual consumer contracts was hand-collected specifically for the empirical part of this book. It was done by simulating 300 online purchases within 2 weeks in September 2019, cancelling the transaction immediately prior to placing the order.

The operational population consists of 300 online purchases sampled from 4 jurisdictions; that is, 75 purchases from each of France, Germany, the Netherlands, and the United Kingdom. The study selected goods-selling traders from 5 industries for this simulation: electronics, sports equipment, print media, fashion, and home decor. These goods were popular among consumers at the time the data were collected.[18] The study counted parent companies and subsidiaries as separate entities.

Before initiating the sampling process, the study drafted a data collection manual outlining several measures to restrict sample biases. For instance, the manual's measure involved deleting all cookies on the computer and searching for almost identical goods typically sold by traders in the market.

The study thoroughly examined the website and terms and conditions of the e-commerce traders and saved them as PDFs. It obtained the company size

[18] Eurostat, 'E-commerce statistics for individuals: Figure 4: Online Purchases, EU28, 2018' (2019) https://ec.europa.eu/eurostat/statistics-explained/index.php/E-commerce_statistics_for_individuals#Most_popular_online_purchases (accessed 29 August 2020).

and date of incorporation from the respective national registries: in France from the Chamber of Commerce (*Chambre de commerce et d'industrie*); in Germany from the Ministry of Justice and Consumer Protection (*Ministerium für Justiz und Verbraucherschutz*);[19] in the Netherlands from the Chamber of Commerce (*Kamer van Koophandel*); and in the United Kingdom from the UK Companies House. The study obtained the most recent annual return for each assessment. In cases where the study could not obtain the relevant data from the above sources, it examined the websites of the selected traders or other reliable sources, such as Statista or major news outlets.

The data on the usage of pre-drafted terms and conditions by public or semi-public authorities was obtained by comparing the terms of the traders with each other and conducting online searches for specific clauses contained in these terms. The study detected a variety of providers in this way.[20] It determined the overlap between each trader's terms and pre-drafted terms, and Chapter 7.2 will present further observations.

6 Data Analysis

The study acquired the relevant data from the operational population using content analysis described in Chapter 1.2. This technique is becoming increasingly popular among empirical legal scholars and is integral to qualitative and experimental legal research.[21]

[19] The Ministry of Justice and Consumer Protection coordinates the register (*Gemeinsames Registerportal der Länder*).

[20] Industrie- und Handelskammer (IHK) Schleswig-Holstein, 'Aufbau eines rechtssicheren Online-Shops' (2017) https://www.ihk-schleswig-holstein.de/blob/swhihk24/servicemarken/serviceleistungen/broschueren/1373948/7235c012267d902ad67dd243d271fdac/Broschuere_Aufbau_eines_rechtssicheren_Onlineshops-data.pdf (accessed 9 April 2019). Thuiswinkel Organisatie, 'Algemene Voorwaarden Thuiswinkel' (2017) https://www.thuiswinkel.org/consumenten/wat-is-thuiswinkel-waarborg/algemene-voorwaarden-thuiswinkel (accessed 9 April 2019). Chambre de commerce et d'industrie (CCI) de Paris Ile-de-France, 'Modèle-type de conditions générales' (2014) https://www.entreprises.cci-paris-idf.fr/web/reglementation/contrats-modeles/commerciaux/conditions-generales-de-vente-entre-professionnels (accessed 9 April 2019). Crown Commercial Services (CCS), 'Guidance: short form terms and conditions' CCS (31 July 2015) https://www.gov.uk/government/publications/short-form-terms-and-conditions (accessed 9 April 2019).

[21] Shari Seidman Diamond and Pam Mueller scrutinized 60 law review journals published between 1998 and 2008. They found a sharp increase in the use of empirical legal methods, accounting for almost half of the methodologies used. See Shari Seidman Diamond and Pam Mueller, 'Empirical Legal Scholarship in Law Reviews' (2010) 6 Annual Review of Law and Social Science 581. The increase and importance of this kind of scholarship was, for example, also pointed out in Anne-Lise Sibony, 'Data and arguments: empirical research in consumer law' in Hans-Wolfgang Micklitz, Anne-Lise Sibony, and Fabrizio Esposito (eds), *Research Methods in Consumer Law: A Handbook* (Edward Elgar Publishing 2018). Examples of recent empirical studies using content analysis include Mark A Hall and Ronald F Wright, 'Systematic Content Analysis of Judicial Opinions' (2008) 96(1) California

As stated in this chapter, the study coded the consumer rights examined in Chapters 3 and 4 and transformed them into dependent variables. It matched each dependent variable with the corresponding contract term and assigned levels of compliance, ranging from 1 to 4.

The study utilized a literal approach to interpret the terms and conditions of the websites, as it represents the sole objective means of contract interpretation. The main reason is that consumers do not individually negotiate the contracts; the contractual text is the only available evidence. The sampled contract terms did not give rise to any serious interpretation issues. The study conducted an inter-rater agreement test with 2 external researchers to ensure that the dependent variables and their compliance scale limit the coder's discretion.[22] Due to this process, the study ensures the correct interpretation and application of the 35 selected rules.

Chapter 6 will utilize descriptive statistics to verify the non-compliance hypothesis (H_1). The study will use several tables to demonstrate with which legal scenarios the instances of non-compliance occurred. Statistical models will be used for the correlation analysis to determine whether the company's size (H_2), the company's age (H_3), and the use of pre-drafted terms and conditions (H_4) affect the levels of non-compliance. The correlation test will use the ordinary least squares or linear least squares (OLS) and the binary logistic regression analysis. Whether the 3 hypothesized factors in H_2–H_4 are making compliance 'more likely' is therefore determined by assessing the traders' instances of non-compliance (OLS) and the probability of non-compliance (binary logistic regression); that is, full compliance versus at least some non-compliance. The OLS will be used with a binary logistic regression to determine the overall levels of correlation.[23] Therefore, the study will use a linear and logistic probability

Law Review 63; James Goudkamp and Donal Nolan, 'Contributory Negligence in the Twenty-First Century: An Empirical Study of First Instance Decisions' (2016) 79(4) Modern Law Review 575; Urska Sadl and Henrik Palmer, 'Can Quantitative Methods Complement Doctrinal Legal Studies? Using Citation Network and Corpus Linguistic Analysis to Understand International Courts' (2017) 30(2) Leiden Journal of International Law 327; Gijs van Dijck, 'The Ordered Apology' (2017) 37(3) Oxford Journal of Legal Studies 562; Adam Chilton and Mila Versteeg, *How Constitutional Rights Matter* (OUP 2020); and Jan Zglinski, *Europe's Passive Virtues: Deference to National Authorities in EU Free Movement Law* (OUP 2020).

[22] For a good example of how the test is applied in practice see Gijs van Dijck, 'Victim-Oriented Tort Law in Action: An Empirical Examination of Catholic Church Sexual Abuse Cases' (2018) 15(1) Journal of Empirical Legal Studies 142. See further Neil J Salkind, 'Reliability of Scores' in Neil J Salkind (ed), *Encyclopedia of Research Design* (SAGE 2010); Thomas Benesch, *Schlüsselkonzepte zur Statistik* (Springer Publishing 2012) 59–60.

[23] For a general overview and comparison of the 2 methods see eg John Pohlman and Dennis Leitner, 'A Comparison of Ordinary Least Squares and Logistic Regression' (2003) 103(5) Ohio Journal of Science 118.

method to measure whether there is a correlation between the instances of non-compliance and the independent variables. The independent variables will also serve as the control variables in the statistical model.

7 Conclusion

This chapter has provided an in-depth account of the empirical case study's research design. As depicted above, data collection and analysis are time-consuming and face methodological challenges. The study made numerous changes based on evaluations, inter-rater tests, and other factors, which similar projects often overlook. Other challenges included the selection of consumer rights, lack of harmonization in several areas of European consumer contract law, and selecting an appropriate dataset size. These challenges have shaped the research design, improving the empirical case study's robustness.

6
Empirical Examination of Trader Compliance

1 Introduction

In the preceding 3 chapters, the book delved into the content of European Union and national consumer protection regulations, as outlined in Chapters 3 and 4, and explored methods accurately to measure compliance with these rules, as discussed in Chapter 5. In the current chapter, the book unveils the outcomes of the statistical analysis, drawing from data collected during the examination of 300 traders' adherence to selected consumer rights, amounting to a total of 11,400 observations. This empirical inquiry uses the data gathered to validate the 4 hypotheses outlined in Chapter 5, employing a combination of descriptive and statistical methodologies. Section 3 of this chapter provides comprehensive insights into compliance with each of the 35 selected consumer rights, shedding light on discernible patterns of non-compliance. The final section delves into additional observations, including violations of consumer protection rules that fall outside the scope of the study.

2 Hypotheses Tests

The empirical inquiry first uses the generated data to examine the H_1 hypothesis, which suggests that e-commerce traders do not fully comply with their legal duties. It uses the same data in the second subsection to assess whether the company's size (H_2), the company's age (H_3), and the use of pre-drafted terms provided by public or semi-public authorities (H_4) affect compliance.

2.1 Hypothesis 1: Non-compliance with Consumer Rights

The empirical inquiry uses descriptive statistics to test the H_1 hypothesis that e-commerce traders do not comply fully with the 35 selected consumer

Compliance with European Consumer Law. Felix Pflücke, Oxford University Press. © Oxford University Press 2024.
DOI: 10.1093/9780198906414.003.0006

Table 6.1 Overall Levels of Trader Compliance

	(1) Lower (%)	(2) Silence (%)	(3) Same (%)	(4) Higher (%)
Country				
France	6.67 (n = 175)	31.50 (n = 827)	60.30 (n = 1,583)	1.52 (n = 40)
Germany	2.40 (n = 63)	28.23 (n = 741)	68.38 (n = 1,795)	0.99 (n = 26)
Netherlands	6.86 (n = 180)	29.10 (n = 764)	63.16 (n = 1,658)	0.88 (n = 23)
United Kingdom	14.63 (n = 384)	29.68 (n = 779)	54.78 (n = 1,438)	0.91 (n = 24)
Industry				
Electronics	6.38 (n = 134)	27.19 (n = 571)	65.52 (n = 1,376)	0.90 (n = 19)
Fashion	6.52 (n = 137)	29.76 (n = 625)	62.57 (n = 1,314)	1.14 (n = 24)
Sports equipment	9.14 (n = 192)	31.62 (n = 664)	57.86 (n = 1,215)	1.38 (n = 29)
Home decor	7.24 (n = 152)	28.05 (n = 589)	63.33 (n = 1,330)	1.38 (n = 29)
Print media	8.90 (n = 187)	31.52 (n = 662)	59.00 (n = 1,239)	0.57 (n = 12)
Company size				
Large	5.62 (n = 232)	27.94 (n = 1,154)	65.06 (n = 2,687)	1.38 (n = 57)
SME	8.95 (n = 570)	30.72 (n = 1,957)	59.45 (n = 3,787)	0.88 (n = 56)
Total	**7.64 (n = 802)**	**29.63 (n = 3,111)**	**61.66 (n = 6,474)**	**1.08 (n = 113)**

Notes: Percentage for each category (independent variable) and rounded to two decimals places. Frequencies in brackets. There are 75 traders for each Member State and 60 traders for each industry. 118 traders are large enterprises and 182 traders are SMEs (45 by default). In total, there are 300 traders.

protection rules. The descriptive analysis uses tables that quantify the overall levels of compliance and the number of instances of non-compliance for each trader. Determining the instances of non-compliance for each trader is particularly important because the hypothesis argues that traders fail to comply in full with the legal duties selected for the present study.

The compliance assessment detected 802 instances of non-compliance on the 300 e-commerce websites (Table 6.1, model (1), Total). On average, this amounts to 2.67 violations for each trader or 7.64 per cent of all the compliance assessments carried out for the study (N = 10,500). It follows that from the 10,500 compliance assessments that were carried out, around 92.36 per cent (n = 9,698) of assessments did not identify a violation of the relevant rules (Table 6.1, model (2–4), Total). In 61.66 per cent (n = 6,474) of assessments, contract terms complied with the rules, while in the case of 29.63 per cent (n = 3,111) of the assessments, the contract was silent on the relevant issue. The inquiry identified a higher level of protection in 1.08 per cent (n = 113) of assessments.

However, the investigation of compliance by trader revealed that most traders had at least 1 or more instances of non-compliance (see Table 6.2 below). More precisely, the empirical examination showed that 80.67 per cent (n = 242) of the 300 simulated e-commerce consumer transactions contained at least 1 or more instances of non-compliance (Table 6.2, models (2–5), Total). This finding means that merely 19.33 per cent (n = 58) of traders complied in full with the selected consumer rights (Table 6.2, model (1), Total). As shown in Table 6.2, 16 per cent of e-commerce traders had 1 instance of non-compliance, 23.67 per cent had 2 instances, 11.67 per cent had 3 instances, and 29.33 per cent had 4 or more violations. 10 traders (3.33 per cent) had 9 or more violations: 1 large enterprise and 8 small and medium-sized enterprises (SMEs) from the United Kingdom and 1 SME from Germany (Table 6.3, model (10)).

The number of instances of full compliance varies, sometimes even significantly, between countries, industries, and company sizes (Table 6.2, model (1)). The lowest level of full compliance was among traders in the United Kingdom. Only 2.67 per cent, so 2 out of 75 UK traders, complied in full with their legal duties. Even in Germany, the most compliant jurisdiction in the present study, only 54.67 per cent (41 out of 75 traders) of traders were in full compliance. Industry compliance varied between 6.67 per cent among the print media enterprises, 4 out of 60 traders, and 30 per cent among the electronics enterprises, 18 out of 60 traders. Compliance among companies of different sizes varied between 13.74 per cent for SMEs, 25 out of 182 traders, and 27.97 per cent for large enterprises, 33 out

Table 6.2 Number of Instances of Non-compliance for each Trader (Part I)

	(1) None (%)	(2) One (%)	(3) Two (%)	(4) 3 (%)	(5) Four (%)
Country					
France	16.00 (n = 12)	21.33 (n = 16)	25.33 (n = 19)	13.33 (n = 10)	10.67 (n = 8)
Germany	54.67 (n = 41)	26.67 (n = 20)	12.00 (n = 9)	2.67 (n = 2)	1.33 (n = 1)
Netherlands	4.00 (n = 3)	13.33 (n = 10)	50.67 (n = 38)	13.33 (n = 10)	12.00 (n = 9)
United Kingdom	2.67 (n = 2)	2.67 (n = 2)	6.67 (n = 5)	17.33 (n = 13)	18.67 (n = 14)
Industry					
Electronics	30.00 (n = 18)	11.67 (n = 7)	26.67 (n = 16)	5.00 (n = 3)	15.00 (n = 9)
Fashion	28.33 (n = 17)	11.67 (n = 7)	25.00 (n = 15)	10.00 (n = 6)	10.00 (n = 6)
Sports equipment	15.00 (n = 9)	13.33 (n = 8)	18.33 (n = 11)	15.00 (n = 9)	10.00 (n = 6)
Home decor	16.67 (n = 10)	26.67 (n = 16)	21.67 (n = 13)	11.67 (n = 7)	8.33 (n = 5)
Print media	6.67 (n = 4)	16.67 (n = 10)	26.67 (n = 16)	16.67 (n = 10)	10.00 (n = 6)
Company size					
Large	27.97 (n = 33)	21.19 (n = 25)	21.19 (n = 25)	9.32 (n = 11)	11.02 (n = 13)
SME	13.74 (n = 25)	12.64 (n = 23)	25.27 (n = 46)	13.19 (n = 24)	10.44 (n = 19)
Total	**19.33 (n = 58)**	**16.00 (n = 48)**	**23.67 (n = 71)**	**11.67 (n = 35)**	**10.67 (n = 32)**

Notes: Percentage for each category (independent variable) and rounded to two decimals places. Frequencies in brackets. There are 75 traders for each Member State and 60 traders for each industry. 118 traders are large enterprises and 182 traders are SMEs (45 by default). In total, there are 300 traders.

Table 6.3 Number of Instances of Non-compliance for each Trader (Part II)

	(6) Five (%)	(7) Six (%)	(8) Seven (%)	(9) Eight (%)	(10) Nine or more (%)
Country					
France	5.33 (n = 4)	5.33 (n = 4)	1.33 (n = 1)	1.33 (n = 1)	0.00 (n = 0)
Germany	1.33 (n = 1)	0.00 (n = 0)	0.00 (n = 0)	0.00 (n = 0)	1.33 (n = 1)
Netherlands	4.00 (n = 3)	1.33 (n = 1)	1.33 (n = 1)	0.00 (n = 0)	0.00 (n = 0)
United Kingdom	12.00 (n = 9)	12.00 (n = 9)	12.00 (n = 9)	4.00 (n = 3)	12.00 (n = 9)
Industry					
Electronics	1.67 (n = 1)	5.00 (n = 3)	1.67 (n = 1)	0.00 (n = 0)	3.33 (n = 2)
Fashion	6.67 (n = 4)	1.67 (n = 1)	3.33 (n = 2)	1.67 (n = 1)	1.67 (n = 1)
Sports equipment	10.00 (n = 6)	6.67 (n = 4)	5.00 (n = 3)	3.33 (n = 2)	3.33 (n = 2)
Home decor	1.67 (n = 1)	3.33 (n = 2)	3.33 (n = 2)	1.67 (n = 1)	5.00 (n = 3)
Print media	8.33 (n = 5)	6.67 (n = 4)	5.00 (n = 3)	0.00 (n = 0)	3.33 (n = 2)
Company size					
Large	2.54 (n = 3)	2.54 (n = 3)	3.39 (n = 4)	0.00 (n = 0)	0.85 (n = 1)
SME	7.69 (n = 14)	6.04 (n = 11)	3.85 (n = 7)	2.20 (n = 4)	4.95 (n = 9)
Total	**5.67 (n = 17)**	**4.67 (n = 14)**	**3.67 (n = 11)**	**1.33 (n = 4)**	**3.33 (n = 10)**

Notes: Percentage for each category (independent variable) and rounded to two decimals places. Frequencies in brackets. There are 75 traders for each Member State and 60 traders for each industry. 118 traders are large enterprises and 182 traders are SMEs (45 by default). In total, there are 300 traders.

of 118 traders. Despite the significant differences between the 3 categories, no jurisdiction, industry, or company size was fully compliant.

In conclusion, the descriptive analysis revealed that the overall levels of compliance were high (92.36 per cent of all compliance assessments, Table 6.1). However, 80.67 per cent (n = 242) of all traders had at least 1 or more instances of non-compliance (Tables 6.2 and 6.3, Total). Therefore, the null hypothesis, that e-commerce traders are fully compliant with the 35 selected consumer protection rights, is rejected, and the first hypothesis (H1) that traders do not comply in full with their legal duties can be confirmed.[1] The empirical findings also confirm the earlier studies that measured trader compliance, but, as discussed in Chapter 5.2, their scope differed from that of the present study.[2]

[1] Section 6.3 of this chapter addresses further observations concerning the levels of compliance with each consumer right.

[2] cf Marco Loos and Joasia A Luzak, 'Wanted: A Bigger Stick. On Unfair Terms in Consumer Contracts with Online Service Providers' (2016) 39(1) Journal of Consumer Policy 63; Aashish Srivastava, 'The New EU Consumer Rights Directive: An Empirical Study on Compliance Issues by E-Tailers' (2017) 32(4) Journal of Business Law 282; Mary Donnelly and Fidelma Whit, 'Digital content and consumer protection: An empirical study of supplier compliance with consumer information obligations' (2019) 35(6) Computer Law & Security Review 1.

2.2 Hypotheses 2 to 4: Factors of Non-compliance

Section 2.1 above revealed that most traders failed to comply fully with their legal duties. This section presents data relating to factors that Chapter 5.2 hypothesized as potentially contributing to non-compliance.[3] The independent variables selected for assessment were the company's size (H_2), the company's age (H_3), and the use of pre-drafted terms prepared by public or semi-public authorities (H_4). As discussed in Chapter 5, the empirical examination addressed the 3 hypotheses jointly because the independent variables also serve as control variables in the Ordinary Least Squares and Binary Logistic Regression models. The Ordinary Least Squares (model (1) in Table 6.4) assessed whether the instances of non-compliance for each trader affect compliance, whereas the Binary Logistic Regression (model (2) in Table 6.4) used the probability of non-compliance, that is, full compliance versus at least some non-compliance.[4] Both tests revealed similar results, and the empirical inquiry discusses them jointly (Table 6.4).

The H_2 hypothesis claims that large enterprises are more likely to be compliant than small and medium-sized enterprises. The coefficient in model (1) on the company size variable is estimated to be positive at the 1 per cent significance level and the 5 per cent significance level in model (2). Values of statistical significance at the 1 or 5 per cent level are a powerful indicator that the findings are unlikely to be observed by chance.[5] In this case, the results indicate that SMEs had, on average, more violations of the consumer protection rules than large enterprises (model (1)) and were less likely to be compliant (model (2)). This finding rejects the null hypothesis that SMEs are more likely to be compliant and confirms the company size hypothesis (H_2) that large enterprises are more likely comply than small and medium-sized enterprises.[6]

The third hypothesis (H_3) claims that e-commerce traders who operated on the market longer are compliant to a greater degree than companies that were incorporated more recently. The hypothesis was tested once with the company

[3] For further details see ch 5.2.

[4] Chapter 5.6 provides further details on these tests and why the study chose them.

[5] This result means that there is only a 1 or 5 per cent risk that the study observed it by chance, which means that the confidence level is at 99 and 95 per cent, respectively.

[6] This result confirms the findings of the UK Competition and Markets Authority's study on traders' awareness of consumer rights in the Consumer Rights Act 2015. The study revealed that company size has an overall positive influence on awareness of obligations. See Competition and Markets Authority/IFF Research, 'Unfair Contract Terms Research' Competition and Markets Authority (19 October 2016) 40 https://assets.publishing.service.gov.uk/government/uploads/system/uploads/attachment_data/file/561518/UK_businesses__understanding_of_unfair_terms_in_consumer_contracts__IFF_Research_.pdf (accessed 29 April 2020).

Table 6.4 Effects of Instances of Non-compliance and Probability of Non-compliance

Independent variable	**Dependent variable**	
	Instances of non-compliance *Ordinary least squares*(1)	**Probability of non-compliance** *Binary logistic regression*(2)
Company size (SME)	1.250***(0.222)	0.800**(0.396)
Company age (uncapped)	0.003(0.006)	0.003(0.012)
Use of pre-drafted terms	-0.705(0.463)	2.040(1.264)
Control variable France	1.612***(0.293)	2.093***(0.416)
Control variable NL	1.870***(0.465)	2.232***(0.810)
Control variable UK	4.407***(0.294)	4.053***(0.769)
Constant	-0.035(0.273)	-0.883**(0.419)
Observations (N)	282	282
R^2	0.509	
Adjusted R^2	0.498	
Log likelihood		-92.651
Akaike information criterion		199.303
Residual standard error	1.696 (df = 275)	
F statistic	47.444*** (df = 6; 275)	

*p<0.1; **p<0.05; ***p<0.01

Notes: The observations dropped from 300 traders to 282 due to missing values; the age variable was impossible to obtain for 13 German traders, 3 Dutch traders (2 used pre-drafted terms), and 2 UK traders. 118 traders are large enterprises and 164 traders are SMEs. Only Dutch traders (n = 56) have used pre-drafted terms and the study accounted for the effect of a trader's origin. Control variables show the likelihood of non-compliance compared to German traders.

age variable uncapped and then the second time capped at 30 years. The empirical inquiry has not detected a statistical difference between capping and not capping the company age. Therefore, the inquiry only reports the results of the uncapped company age in Table 6.4. In either statistical test (models (1) and (2)), company age has not statistically affected non-compliance. The third hypothesis (H_3), that the company's age is affecting compliance, can thus not be confirmed.[7]

Surprisingly, the traders' use of terms pre-drafted by public or semi-public authorities (H_4) does not statistically affect compliance once the study has accounted for the effect of the trader's origin. The 4th hypothesis

[7] The Competition and Markets Authority could also not establish any statistical significance in its study. See Competition and Markets Authority/IFF Research (n 6) 20–21.

is consequently not confirmed.[8] It is nonetheless worth mentioning that, although not at a statistically significant level, model (1) suggests from an effect size perspective that e-commerce traders who based their terms and conditions on pre-drafted standard contract terms prepared by public or semi-public authorities have on average fewer violations compared to traders who do not. However, from an effect size perspective, model (2) suggests that traders using pre-drafted terms have a higher probability of non-compliance than traders who draft their own terms. Although there is no statistical significance at the usual levels, the results, nevertheless, could suggest 2 scenarios: (1) the pre-drafted terms already contained provisions that were in breach of consumer protection standards (although, on average, fewer than traders who drafted their own); or (2) that traders using them had collectively failed to implement them faithfully on their websites. Chapter 7.2 will critically examine both options.

It follows that a company's size statistically affects compliance, while a company's age or the use of terms pre-drafted by (semi-)public authorities is not statistically significant. Section 3 below provides further details on the non-compliance with each consumer right, and the next chapter outlines the implications of the findings on EU consumer contract law.

3 Compliance with Consumer Rights

A closer look at the data revealed that 60.60 per cent (n = 486) of the 802 detected violations concerned mandatory disclosures, 21.95 per cent (n = 176) unfair contract terms, 16.58 per cent (n = 133) the consumers' right of withdrawal, and 0.87 per cent (n = 7) the rules governing the passing of risk (Table 6.5, Total). The data also suggests that traders, regardless of their origin, industry, or company size, struggled the most with mandatory disclosures. It is followed, except in Germany, by the right of withdrawal, unfair contract terms, and the passing of risk.

This section examines the exact levels of compliance with each consumer right. It discusses patterns and individual instances where traders failed to comply with consumer protection standards by examining and referring to the compliance assessments.

[8] The empirical inquiry included the4 jurisdictions as control variables. The level of compliance is compared to German traders because they were the most compliant. French, Dutch, and UK traders had, on average, more instances of non-compliance compared to German traders (see Table 6.4, model (1)); German traders were also more likely to comply with their legal duties (see Table 6.4, model (2)).

Table 6.5 Instances of Non-compliance by Legal Category

	(1) Unfair contract terms (%)	(2) Mandatory disclosures (%)	(3) Right of withdrawal (%)	(4) Passing of risk (%)
Country				
France	14.29 (n = 25)	71.43 (n = 125)	13.71 (n = 24)	0.57 (n = 1)
Germany	9.52 (n = 6)	79.37 (n = 50)	11.11 (n = 7)	0.00 (n = 0)
Netherlands	31.67 (n = 57)	55.56 (n = 100)	12.78 (n = 23)	0.00 (n = 0)
United Kingdom	22.92 (n = 88)	54.95 (n = 211)	20.57 (n = 79)	1.56 (n = 6)
Industry				
Electronics	31.34 (n = 42)	52.24 (n = 70)	15.67 (n = 21)	0.75 (n = 1)
Fashion	21.17 (n = 29)	59.85 (n = 82)	18.25 (n = 25)	0.73 (n = 1)
Sports equipment	15.63 (n = 30)	64.58 (n = 124)	18.75 (n = 36)	1.04 (n = 2)
Home decor	23.68 (n = 36)	57.24 (n = 87)	17.11 (n = 26)	1.97 (n = 3)
Print media	20.86 (n = 39)	65.78 (n = 123)	13.37 (n = 25)	0.00 (n = 0)
Company size				
Large	25.86 (n = 60)	57.76 (n = 134)	14.66 (n = 34)	1.72 (n = 4)
SME	20.35 (n = 116)	61.75 (n = 352)	17.37 (n = 99)	0.53 (n = 3)
Total	**21.95 (n = 176)**	**60.60 (n = 486)**	**16.58 (n = 133)**	**0.87 (n = 7)**

Notes:

(1) Percentage for each category (independent variable) and rounded to two decimals places. Frequencies in brackets. There are 75 traders for each Member State and 60 traders for each industry. 118 traders are large enterprises and 182 traders are SMEs (45 by default). In total, there are 300 traders.

(2) Model (1) are dependant variables X1-X11. Model (2) are Y1-Y4; Z1a-Zl1; Z4. Model (3) are Z2a(i)-Z2f. Model (4) are Z3a and Z3b. See Chapter 5.3 for further details.

3.1 Unfair Contract Terms

The empirical inquiry detected 176 instances of non-compliance in the 3,300 compliance assessments in search of unfair contract terms (Table 6.5, model (1)). The empirical findings suggest substantial differences between the jurisdictions, industries, and company sizes. Out of 3,300 compliance assessments (with 825 assessments for each jurisdiction), only 6 instances of unfair terms were found in Germany (0.73 per cent), 25 in France (3.01 per cent), 57 in the Netherlands (6.91 per cent), and 88 in the United Kingdom (10.67 per cent). The number of unfair terms by industries varied between 4.39 per cent in fashion (29 out of 660 compliance assessments) and 6.36 per cent in electronics (42 out of 660 compliance assessments), and 4.62 per cent for large companies (60 out of 1,298 compliance assessments) and 5.79 per cent for SMEs (116 out of 2,002 compliance assessments).

At first glance, the overall number of unfair terms seems low. Only 8.34 per cent out of the 300 traders' websites contained 2 or more unfair contract

Table 6.6 Number of Unfair Contract Terms for each Trader

	(1) None (%)	(2) One (%)	(3) Two (%)	(4) Three (%)	(5) Four (%)
Country					
France	66.67 (n = 50)	33.33 (n = 25)	0.00 (n = 0)	0.00 (n = 0)	0.00 (n = 0)
Germany	92.00 (n = 69)	8.00 (n = 6)	0.00 (n = 0)	0.00 (n = 0)	0.00 (n = 0)
Netherlands	28.00 (n = 21)	68.00 (n = 51)	4.00 (n = 3)	0.00 (n = 0)	0.00 (n = 0)
United Kingdom	21.33 (n = 16)	49.33 (n = 37)	22.67 (n = 17)	4.00 (n = 3)	2.67 (n = 2)
Industry					
Electronics	45.00 (n = 27)	45.00 (n = 27)	6.67 (n = 4)	1.67 (n = 1)	1.67 (n = 1)
Fashion	58.33 (n = 35)	35.00 (n = 21)	6.67 (n = 4)	0.00 (n = 0)	0.00 (n = 0)
Sports equipment	63.33 (n = 38)	26.67 (n = 16)	8.33 (n = 5)	0.00 (n = 0)	1.67 (n = 1)
Home decor	51.67 (n = 31)	40.00 (n = 24)	5.00 (n = 3)	3.33 (n = 2)	0.00 (n = 0)
Print media	41.67 (n = 25)	51.67 (n = 31)	6.67 (n = 4)	0.00 (n = 0)	0.00 (n = 0)
Company size					
Large	55.93 (n = 66)	38.14 (n = 45)	5.08 (n = 6)	0.85 (n = 1)	0.00 (n = 0)
SME	49.45 (n = 90)	40.66 (n = 74)	7.69 (n = 14)	1.10 (n = 2)	1.10 (n = 2)
Total	**52.00 (n = 156)**	**39.67 (n = 119)**	**6.67(n = 20)**	**1.00(n = 3)**	**0.67(n = 2)**

Notes: Percentage for each category (independent variable) and rounded to two decimals places. Frequencies in brackets. There are 75 traders for each Member State and 60 traders for each industry. 118 traders are large enterprises and 182 traders are SMEs (45 by default). In total, there are 300 traders. Total of 11 Unfair Contract Terms scenarios.

terms (Table 6.6, Total). However, only 52 per cent of all traders had no unfair contract terms on their websites. The data showed the greatest differences among jurisdictions. Only 21.33 per cent of UK traders had no unfair term on their websites compared to 92 per cent of German traders.

Another difference between the jurisdictions concerns the nature of the violations. As explained in Chapters 3 and 5, different techniques for controlling unfair terms exist in the 4 jurisdictions, as the Unfair Contract Terms Directive is only a minimum harmonization instrument, and Member States are allowed to enact stricter rules.[9] The Directive contains a general test of fairness and a non-exhaustive and indicative list of potentially unfair contract terms.[10] France, Germany, and the Netherlands police unfair terms with a

[9] Unfair Contract Terms Directive, art 8.
[10] ibid arts 3 and 4 in connection with Annex I.

general test complemented by 'grey lists', that is, by creating a presumption that a term included in a 'grey list' is unfair and limiting the judicial discretion on the matter, and by 'black lists', that is by declaring terms included in the 'black list' as void and thus precluding any judicial discretion. However, the content and extent of the lists vary significantly between the 3 jurisdictions, as depicted in Chapters 3 and 5. Conversely, the United Kingdom controls unfair terms with a general test of fairness accompanied by an indicative list of potentially unfair terms and several statutory and common law prohibitions resembling a 'black list'. The different consumer protection standards between the jurisdictions also explain why the compliance assessments have not detected any violations with the general test in France, Germany, and the Netherlands. These 3 jurisdictions have included the potentially unfair terms in the Annex to the Unfair Contract Terms Directive in their 'grey lists' and 'black lists', thus limiting the need to rely only on the general test. One consequence of the different standards is that the results presented in Table 6.7 do not allow for a direct comparison between the jurisdictions, industries, and company size. Thus, a more nuanced examination of the data is necessary.

Table 6.7 Non-compliances with Unfair Contract Terms

	(1) Violation 'General test' (%)	(2) Violation 'Grey list' (%)	(3) Violation 'Black list' (%)	Overall
Country				
France	0.00 (n = 0)	0.00 (n = 0)	100.00 (n = 25)	25
Germany	0.00 (n = 0)	0.00 (n = 0)	100.00 (n = 6)	6
Netherlands	0.00 (n = 0)	7.02 (n = 4)	92.98 (n = 53)	57
United Kingdom	12.50 (n = 11)	0.00 (n = 0)	87.50 (n = 77)	88
Industry				
Electronics	9.52 (n = 4)	7.14 (n = 3)	83.33 (n = 35)	42
Fashion	3.45 (n = 1)	0.00 (n = 0)	96.55 (n = 28)	29
Sports equipment	13.33 (n = 4)	3.33 (n = 1)	83.33 (n = 25)	30
Home decor	5.56 (n = 2)	0.00 (n = 0)	94.44 (n = 34)	36
Print media	0.00 (n = 0)	0.00 (n = 0)	100.00 (n = 39)	39
Company size				
Large	1.67 (n = 1)	1.67 (n = 1)	96.67 (n = 58)	60
SME	8.62 (n = 10)	2.59 (n = 3)	88.79 (n = 103)	116
Total	**6.25 (n = 11)**	**2.27 (n = 4)**	**91.48 (n = 161)**	**176**

Notes: Percentage for each category (independent variable) and rounded to two decimals places. Frequencies in brackets. There are 75 traders for each Member State and 60 traders for each industry. 118 traders are large enterprises and 182 traders are SMEs (45 by default). In total, there are 300 traders. The level of protection varies between the Member States, see Tables 2 to 4 in Chapter 5.

Table 6.8 Instances of Unfair Contract Terms by Legal Category

	X1	X2	X3	X4	X5	X6	X7	X8	X9	X10	X11	Overall
Country												
France	0	0	0	0	0	0	0	0	0	0	25	25
Germany	0	0	0	2	0	0	0	0	0	0	4	6
Netherlands	2	1	0	1	0	0	0	0	0	0	53	57
United Kingdom	2	0	0	3	4	3	1	0	0	22	53	88
Industry												
Electronics	2	1	0	1	2	2	0	0	0	4	30	42
Fashion	1	0	0	0	1	0	0	0	0	6	21	29
Sports equipment	1	0	0	2	1	1	1	0	0	3	21	30
Home decor	0	0	0	3	0	0	0	0	0	5	28	36
Print media	0	0	0	0	0	0	0	0	0	4	35	39
Company size												
Large	1	1	0	1	0	0	0	0	0	9	48	60
SME	3	0	0	5	4	3	1	0	0	13	87	116
Non-compliance												
'General test'	0	0	0	3	4	3	1	0	0	0	0	11
'Grey list'	2	1	0	1	0	0	0	0	0	0	0	4
'Black list'	2	0	0	2	0	0	0	0	0	22	135	161
Total	**4**	**1**	**0**	**6**	**4**	**3**	**1**	**0**	**0**	**22**	**135**	**176**

Notes:

(1) Frequencies of unfair contract terms. There are 75 traders for each Member State and 60 traders for each industry. 118 traders are large enterprises and 182 traders are SMEs (45 by default). In total, there are 300 traders.

(2) X1 limitation of liability in case of death or personal injury. X2 exclusion or limitation of compensation in case of total or partial non-performance. X3 one-sided compensation for cancellation. X4 excessive compensation. X5 one-sided changes to the contract. X6 one-sided changes to the product. X7 price variations. X8 one-sided interpretation of the contract. X9 one-sided compliance with obligations. X10 transfer of contracts to other traders under less favourable conditions. X11 limitation of rights to legal action.

The empirical findings in Table 6.8 suggest that the 176 violations concerned 8 out of the 11 selected scenarios of (potentially) unfair terms and that most of the detected unfair contract terms concerned a small number of consumer rights. Most unfair terms were invalid jurisdiction or choice of law clauses (Table 6.8, X11). These clauses attempted to deprive consumers of their right to bring a claim at their habitual residence and also to rely on their national consumer protection rules.[11] Although consumers are not bound by such clauses,

[11] See ch 3.4.11 of this monograph. The observation confirms the findings of Loos and Luzak (n 2) 85–86.

such a high number of violations is alarming. A good illustrative example of a non-compliant jurisdiction clause is the contract term of a Dutch trader, which provided its terms and conditions partly in Dutch and partly in English. The English version stated that Spanish law exclusively governed the contract, and disputes could only be resolved by the courts of Barcelona, except when the customer was a consumer. In this case, the trader accepted that customers could submit their claim at their habitual residence in Spain. The Dutch version provided almost the same content but allowed customers to go to court at their habitual residence, not only in Spain. Even if one were to interpret these clauses in favour of the trader, that is to say, by only taking into account the content of the Dutch clause, consumers would only be able to rely on Spanish law, which is a clear breach of the consumers' rights, as indicated by dependent variable X11.[12]

The second most common type of unfair contract terms in the traders' standard terms concerned the transfer of rights and obligations (variable X10). As shown in Table 6.8, all 22 violations occurred in the United Kingdom. Almost one-third of all UK traders' contracts had such a clause in their terms and conditions. It was pointed out in Chapter 3 that, according to the common law doctrine of assignment, these clauses do not bind consumers.[13]

6 clauses allowing traders to charge consumers a disproportionately high compensation if consumers fail to fulfil their contractual obligations (variable X4) were detected in the terms and conditions of 2 German traders, 1 Dutch trader, and 3 UK traders. The clauses of the German and UK traders yield relevant results. In Germany, such clauses generally breach § 309 No 6 of the BGB. Traders are, however, allowed to charge interest in case consumers fail to pay for the goods delivered. The BGB caps the interest rate at 5 percentage points above the basic interest rate in business-to-consumer contracts and 9 percentage points above the basic rate of interest in business-to-business contracts.[14] All German traders in the study complied with the latter requirement. The empirical inquiry found clauses where traders charged consumers to return the goods in the United Kingdom. For instance, 1 trader failed to provide the correct withdrawal period (7 days instead of 14) and required consumers to get written permission before returning the goods and to pay 25 per cent

[12] Loos and Luzak also found such clauses. See Loos and Luzak (n 2) 82–84. Invalid choice of law clauses are contrary to art 6(1) of Regulation (EU) 593/2008 (Rome I); invalid jurisdiction clauses are in breach of art 18(2) of Regulation (EU) 1215/2012, also referred to as the Brussels I Regulation (Recast). Chapter 3.4.11 in this volume provides further context.

[13] See ch 3.4.10.

[14] BGB, § 288. See generally Christian Ernst, '§ 288' in Wolfgang Krüger (ed), *Münchner Kommentar zum Bürgerlichen Gesetzbuch Band 2: Schuldrecht Allgemeiner Teil 1 §§ 241-310* (8th edn, CH Beck 2019) BGB § 288 [1–5].

of the purchase price as a penalty. 1 trader also charged a 25 per cent 'handling and restocking' fee. Another trader charged consumers a 'restocking fee' of up to 25 per cent. The exact percentage does not matter in this case, as traders cannot charge consumers in case of a return.[15] However, the consumer must pay to return the goods unless the trader's terms provide otherwise or in case the trader failed to inform the consumer of the cost.[16] The question is whether such a term is a penalty clause. As stated above (Chapter 3.4.4), a penalty clause exists where there is no legitimate interest in deterring the contractual breach and the clause serves as an exorbitant or unconscionable alternative to common law damages. Traders have a generous margin of error, so it seems unlikely that it is a penalty clause. Instead, section 62 of the Consumer Rights Act 2015 in connection with Schedule 2 Part 1(5) and (6) of the Act applies, and the UK courts would probably set aside such a clause.

The empirical inquiry detected several violations concerning variable X1 (n = 4), that is, the traders' limitation of negligence liability in case of death or personal injury of consumers,[17] variable X5 (n = 4), that is, clauses allowing traders to modify the contract unilaterally,[18] and variable X6 (n = 3), that is one-sided compensation for cancellation clauses.[19] One violation concerned clauses excluding or limiting the consumer's compensation in case of total or partial non-performance of the trader (variable X2). Another one concerned a price variation clause (variable X7).[20]

In conclusion, examining trader compliance with unfair terms revealed that traders struggled the most with providing only the permitted jurisdiction and choice of law clauses (variable X11) and clauses that would allow traders to transfer their rights and obligations to third parties (variable X10). Both scenarios accounted for 89.20 per cent (157 out of 176) of the identified unfair contract terms in the present study. Another discovery was that traders in the United Kingdom had the greatest number of unfair terms on their websites. The same applied to traders in electronics and small and medium-sized enterprises. Overall, 52 per cent of 300 traders (n = 156) had no unfair contract term on their websites. However, the non-compliance level at 5.33 per cent is reasonably low (176 unfair contract terms out of 3,300 compliance assessments).

[15] Directive 2011/83/EU, art 9(1), implemented in the United Kingdom by s 29(1) of the Consumer Contracts (Information, Cancellation and Additional Charges) Regulations 2013.
[16] Directive 2011/83/EU, art 14(1), implemented in the United Kingdom by section 35(5) of the Consumer Contracts (Information, Cancellation and Additional Charges) Regulations 2013.
[17] See ch 3.4.1.
[18] See ch 3.4.5.
[19] See ch 3.4.6.
[20] See chs 3.4.2 and 3.4.7.

3.2 Mandatory Disclosures

This section explores the findings concerning non-compliance with the 15 selected mandatory disclosures, including details on whether traders provided the required information incorrectly. Out of 4,500 compliance assessments regarding mandatory disclosures alone, 486 non-compliances (94 violations and 392 omissions) and 4,014 compliances were detected (Table 6.9, Total; Table 6.10, Overall).

Table 6.9 Number of Instances of Non-compliance with Mandatory Disclosures for each Trader

	(1) None (%)	(2) One (%)	(3) Two (%)	(4) Three (%)	(5) Four (%)	(6) Five (%)	(7) Six (%)	(8) Seven (%)
Country								
France	25.33 (n = 19)	20.00 (n = 15)	34.67 (n = 26)	9.33 (n = 7)	5.33 (n = 4)	4.00 (n = 3)	1.33 (n = 1)	0.00 (n = 0)
Germany	66.67 (n = 50)	14.67 (n = 11)	13.33 (n = 10)	1.33 (n = 1)	1.33 (n = 1)	1.33 (n = 1)	0.00 (n = 0)	1.33 (n = 1)
Netherlands	15.00 (n = 11)	56.00 (n = 42)	18.67 (n = 14)	5.33 (n = 4)	2.67 (n = 2)	2.67 (n = 2)	0.00 (n = 0)	0.00 (n = 0)
United Kingdom	8.00 (n = 6)	21.33 (n = 16)	10.67 (n = 8)	20.00 (n = 15)	24.00 (n = 18)	13.33 (n = 10)	2.67 (n = 2)	0.00 (n = 0)
Industry								
Electronics	41.67 (n = 25)	30.00 (n = 18)	13.33 (n = 8)	5.00 (n = 3)	5.00 (n = 3)	5.00 (n = 3)	0.00 (n = 0)	0.00 (n = 0)
Fashion	33.33 (n = 20)	28.33 (n = 17)	20.00 (n = 12)	10.00 (n = 6)	5.00 (n = 3)	1.67 (n = 1)	1.67 (n = 1)	0.00 (n = 0)
Sports equipment	20.00 (n = 12)	23.33 (n = 14)	21.67 (n = 13)	11.67 (n = 7)	15.00 (n = 9)	6.67 (n = 4)	0.00 (n = 0)	1.67 (n = 1)
Home decor	33.33 (n = 20)	30.00 (n = 18)	16.67 (n = 10)	6.67 (n = 4)	6.67 (n = 4)	5.00 (n = 3)	1.67 (n = 1)	0.00 (n = 0)
Print media	15.00 (n = 9)	28.33 (n = 17)	25.00 (n = 15)	11.67 (n = 7)	10.00 (n = 6)	8.33 (n = 5)	1.67 (n = 1)	0.00 (n = 0)
Company size								
Large	39.83 (n = 47)	30.51 (n = 36)	15.25 (n = 18)	6.78 (n = 8)	5.93 (n = 7)	1.69 (n = 2)	0.00 (n = 0)	0.00 (n = 0)
SME	21.43 (n = 39)	26.37 (n = 48)	21.98 (n = 40)	10.44 (n = 19)	9.89 (n = 18)	7.69 (n = 14)	1.65 (n = 3)	0.55 (n = 1)
Total	**28.67 (n = 86)**	**28.00 (n = 84)**	**19.33 (n = 58)**	**9.00 (n = 27)**	**8.33 (n = 25)**	**5.33 (n = 16)**	**1.00 (n = 3)**	**0.33 (n = 1)**

Notes: Percentage for each category (independent variable) and rounded to two decimals places. Frequencies in brackets. There are 75 traders for each Member State and 60 traders for each industry. 118 traders are large enterprises and 182 traders are SMEs (45 by default). In total, there are 300 traders.

Table 6.10 Instances of Non-compliance with Mandatory Disclosures

	Y1	Y2	Y3	Y4	Z1a	Z1b	Z1c	Z1d	Z1e	Z1f	Z1g(i)	Z1g(ii)	Z1h	Z1i	Z4	Overall
Country																
France	0	17	0	1	0	0	0	0	3	19	0	27	16	0	42	125
Germany	8	5	0	0	0	1	1	0	0	8	2	5	10	0	10	50
Netherlands	2	5	0	1	0	0	0	0	1	3	1	17	12	0	58	100
United Kingdom	24	50	0	0	0	0	3	0	0	5	1	37	43	0	48	211
Industry																
Electronics	7	13	0	0	0	0	1	0	1	1	1	11	8	0	27	70
Fashion	3	18	0	1	0	0	0	0	2	5	0	14	15	0	24	82
Sports equipment	11	14	0	1	0	1	1	0	1	7	0	22	25	0	41	124
Home decor	8	17	0	0	0	0	1	0	0	6	1	15	13	0	26	87
Print media	5	15	0	0	0	0	1	0	0	16	2	24	20	0	40	123
Company size																
Large	10	28	0	0	0	0	0	0	1	9	1	20	23	0	42	134
SME	24	49	0	2	0	1	4	0	3	26	3	66	58	0	116	352

(*continued*)

Table 6.10 Continued

	Y1	Y2	Y3	Y4	Z1a	Z1b	Z1c	Z1d	Z1e	Z1f	Z1g(i)	Z1g(ii)	Z1h	Z1i	Z4	Overall
Non-compliance																
Violation	16	26	0	2	0	0	0	0	0	0	1	0	1	0	48	94
Omission	18	51	0	0	0	1	4	0	4	35	3	86	80	0	110	392
Total	**34**	**77**	**0**	**2**	**0**	**1**	**4**	**0**	**4**	**35**	**4**	**86**	**81**	**0**	**158**	**486**

Notes:

(1) There are 75 traders for each Member State and 60 traders for each industry. 118 traders are large enterprises and 182 traders are SMEs (45 by default). In total, there are 300 traders.

(2) Violation, that is, trader has incorrectly provided information, results in score of 1. Omission, that is, trader has failed to display the information, results in score of 1.4. Overall 'lower' score.

(3) Y1 company registration number. Y2 VAT number, Y3 technical steps to conclude contract. Y4 languages offered for conclusion of contract.

(4) Z1a main characteristics of the goods. Z1b trading name, Z1c geographical address. Z1d total price of goods inclusive of taxes. Z1e arrangements for payments. Z1f time by which the traders undertake to deliver the goods. Z1g(i) conditions for right of withdrawal. Z1g(ii) model withdrawal form. Z1h reminder of the existence of a legal guarantee of conformity of goods. Z1i information provided on durable medium. Z4 providing the hyperlink to the Europe Commission's Online Dispute Resolution Platform.

Overall, 28.67 per cent of all traders complied with all examined mandatory disclosures (Table 6.9, model (1)). 66.67 per cent of German traders complied in full compared to only 8 per cent of UK traders. The empirical inquiry observed substantial differences between the different industries, with 41.67 per cent compliance in electronics versus 15 per cent in print media, and between large enterprises (39.83 per cent) and SMEs (21.43 per cent).

The greatest number of instances of non-compliance occurred concerning the requirement to display the link to the European Commission's Online Dispute Resolution platform (variable Z4). As discussed in Chapter 3.3.1.6, traders are allowed to opt out of online dispute resolution (ODR), but they are legally required to provide a link to the Commission's platform and their business email address.[21] As shown in Table 6.9, more than half (52.67 per cent) of all 300 traders failed to comply with this mandatory requirement (n = 158), although the number is much lower in Germany (13.33 per cent, so 10 out 75). A closer look at the data revealed that 110 traders failed to provide the link on their websites, while 48 traders did so incorrectly (Table 6.10, model (Z4)).[22] The 48 traders who incorrectly provided the information requirement referred to a national or industry ODR body. Referring only to a national or industry body is highly problematic in cross-border disputes, as consumers might not speak the national language.

The second most frequent type of non-compliance with mandatory disclosures concerned the traders' failure to provide a withdrawal form on their websites (Table 6.10, model (Z1g(ii))).[23] An example of how a model withdrawal form should look is in the Annex to the Consumer Rights Directive, but traders can draft their own forms or provide an electronic alternative. As illustrated in Table 6.10, 86 traders failed to provide such a form on their websites, including almost half of all UK traders (37 out of 75) and more than 1-3 of all French traders (27 out of 75).

The inquiry detected another alarming level of non-compliance with the requirement to remind consumers of the existence of a legal guarantee of conformity of goods (Table 6.10, model (Z1h)).[24] As many as 81 traders failed to comply with this mandatory disclosure: 80 traders failed

[21] Directive 2011/83/EU, art 6(1)(t) in connection with Regulation (EU) 524/2013, art 14.

[22] This result confirms the findings of the European Commission's study where nearly 45 per cent of traders failed to comply with this information requirement. See European Commission, 'Online shopping: Commission and Consumer Protection authorities urge traders to bring information policy in line with EU law' (31 January 2020) https://ec.europa.eu/commission/presscorner/detail/en/IP_20_156 (accessed 12 August 2020).

[23] Directive 2011/83/EU, art 6(1)(h). See ch 3.3.1.1.

[24] Directive 2011/83/EU, art 6(1)(l). See ch 4.3.1.1.

to include the reminder on their websites; 1 Dutch trader stipulated that consumers automatically waived their statutory rights if they failed to report the non-conformity within 5 days of delivery.[25]

Traders must also display their VAT number on their websites (variable Y2).[26] In this regard, 77 traders breached this requirement, 50 alone in the United Kingdom (Table 6.10, model (Y2)). Of the 77 traders who failed to comply with this requirement, 26 traders failed to provide the country code, for instance, NL for the Netherlands, and 51 traders did not include their VAT number on their websites. Only 223 traders had correctly displayed the VAT number on their websites.

Turning to the requirement concerning the display of traders' register numbers on their websites (variable Y1),[27] 34 traders failed to comply with this requirement, 24 of them from the United Kingdom. 18 of these 34 traders failed to include the registration number on their websites, while 16 did so incorrectly. In all, 266 traders complied with this requirement (Table 6.10, model (Y1)). All 16 traders who incorrectly provided the information failed to indicate in which register they were listed. This omission has far-reaching consequences in case of a dispute, making it extremely difficult to establish or verify the identity of traders.

Another surprise was that 35 traders did not provide the estimated delivery time, out of which more than half of the traders (n = 19) were French (Table 6.10, model (Z1f)).[28]

Traders also failed to comply with 5 additional mandatory disclosures, although not so significantly. 4 traders failed to include their addresses on their websites (Table 6.10, model (Z1c)),[29] 3 traders failed to inform consumers of their right of withdrawal, and 1 trader stated that consumers had no right of withdrawal (Z1g(i)).[30] 4 traders failed to provide any payment

[25] The trader relied on art 6:89 and art 7:23 of the BW, although 5 days seem rather short for a reasonable period to inspect the goods. Therefore, it breached the consumer protection right covered by the dependent variable Z1h. The Dutch Supreme Court (*Hoge Raad*) ruled in 2010 that all the circumstances of the case must be taken into account to determine whether a period is reasonable, including the expertise and relationship of the parties (HR 8 October 2010, ECLI:NL:HR:2010:BM9615, para 3.4). The assessment is thus always context specific; in the case of financial services, the Dutch Supreme Court ruled that even 3 years is a reasonable period because of the ongoing client–consumer relationship (HR 8 February 2013, ECLI:NL:HR:2013:BY4600). cf Jacob Hijma, 'HR 08-02-2013, ECLI:NL:HR:2013:BY4600' (2014) Nederlandse Jurisprudentie 497. In the European Commission's study (n 22), over a third of traders did not inform consumers about their statutory rights concerning conformity of goods.

[26] Directive 2000/31/EC, art 5(1)(g). See ch 4.2.1.

[27] Directive 2000/31/EC, art 5(1)(d). See ch 4.2.1.

[28] Directive 2011/83/EU, art 6(1)(g). See ch 4.3.1.1.

[29] Directive 2011/83/EU, art 6(1)(c) and (d). See ch 4.3.1.1.

[30] Directive 2011/83/EU, art 6(1)(h), (j), and (k). See ch 4.3.1.1.

options on their websites, which means that consumers would presumably only find out how they could pay for their goods after purchasing them (Table 6.10, model (Z1e)).[31] Another 2 traders provided vital parts of their terms and conditions in a language other than the remaining parts of the contract (Table 6.10, model (Y4)).[32] For instance, 1 French trader included the ODR clause only in English in the terms and conditions. Another trader, based in the Netherlands, provided the entire website in Dutch, but most of the terms and conditions were in English. Importantly, the right of withdrawal and rules on trader liability were not in Dutch. As mentioned above (Chapter 6.3.1), it is of even greater concern that the choice of law clause differed between the Dutch and English versions. The English version provided that law exclusively governed the contract, and disputes could only be resolved by the courts of Barcelona unless the customer was a consumer. In this case, the trader accepted that customers could submit their claim at the place of their habitual residence in Spain. The Dutch version provided almost the same content but allowed customers to go to court at the place of their habitual residence, not only in Spain. Lastly, 1 trader failed to provide its trading name (Table 6.10, model (Z1b)).[33]

All 300 traders, however, complied with 4 of the 15 information and formal requirements. These requirements concerned the technical steps to conclude the contract (Table 6.10, model (Y3)),[34] the main characteristics of the goods (Table 6.10, model (Z1a)),[35] the total price of the goods inclusive of taxes (Table 6.10, model (Z1d)),[36] and to provide the contractual information on a durable medium (Table 6.10, model (Z1i)).[37]

Overall, compliance with the 15 mandatory disclosures was high. In absolute terms, 10.8 per cent (486 out of 4,500) of the compliance assessments concerning disclosures were instances of non-compliance (Table 6.10, Overall). As shown in Table 6.10, 94 of the 486 instances of non-compliance were violations, which means that traders provided the information incorrectly, while 392 instances of non-compliance were omissions. However, only 28.67 per cent of all traders complied in full with the mandatory disclosures (Table 6.9, model (1)), which was even lower in the United

[31] Directive 2011/83/EU, art 6(1)(g). See ch 4.3.1.1.
[32] Directive 2000/31/EC, art 10(1)(d). See ch 4.2.1.
[33] Directive 2011/83/EU, art 6(1)(b). See ch 4.3.1.1.
[34] Directive 2000/31/EC, art 10(1)(a). See ch 4.2.1.
[35] Directive 2011/83/EU, art 6(1)(a). See ch 4.3.1.1.
[36] Directive 2011/83/EU, art 6(1)(e). See ch 4.3.1.1.
[37] Directive 2011/83/EU, art 8(1) in connection with art 2(10). See ch 4.3.1.2.

Kingdom (8 per cent), the print media industry (15 per cent), and among SMEs (21.43 per cent).

3.3 Right of Withdrawal

The previous section examined the traders' duty to inform consumers of their right of withdrawal and include a withdrawal form on their websites. This section focuses on how faithfully the 300 traders implemented each obligation of the right of withdrawal. Unlike the 2 right of withdrawal provisions in the mandatory disclosure section, legally traders do not need to provide all the details about the right of withdrawal on their websites. However, if traders do address this right, they must comply with the provisions or provide a higher standard for consumers.

As shown in Table 6.11, 133 out of 2,100 compliance assessments, that is 6.33 per cent, reflected a lower level of protection. The most significant differences were between the 4 jurisdictions. The UK traders accounted for the most instances of non-compliance with consumers' right of withdrawal (15.05 per cent), which is more than the French (4.57 per cent), German (1.33 per cent), and Dutch traders (4.38 per cent) combined. Differences between the industries and company sizes were present but not as substantial. On average, the difference was around 3.5 percentage points between electronics (5.00 per cent) and sports equipment (8.57 per cent), and large enterprises (4.12 per cent) and SMEs (7.77 per cent). In 5.38 per cent of all compliance assessments, traders provided a higher standard for consumers than required by the national rules implementing the Consumer Rights Directive.[38]

Violations of the right of withdrawal occurred with all 7 requirements selected for the study. However, a closer look at the data revealed that most non-compliance instances concerned a small number of legal duties (Table 6.12, Lower). The empirical inquiry detected the greatest number of violations in the context of the traders' obligation to reimburse consumers within 14 days (71 out of 133 violations)[39] and the 14-day statutory withdrawal period (34 out of 133 violations).[40] These 2 provisions alone accounted for almost 80 per cent of all violations of the right of withdrawal (105 out of 133 violations). Moreover, the inquiry found this pattern in the overall results for each jurisdiction, except for Germany, industry, and company size.

[38] See ch 4.3.1.3.
[39] Consumer Rights Directive, art 13(1); dependent variable Z2f.
[40] Consumer Rights Directive, art 9(1); dependent variable Z2a(i).

Table 6.11 Levels of Compliance with Right of Withdrawal

	Lower (%)	Silence (%)	Same (%)	Higher (%)
Country				
France	4.57 (n = 24)	27.81 (n = 146)	60.00 (n = 315)	7.62 (n = 40)
Germany	1.33 (n = 7)	7.24 (n = 38)	86.48 (n = 454)	4.95 (n = 26)
Netherlands	4.38 (n = 23)	17.52 (n = 92)	73.71 (n = 387)	4.38 (n = 23)
United Kingdom	15.05 (n = 79)	35.24 (n = 185)	45.14 (n = 237)	4.57 (n = 24)
Industry				
Electronics	5.00 (n = 21)	17.62 (n = 74)	72.86 (n = 306)	4.52 (n = 19)
Fashion	5.95 (n = 25)	21.43 (n = 90)	66.90 (n = 281)	5.71 (n = 24)
Sports equipment	8.57 (n = 36)	25.71 (n = 108)	58.81 (n = 247)	6.90 (n = 29)
Home decor	6.19 (n = 26)	19.52 (n = 82)	67.38 (n = 283)	6.90 (n = 29)
Print media	5.95 (n = 25)	25.48 (n = 107)	65.71 (n = 276)	2.86 (n = 12)
Company size				
Large	4.12 (n = 34)	18.89 (n = 156)	70.10 (n = 579)	6.90 (n = 57)
SME	7.77 (n = 99)	23.94 (n = 305)	63.89 (n = 814)	4.40 (n = 56)
Total	**6.33 (n = 133)**	**21.95 (n = 461)**	**66.33 (n = 1,393)**	**5.38 (n = 113)**

Notes:

(1) Percentage for each category (independent variable) and rounded to two decimals places. Frequencies in brackets. There are 75 traders for each Member State and 60 traders for each industry. 118 traders are large enterprises and 182 traders are SMEs (45 by default). In total, there are 300 traders.

(2) Overall 2,100 compliance assessments, 525 for each jurisdiction, 420 for each industry, 826 for each large companies, 1,274 for each SME.

(3) 7 dependent variables have been included: Z2a(i) 14-day withdrawal period. Z2a(ii) withdrawal without giving any reason. Z2b definition when the withdrawal period commences. Z2c definition when the withdrawal period commences in case consumers order multiple goods. Z2d withdrawal may not incur any costs. Z2e 14-day period to send back goods. Z2f 14-day period to reimburse consumer.

Furthermore, the inquiry observed 2 patterns among the 71 traders' who failed to comply with the consumers' right to get reimbursed within '14 days from the day on which [they are] informed of the consumer's decision to withdraw from the contract'.[41] The most common form of non-compliance was that traders would only reimburse consumers once they received the goods and had time to inspect them. Consumers have a right to be reimbursed as soon as they provide evidence about the return of the goods to traders.[42] The remaining violations of the right of withdrawal concerned the time traders have to reimburse consumers. Some traders stated that they might take up to 30 days to reimburse consumers, another clear breach of the national rules implementing Article 13 of the Consumer Rights Directive.

[41] Consumer Rights Directive, art 13(1); dependent variable Z2f.

[42] Consumer Rights Directive, art 13(3.

Table 6.12 Instances of Non-compliance and Levels of Compliance with Right of Withdrawal

	Z2a(i)	Z2a(ii)	Z2b	Z2c	Z2d	Z2e	Z2f	Overall
Instances of Non-compliance								
Country								
France	7	0	1	0	0	1	15	24
Germany	0	0	0	1	1	1	4	7
Netherlands	7	0	2	0	0	1	13	23
United Kingdom	20	6	6	1	4	3	39	79
Industry								
Electronics	8	1	2	0	0	2	8	21
Fashion	5	1	2	0	0	1	16	25
Sports equipment	7	0	2	2	2	2	21	36
Home decor	6	1	0	0	3	1	15	26
Print media	8	3	3	0	0	0	11	25
Company size								
Large	9	2	1	1	1	1	19	34
SME	25	4	8	1	4	5	52	99
Total	**34**	**6**	**9**	**2**	**5**	**6**	**71**	**133**
Levels of Compliance								
Lower	34	6	9	2	5	6	71	133
Silence	3	74	15	162	83	85	39	461
Same	172	220	276	136	212	195	182	1,393
Higher	91	n/a	0	0	0	14	8	113

Notes:

(1) There are 75 traders for each Member State and 60 traders for each industry. 118 traders are large enterprises and 182 traders are SMEs (45 by default). In total, there are 300 traders.

(2) Violation, that is, trader has incorrectly provided information, results in score of 1. Omission, that is, trader has failed to display the information, results in score of 1.4. Overall 'lower' score.

(3) Overall, 2,100 compliance assessments, 525 for each jurisdiction, 420 for each industry, 826 for each large companies, 1,274 for each SMEs.

(4) Z2a(i) 14-day withdrawal period. Z2a(ii) withdrawal without giving any reason. Z2b definition when the withdrawal period commences. Z2c definition when the withdrawal period commences in case consumers order multiple goods. Z2d withdrawal may not incur any costs. Z2e 14-day period to send back goods. Z2f 14-day period to reimburse consumer.

The inquiry detected 2 patterns in the examination of compliance with the statutory withdrawal period (variable Z2a(i)).[43] The first pattern was compliance with outdated legislation, namely the (at least) 7-day withdrawal

[43] Consumer Rights Directive, art 9(1). This finding confirms parts of the Commission's study. See European Commission (n 22).

Table 6.13 Length of Right of Withdrawal

	Invalid (%)	7 days (%)	10 days (%)	14 days (%)	More than 14 days (%)
Country					
France	4.00 (n = 3)	5.33 (n = 4)	0.00 (n = 0)	53.33 (n = 40)	37.33 (n = 28)
Germany	2.67 (n = 2)	0.00 (n = 0)	0.00 (n = 0)	65.33 (n = 49)	32.00 (n = 24)
Netherlands	5.33 (n = 4)	4.00 (n = 3)	1.33 (n = 1)	65.33 (n = 49)	24.00 (n = 18)
United Kingdom	18.67 (n = 14)	8.00 (n = 6)	0.00 (n = 0)	45.33 (n = 34)	28.00 (n = 21)
Industry					
Electronics	13.33 (n = 8)	0.00 (n = 0)	0.00 (n = 0)	60.00 (n = 36)	26.67 (n = 16)
Fashion	6.67 (n = 4)	1.76 (n = 1)	0.00 (n = 0)	60.00 (n = 36)	31.67 (n = 19)
Sports equipment	3.33 (n = 2)	8.33 (n = 5)	0.00 (n = 0)	53.33 (n = 32)	35.00 (n = 21)
Home decor	5.00 (n = 3)	5.00 (n = 3)	1.76 (n = 1)	48.33 (n = 29)	40.00 (n = 24)
Print media	10.00 (n = 6)	6.67 (n = 4)	0.00 (n = 0)	65.00 (n = 39)	18.33 (n = 11)
Company size					
Large	6.78 (n = 8)	1.69 (n = 2)	0.00 (n = 0)	51.69 (n = 61)	39.83 (n = 47)
SME	8.24 (n = 15)	6.04 (n = 11)	0.55 (n = 1)	60.99 (n = 111)	24.18 (n = 44)
Total	**7.67 (n = 23)**	**4.33 (n = 13)**	**0.33 (n = 1)**	**57.33 (n = 172)**	**30.33 (n = 91)**

Notes:

(1) Length with right of withdrawal is dependent variable Z2a(i). There are 75 traders for each Member State and 60 traders for each industry. 118 traders are large enterprises and 182 traders are SMEs (45 by default). In total, there are 300 traders.

(2) More than 14 days includes: 6 × 15 days; 12 × 16 days; 5 × 21 days; 2 × 28 days; 53 × 30 days; 2 × 31; 1 × 44 days; 2 × 60 days; 2 × 90 days; 6 × 100.

(3) Invalid does not automatically mean traders failed to provide 14 days. Instead, traders either failed to provide the correct starting date (violation: n = 9), explicitly excluded the right of withdrawal (violation: n = 4), or simply provided that consumers have a statutory right of withdrawal without providing any further details (compliance: n = 10).

period, which Article 6(1) of the Distance Selling Directive (see Table 6.13, 7 days) used to impose. On a positive note, the empirical examination revealed that more traders provided a higher level of protection than a lower one (Table 6.13, more than 14 days). In particular, traders in France provided a more extended withdrawal period (37.33 per cent), as well as traders in the home decor industry (40.00 per cent)[44] and large enterprises (39.83 per cent). 6 traders provided consumers with as long as 100 days to return the goods (Table 6.13, Notes (2)).

[44] This result confirms the proposition of Omri Ben-Shahar and Eric A Posner, who argued that withdrawal rights make 'economic sense when the buyer most efficiently learns of a product through use

The remaining 5 violations accounted for 28 out of 133 instances of non-compliance with the consumers' right of withdrawal. 9 traders incorrectly provided the starting date of the withdrawal period (variable Z2b),[45] 2 traders provided it incorrectly in a situation where multiple goods had been ordered (variable Z2c),[46] 6 traders required consumers to justify their decision when withdrawing from the contract (variable Z2a(ii)),[47] 5 charged consumers for their withdrawal, and 6 traders gave consumers fewer than 14 days to return the goods (variable Z2e).[48]

A breakdown of the instances of non-compliance by trader revealed that, overall, 70 per cent of traders had no violation of the consumers' right of withdrawal (Table 6.14, model (1)). Compliance, however, varied substantially between the jurisdictions, the industries, and between large enterprises and SMEs. The highest level of compliance was observed in Germany (92 per cent), electronics (76.67 per cent), and among the large enterprises (77.97 per cent). Conversely, the lowest level of compliance was detected in the United Kingdom (37.33 per cent), in the sports equipment industry (58.33 per cent), and among the SMEs (64.84 per cent). Another important finding is that UK traders accounted for all instances with the highest number of violations; that is, 3 or more violations (Table 6.14, models (4)–(6)).

3.4 Passing of Risk

The inquiry assessed trader compliance with rules governing the passing of risk with 2 variables. According to the first variable (Z3a), traders are liable for the risk of loss or damage to the goods before consumers, or a third party indicated by them, have acquired physical possession of the goods. The second variable (Z3b) is an exception to the first variable (Z3a) when consumers have commissioned their carriers.[49] In this case, the risk passes to consumers when their commissioned carrier takes possession of the goods. Traders are not

or inspection at home and the product either does not depreciate rapidly or does depreciate but in a fashion that can be easily measured and compensated for'. See Omri Ben-Shahar and Eric A Posner, 'The Right to Withdraw in Contract Law' (2011) 40(1) Journal of Legal Studies 145.

45 Consumer Rights Directive, art 9(2)b.

46 ibid art 9(2)(b)(i).

47 ibid art 9(1).

48 ibid art 14(1).

49 The former scenario is dependent variable Z3a and the latter Z3b (Consumer Rights Directive, art 20). See ch 4.3.1.4.

Table 6.14 Number of Instances of Non-compliance with Right of Withdrawal for each Trader

	(1) None (%)	(2) One (%)	(3) Two (%)	(4) Three (%)	(5) Four (%)	(6) Five (%)
Country						
France	73.33 (n = 55)	21.33 (n = 16)	5.33 (n = 4)	0.00 (n = 0)	0.00 (n = 0)	0.00 (n = 0)
Germany	92.00 (n = 69)	6.67 (n = 5)	1.33 (n = 1)	0.00 (n = 0)	0.00 (n = 0)	0.00 (n = 0)
Netherlands	77.33 (n = 58)	14.67 (n = 11)	8.00 (n = 6)	0.00 (n = 0)	0.00 (n = 0)	0.00 (n = 0)
United Kingdom	37.33 (n = 28)	38.67 (n = 29)	12.00 (n = 9)	8.000 (n = 6)	1.33 (n = 1)	2.67 (n = 2)
Industry						
Electronics	76.67 (n = 46)	15.00 (n = 9)	5.00 (n = 3)	3.33 (n = 2)	0.00 (n = 0)	0.00 (n = 0)
Fashion	70.00 (n = 42)	25.00 (n = 15)	1.67 (n = 1)	1.67 (n = 1)	0.00 (n = 0)	1.67 (n = 1)
Sports equipment	58.33 (n = 35)	30.00 (n = 18)	8.33 (n = 5)	1.67 (n = 1)	0.00 (n = 0)	1.67 (n = 1)
Home decor	70.00 (n = 42)	18.33 (n = 11)	10.00 (n = 6)	1.67 (n = 1)	0.00 (n = 0)	0.00 (n = 0)
Print media	75.00 (n = 45)	13.33 (n = 8)	8.33 (n = 5)	1.67 (n = 1)	1.67 (n = 1)	0.00 (n = 0)
Company size						
Large	77.97 (n = 92)	16.10 (n = 19)	5.08 (n = 6)	0.85 (n = 1)	0.00 (n = 0)	0.00 (n = 0)
SME	64.84 (n = 118)	23.08 (n = 42)	7.69 (n = 14)	2.75 (n = 5)	0.55 (n = 1)	1.10 (n = 2)
Total	**70.00 (n = 210)**	**20.33 (n = 61)**	**6.67 (n = 20)**	**2.00 (n = 6)**	**0.33 (n = 1)**	**0.67 (n = 2)**

Notes: Percentage for each category (independent variable) and rounded to two decimals places. Frequencies in brackets. There are 75 traders for each Member State and 60 traders for each industry. 118 traders are large enterprises and 182 traders are SMEs (45 by default). In total, there are 300 traders.

required to include this information on their websites but must not provide a lower standard in their terms and conditions.

Almost all traders complied with the first variable governing the passing of risk. In all, 155 traders addressed the passing of risk issue in their terms by including the correct information, 138 were silent, and 7 traders provided the information incorrectly. The 7 violations occurred in France (n = 1) and the

United Kingdom (n = 6). The inquiry detected no patterns in terms of the violations' distribution across the industries and the company sizes: 3 violations in home decor, 2 in sports equipment, 1 in electronics, and 1 in fashion. The French trader in breach was a large enterprise (out of 33) and the 6 UK traders in breach were 3 (out of 35) large enterprises and 3 (out of 40) SMEs. Importantly, no trader failed to comply with the second requirement: 7 traders stated it correctly, and 293 traders did not address it at all in their terms and conditions. The prevalence of silence, however, comes as no surprise, as traders typically commission the carrier, not consumers.

The traders' clauses, which were non-compliant with the first passing of risk rule, provided that the risk passes to consumers before delivery, for instance, when consumers place their order or when the goods are shipped. Including either of the clauses in the terms and conditions is not allowed, and consumers are, because of the imperative nature of the rules implementing the Consumer Rights Directive, at no time bound by it.[50] The Consumer Rights Directive fully harmonized the rules on the passing of risk. It seems that the 6 UK traders and the 1 French trader had not updated their terms and conditions since the implementation of the Directive's rules into national law.

4 Additional Observations

This subsection steps outside the formal bounds of the empirical inquiry. It puts forward several additional observations made during the compliance assessment process, which, although interesting, did not directly address any of the hypotheses. These observations concerned violations of other consumer protection rules not included in the present study. However, some of them provided illustrations of more general trader behaviour. This section mentions the 4 most interesting additional observations.

The first additional observation concerns the delivery time of goods. The previous section of this chapter revealed that 35 traders failed to provide any delivery date (Table 6.10, model (Z1f)). What has been left undiscussed is the exact time by which traders aimed to deliver the goods. As examined in Chapter 4.3.1.5, Article 18 of the Consumer Rights Directive provides that traders must transfer the physical possession of the goods to consumers within 30 days. However, consumers and traders can agree that the delivery date could exceed 30 days, so the obligation to deliver within 30

[50] Consumer Rights Directive, art 25.

days becomes mandatory only if they have not stipulated otherwise. Although traders could take as long as 30 days if the terms were silent on the issue, almost all the 300 traders, except for 1 Dutch trader, provided for a delivery period of less than 30 days.[51] Most traders promised to deliver the goods the following day; some even offered same-day delivery.

The compliance inquiry detected 2 potential scam websites. The 2 websites pretended to be traders based in the United Kingdom, but the 2 shops are probably based in Hong Kong and failed to comply with very basic UK and EU consumer law rules. Several online reviews suggested that these shops sell counterfeit items and ship the goods from outside the United Kingdom, mainly from Hong Kong. These claims could not be verified, but there is strong evidence that the 2 traders operate a scam business outside the United Kingdom.[52]

The third observation concerns commercial guarantees, which consumers can purchase irrespective of their statutory rights. In theory, these guarantees offer consumers additional rights if the goods become faulty or damaged after the statutory guarantee period expired. The inquiry revealed that traders offered guarantees which merely reflected the consumers' statutory rights and thus were a bad bargain for consumers.

Another observation was that dozens of traders excluded the application of the United Nations Convention on Contracts for the International Sale of Goods, also called CISG or the Vienna Convention.[53] The harmonized CISG framework aims to reduce transaction costs in international trade[54] and thus applies to cross-border[55] and business-to-business transactions.[56] Traders operating in countries that have ratified the Convention are automatically bound by the CISG unless they explicitly opt out.[57] Almost all European Union Member States are party to the Vienna Convention, including France, Germany, and the Netherlands.[58] The United Kingdom has not acceded to the

[51] One trader provided a delivery date of 6 to 8 weeks.

[52] The emergence of bad faith actors in e-commerce is a global problem and requires further international initiatives. See eg Gail Pearson, 'Further Challenges for Australian Consumer Law' in Claudia Lima Marques and Dan Wei (eds), *Consumer Law and Socioeconomic Development: National and International Dimensions* (Springer Publishing 2017) 303–305.

[53] United Nations Convention on Contracts for the International Sale of Goods, Vienna (11 April 1980).

[54] ibid preamble.

[55] ibid art 1.

[56] ibid art 2.

[57] ibid art 6.

[58] The CISG has been in force in France since 1 January 1988, in Germany since 1 January 1991, and in the Netherlands since 1 January 1992. United Nations, 'Status: United Nations Convention on Contracts for the International Sale of Goods (Vienna, 1980) (CISG)' United Nations Commission on International Trade Law (20 April 2021) https://uncitral.un.org/en/texts/salegoods/conventions/sale_of_goods/cisg/status (accessed 20 April 2021).

Convention, and this is unlikely to change in the near future.[59] It might explain why only 1 UK trader explicitly excluded the application of the CISG. Overall, none of the 300 traders has explicitly opted into the CISG, some only by default, and dozens of traders, particularly German ones, have excluded the application of the Vienna Convention.

5 Conclusion

This chapter has tested the hypotheses that traders are not fully compliant with their legal duties (H_1) and the proposition that factors such as the company's size (H_2), the company's age (H_3), or the use of terms pre-drafted by public or semi-public organizations (H_4) influence compliance. Descriptive statistics have confirmed the first hypothesis that traders are not fully complying with their legal duties, as 80.67 per cent (242 out of 300) of the simulated e-commerce consumer transactions contained at least 1 or more instances of non-compliance (Table 6.2, models (2–5), Total). The ordinary least square and binary logistic regression tests in section 2 revealed that SMEs had, on average, more violations of the consumer protection rules than large enterprises (Table 6.4 model (1)) and were less likely to be compliant (Table 6.4 model (2)). However, the statistical tests (Table 6.4) could not establish any statistically significant correlation between compliance and the company's age or the use of pre-drafted terms and conditions. Another finding was that the traders' origin significantly affected compliance, with UK traders being more likely not to comply compared to German (most compliant), French (second most compliant), and Dutch (third most compliant) traders. Section 3 provided further details about the level of trader compliance by each consumer right. Out of 802 instances of non-compliance, 60.60 per cent (n = 486) concerned mandatory disclosures, 21.95 per cent (n = 176) unfair contract terms, 16.58 per cent (n = 133) the consumers' right of withdrawal, and 0.87 per cent (n = 7) the rules governing the passing of risk (Table 6.5, Total). Section 4 offered a few additional observations concerning other violations found on the traders' websites but fell outside the scope of the present study. Overall, the compliance assessments and statistical tests revealed some interesting patterns of non-compliance, which the following chapter will translate into targeted and actionable policy recommendations.

[59] Reasons for and against the UK's accession were discussed in Benjamin Hayward, Bruno Zeller, and Camilla Baasch Andersen, 'The CISG and the United Kingdom: Exploring Coherency and Private International Law' (2018) 67(3) International and Comparative Law Quarterly 607.

7
Policy Recommendations

1 Introduction

The compliance assessments carried out for the empirical inquiry of this book have revealed that only 58 of the 300 e-commerce traders, 19.33 per cent, were fully compliant with applicable consumer rights.[1] The empirical examination not only shed light on the levels of trader compliance but also detected patterns of (non-)compliance. For instance, statistical tests revealed that large companies are more likely to be compliant than small and medium-sized enterprises (SMEs). Conversely, from a statistical perspective, company age and utilization of standard contract terms drafted and provided by public or semi-public authorities did not affect compliance.[2]

This chapter aims to translate the study's empirical findings into targeted and actionable policy recommendations to increase the efficiency of EU consumer contract law and trader compliance. However, it is not an exhaustive list of necessary reforms. All policy recommendations build on the findings of the book's empirical inquiry or similar studies in the field, comply with the EU's principles of conferral, subsidiarity, and proportionality, adhere to the Better Regulation guidelines, and align with existing proposals or laws on the EU and national level.[3] The chapter addresses all policy recommendations to the relevant stakeholders, the EU legislator, the Member States, and other groups, such as e-commerce traders or consumer organizations. The chapter is, however, not exploring the possible influences of Brexit on UK or EU consumer contract

[1] Table 6.2.
[2] Table 6.4.
[3] TEU, art 5; TFEU, arts 2(2), 4(1) and (2), and 114. For an overview of the EU's competence in consumer contract law see eg Stephen Weatherill, *EU Consumer Law and Policy* (2nd edn, Edward Elgar Publishing 2013) 15–24; Stephen Weatherill, 'Finding the Internal Market in the Treaty' in Stephen Weatherill (ed), *The Internal Market as a Legal Concept* (OUP 2017). Chapter 2 of this book critically examines the Better Regulation guidelines and whether they generate evidence-based policy. It also defines what good evidence should look like.

Compliance with European Consumer Law. Felix Pflücke, Oxford University Press. © Oxford University Press 2024.
DOI: 10.1093/9780198906414.003.0007

law, as not only would this go beyond the scope of inquiry of the study, but it is also too early to determine any future developments.[4]

The chapter first explores the idea of promoting compliant standard contract terms pre-drafted by public and semi-public organizations. This section examines the levels of compliance of e-commerce traders who based their terms and conditions on pre-drafted standard contract terms. It investigates why most traders still failed to comply fully with their legal duties. The chapter then turns to the issue of higher levels of non-compliance among SMEs. It considers instances where SMEs failed to comply and recommends solutions to improve their compliance. Finally, the chapter discusses the idea of increasing access to justice for consumers by granting consumers the option to resolve their disputes via online dispute resolution (ODR) without allowing traders to opt out.

2 Promoting Compliant Pre-drafted Standard Contract Terms

The dataset of the book's empirical inquiry revealed that only traders based in the Netherlands used standard contract terms drafted and provided by public or semi-public organizations. Of these, 56 out of 75 based their terms and conditions on standard contract terms provided by 4 semi-public organizations.[5] The most commonly used standard terms were by *Thuiswinkel* (n = 32).[6] Other standard terms used by traders of the present study were by the *Stichting Webshop Keurmerk* (n = 20),[7] the *Centrale*

[4] For instance, Horst Eidenmüller discussed possible scenarios. Horst Eidenmüller, 'Collateral Damage: Brexit's Negative Effects on Regulatory Competition and Legal Innovation in Private Law' (2018) 26(4) Zeitschrift für Europäisches Privatrecht 868.

[5] Table 5.7.

[6] Thuiswinkel Organisatie, 'Algemene Voorwaarden Thuiswinkel' (1 June 2014) https://www.thuiswinkel.org/veilig-online-shoppen/wat-is-thuiswinkel-waarborg/algemene-voorwaarden-thuiswinkel/ (accessed 22 May 2021). It is the latest published version of pre-drafted standard contract terms provided by the Thuiswinkel Organisatie, drafted in collaboration with the organisation Coördinatiegroep Zelfreguleringsoverleg (Coordination Group on Negotiation for Self-Regulation) in 2014. This organization was founded in 1996 to liaise between industry and consumer organizations, act as a self-regulation body for traders, and most importantly, increase consumer confidence in e-commerce transactions, cf Esther van Schagen, 'The Draft Common Frame of Reference and Multilevel Governance' (2010) 1(3) Edinburgh Student Law Review 92; Franziska Weber and Christopher Hodges, 'The Netherlands' in Christopher Hodges, Iris Benöhr, and Naomi Creutzfeldt-Banda (eds), *Consumer ADR in Europe* (Hart Publishing 2012) 152–53.

[7] Stichting Webshop Keurmerk, 'Algemene Voorwaarden voor Webshops' (1 June 2014) https://www.keurmerk.info/nl/home/gratis-algemene-voorwaarden/ (accessed 22 May 2021). Exactly like the Thuiswinkel standard terms, the Stichting Webshop Keurmerk drafted its standard terms in collaboration with the consumer organization Coördinatiegroep Zelfreguleringsoverleg in 2014.

Branchevereniging Wonen (n = 3),[8] and 1 by the International Chamber of Commerce[9] (Incoterms®).

A closer look at the data collected on the use of pre-drafted standard contract terms by Dutch traders suggests that large enterprises are more likely to use them (87.5 per cent, that is 14 out of 16 traders) than SMEs (71.19 per cent, that is 42 out of 59 traders). 12 large enterprises based their terms on Thuiswinkel, 1 on Centrale Branchevereniging Wonen, and 1 on Incoterms, whereas 20 SMEs based their terms on Thuiswinkel, 20 on Stichting Webshop Keurmerk, and 2 on Centrale Branchevereniging Wonen.

However, the 56 Dutch traders who based their terms on pre-drafted standard contract terms were, from a statistical viewpoint, not more likely to be compliant than traders who drafted their terms.[10] Nonetheless, the first statistical test in Table 6.4 suggested from an effect size perspective that e-commerce traders who based their terms and conditions on standard contract terms prepared by public or semi-public authorities had, on average, fewer violations compared to traders who did not.[11] The second test in Table 6.4, however, revealed that traders who used pre-drafted terms had a higher probability of non-compliance than traders who drafted their terms.[12] As mentioned in the previous chapter, this might suggest that the pre-drafted terms already contained provisions which were in breach of consumer protection standards, although they had, on average, fewer violations than traders who drafted their terms. Alternatively, traders using the pre-drafted terms had collectively failed to implement them faithfully on their websites. It is, therefore, crucial to assess whether the original standard contract terms drafted and provided by public or semi-public organizations complied with the consumer protection rights selected for the present study.

The following sections scrutinize the pre-drafted contract terms supplied by semi-public organizations in the Netherlands. However, it remains unclear whether these organizations provide traders with additional information beyond publicly accessible information on their websites.

[8] Centrale Branchevereniging Wonen, 'Download de CBW-erkende voorwaarden' (31 December 2019) https://www.cbw-erkend.nl/garanties-wonen (accessed 22 May 2021). The Centrale Branchevereniging Wonen published new pre-drafted standard contract terms, which have been in use since 1 January 2020. However, the study only considers the previous set of terms used by traders.

[9] The trader specifically referred to and used the Incoterms® 2010, particularly the Delivered at Place (DAP) Incoterms®. See International Chamber of Commerce, 'What are Incoterms® rules?' (2020) https://iccwbo.org/resources-for-business/incoterms-rules/incoterms-2020/ (accessed 22 May 2021).

[10] Table 6.4.

[11] Table 6.4 model (1).

[12] Table 6.4 model (2).

2.1 Empirical Evidence

2.1.1 Thuiswinkel

The first standard contract terms examined were drafted and provided by Thuiswinkel. These terms were prevalent among large enterprises (12 out of 14 traders used pre-drafted terms), but also almost half of SMEs (20 out of 42) used them. Traders who based their terms on Thuiswinkel's standard contracts terms violated in total 5 consumer rights, which overall accounted for 59 instances of non-compliance (Table 7.1 below). The violations concerned choice of law clauses, right of withdrawal, failure to provide the hyperlink to the EU Commission's Online Dispute Resolution platform, failure to provide the right of withdrawal form, and failure to display the company's registration number on the website.

Examining the original version of the Thuiswinkel standard contract terms showed that they contained 2 instances of non-compliance. The first one concerned the choice of law clause in the pre-drafted standard contract terms, which stated that exclusively Dutch law applies.[13] Consumers can rely on the law of the place of their habitual residence, and such a clause is unlikely to stand should consumers be based outside of the Netherlands.[14] 31 out of 32 traders who used the pre-drafted terms adopted Thuiswinkel's choice of law clause.[15] It is unclear whether Thuiswinkel provides traders with different pre-drafted terms or guidance for cross-border transactions that are not publicly available. Thus, the clause should be corrected and state that consumers based in the European Union can rely on the law of the place of their habitual residence. The second instance where Thuiswinkel failed to respect one of the selected consumer rights is its failure to include a term that informs consumers about the existence of the EU Commission's Online Dispute Resolution platform. Traders are not required to take part in ODR, but they must inform consumers of the existence of the European Commission's platform and also display the hyperlink to the platform.[16] Thuiswinkel, however, only provided

[13] 'Op overeenkomsten tussen de ondernemer en de consument waarop deze algemene voorwaarden betrekking hebben, is uitsluitend Nederlands recht van toepassing.' [Only Dutch law applies to agreements between the trader and the consumer including to these general terms and conditions] art 17(1) of Thuiswinkel (n 6).

[14] Article 6(1) of the Regulation (EC) 593/2008 (Rome I), included in dependent variable X11 of the present study. Chapter 3.4.11 of the book provides further legal context.
Traders who had used this clause in their terms all shipped within and outside the Netherlands. Loos and Luzak also found incompliant choice of law clauses in the empirical study on consumer service agreements, Marco Loos and Joasia A Luzak, 'Wanted: a Bigger Stick. On Unfair Terms in Consumer Contracts with Online Service Providers' (2016) 39(1) Journal of Consumer Policy 85.

[15] 1 trader excluded this clause from its terms.

[16] Consumer Rights Directive, art 6(1)(t); dependent variable Z4.

the hyperlink to their own ODR and alternative dispute resolution (ADR) systems (Geschillencommissie Thuiswinkel) and explained how consumers could access their ODR and ADR procedures.[17] Failing to provide information on the EU's ODR platform is another violation of a consumer protection rule. Despite the error in Thuiswinkel's standard contract terms, 7 out of 32 traders correctly referred to the EU's ODR platform.

Traders violated 3 consumer rights because they failed to implement Thuiswinkel's pre-drafted standard terms and conditions faithfully. The first instance concerned a trader who failed to include their company registration number on the website.[18] Another instance was where a trader failed faithfully to implement Thuiswinkel's pre-drafted terms concerning the consumer's right of withdrawal. The trader provided in its terms that consumers would only be reimbursed after 30 days. Consumers, however, have a right to be reimbursed within 14 days.[19] The third instance concerned the traders' duty to provide a model withdrawal form on their websites.[20] The Annex to the Thuiswinkel terms and conditions provides a model withdrawal form. Almost all traders who used Thuiswinkel's terms included such a form on their website; only 2 traders failed to do so.[21]

The empirical inquiry can only attribute the violations regarding the choice of law issue and the mandatory disclosure concerning the EU's ODR platform to Thuiswinkel. All 3 remaining violations occurred because traders failed to implement Thuiswinkel's standard terms and conditions faithfully. Nonetheless, the 2 violations in the pre-drafted standard contract terms accounted for 55 out of 58 instances of non-compliance.

2.1.2 Stichting Webshop Keurmerk

Stichting Webshop Keurmerk provided the second most popular standard contract terms used exclusively by SMEs (20 out of 42 SMEs used pre-drafted terms). Traders who based their terms on these pre-drafted standard terms violated 4 mandatory disclosures and 3 consumer rights concerning withdrawals (see Table 7.1 below).

Similarly to Thuiswinkel, the terms pre-drafted and provided by the Stichting Webshop Keurmerk stated that exclusively Dutch law applies,[22]

[17] Thuiswinkel (n 6) art 17 (Geschillen).
[18] E-Commerce Directive, art 5(1)(d) of; dependent variable Y1.
[19] Consumer Rights Directive, art 13(1); dependent variable Z2f.
[20] Consumer Rights Directive, art 6(1)(h); dependent variable Z1g(ii).
[21] The study could not verify whether traders provide consumers with such a withdrawal form should customers purchase goods.
[22] Regulation (EC) 593/2008 (Rome I), art 6(1); dependent variable X11. 5 traders who used Stichting Webshop Keurmerk's terms and conditions had not included such a clause.

and their terms also only referred to their own ODR and ADR systems (here Geschillencommissie Webshop).[23] Most traders had adopted these 2 provisions, which together resulted in 34 instances of non-compliance (Table 7.1). As with Thuiswinkel, it is unclear whether Stichting Webshop Keurmerk provides traders with different pre-drafted terms or guidance for cross-border transactions that are not publicly available.

In addition to the violations mentioned above, traders violated 6 consumer rights because they failed faithfully to implement the pre-drafted standard contract terms of Stichting Webshop Keurmerk: 1 trader omitted the payment arrangement on its website;[24] 2 traders failed to provide the estimated delivery date of the goods;[25] 5 traders failed to provide the model withdrawal form;[26] 3 traders failed to provide the consumers right of withdrawal correctly (14-day period);[27] 1 trader incorrectly provided that the consumer had to return the goods within 10 days, even though consumers have up to 14 days;[28] and 6 traders provided that consumers would not be reimbursed within the statutory 14-day period, but only within 30 days.[29]

34 out of 52 instances of non-compliance can thus be attributed directly to the pre-drafted terms and conditions provided by the Stichting Webshop Keurmerk. In contrast, traders caused the remaining 18 violations by failing to implement the pre-drafted terms and conditions faithfully.

2.1.3 Centrale Branchevereniging Wonen

3 traders used the terms and conditions provided by the Centrale Branchevereniging Wonen. The Centrale Branchevereniging Wonen's terms complied almost in full with the selected consumer rights; they only failed to include a model withdrawal form in their terms or its Annex (Table 7.1 below).[30] But unlike Thuiswinkel and Stichting Webshop Keurmerk, the Centrale Branchevereniging Wonen did not include an invalid choice of law clause in

[23] Stichting Webshop Keurmerk (n 7) art 17 (Geschillen). As pointed out earlier, this clearly breaches art 6(1)(t) of the Consumer Rights Directive; dependent variable Z4.
1 trader correctly provided the EU's ODR platform link.

[24] Consumer Rights Directive, art 6(1)(g); dependent variable Z1e.

[25] Consumer Rights Directive, art 6(1)(g); dependent variable Z1f.

[26] Consumer Rights Directive, art 6(1)(h); dependent variable Z1g(ii).

[27] Consumer Rights Directive, art 9(1); dependent variable Z2a(i). 1 trader provided 10 days (Trader 205) and 2 traders provided 7 days.

[28] Consumer Rights Directive, art 14(1); dependent variable Z2e.

[29] Consumer Rights Directive, art 13(1); dependent variable Z2f.

[30] It is unclear whether Centrale Branchevereniging Wonen directly provides traders with this form; it was not included in their pre-drafted terms on the publicly available part of their website. Nonetheless, 2 of 3 traders had a model withdrawal form on their websites (Traders 203 and 210). Only 1 trader had not included one as required by art 6(1)(h) of the Consumer Rights Directive; dependent variable Z1g(ii).

Table 7.1 Instances of Non-compliance by Standard Contract Terms Providers and Traders

	Unfair Terms	Mandatory Disclosures	Right of Withdrawal	Passing of Risk
Thuiswinkel	1	1	0	0
Traders	1 (n = 31)	3 (n = 27)	1 (n = 1)	0 (n = 0)
Stichting Webshop Keurmerk	1	1	0	0
Traders	1 (n = 15)	4 (n = 27)	3 (n = 10)	0 (n = 0)
Centrale Brancheverenìging Wonen	0	1	0	0
Traders	0 (n = 0)	2 (n = 2)	1 (n = 1)	0 (n = 0)
Incoterms® Delivery at Place	0	0	0	0
Traders	2 (n = 2)	2 (n = 2)	0 (n = 0)	0 (n = 0)

Notes:

(1) Consumer rights violated and instances in bracket, subdivided by legal category and standard contract terms providers and traders who used them.

(2) Number of traders who based their terms on pre-drafted standard contract terms (total of 56 (N)) by provider: *Thuiswinkel* (n = 32); *Stichting Webshop Keurmerk* (n = 20); *Centrale Brancheverenìging Wonen* (n = 3), and Incoterms® by the International Chamber of Commerce (n = 1).

(3) Dependent variables that traders failed to comply with (instances in bracket):

Thuiswinkel traders: X11 (n = 31), Y1 (n = 1), Z1g(ii) (n = 1), Z2f (n = 1), Z4 (n = 25).

Stichting Webshop Keurmerk traders: X11 (n = 15), Z1e (n = 1), Z1f (n = 2), Z1g(ii) (n = 5), Z2a(i) (n = 3), Z2e (n = 1), Z2f (n = 6), Z4 (n = 19).

Centrale Brancheverenìging Wonen traders: Y2 (n = 1), Z1g(ii) (n = 1), Z2f (n = 1).

Incoterms® Delivery at Place trader: X2 (n = 1), X11 (n = 1), Z1h (n = 1), Z4 (n = 1).

(4) Dependent variables that providers of pre-drafted terms failed to comply with:

Thuiswinkel: X11, Z4.

Stichting Webshop Keurmerk: X11, Z4.

Centrale Brancheverenìging Wonen: Z1g(ii).

(5) X2: contract terms inappropriately excluding or limiting the legal rights of consumers in case of total, partial, or inadequate performance by traders or suppliers; X11: contract terms excluding or hindering consumers to take legal action (eg unfair choice of law clauses); Y1: providing the trade register number; Y2: providing the VAT number; Z1e: providing the payment arrangements; Z1f: providing the delivery time; Z1g(ii): providing a model withdrawal form; Z1h: providing a reminder of the existence of a legal guarantee of conformity of goods; Z2a(i): consumers have 14 days to withdraw from distance contracts; Z2e: consumers have 14 days to return the goods after they communicated their decision to withdraw from the contract; Z2f: traders have to reimburse consumer after 14 days of being informed of the latter's decision to withdraw from the contract; Z4: providing the hyperlink and method to access the EU's ODR platform. Chapter 5 provides further details on each variable.

their terms. Traders who used them did also not include it of their own motion on their websites.[31] The Centrale Branchevereniging Wonen's standard terms correctly provided that consumers based in the European Union can rely on the laws of the place of their habitual residence.[32] Centrale Branchevereniging Wonen's terms also included a hyperlink to the EU's ODR platform, which, as explained above, was missing from the terms of the other 2 providers of pre-drafted terms.[33] Some of the traders, however, failed to implement the Centrale Branchevereniging Wonen's terms faithfully: 1 trader failed to provide its VAT number,[34] and another trader incorrectly provided that it would only reimburse customers withdrawing from the contract once it had received back the goods, even though consumers have the right to be reimbursed within 14 days of sending proof that they have returned the goods.[35] Consequently, the empirical inquiry could only attribute 1 out of 3 consumer rights violations to the Centrale Branchevereniging Wonen's terms.

2.1.4 Incoterms®

1 trader used the Incoterms® Deliver at Place (DAP) provided by the International Chamber of Commerce.[36] Incoterms® are very different from the pre-drafted terms examined above, as Incoterms® deal with different legal issues, and traders can include or exclude them. Incoterms® Deliver at Place (DAP) govern the delivery of goods, namely that the seller is in charge of arranging the delivery at the consumers' address and that the risk of loss or damage to the goods transfers from seller to buyer as soon as the goods are delivered.[37] This demonstrates that Incoterms® do not have the ambition to govern the entire contractual relationship but only certain areas, such as the delivery phase.

The trader using the Incoterms® had 2 unfair contract terms on its website and failed to comply with 2 mandatory disclosures (see Table 7.1).[38] Incoterms® DAP, however, do not address these particular issues, and non-compliance

[31] Neither did 1 of the 3 traders violate art 6(1) of Regulation (EC) 593/2008 (Rome I); dependent variable X11.

[32] Centrale Branchevereniging Wonen (n 8) art 22.

[33] All traders correctly implemented it.

[34] E-Commerce Directive, art 5(1)(g); dependent variable Y2.

[35] Consumer Rights Directive, art 13(1); dependent variable Z2f.

[36] International Chamber of Commerce (n 9).

[37] World Trade Press, *Incoterms 2010: A Comprehensive Guide to the INCOTERMS 2010* (World Trade Press 2010) 24–25.

[38] The first unfair contract term concerned dependent variable X2, which does not allow the consumer to offset a debt, contrary to the national rules implementing art 3 in connection with Point 1(b) Annex to the Unfair Contract Terms Directive. The second unfair term concerned a jurisdiction clause: the trader included a clause that consumers could only bring a claim at the local court in Groningen, which is in breach of art 18(2) of Regulation (EU) 1215/2012 (dependent variable X11 of

cannot be attributed to the International Chamber of Commerce but directly to the trader.

2.2 Observations

The examination of trader and provider compliance indicates that providers of pre-drafted terms, rather than the traders who utilized them, account for more instances of non-compliance (91 out of 118). Their pre-drafted terms contained many consumer rights violations, and the number of traders who failed to implement the terms and conditions faithfully was significantly lower (27 out of 118).[39] These findings confirm one of the earlier observations in Chapter 6, where the empirical data suggested that the pre-drafted terms already contained provisions that breached consumer protection standards. However, on average, they had fewer traders who fully drafted their terms. It also rejects the second observation from Chapter 6, that traders' non-compliance resulted from their failure to implement the pre-drafted terms faithfully.[40]

2.3 Policy Recommendations

The European Commission first proposed the broader use of standard contract terms pre-drafted and provided by public or semi-public organizations in the early 2000s.[41] In theory, this approach allows traders to use standard terms that are fully compliant with all legal duties while simultaneously upholding the contractual freedom of traders. Traders are still allowed to tailor these terms to their needs, for instance, by adopting only parts of the pre-drafted terms or modifying them. Traders may also draft their terms and conditions. The European Commission's proposals have not focused on whether

the study). The trader also failed to inform consumers of the existence of a legal guarantee of conformity for goods (art 6(1)(l) of the Consumer Rights Directive; dependent variable Z1h) and the methods of accessing the EU's ODR platform (art 6(1)(t) of the Consumer Rights Directive; dependent variable Z4).

[39] Table 7.1 above.

[40] Chapter 6.2.2 put forward both observations.

[41] European Commission, 'European contract law' (Communication) COM(2001) 398 final, para 56; European Commission, 'A more coherent European contract law: An action plan' (Communication) COM(2003) OJ C63/1; European Commission, 'European contract law and the revision of the acquis: the way forward' (Communication) COM(2004) 651 final, para 2.2.3.

these pre-drafted terms comply with consumer rights nor their correct implementation by traders. It might mislead consumers into believing that such pre-drafted standard contract terms are fully compliant because of the public or semi-public provenance. As shown earlier in this part of the chapter, the pre-drafted standard terms contained consumer rights violations, and, additionally, several traders failed to implement these pre-drafted terms faithfully. Therefore, this section's policy recommendations put forward proposals to increase compliance with pre-drafted standard contract terms and ensure that traders implement such pre-drafted terms correctly.

Ensuring compliance of pre-drafted standard terms and their correct implementation by traders are within the Member States' competence. The European Commission can propose new substantive rules[42] but also, as it has done, coordinate enforcement actions within the EU.[43] The Commission could publish standard contract terms that comply with the strictest national consumer protection rules in the EU's single market. These standard terms could be published as a soft-law instrument and serve as an alternative to further harmonization of the national contract laws.[44] Taking the strictest national rules would be necessary because the EU has yet to harmonize all consumer rules, and the Member States can still adopt stricter rules.[45] However, the European Commission dismissed such a proposal in 2005 as, in its view, using the strictest national rules might make its model standard contract terms less attractive for traders.[46] Giuditta Cordero-Moss highlighted another shortcoming of this approach, arguing that the main problem would be the

[42] However, the European Commission must stay within the limits of art 114 of the TFEU. For a general historical account of the European Commission's competence to harmonize national (consumer contract) laws see eg Weatherill (n 1) ch 3.

[43] For instance, Regulation (EU) 2017/2394 of 12 December 2017 on cooperation between national authorities responsible for the enforcement of consumer protection laws and repealing Regulation (EC) No 2006/2004 [2017] OJ L345/1.

[44] Jens Karsten and Ali R Sinai argue that 'models' should be drawn up for every jurisdiction and monitored accordingly. They also highlight the relevance of consumer organizations and their potential involvement in drafting and providing such terms, Jens Karsten and Ali R Sinai, 'The Action Plan on European Contract Law: Perspectives for the Future of European Contract Law and EC Consumer Law' (2003) 26(2) Journal of Consumer Policy 168. The discussion at the time included similar proposals of framework legislation and non-binding measures as opposed to complete harmonization; see eg Josef Drexl, 'Community Legislation Continued: Complete Harmonisation, Framework Legislation or Non-Binding Measures:
Alternative Approaches to European Contract Law, Consumer Protection and Unfair Trade Practices?' (2002) 13(6) European Business Law Review 557.

[45] Especially regarding the Unfair Contract Terms Directive and the E-Commerce Directive see ch 3 and ch 4.2 of this book. The minimum harmonization Consumer Sales and Guarantees Directive 1999/44/EC was replaced and repealed by a maximum harmonization Directive under the European Commission's New Deal for Consumers, discussed further below.

[46] The European Commission also argued that these standard terms require constant updates, and the general maintenance for a website providing standard contract terms would be very costly. Hence,

diverging rules on contractual interpretation.[47] In her view, even transnational instruments, such as the principles of European contract law (PECL)[48] and the principles of international commercial contracts (UPICC),[49] could not resolve this issue,[50] as they 'do not contribute considerably to a harmonised standard of interpretation'.[51] She argued that Incoterms® could be an alternative to providing pre-drafted standard contract terms, as they operate independently of national general contract laws. However, this benefit is non-existent in B2C contracts because consumers can always rely on national law in case of a dispute;[52] any contractual clauses attempting to restrict or exclude this are not binding on consumers.[53] In addition to adopting pre-drafted standard contract terms, one could propose an instrument which would also exhaustively govern issues of contractual interpretation, such as a European Civil Code.[54] Earlier proposals of such a project, the Proposal for a Common European Sales Law (CESL),[55] failed due to political opposition, even as an optional instrument.[56] The optional CESL would have fully harmonized all the rules governing e-commerce, including contractual interpretation,[57] but only should

the European Commission ultimately abandoned this idea. European Commission, 'First Annual Progress Report on European Contract Law and the Acquis Review' COM(2005) 456 final, para 4.1; Ulf Bernitz, 'The Commission's Communications and Standard Contract Terms' in Stefan Vogenauer and Stephen Weatherill (eds), *The Harmonisation of European Contract Law: Implications for European Private Laws, Business and Legal Practice* (Hart Publishing 2006) 190.

[47] Giuditta Cordero-Moss, 'Standard contract terms as an alternative to legislation' in Christian Twigg-Flesner (ed), *Research Handbook on EU Consumer and Contract Law* (Edward Elgar Publishing 2016) 489, 495–502.

[48] For the principles of European contract law (PECL) see Ole Lando and Hugh Beale (eds), *Principles of European Contract Law, Parts I and II* (Kluwer Law International 2000); Ole Lando, Eric Clive, André Prüm, and Reinhard Zimmermann (eds), *Principles of European Contract Law Parts III* (Kluwer Law International 2003).

[49] International Institute for the Unification of Private Law, 'The Principles of International Commercial Contracts' (Rome, 2016).

[50] Cordero-Moss (n 47) 503–505.

[51] ibid 506.

[52] Regulation (EC) 593/2008 (Rome I), art 6(1).

[53] For instance, art 25 of the Consumer Rights Directive and art 6(1) of the Unfair Contract Terms Directive.

[54] This approach would be necessary for consumer contracts, but, of course, not for business-to-business contracts, as they can simply adopt INCOTERMS®.

[55] European Commission, 'Proposal for a Regulation of the European Parliament and of the Council on a Common European Sales Law (CESL)' COM(2011) 635 final.

[56] For background information on the Common European Sales Law see Weatherill (n 1) 197–99. However, the European Parliamentary Research Service estimates that the long-term opportunity costs of trade within the Single Market are between 183 and 269 billion Euros annually. The researchers identified the lack of harmonization of the rules concerning online and distance sales as one of the main barriers, European Parliamentary Research Service, 'The Costs of Non-Europe in the Single Market: Free Movement of Goods' (September 2014) 7 ff http://www.europarl.europa.eu/EPRS/EPRS_STUDY_536353_CoNE_Single_Market_I.pdf (accessed 3 November 2020).

[57] Part III of the Common European Sales Law. See generally Gerard McMeel and Hans Christoph Grigoleit, 'Interpretation of Contracts' in Gerhard Dannemann and Stefan Vogenauer (eds), *The*

traders decide to opt in.[58] It would have also provided traders with greater choice,[59] but, as pointed out earlier in the book, another attempt to adopt the CESL seems, from a political viewpoint, very unlikely. Moreover, it is not clear whether Article 114 of the Treaty on the Functioning of the European Union supports the adoption of such an instrument.[60]

Instead of drastically reforming the EU consumer contract law acquis, the European Commission went ahead with its more conventional New Deal for Consumers.[61] The recently adopted Directive 2019/770/EU and Directive 2019/771/EU are maximum harmonization instruments[62] but are not as ambitious as the CESL: Directive 2019/770/EU harmonizes rules regarding digital content and services; 2019/771/EU repealed and replaced the minimum harmonization Consumer Sales and Guarantees Directive 1999/44/EC. Directive 2019/2161/EU also only amended the Unfair Contract Terms Directive concerning the rules on penalties (Article 1 of Directive 2019/2161/EU) and introduced

Common European Sales Law in Context: Interactions with English and German Law (OUP 2013) 369–72; Stefan Vogenauer, 'Interpretation' in Nils Jansen and Reinhard Zimmermann (eds), *Commentaries on European Contract Laws* (OUP 2018).

[58] cf Richard Epstein, 'Harmonization, heterogeneity and regulation: CESL, the lost opportunity for constructive harmonization' (2013) 50(Special Issue) Common Market Law Review 207.

[59] See eg Karsten and Sinai (n 44) 170; Jan M Smits, 'Party choice and the Common European Sales Law, or: How to prevent the CESL from becoming a lemon on the law market' (2013) 50(Special Issue) Common Market Law Review 51; Horst Eidenmüller, 'What can be wrong with an option? An optional Common European Sales Law as a regulatory tool' (2013) 50(Special Issue) Common Market Law Review 69. Christian Twigg-Flesner proposed a (mandatory) B2C cross-border-only regulation in the EU's Single Market, which, according to Stephen Weatherill, would limit the spill-over effect of EU measures into domestic affairs and protect national regulatory autonomy. See Christian Twigg-Flesner, *A Cross-Border-Only Regulation for Consumer Transactions in the EU: A Fresh Approach to EU Consumer Law* (Springer Publishing 2011) 26 ff; Weatherill (n 1) 81–82.

[60] As pointed out in ch 4.3, the CESL would have further unified the EU consumer contract rules. Still, the EU withdrew its proposal and the Consumer Rights Directive's first and more ambitious proposal. Nonetheless, empirical evidence on trader preference indicated that traders favoured further harmonization of consumer contract rules. Stefan Vogenauer and Stephen Weatherill, 'The European Community's Competence to Pursue the Harmonisation of Contract Law: An Empirical Contribution to the Debate' in Stefan Vogenauer and Stephen Weatherill (eds), *The Harmonisation of European Contract Law: Implications for European Private Laws, Business and Legal Practice* (Hart Publishing 2006) 132–33.

[61] European Commission, 'A New Deal for Consumers' (Communication) COM(2018) 183 final. Directive (EU) 2019/770 of 20 May 2019 on certain aspects concerning contracts for the supply of digital content and digital services [2019] OJ L136/1; Directive (EU) 2019/771 of 20 May 2019 on certain aspects concerning contracts for the sale of goods, amending Regulation (EU) 2017/2394 and Directive 2009/22/EC, and repealing Directive 1999/44/EC [2019] OJ L136/28; Directive (EU) 2019/2161 of 27 November 2019 amending Council Directive 93/13/EEC and Directives 98/6/EC, 2005/29/EC and 2011/83/EU of the European Parliament and of the Council as regards the better enforcement and modernisation of Union consumer protection rules [2019] OJ L328/7 (Omnibus Directive). For further background information on the New Deal for Consumers see Mateusz Grochowski, 'European Consumer Law after the New Deal: A Tryptich' (2020) 39(1) Yearbook of European Law 387.

[62] Directive 2019/770/EU, art 4; Directive 2019/771/EU, art 4. Stephen Weatherill notes that Directive 2019/771/EU 'harmonises *some* matters according to the maximum harmonization model'. However,

information requirements for contracts concluded on online marketplaces (Article 4(5) of Directive 2019/2161/EU). Despite being less ambitious than the CESL, the 3 Directives will significantly increase the harmonization of the Member State's consumer contract laws. The instruments contain several optional provisions that fragment the Acquis.[63] However, one fundamental unresolved issue is that the 3 Directives have not addressed the earlier issue of apparent divergences in contractual interpretation. Nonetheless, as shown in Chapter 3, there is significant harmonization concerning the fairness assessment of contract terms through Court of Justice case law.[64]

Making pre-drafted standard terms and conditions which adopt the strictest national rules accessible seems, therefore, the best option. Most importantly, the Commission's concern that opting for the strictest standard disincentivizes its use is not applicable anymore, as the playing field changed in recent years. Chapter 4.3 of the present book revealed that the Member States' consumer contract laws have been significantly harmonized, for instance, concerning the consumers' right of withdrawal or the rules governing the passing of risk. The only remaining concern over this approach would be the diverging rules regarding contractual interpretation, including potentially unfair contract terms. As shown in Chapter 3, the CJEU case law harmonizes the national judicial practice of controlling unfair contract terms. The examination of the national rules implementing the Unfair Contract Terms Directive further revealed that there is also considerable overlap among the 4 Member States. However, some significant differences remain, which were also not addressed by the New Deal for Consumers. The most pragmatic solution would be to leave the legal issues covered by the national rules implementing the Unfair Contract Terms Directive out of the pre-drafted terms. Traders are not required to include the information in these provisions in their terms and conditions, and EU consumers can, by default, rely on the law of the place of their habitual residence.[65]

the Directive also contains several limitations regarding the material scope and options, as in the Consumer Rights Directive and other minimum provisions (especially arts 3, 17, and 18 of Directive 2019/771/EU). He argues that this preserves at least some diversity at the national level, and the choice of the 'model of harmonisations' shows the sensitive nature of harmonizing consumer contract law. Stephen Weatherill, 'Is maximum harmonisation a myth? The story of Directive 2019/771 on contracts for the sale of goods' (2021) 16(2) Revue européenne de droit de la consommation 239.

[63] See eg Felix Pflücke, 'The Implementation of the EU Directives 2019/770 and 2019/771 in Luxembourg' (2022) 11(3) Journal of European Consumer and Market Law 114.

[64] For a detailed examination of divergences regarding the contractual interpretation see eg Jacques H Herbots, 'Interpretation of Contracts' in Jan M Smits (ed), *Elgar Encyclopedia of Comparative Law* (2nd edn, Edward Elgar Publishing 2012) 421 ff; Hein Kötz, *European Contract Law* (2nd edn, OUP 2017) 91 ff.

[65] Regulation (EU) 593/2008 (Rome I), art 6(1).

The pre-drafted standard contract terms could thus only cover the terms required by the mandatory information and formal requirements.

The European Commission, national authorities, or consumer and trader organizations could draft and provide standard contract terms with the strictest national standard as their benchmark.[66] This approach would be particularly beneficial in cross-border transactions and could complement or even be an alternative to further harmonization on the EU level.[67] Chapter 5.5 showed that such terms are widely available in all 4 jurisdictions included in the present study. However, Dutch traders were the only ones using them (see Table 5.7). There is no data on whether such pre-drafted standard contract terms are available in all the remaining Member States, nor is there any reliable information on their quality. The latter is significant, as the pre-drafted standard contract terms sampled for the present study were not fully compliant with the relevant consumer protection rules (see Table 7.1 above). Surprisingly, these terms, pre-drafted by semi-public organizations, did not comply in full, considering the involvement of consumer and trader representatives and academics in their preparation.[68] In many Member States, membership in such industry organizations is compulsory, and the question arises whether providers of standard contract terms should also ensure that traders correctly implement[69] and regularly update them.[70]

However, these semi-public organizations would need further regulatory powers to ensure that their members complied with legal duties. Franziska Weber and Christopher Hodges examined how Thuiswinkel operates and

[66] Ulf Bernitz notes that pre-drafted standard contract terms are unlikely to breach EU competition rules (art 101 of the TFEU, ex art 81 of the EC Treaty), unless these standard terms contain terms such as index clauses. Bernitz (n 46) 186.

[67] Fabrizio Cafaggi examined different forms of self-regulation regarding standard contract terms. He distinguished between standard terms that would substitute or complement existing legislation, or that would be more sector-specific. Fabrizio Cafaggi, 'Self-Regulation in European Contract Law' in Hugh Collins (ed), *Standard Contract Terms in Europe: A Basis for and a Challenge to European Contract Law* (Kluwer Law International 2008) 93 ff.

[68] There have been other instances where this had happened before in the Netherlands. Esther van Schagen, '"Better" Enforcement of EU Consumer Law: Exploring Responsive Enforcement' in Esther van Schagen and Stephen Weatherill (eds), *Better Regulation in EU Contract Law: The Fitness Check and the New Deal for Consumers* (Hart Publishing 2019) 152–54.

[69] As shown in ch 6, many traders also exceeded the required legal standard, which these semi-public organizations should encourage.

[70] A study by the CMA revealed that the frequency of how often traders reviewed their terms and conditions was of particular importance. See Competition and Markets Authority/IFF Research, 'Unfair Contract Terms Research' Competition and Markets Authority (19 October 2016) 40 https://assets.publishing.service.gov.uk/government/uploads/system/uploads/attachment_data/file/561518/UK_businesses__understanding_of_unfair_terms_in_consumer_contracts__IFF_Research_.pdf (accessed 29 April 2020). Several traders also referred to outdated legislation, such as the 7-day right to withdraw under the Distance Selling Directive (see ch 6.3.3).

found that its members must adopt the standard contract terms drafted by Thuiswinkel.[71] Thuiswinkel's members are also independently audited for compliance before they are even allowed to join the organization, and its members are then subject to an annual compliance check-up.[72] The Dutch approach could thus serve as a good model of self-regulation for other jurisdictions. The only issue was that these pre-drafted terms contained some consumer rights violations.

Compliance of and with pre-drafted standard contract terms could generally be ensured through the deployment of artificial intelligence (AI), for instance, the one introduced by the CLAUDETTE programme at the European University Institute.[73] CLAUDETTE allows users to check the fairness of a contract term, although the programme still requires significant input before it could replace legal professionals.[74] Deploying AI-based automated decision-making systems to examine whether traders faithfully implement pre-drafted terms would not be as ambitious as the CLAUDETTE programme, as one could simply detect divergences by comparing the pre-drafted standard contract with the trader's terms and conditions. National enforcement and consumer organizations could also use such technology in the future. It appears that they will need to continue manually assessing trader compliance for the foreseeable future.[75]

3 Supporting Small and Medium-sized Enterprises

3.1 Empirical Evidence

The descriptive analysis in Chapter 6 revealed that 27.97 per cent of large enterprises complied in full with their legal duties compared to 13.74 per cent of

[71] Weber and Hodges (n 6) 152.

[72] ibid.

[73] European University Institute, 'CLAUDETTE: Machine Learning Powered Analysis of Consumer Contracts and Privacy Policies' (2019) http://claudette.eui.eu/ (accessed 23 May 2021). For further information on the software programme see Hans-Wolfgang Micklitz, Przemyslaw Palka, and Yannis Panagis, 'The Empire Strike Back: Digital Control of Unfair Terms of Online Services' (2017) 40(3) Journal of Consumer Policy 367 ff; Vanessa Mak, *Legal Pluralism in European Contract Law* (OUP 2020) 146–49.

[74] Vanessa Mak detected several inaccuracies in the CLAUDETTE software. See Mak (n 73) 181. Unfair contract terms found in the empirical examination in this book were also not picked up as unfair by the software.

[75] These organizations could then take collective enforcement action under the new Omnibus Directive 2019/2161/EU, part of the EU's New Deal for Consumers. See eg Hilde K Ellingsen, *Standing to Enforce European Union Law before National Courts* (Hart Publishing 2021) 191–93. Regulators

Table 7.2 Top 10 Instances of Non-compliance by SMEs and Large Enterprises

	Z4	X11	Z1g(ii)	Z1h	Z2f	Y2	Z1f	Z2a(i)	Y1	X10
SME	116	87	66	58	52	49	26	25	24	13
	X11	Z4	Y2	Z1h	Z1g(ii)	Z2f	Y1	X10	Z1f	Z2a(i)
Large	48	42	28	23	20	19	10	9	9	9

Notes:

(1) 118 traders are large enterprises and 182 traders are SMEs (45 by default). In total, there are 300 traders.

(2) X10: contract terms allowing traders to transfer their rights and obligations to third parties; X11: contract terms excluding or hindering consumers to take legal action (eg choice of law clauses); Y1: providing the trade register number; Y2: providing the VAT number; Z1f: the providing delivery time; Z1g(ii): providing a model withdrawal form; Z1h: providing a reminder of the existence of a legal guarantee of conformity of goods; Z2a(i): consumers have 14 days to withdraw from distance contracts; Z2f: traders have to reimburse consumer after 14 days of being informed of the latter's decision to withdraw from the contract; Z4: providing the hyperlink and method to access the EU's ODR platform. Chapter 5 provides further details on each variable.

SMEs (Table 6.2). This pattern was also confirmed in the statistical analysis, which showed that SMEs had committed, on average, more violations of the consumer protection rules than large enterprises (Table 6.4 model (1)) and were overall less likely to be compliant (Table 6.4 model (2)).[76] Most instances of non-compliance for SMEs and large enterprises occurred with mandatory disclosures, followed by unfair contract terms, the right of withdrawal, and the passing of risk (Table 6.5). This pattern was also reflected in the list of the top 10 instances of non-compliance, although the order and quantity of violations between SMEs and large enterprises differed (Table 7.2). The findings in Table 7.2 show that traders struggled with the same legal duties regardless of the company size.

3.2 Policy Recommendations

The empirical findings are not surprising. SMEs lack the expertise and resources to comply with all legal requirements, especially in cross-border transactions.[77] Stephen Weatherill argued that SMEs and consumers benefit

increasingly use RegTech, for instance, in financial law. See Herwig CH Hofmann, Dirk A Zetzsche, and Felix Pflücke, 'The Changing Nature of "Regulation by Information": Towards Real-time Regulation?' (2023) 28(4–6) European Law Journal 172.

[76] Chapter 6.2.2 contains Table 6.4 and the interpretation of its findings.

[77] cf Catalina Goanta, *Convergence in European Consumer Sales Law: A Comparative and Numerical Approach* (Intersentia 2016) 124.

the most from harmonized rules in the EU's single market but also suggested that traders will probably favour an optional EU instrument over mandatory rules.[78] SMEs might be willing to adopt pre-drafted standard contract terms, which take the strictest national rules as a benchmark. This approach would allow SMEs to comply fully with all the legal duties while only marginally increasing their transaction costs.[79] There has also been an academic debate about the possibility of treating SMEs differently in B2C and B2B transactions.[80] As discussed in Chapter 4.3, the EU legislator included optional provisions in the Consumer Rights Directive, which allow Member States to adopt stricter rules for certain situations, including extending the Directive's level of protection to SMEs.[81] Guido Alpa argued that SMEs should be treated differently in consumer transactions for consistency.[82] However, such an approach would lead to further inconsistencies in the European consumer contract law acquis, and thus possibly create further confusion among SMEs and decrease consumer confidence.[83]

The empirical evidence also suggested that SMEs struggled with the same legal duties as large enterprises (Table 7.2 above). The only difference was the number of instances of non-compliance, so providing pre-drafted standard contract terms and conditions which comply with the strictest national rules in the EU's single market would probably have the most significant impact in

[78] Stephen Weatherill, 'Competence and European Private Law' in Christian Twigg-Flesner (ed), *The Cambridge Companion to European Union Private Law* (CUP 2010) 68–69. Hugh Beale also expressed this view about B2B transactions and argued that SMEs might be willing to pay higher transaction costs in favour of greater protection. Hugh Beale, 'The Role for European Contract Law: Uniformity or Diversity?' in Francisco de Elizalde (ed), *Uniform Rules for European Contract Law? A Critical Assessment* (Hart Publishing 2018) 25–26.

[79] The previous section pointed out that the divergences between Member States are marginal after the adoption of the Consumer Rights Directive and the EU's New Deal for Consumers. Interpretation issues are unlikely to occur when the pre-drafted terms only focus on the required legal duties as discussed in the previous section.

[80] See eg Marco Loos and Ilse Samoy, 'The Position of Small and Medium-Sized Enterprises in European Contract Law: An Introduction' in Marco Loos and Ilse Samoy (eds), *The Position of Small and Medium-Sized Enterprises in European Contract Law* (Intersentia 2014) 3–6; Matthias Lehmann and Johannes Ungerer, 'Save the "Mittelstand": How German Courts Protect Small and Medium-Sized Enterprises from Unfair Terms' (2017) 25(2) European Review of Private Law 313 ff; Beale (n 78) 25--26; Mak (n 73) 110–11.

[81] Consumer Rights Directive, preamble 13.

[82] Guido Alpa, 'Towards a European Contract Law' in Reiner Schulze and Jules Stuyck (eds), *Towards a European Contract Law* (Sellier European Law Publishers 2011) 30–31.

[83] It is worth mentioning that the European Commission suggested that it might exclude micro-enterprises from the scope of future legislative measures in cases where applying the rules to them would not be proportionate. European Commission, 'Minimizing regulatory burden for SMEs: Adapting EU regulation to the needs of micro-enterprises' COM(2011) 803 final, para 4. This approach was, for instance, applied in the European Commission's Regulatory Fitness and Performance exercise. See European Commission, 'Regulatory Fitness and Performance (REFIT): Results and Next Steps' COM(2013) 685 final, para 2.1.

increasing not only SMEs' but also the overall levels of compliance. In light of the evidence presented in the previous section, this approach is more realistic than attempting to adopt a new version of the (optional) CESL.[84]

Providing SMEs with pre-drafted standard terms that are frequently updated, available in all EU languages, and accompanied by guidance notes would not only lead to greater compliance but would probably also increase the willingness of SMEs to engage in cross-border transactions in the first place.[85] The European Commission's Executive Agency for Small and Medium-sized Enterprises has already provided guidance and support to SMEs in understanding EU legislation as a core priority in their Competitiveness of Enterprises and Small and Medium-sized Enterprises programme launched from 2014 to 2020.[86] SMEs can already access information on rules governing cross-border transactions via the Commission's 'Your Europe Business Portal', and this portal could provide the proposed pre-drafted terms to SMEs.

4 Increasing Access to Justice by Promoting Online Dispute Resolution

The final policy recommendation concerns increasing access to justice through ODR. Most business-to-consumer contracts are low-value transactions, and consumers are thus less likely to take disputes to court.[87] ODR may provide a cheap and efficient remedy where a trader has failed to comply with legal duties. The main concern about the current EU ODR regime is that traders are only required to provide a hyperlink to the platform and explain the methods of accessing it, but traders do not need to subject themselves to ODR.[88] The latest reform under Article 5 of Directive 2019/2161 is going in the right direction. However, reforms need to go further as it merely requires one online entry point where consumers can access information about their rights and access ODR and the European Consumer Centres Network.

84 Although at least 78 per cent of SMEs suggested in several surveys that they would be willing to use such an optional instrument in cross-border transactions. See Alexander J Wulf, *Institutional Competition Between Optional Codes in European Contract Law: A Theoretical and Empirical Analysis* (Springer Publishing 2014) 80–84.

85 See the previous section of this chapter for further details.

86 European Commission, 'COSME: Europe's programme for small and medium-sized enterprises' (2021) https://ec.europa.eu/growth/smes/cosme_en (accessed 20 May 2021).

87 Pablo Cortés and Fernando Esteban de la Rosa even proposed introducing a global ODR system. See Pablo Cortés and Fernando Esteban de la Rosa, 'Building a global redress system for low-value cross-border disputes' (2013) 62(2) The International and Comparative Law Quarterly 407 ff.

88 Traders can choose to opt out of the EU's ODR scheme. See Consumer Rights Directive, art 6(1)(t) in connection with art 14(1) of Regulation (EU) 524/2013.

4.1 Empirical Evidence

In the book's empirical inquiry, 52.67 per cent of traders (158 out of 300) failed to inform consumers of the existence and possibility of resolving disputes via the European Commission's ODR platform.[89] Compliance with this mandatory disclosure requirement varied significantly between jurisdictions, industries, and company sizes.[90] Among the 4 jurisdictions, Germany was the most compliant (86.67 per cent), followed by France (44 per cent), the United Kingdom (36 per cent), and the Netherlands (22.67 per cent).[91] Among the 5 industries, fashion was the most compliant (60 per cent), closely followed by home decor (56.67 per cent) and electronics (55 per cent); print media (33.33 per cent) and sports equipment (31.67 per cent) were the least compliant.[92] Finally, large enterprises (64.41 per cent) were more compliant with this duty than SMEs (36.26 per cent).[93]

Another worrying trend was that 39.44 per cent (56 out of 142) of traders who complied with the disclosure requirement had opted out of the EU's ODR scheme,[94] and only 4 had expressly opted in.[95] Surprisingly, 89 traders provided in their terms and conditions the method for accessing a national ODR provider;[96] 73 of them provided that they were willing to resolve any disputes using this national provider.[97] These observations show that traders are interested in resolving their disputes via ODR, although the empirical inquiry observed significant differences between the Member States. In particular, 53.33 per cent of Dutch traders and 34.67 per cent of French traders were willing to resolve their disputes via online dispute resolution, compared to only 6.67 per cent of German traders and 2.67 per cent of UK traders.[98] Interest in ODR by industry was relatively constant between 26.67 per cent and 28.33 per cent; it only dropped to 13.33 per cent in the case of sports equipment.[99] Similarly, interest in ODR was almost the same between

[89] Table 7.3 (model (1) Total). As pointed out above, this finding confirms a study by the European Commission, which revealed that nearly 45 per cent of traders failed to comply with this requirement. European Commission, 'Online shopping: Commission and Consumer Protection authorities urge traders to bring information policy in line with EU law' (31 January 2020) https://ec.europa.eu/commission/presscorner/detail/en/IP_20_156 (accessed 12 August 2020).
[90] Table 7.3 (model (2)).
[91] Table 7.3 (model (2) Country).
[92] Table 7.3 (model (2) Industry).
[93] Table 7.3 (model (2) Company Size).
[94] Table 7.3 (model (3)).
[95] Table 7.3 (model (4)).
[96] Table 7.3 (model (5) Total).
[97] Table 7.3 (model (6) Total).
[98] Table 7.3 (model (6) Country).
[99] Table 7.3 (model (6) Industry).

Table 7.3 Trader Compliance and Trader Willingness to Take Part in ODR

	(1) Failed to Provide it	(2) Provided it	(3) Provided it but Opt-Out	(4) Provided it and Opt-In	(5) Provided National ODR	(6) Opt-In National ODR
Country						
France	42	33	0	0	37	26
Germany	10	65	49	3	5	5
The NL	58	17	2	0	41	40
The United Kingdom	48	27	2	1	6	2
Industry						
Electronics	27	33	12	0	21	16
Fashion	24	36	12	2	20	17
Sport Eq.	41	19	7	1	9	8
Home D.	26	34	12	1	22	16
Print Media	40	20	10	0	17	16
Company size						
Large	42	76	29	1	39	29
SME	116	66	24	3	50	44
Total	**158**	**142**	**56**	**4**	**89**	**73**

Notes:

(1) Model (1): traders who failed to display the hyperlink to the EU Commission's ODR platform and methods of accessing it (dependent variable Z4 of the study); model (2) traders complied with dependent variable Z4; model (3) traders provided the required information but opted out of the EU's ODR scheme; model (4) traders provided information and opted into the EU's ODR scheme; model (5) traders provided a hyperlink and how to access ODR of a national provider; model (6) traders provided information about national ODR scheme and indicated their willingness to take part in ODR proceedings with a national provider.

(2) There are 75 traders for each Member State and 60 traders for each industry. 118 traders are large enterprises and 182 traders are SMEs (45 by default). In total, there are 300 traders and 16 national ODR providers. The French national ODR providers referred to were: Fédération du e-commerce et de la vente à distance (provided: 24; provided and opt-in: 21); Médiateur du Commerce Coopératif et Associé (provided: 1); Centre de Médiation et de Cyber-Services de Règlement Amiable des Huissiers de Justice MEDICYS (provided: 5; provided and opt-in: 2); Fédération du Commerce et de la Distribution (provided: 1); TELECOM le Médiateur des Communications Électroniques (provided: 1); Centre de médiation de conciliateurs de justice CM2C (provided: 1); Association des médiateurs européens (provided: 1; provided and opt-in: 1); MEDIATION-NET(provided: 3; provided and opt-in: 2). The German national ODR providers referred to were: Allgemeine Verbraucherschlichtungsstelle beim Zentrum für Schlichtung eV (provided: 3; provided and opt-in: 3); janoFair (provided: 2; provided and opt-in: 2). The Dutch national ODR providers referred to were: Geschillencommissie Thuiswinkel Organisatie (provided: 27; provided and opt-in: 26); Geschillencommissie Stichting Webshop Keurmerk (provided: 12; provided and opt-in: 12); Geschillencommissie Centrale Branchevereniging Wonen (provided: 2; provided and opt-in: 2). The UK national ODR providers referred to were: RetailADR (provided: 3; provided and opt-in: 2); Consumer Ombudsman (provided: 1); Furniture Ombudsman (provided: 2).

large enterprises (24.58 per cent) and SMEs (24.18 per cent).[100] In total, traders referred to 16 different national ODR providers.[101]

4.2 Policy Recommendations

ODR can be a fast and cost-efficient option to resolve a dispute, especially in low-value and cross-border B2C cases.[102] It is worrying that most traders failed to provide the link to the EU's ODR platform or opted out of the scheme. The question which remains unanswered is why traders referred to a national ODR provider of their choice and not to the EU's ODR platform. It could be that the traders were unaware of the EU's platform, as a study by the European Commission pointed out that almost 40 per cent of traders were unaware of the possibility of resolving disputes via an out-of-court mechanism.[103] Pablo Cortés highlighted other shortcomings of the current regime. He observed that the EU's ODR platform places the burden of providing the trader's email address on the consumer, the platform does not contact the consumer should traders opt out of ODR, and ODR proceedings can only take place if the trader replies to the platform's email.[104] It remains unclear whether authorities addressed these issues in the meantime. If not, policy-makers should consider these and additional observations about the efficacy of the EU's ODR mechanism when enhancing the platform's user-friendliness and implementing it on a larger scale. Otherwise, traders and consumers will refrain from using the platform, as indicated by the extremely poor performance in the European Commission's review of the ADR and ODR systems.[105]

[100] Table 7.3 (model (6) Company Size).

[101] Table 7.3 (Notes (3)).

[102] A recent European Commission study highlighted that high litigation costs reduced access to justice; the Commission also provided concrete numbers of litigation expenses (including small-value claims) by Member States. European Commission, 'The 2021 EU Justice Scoreboard' (Communication) COM(2021) 389 final, 20–22. Alternatives to ODR are collective redress or enforcement action by national authorities, but both have a much higher threshold for consumers.

[103] European Commission, 'Consumer Conditions Scoreboard: Consumers at home in the Single Market' (October 2017) 66 (Figure 42) http://ec.europa.eu/newsroom/just/document.cfm?action=display&doc_id=45983 (accessed 3 September 2020).

[104] Pablo Cortés, 'The New Landscape of Consumer Redress: The European Directive on Consumer Alternative Dispute Resolution and the Regulation on Online Dispute Resolution' in Pablo Cortés (ed), *The New Regulatory Framework for Consumer Dispute Resolution* (OUP 2016) 33–34.

[105] European Commission, 'Report on the application of Directive 2013/11/EU of the European Parliament and of the Council on alternative dispute resolution for consumer disputes and Regulation (EU) No 524/2013 of the European Parliament and of the Council on online dispute resolution for consumer disputes' COM(2023) 648 final, 8: 'The platform amassed 180 000 complaints since its launch in 2016, as a result 19 000 companies, from large platforms to SMEs, have registered on the platform since

In the book's empirical inquiry, most traders failed to provide the method of accessing the EU's ODR platform, and only 4 out of 300 traders stated that they were willing to resolve disputes via this platform. Opting out of the EU's platform is perfectly legal as long as traders provide a hyperlink to the EU's platform, state that they opt out of the EU's scheme, and provide a hyperlink and description of how to access a nationally regulated ODR or ADR provider.[106] The recommendation first focuses on gathering empirical data on why traders choose their national ODR platforms over the EU's platform. Such a study is not in existence at the time of writing. One could conduct this through a survey and improve the EU's ODR platform based on the survey's findings. Another development in recent years has been that some platforms, for instance, eBay, have developed their own ODR schemes.[107] Such mechanisms can resolve disputes between traders and consumers at a fingertip, including direct enforcement action by the platform.[108] This form of platform governance can be seen as another valuable tool in resolving disputes, as long as it does not infringe on consumer protection rights, which would undermine the authority of states and their independent judiciary.[109]

In conclusion, the empirical observations revealed that most traders failed to comply with the mandatory disclosure rules regarding the method for accessing the EU's ODR platform and that only 4 out of 300 traders opted into the scheme. There is compelling evidence that ODR should be made

that year. Yet, 80 to 85% of complaints, go unanswered on the platform, and only about of 1% of the complaints (i.e. less than 200 cases) result in an ADR outcome.'

[106] Concerning ADR see art 6(1)(t) of the Consumer Rights Directive in connection with art 13 of Directive 2013/11/EU. Concerning ODR see art 6(1)(t) of the Consumer Rights Directive in connection with art 14 of Regulation (EU) 524/2013.

[107] As discussed in ch 4.3.1.6. See eg Louis F Del Duca, Colin Rule, and Kathryn Rimpfel, 'eBay's De Facto Low Value High Volume Resolution Process: Lessons and Best Practices for ODR Systems Designers' (2014) 6 Yearbook on Arbitration and Mediation 204.

[108] Platforms are also required to remove any illegal listings or content on their website as soon as they become aware of it (art 14(1)(b) of the E-Commerce Directive). There is, however, no general duty to monitor a website for illegal content under the E-Commerce Directive nor are Member States allowed to introduce such a requirement (art 15 of the E-Commerce Directive). Surprisingly, the Court of Justice provided in *Glawischnig-Piesczek* that there can be a positive duty to monitor a website for illegal content containing identical or equivalent information. The Court also clarified that such content must be removed from the website globally, sparking a public outcry about its implications on non-EU citizens, especially regarding free speech on social media. For e-commerce platforms, this duty could be disabling access to a fraudulent trading account on an e-commerce platform like eBay. Case C-18/18 *Eva Glawischnig-Piesczek v Facebook Ireland Limited* ECLI:EU:C:2019:821. See eg Tobias Lutzi, *Private International Law Online: Internet Regulation and Civil Liability in the EU* (OUP 2020) paras 2.21–2.22, 2.37, 2.54, 6.04; Aleksandra Kuczerawy and Clara Rauchegger, 'Court of Justice Injunctions to remove illegal online content under the eCommerce Directive: Glawischnig-Piesczek' (2020) 57(5) Common Market Law Review 1495.

[109] See eg Tarleton Gillespie, *Custodians of the Internet: Platforms, Content Moderation, and the Hidden Decisions that Shape Social Media* (Yale UP 2018) ch 8.

mandatory for small-value claims or that consumers should be given the final say on whether they prefer to enter into ODR instead of regular court proceedings.[110] Neither ADR nor ODR is mandatory in e-commerce consumer contract disputes in France, Germany, the Netherlands, and the United Kingdom at the time of writing.[111] Making ODR or ADR mandatory is not a novel idea. For instance, the implementation of the Mediation Directive in Italy made it compulsory to enter mediation in cross-border and domestic civil cases before proceedings before a court could take place (between 2009 and 2012).[112] Several years later, the rule was found unconstitutional and limited in scope. After the reform, parties in certain legal disputes concerning low-value claims, such as low-value claims arising from traffic accidents, B2C contracts, and insurance disputes, must attend at least 1 introductory mediation session before they are allowed to start legal proceedings in a court. According to the data obtained by Sue Prince, almost 60,000 mediations took place in the first 3 months of 2014, resolving approximately half of the disputes.[113] A legal assessment of such a measure by the Court of Justice of the European Union, as well as on the national level in Germany and the United Kingdom, found that mandatory ADR would conform with Article 6 of the European Convention on Human Rights and Article 47 of the Charter of Fundamental Rights of the

[110] See also the discussion in Stefan Wrbka, *European Consumer Access to Justice Revisited* (CUP 2015) 95–97; Pablo Cortés, 'Enforcing EU Consumer Policy More Effectively: A 3 Pronged Approach' in Sara Drake and Melanie Smith (eds), *New Directions in the Effective Enforcement of EU Law and Policy* (Edward Elgar Publishing 2016) 222–23; Michael Stürner, 'ADR and Adjudication by State Courts: Competitors or Complements?' in Michael Stürner, Fernando Gascón Inchausti, and Remo Caponi (eds), *The Role of Consumer ADR in the Administration of Justice: New Trends in Access to Justice under EU Directive 2013/11* (Sellier European Law Publishers 2015) 18–20; Richard Susskind, *Online Courts and the Future of Justice* (OUP 2019) 187–89; Ethan Katsh and Orna Rabinovich-Einy, *Digital Justice: Technology and the Internet of Disputes* (OUP 2017) 159–62. Vanessa Mak argues that the data gathered from ODR proceedings could also shape future legislation, as it provides detailed data on consumer and trader behaviour. See Mak (n 73) 150.

[111] For an overview of the out-of-court redress landscape in the 4 jurisdictions see eg Sabine Bernheim-Desvaux and Patricia Foucher, 'L'effectivité du droit français de la consommation'; Vanessa Mak, 'Enforcement and Effectiveness of Consumer Law: The Netherlands'; and Christine Riefa and Chris Willett, 'Enforcement and Effectiveness of Consumer Law in the UK', all in Hans-Wolfgang Micklitz and Geneviève Saumier (eds), *Enforcement and Effectiveness of Consumer Law* (Springer Publishing 2018); Eline Verhage, 'The Implementation of the Consumer ADR Directive in the Netherlands'; Emmanuel Guinchard, 'The Implementation of the Consumer ADR Directive in France'; and Roa Miquel, 'The Implementation of the Consumer ADR Directive in Germany', all in Pablo Cortés (ed), *The New Regulatory Framework for Consumer Dispute Resolution* (OUP 2016).

[112] Directive (EC) 2008/52 of 21 May 2008 on certain aspects of mediation in civil and commercial matters [2008] OJ L136/3 (Mediation Directive). Sue Prince, 'Access to Court? "Encouraging" Consumers to Use Court-Connected Mediation in Small Claims and Other Cases' in Pablo Cortés, 'The New Landscape of Consumer Redress: The European Directive on Consumer Alternative Dispute Resolution and the Regulation on Online Dispute Resolution' in Pablo Cortés (ed), *The New Regulatory Framework for Consumer Dispute Resolution* (OUP 2016) 86–88. The same book provides additional examples from other jurisdictions.

[113] Prince (n 112).

European Union.[114] The European Commission is collecting evidence on possible reforms via an impact assessment, and it remains to be seen how the Commission aims to make the system fit for purpose.[115]

5 Conclusion

This chapter has sought to translate the empirical findings of the book into targeted and actionable policy recommendations. The chapter has examined 3 policy recommendations in light of the empirical results of the book's empirical inquiry. The first policy recommendation concerned using standard contract terms drafted and provided by public or semi-public organizations. The empirical case study determined that the providers of pre-drafted standard terms are responsible for most instances of non-compliance, with only a handful of violations attributed to traders who did not faithfully implement them. The examination unveiled that for these pre-drafted terms to enhance compliance levels effectively, they must remain free from any breaches of consumer protection rules, undergo frequent updates, and be subject to regular monitoring, for example, through a self-regulation scheme like the one in the Netherlands. The second policy recommendation addressed that SMEs were less likely to comply with their legal duties. The empirical evidence suggested that SMEs struggled with the same legal duties as large enterprises, only the quantity of violations was higher among SMEs. The critical analysis of the empirical findings demonstrated that pre-drafted terms would benefit SMEs the most. The third and final recommendation focused on the fact that most traders failed to provide the hyperlink to the EU's ODR platform, and only 4 out of 300 traders

[114] Joined Cases C-317/08, C-318/08, C-319/08 and C-320/08, *Rosalba Alassini v Telecom Italia SpA (C-317/08) and Filomena Califano v Wind SpA (C-318/08) and Lucia Anna Giorgia Iacono v Telecom Italia SpA (C-319/08) and Multiservice Srl v Telecom Italia SpA (C-320/08)* ECLI:EU:C:2010:146. Convention for the Protection of Human Rights and Fundamental Freedoms of 4 November 1950 (European Convention on Human Rights, as amended Protocol No 15 on 1 August 2021) (ECHR). Charter of Fundamental Rights of the European Union [2012] OJ C326/391. Concerning compliance with the ECHR and EU law see Iris Benöhr, *EU Consumer Law and Human Rights* (OUP 2013) 196–99. Regarding the United Kingdom see Civil Justice Council, 'Compulsory ADR' (June 2021) https://www.judiciary.uk/wp-content/uploads/2021/07/Civil-Justice-Council-Compulsory-ADR-report-1.pdf (accessed 15 June 2021). Michael Stürner suggests that it would comply with the German constitution (art 20(3) of the Grundgesetz) and the Court of Justice case law. See Joined Cases C-317/08, C-318/08, C-319/08 and C-320/08, *Rosalba Alassini v Telecom Italia SpA (C-317/08) and Filomena Califano v Wind SpA (C-318/08) and Lucia Anna Giorgia Iacono v Telecom Italia SpA (C-319/08) and Multiservice Srl v Telecom Italia SpA (C-320/08)* (n 114); Stürner (n 110) 19.

[115] European Commission, 'Impact Assessment Report: Proposal for a Directive amending Directive 2013/11/EU on alternative dispute resolution for consumer disputes, as well as Directives (EU) 2015/2302, (EU) 2019/2161 and (EU) 2020/1828' SWD(2023) 335 final, Pts 1 and 2.

stated that they were willing to resolve disputes with their customers via the EU's platform. Another observation was that traders referred to national ODR providers, meaning they preferred to choose a national provider over the EU's ODR platform. Further empirical evidence, for instance, in a survey, needs to be carried out to understand why traders opted out of the EU's ODR platform but opted into a national ODR scheme. In addition, the recommendations proposed that ODR should be mandatory in e-commerce consumer disputes or that consumers should at least have the final say on whether they wanted to resolve their disputes online.

In conclusion, acquiring further evidence regarding e-commerce trader compliance and behaviour is crucial to bolster the effectiveness of EU consumer contract law. While some traders' websites may exhibit compliance with all legal duties, the real test lies in their ability to maintain these standards when consumers engage in actual purchases. To address this, the relevant stakeholders should prioritize the collection of additional experimental evidence, ultimately contributing to a more robust and responsive framework.

8
Conclusion

1 Introduction

The previous chapters explored how the European Union and 4 selected European jurisdictions regulate e-commerce business-to-consumer transactions and whether the legislative choices have been evidence-based. For this purpose, a hand-collected dataset helped assess whether traders complied with the underlying rules, which has been unexplored to date. This chapter concludes the book and summarizes the main findings, outlines some of the book's implications, addresses unanswered questions, and offers some concluding remarks.

2 Summary of the Argument

Chapter 1 first briefly reviewed the academic landscape and outlined that a study which measures levels and factors of compliance still needed to be conducted. The chapter outlined why content analysis is the most suitable methodology to determine the levels of trader compliance because it enables the thorough evaluation of e-commerce websites against the European consumer contract rules, ensuring a comprehensive and nuanced assessment. It also provided explanations for further methodological choices made in the project and outlined the different limitations of the present study, especially concerning the dataset size. The study included 300 traders from 4 jurisdictions, as well as 35 applicable national rules implementing the Unfair Contract Terms Directive, the E-Commerce Directive, and the Consumer Rights Directive, leaving other traders, jurisdictions, and rules out of the picture.

The second chapter depicted the transition towards an evidence-based approach in European consumer contract law. The chapter highlighted that the EU based early instruments on national practices rather than scientifically grounded evidence. It demonstrated that the transition towards an evidence-based approach gained momentum with REFIT and the Better Regulation agenda, although several caveats remain. In particular, it could be argued

Compliance with European Consumer Law. Felix Pflücke, Oxford University Press. © Oxford University Press 2024.
DOI: 10.1093/9780198906414.003.0008

on multiple occasions that the Commission adopted legislation on policy-based evidence rather than evidence-based policy. One example was when the Commission collected evidence on trader compliance by surveying e-commerce traders, asking them whether they believed their competitors complied with EU law.[1] The Commission enacted legislation based in part on this evidence, which strongly questions the quality of some of the assessments. After defining how good evidence should look, the chapter highlighted that evidence should only inform the political discourse rather than dictate it.

The third and fourth chapters provided doctrinal accounts of the consumer protection rights derived from the implementation of the 3 selected Directives and whether evidence and consumer theories confirm or reject the legislative choices. Chapter 3 focused on the implementation of the minimum harmonization Unfair Contract Terms Directive. The chapter examined how the general test used in the Directive (Articles 3 and 4) operates on the European Union and national level. The chapter detected several national nuances among the rules implementing the Directive, a discovery which has significantly shaped the research design of the empirical part of the book. The doctrinal examination revealed different approaches to controlling unfair contract terms for unfairness in the jurisdictions under examination. One key observation has been that, unlike in France,[2] Germany,[3] and the Netherlands,[4] the United Kingdom does not have a list of terms presumed unfair ('grey list' character) or unfair under all circumstances ('black list' character). Instead, UK judges assess contract terms under the general test of fairness, which, as in the Directive, is supplemented by an indicative list of potentially unfair terms.[5] However, in addition to this general test, some contract terms, such as penalty clauses and assignments,[6] are unfair because of common law rules or other statutory provisions.[7] Another observation has been that some terms are unfair under the Court of Justice case law.[8] These different regulatory techniques for controlling unfair contract terms shaped the research design of the study, which divided the levels of unfairness into 3 categories: (1) a term may be regarded as unfair under the general test; (2) a term is presumed unfair under a 'grey list' with limited judicial discretion; (3) a term is considered

[1] See ch 2.3.2; Impact Assessment SWD(2018) 96 final, s 2.3.1.
[2] Code de la consommation, art L212-1 in connection with arts R212-1 and R212-2.
[3] BGB, §§ 308–309.
[4] BW, art 6:233(a) in connection with arts 6:236 and 6:237.
[5] Consumer Rights Act 2015, s 62 in connection with Sch 2.
[6] See chs 3.4.4 and 3.4.10.
[7] Consumer Rights Act 2015, ss 31 and 65. See chs 3.4.1 and 3.4.11.
[8] See chs 3.4.4, 3.4.5, 3.4.7, and 3.4.11.

unfair without the possibility of (re)evaluation ('black-listed'). Analysing the rules on unfair contract terms elucidated that the legislative framework relied not on scientifically grounded evidence but instead on alternative foundations. Initially, law-makers formulated these rules upon the presumption of consumer rationality, subsequently empowering consumers through information rights emanating from the neo-classical economic theory. Subsequently, they created the legislative framework by incorporating national practices into its foundation.

Chapter 4 focused on the rights consumers derive from the national rules implementing the minimum harmonization E-Commerce Directive and the maximum harmonization Consumer Rights Directive. The chapter's section on the E-Commerce Directive examined whether the Member States had decided to go beyond the Directive's level of protection. Only France opted for a higher standard regarding the language requirement, requiring traders to provide the terms and conditions at least in French.[9] This section revealed minor observations and included them in the compliance assessment. Unlike the section on the E-Commerce Directive, the part of the chapter exploring consumer rights of the Consumer Rights Directive has focused only on the EU level since Member States are not allowed to deviate from the Directive's standard.[10] The section did, however, point out the increased level of harmonization after adopting the Directive, particularly regarding mandatory disclosures and withdrawal rights; rules governing the passing of risk did not even exist on the EU level. In terms of empirical evidence and alignment with consumer theories, the chapter illustrated a growing trend in both the utilization and improvement of evidence from the E-Commerce Directive to the Consumer Rights Directive. The E-Commerce Directive presented some evidence with limited scope and lower scientific rigour, whereas the Consumer Rights Directive exhibited breadth and sophistication with minor caveats. This analysis also demonstrated that not all consumer theories and behavioural evidence support the legislative choices.

Chapter 5 presented the study's research design. It explained that the study used empirical methods to verify 4 hypotheses that the chapter located in the broader academic debate. The H_1 hypothesis claimed that e-commerce traders fail to comply in full with their legal duties; the H_2–H_4 hypotheses argued that the company's size (H_2), the company's age (H_3), and the use of pre-drafted

[9] Code de la consommation, art L224-76. See ch 4.2.1 (Language Requirement).

[10] The optional provisions allowing the Member States to deviate from the Directive's standard were not found to be applicable to the present study.

terms provided by public or semi-public authorities (H_4) affects compliance. The chapter then outlined how compliance with the selected rules would be measured and why this is the correct assessment method.

The sixth chapter examined the 4 hypotheses using both descriptive and statistical methods. It confirmed the first hypothesis (H_1) that traders do not comply in full with their legal duties: 80.67 per cent of all traders had at least 1 or more instances of non-compliance.[11] The chapter examined the second, third, and fourth hypotheses jointly in an ordinary least squares and binary logistic regression model.[12] It confirmed H_2 in both statistical tests (at the 1 and 5 per cent level of statistical significance) that large enterprises are more likely to be compliant than small and medium-sized enterprises (SMEs). The assessment of H_3 rejected that older companies are more compliant than younger ones. The examination of H_4 also rejected that traders using standard contract terms that public or semi-public organizations provide and draft are more compliant than traders who draft their terms themselves. The data on H_4 suggested that traders using pre-drafted terms had, on average, fewer violations than traders who drafted their own terms but also that traders using such terms had a higher probability of non-compliance. This finding has been examined further in Chapter 7. Section 6.3 provided a fuller account of how traders violated particular consumer rights. It observed that most instances of non-compliance concerned mandatory disclosures (60.60 per cent), followed by unfair contract terms (21.95 per cent), the right of withdrawal (16.58 per cent), and the passing of risk (0.87 per cent).[13] A closer look at the data showed that only 52 per cent of all traders had no unfair contract terms on their websites[14] and that most of the unfair terms detected were non-compliant choice of law and jurisdiction clauses.[15] Even more surprising were the findings concerning mandatory disclosures: only 28.67 per cent of all traders complied with all legal requirements. This number was even lower in the United Kingdom—at only 8 per cent. The greatest failure to comply with mandatory disclosures concerned the requirements to display the hyperlink to the EU's online dispute resolution (ODR) platform, to provide a model withdrawal form, to remind consumers of a legal guarantee concerning the conformity of goods, and to display the VAT number.[16] Compliance with the consumers' right of withdrawal was again a

[11] That is, 242 out of 300 traders. See Tables 6.2 and 6.3, Total.
[12] Table 6.4.
[13] Table 6.5.
[14] Table 6.6.
[15] Table 6.8 model (X11).
[16] Table 6.10.

bigger problem in the United Kingdom: 15.05 per cent of assessments carried out on UK traders detected violations compared to an average of 6.33 per cent elsewhere.[17] However, regarding the length of the right of withdrawal, 30.33 per cent of traders provided consumers with more time than the 14-day statutory period.[18] Overall, 70 per cent of traders had not violated any provision relating to the consumer's right of withdrawal; the lowest score was observed in the United Kingdom (37.33 per cent) and the highest in Germany (92 per cent). Finally, the chapter examined how the contractual terms regulated the passing of risk. Only 7 out of 300 traders violated the underlying consumer protection rules, but it could not detect a pattern explaining these instances.[19] The chapter concluded with additional observations on trader compliance, including a discussion of detected violations of consumer protection rules that fell outside the scope of the present study or of other trader preferences, such as that many traders opted out of the United Nations Convention on Contracts for the International Sale of Goods.

Chapter 7 translated the empirical findings into targeted and actionable policy recommendations. This chapter explored 3 policy recommendations likely to have the most significant impact on trader compliance. The first recommendation examined the wider use of standard contract terms drafted and provided by public or semi-public organizations. Such terms were available in all 4 jurisdictions, but the examination of the dataset revealed that only Dutch traders used them (56 out of 75 Dutch traders). The chapter looked into one of the additional observations in Chapter 6 that traders using pre-drafted terms had, on average, fewer violations but were at the same time more likely to be in breach of consumer protection standards. Chapter 7 examined possible reasons for this and revealed that 3 of the 4 pre-drafted contract terms breached consumer protection rules. In addition, the examination could not attribute it to traders failing to faithfully implement these terms because such conduct was detected only in very few instances. Therefore, the policy recommendations focused on increasing compliance of pre-drafted standard contract terms and ensuring their correct implementation. The European Commission, national authorities, or semi-public actors should provide and constantly update pre-drafted standard contracts complying with the strictest national rules, which traders could optionally use. This approach is the most

[17] Table 6.11.
[18] Table 6.13.
[19] See ch 6.3.4.

reasonable way of addressing the issue of non-compliance, especially considering the lack of political appetite for a European Civil Code in recent years. Several shortcomings were, nonetheless, highlighted, especially issues regarding different standards of contract interpretation at the national level. The chapter argued that pre-drafted standard terms should include all the mandatory information required under EU law. This approach would help to address the problem of diverging rules on contract interpretation. Compliance of and with these pre-drafted terms could also be achieved by introducing more self-regulation mechanisms, as is the case in the Netherlands. The second policy recommendation focused on SMEs, given that the examination revealed that they were less compliant than large enterprises. SMEs and large enterprises struggled to comply with almost the same legal provisions; only the quantity of violations was higher in the case of SMEs.[20] Providing SMEs with pre-drafted standard contract terms that comply with the strictest national rules was proposed as having the most likely impact on compliance while not significantly increasing transaction costs. Some academics and practitioners proposed less restrictive rules for SMEs, which others criticized for undermining consumer confidence and leading to further confusion among traders and consumers. The third and last policy recommendation focused on increasing consumers' access to justice through mandatory ODR. Under the current regime, traders can choose whether to participate in the EU's ODR scheme. Only 4 out of 300 traders stated that they would be willing to resolve any issues through the EU's ODR platform: 158 failed to comply with the requirement to provide the hyperlink to the platform, while 56 explicitly opted out.[21] Another interesting observation was that 73 traders stated that they were willing to resolve disputes via a national ODR provider of their choice.[22] This observation shows at least some interest in resolving disputes via ODR on the part of traders, which suggests that the EU's ODR platform is (for unknown reasons) not attractive enough. Consequently, the recommendation suggested making ODR mandatory either for both traders and consumers or only for traders and optional for consumers. Otherwise, it deprives consumers of their opportunity to access justice online, leading to less compliance in e-commerce.

[20] Table 7.2.
[21] Table 7.3.
[22] ibid.

3 Unanswered Questions

The book has led to both substantive and methodological results. As discussed in the previous section, the empirical evidence revealed several findings concerning the levels of trader compliance and the factors underlying it. The book has translated these observations into targeted and actionable policy recommendations with academic and practical use. The book has more widely advocated for an evidence-based approach to regulating consumer contracts and hopes to inspire future law-in-action studies.

The methodology of the present study has also contributed to the academic discussion on how compliance should be empirically measured. In particular, no other study had so far addressed how empirical research should measure national divergences. Other scholars will be able to use the methodology to address issues beyond the inquiry's scope. The new empirical approach also enables a more nuanced differentiation between severe and minor violations, allowing for a targeted response from legislators and policy-makers.

Chapter 1 highlighted several issues that have had to remain uncharted. First and foremost, the present book focused only on 4 jurisdictions, and the need remains to explore other jurisdictions, industries, or rules. The book could also not investigate all possible non-compliance factors and instead selected the most relevant ones. Future research projects might focus on the above-outlined issues and base their methodology on the research design of the present study.

4 Conclusion

Contributing to the ongoing discourse surrounding the harmonization of European consumer contract law, this book has offered new empirical insights into trader compliance in e-commerce and the potential determinants of traders' adherence or non-adherence to established rules. In pursuit of this objective, the book has aspired to augment the current academic landscape and establish a robust foundation upon which future empirical research in European consumer contract law can build. An insatiable need remains for more extensive and comprehensive investigations to unravel the complexities surrounding trader compliance, also in areas the book has not covered, like personalized pricing, dark patterns, and nudging that affect the future of e-commerce regulation. The insights from this endeavour illuminate that the quest for an effective European consumer contract law continues to demand further research, analysis, and inquiry.

Bibliography

Adams J and Brownsword R, 'The Unfair Contract Terms Act: A Decade of Discretion' (1988) 104 Law Quarterly Review 94

Alemanno A, 'How Much Better is Better Regulation? Assessing the Impact of the Better Regulation Package on the European Union: A Research Agenda' (2015) 6(3) European Journal of Risk Regulation 344

Alpa G, 'Towards a European Contract Law' in Schulze R and Stuyck J (eds), *Towards a European Contract Law* (Sellier European Law Publishers 2011)

Arnull A, 'The Principle of Effective Judicial Protection in EU law: an Unruly Horse?' (2011) 36(1) European Law Review 51

Arras S and Braun C, 'Stakeholders wanted! Why and how European Union agencies involve non-state stakeholders' (2018) 25(9) Journal of European Public Policy 1261

Arroyo Amayuelas E, 'Directive 2000/31/EC: Article 10 Information to be provided' in Schulze R and Staudenmayer D (eds), *EU Digital Law: Article-by-Article Commentary* (Bloomsbury 2020)

Aubert de Vincelles C, 'Consumer Sales in France after the Implementation of the Consumer Rights Directive' in de Cristofaro G and de Franceschi A (eds), *Consumer Sales in Europe: After the Implementation of the Consumer Rights Directive* (Intersentia 2016)

Bakos Y, Marotta-Wurgler F, and Trossen DR, 'Does Anyone Read the Fine Print? Consumer Attention to Standard Form Contracts' (2014) 43(1) Journal of Legal Studies 1

Bar-Gill and Ben-Shahar O, 'Regulatory Techniques in Consumer Protection: A Critique of European Consumer Contract Law' (2013) 50(Special Issue) Common Market Law Review 109

Bartels S, 'Substitution of New Debtor: Transfer of Contract' in Busch D and others (eds), *The Principles of European Contract Law and Dutch Law: A Commentary II* (Kluwer Law International 2006)

Becher SI, 'Unintended Consequences and the Design of Consumer Protection Legislation' (2018) 93(1) Tulane Law Review 105

Beale H, 'Unfair Contract Terms Act 1977' (1978) 5(1) British Journal of Law and Society 114

Beale H, 'Unfair Contracts in Britain and Europe' (1989) 42(1) Current Legal Problems 197

Beale H, 'Legislative Control of Fairness: The Directive on Unfair Terms in Consumer Contracts' in Beatson J and Friedmann D (eds), *Good Faith and Fault in Contract Law* (Oxford Clarendon Press 1995)

Beale H, 'Art. 66-68: The Sources of Contract Terms Under the CESL' in Colombi Ciacchi A (ed), *Contents and Effects of Contracts-Lessons to Learn from the Common European Sales Law* (Springer Publishing 2016)

Beale H, 'The Role for European Contract Law: Uniformity or Diversity?' in de Elizalde F (ed), *Uniform Rules for European Contract Law?: A Critical Assessment* (Hart Publishing 2018)

Beale H, and Ringe WG, 'Transfer of Rights and Obligations' in Dannemann G and Vogenauer S (eds), *The Common European Sales Law in Context: Interactions with English and German Law* (OUP 2013)

Beatson J, Burrows A, and Cartwright J, *Anson's Law of Contract* (30th edn, OUP 2016)

Ben-Shahar O and Posner EA, 'The Right to Withdraw in Contract Law' (2011) 40(1) Journal of Legal Studies 115
Bénabent A, 'Clauses Abusives: le droit français et ses réactions à la directive européenne' (1995) 3(2) European Review of Private Law 211
Benesch T, *Schlüsselkonzepte zur Statistik* (Springer Publishing 2012)
Benöhr I, *EU Consumer Law and Human Rights* (OUP 2013)
Bernheim-Desvaux S and Foucher P, 'L'effectivité du droit français de la consommation' in Micklitz HW and Saumier G (eds), *Enforcement and Effectiveness of Consumer Law* (Springer Publishing 2018)
Bernitz U, 'The Commission's Communications and Standard Contract Terms' in Vogenauer S and Weatherill S (eds), *The Harmonisation of European Contract Law: Implication for European Private Laws, Business and Legal Practice* (Hart Publishing 2006)
Beyers J and Arras S, 'Who feeds information to regulators? Stakeholder diversity in European Union regulatory agency consultations' (2020) 40(4) Journal of Public Policy 573
Borges G, *Die Inhaltskontrolle von Verbraucherverträgen* (Dunckler & Humblot 2000)
Brandner HE and Ulmer P, 'The Community Directive on Unfair Terms in Consumer Contracts: Some Critical Remarks on the Proposal Submitted by the EC Commission' (1991) 28(3) Common Market Law Review 647
Bricks H, *Les Clauses Abusives* (Librairie générale de droit et de jurisprudence 1982)
Bright S, 'Winning the Battle Against Unfair Contract Terms' (2000) 20(3) Legal Studies 331
Bright S, 'Unfairness and the Consumer Contract Regulations' in Burrows A and Peel E (eds), *Contract Terms* (OUP 2007)
Brunaux G, 'La protection dépendante du contexte contractuel' in Sauphanor-Brouillaud N and others, *Les contrats de consommation: Règles communes* (2nd edn, Librairie générale de droit et de jurisprudence 2018)
Bulletin of the European Communities, 'Statement from the Paris Summit 19 to 21 October 1972' (October 1972, No 10) Luxembourg: Office for official publications of the European Communities
Bunea A, 'Designing stakeholder consultations: Reinforcing or alleviating bias in the European Union system of governance?' (2017) 56(1) European Journal of Political Research 46
Burrows A, *A Casebook on Contracts* (6th edn, Hart Publishing 2018)
Busch C, 'Implementation of the Consumer Rights Directive Germany' (2014) 3(2) Journal of European Consumer and Market Law 119
Busch C, 'The future of pre-contractual information duties: from behavioural insights to big data' in Twigg-Flesner C (ed), *Research Handbook on EU Consumer and Contract Law* (Edward Elgar Publishing 2016)
Busseuil G, 'Implementation of the Consumer Rights Directive: France' (2014) 3(4) Journal of European Consumer and Market Law 270
Cafaggi F, 'Self-Regulation in European Contract Law' in Collins H (ed), *Standard Contract Terms in Europe: A Basis for and a Challenge to European Contract Law* (Kluwer Law International 2008)
Cartwright J, 'Information Obligations and Disinformation of Consumers: English Law Report' in Straetmans G (ed), *Information Obligations and Disinformation of Consumers* (Springer Publishing 2019)
Caruso D, 'Black Lists and Private Autonomy in EU Contract Law' in Dorota Leczykiewicz and Stephen Weatherill (eds), *The Involvement of EU Law in Private Law Relationships* (Hart Publishing 2013)

Cauffman C, 'The Consumer Rights Directive Adopted' (2012) 19(1) Maastricht Journal of European and Comparative Law 212

Cauffman C, Faure M, and Hartlief T, *Harmonisatie van het consumentencontractenrecht in Europa: consequenties voor Nederland* (Boom Juridische Uitgevers 2009)

Centrale Brancheverenigin Wonen, 'Download de CBW-erkende voorwaarden' (31 December 2019) https://www.cbw-erkend.nl/garanties-wonen (accessed 22 May 2021)

Chambre de commerce et d'industrie (CCI) de Paris Ile-de-France, 'Modèle-type de conditions générales' (2014) https://www.entreprises.cci-paris-idf.fr/web/reglementation/contrats-modeles/commerciaux/conditions-generales-de-vente-entre-professionnels (accessed 9 April 2019)

Chambres de Métiers et de l'Artisanat, 'Le portail des Chambres de Métiers et de l'Artisanat: Immatriculation au Répertoire des métiers' (2020) https://www.artisanat.fr/porteur-de-projet/lancer-mon-activite/immatriculation-au-repertoire-des-metiers (accessed 5 October 2020)

Chen-Wishart M, 'Regulating Unfair Terms' in Gullifer L and Vogenauer S (eds), *English and European Perspectives on Contract and Commercial Law: Essays in Honour of Hugh Beale* (Hart Publishing 2014)

Chen-Wishart M, *Contract Law* (6th edn, OUP 2018)

Chilton A and Versteeg M, *How Constitutional Rights Matter* (OUP 2020)

Civil Justice Council, 'Compulsory ADR' (Civil Justice Council, June 2021) https://www.judiciary.uk/wp-content/uploads/2021/07/Civil-Justice-Council-Compulsory-ADR-report-1.pdf (accessed 15 June 2021)

Coglianese C, 'Building Better Compliance' (2022) 100 Texas Law Review 192

Collins H, 'Good Faith in European Contract Law' (1994) 14(2) Oxford Journal of Legal Studies 229

Collins H, 'The Directive on Unfair Contract Terms: Implementation, Effectiveness, and Harmonization' in Collins H (ed), *Standard Contract Terms in Europe: A Basis for and a Challenge to European Contract Law* (Kluwer Law International 2008)

Colombi Ciacchi A, 'Good Governance and the Fitness Check of EU Consumer Law' in van Schagen E and Weatherill S (eds), *Better Regulation in EU Contract Law: The Fitness Check and the New Deal for Consumers* (Hart Publishing 2019)

Commission des clauses abusives, 'Contrats de fourniture de gaz et d'électricité' (Commission des clauses abusives, July 2020) http://www.clauses-abusives.fr/theme_recommandation/eau-electricite-gaz-gpl/ (accessed 20 July 2020)

Competition and Markets Authority, 'Unfair Contract Terms Guidance: Guidance on the unfair terms provisions in the Consumer Rights Act 2015' (31 July 2015) https://assets.publishing.service.gov.uk/government/uploads/system/uploads/attachment_data/file/450440/Unfair_Terms_Main_Guidance.pdf (accessed 26 July 2020)

Competition and Markets Authority and IFF Research, 'Unfair Contract Terms Research' Competition and Markets Authority (19 October 2016) https://assets.publishing.service.gov.uk/government/uploads/system/uploads/attachment_data/file/561518/UK_businesses__understanding_of_unfair_terms_in_consumer_contracts__IFF_Research_.pdf (accessed 29 April 2020)

Copenhagen Economics, 'Study on the economic impact of the electronic commerce Directive' (September 2007)

Cordero-Moss G, 'Standard contract terms as an alternative to legislation' in Twigg-Flesner C (ed), *Research Handbook on EU Consumer and Contract Law* (Edward Elgar Publishing 2016)

Cortés P, 'Enforcing EU Consumer Policy More Effectively: A Three Pronged Approach' in Drake S and Smith M (eds), *New Directions in the Effective Enforcement of EU Law and Policy* (Edward Elgar Publishing 2016)

Cortés P, 'The New Landscape of Consumer Redress: The European Directive on Consumer Alternative Dispute Resolution and the Regulation on Online Dispute Resolution' in Cortés P (ed), *The New Regulatory Framework for Consumer Dispute Resolution* (OUP 2016)

Cortés P and de la Rosa FE, 'Building a global redress system for low-value cross-border disputes' (2013) 62(2) The International and Comparative Law Quarterly 407

Creutzfeldt N, 'Alternative Dispute Resolution for Consumers' in Stürner M, Gascón Inchausti F, and Caponi R (eds), *The Role of Consumer ADR in the Administration of Justice: New Trends in Access to Justice under EU Directive 2013/11* (Sellier European Law Publishers 2015)

Crown Commercial Services (CCS), 'Guidance: short form terms and conditions' (31 July 2015) https://www.gov.uk/government/publications/short-form-terms-and-conditions (accessed 9 April 2019)

Dalloz, *Code de la consommation: annote & commenté* (24th edn, Dalloz 2020)

Dalloz, *Commentaire Code de la consommation* (Dalloz 5 February 2020)

Davo H, 'Clauses Abusives: loi du février 1995 transportant la directive 93/13/CCE en droit français' (1997) 5(2) European Review of Private Law 157

de Cristofaro G, 'After Implementing Directive 2011/83/EU in the Member States: Are the National Provisions on Consumer Contracts Really Harmonised? Some Critical Remarks' (2014) 3(4) Journal of European Consumer and Market Law 217

de Cristofaro G and de Franceschi A (eds), *Consumer Sales in Europe: After the Implementation of the Consumer Rights Directive* (Intersentia 2016)

De Matos AM, *Les contrats transfrontières conclus par les consommateurs au sein de l'Union européenne* (Presses Universitaires d'Aix-Marseille 2001)

de Moor A, 'Common and Civil Law Conceptions of Contract and European Law of Contract: The Case of the Directive on Unfair Terms in Consumer Contracts' (1995) 3(2) European Review of Private Law 257

Del Duca LF, Rule C, and Rimpfel K, 'eBay's De Facto Low Value High Volume Resolution Process: Lessons and Best Practices for ODR Systems Designers' (2014) 6 Yearbook on Arbitration and Mediation 204

Direction de l'information légale et administrative, 'Recherche sur les entreprises immatriculées au registre du commerce et des sociétés (RCS)' (Direction de l'information légale et administrative, 2019) https://www.service-public.fr/professionnels-entreprises/vosdroits/R19859 (accessed 4 October 2019)

Donnelly M and Whit F, 'Digital content and consumer protection: An empirical study of supplier compliance with consumer information obligations' (2019) 35(6) Computer Law & Security Review 1

Drexl J, 'Community Legislation Continued: Complete Harmonisation, Framework Legislation or Non-Binding Measures: Alternative Approaches to European Contract Law, Consumer Protection and Unfair Trade Practices?' (2002) 13(6) European Business Law Review 557

Dutilleul FH and Delebecque P, 'Introduction: Le droit spécial des contrats' in Dutilleul FC and Delebecque P, *Contrats civils et commerciaux* (11th edn, Dalloz 2019)

Ebers M, 'From *Océano* to *Asturcom*: Mandatory Consumer Law, Ex Officio Application of European Union Law and Res Judicata' (2010) 18(4) European Review of Private Law 823

Eidenmüller H, 'Why Withdrawal Rights?' (2011) 7(1) European Review of Contract Law 1

Eidenmüller H, 'What can be wrong with an option? An optional Common European Sales Law as a regulatory tool' (2013) 50(Special Issue) Common Market Law Review 69

Eidenmüller H, 'Collateral Damage: Brexit's Negative Effects on Regulatory Competition and Legal Innovation in Private Law' (2018) 26(4) Zeitschrift für Europäisches Privatrecht 868

Eleftheriadis P, 'Eleven Types of post-Brexit EU Law' (Oxford Business Law Blog, 8 January 2021) https://www.law.ox.ac.uk/business-law-blog/blog/2021/01/eleven-types-post-brexit-eu-law (accessed 30 January 2021)

Ellingsen HK, *Standing to Enforce European Union Law before National Courts* (Hart Publishing 2021)

Epstein L and Martin AD, 'Quantitative Approaches to Empirical Legal Research' in Cane P and Kritzer H (eds), *The Oxford Handbook of Empirical Legal Research* (OUP 2010)

Epstein R, 'Harmonization, heterogeneity and regulation: CESL, the lost opportunity for constructive harmonization' (2013) 50(Special Issue) Common Market Law Review 207

Ernst C, '§ 288' in Wolfgang Krüger (ed), *Münchner Kommentar zum Bürgerlichen Gesetzbuch Band 2: Schuldrecht Allgemeiner Teil 1 §§ 241-310* (8th edn, CH Beck 2019)

Ernst S and others (eds), *AGB-Recht: Kommentar* (12th edn, Otto Schmidt Verlag 2016)

Esposito F, *The Consumer Welfare Hypothesis in Law and Economics: Towards a Synthesis for the 21st Century* (Edward Elgar Publishing 2022)

European Parliamentary Research Service, 'The Costs of Non-Europe in the Single Market: Free Movement of Goods' (September 2014) http://www.europarl.europa.eu/EPRS/EPRS_STUDY_536353_CoNE_Single_Market_I.pdf (accessed 3 November 2020)

European University Institute, 'CLAUDETTE: Machine Learning Powered Analysis of Consumer Contracts and Privacy Policies' (2019) http://claudette.eui.eu/ (accessed 23 May 2021)

Eurostat, 'E-commerce statistics for individuals - Figure 4: Online Purchases, EU28, 2018' (2019) https://ec.europa.eu/eurostat/statistics-explained/index.php/E-commerce_statistics_for_individuals#Most_popular_online_purchases (accessed 29 August 2019)

Fastrich L, *Richterliche Inhaltskontrolle im Privatrecht* (CH Beck 1992)

Fernie J, Sparks L, and McKinnon A, 'Retail logistics in the UK: past, present and future' (2010) 38(11) International Journal of Retail & Distribution Management 894

Garben S and Govaere I (eds), *The EU Better Regulation Agenda: A Critical Assessment* (Hart Publishing 2018)

Giliker P, 'The Transposition of the Consumer Rights Directive into UK Law: Implementing a Maximum Harmonization Directive' (2015) 23(1) European Review of Private Law 5

Giliker P, 'The Consumer Rights Act 2015: a bastion of European Consumer Rights' (2017) 37(1) Legal Studies 78

Gillespie T, *Custodians of the Internet: Platforms, Content Moderation, and the Hidden Decisions that Shape Social Media* (Yale UP 2018)

Gillies LE, 'Recent developments in the approximation of EU private international laws: towards mutual trust, mutual recognition and enhancing social justice in civil and commercial matters' in Twigg-Flesner C (ed), *Research Handbook on EU Consumer and Contract Law* (Edward Elgar Publishing 2016)

Goanta C, *Convergence in European Consumer Sales Law: A Comparative and Numerical Approach* (Intersentia 2016)

Goudkamp J and Nolan D, 'Contributory Negligence in the Twenty-First Century: An Empirical Study of First Instance Decisions' (2016) 79(4) Modern Law Review 575

Grundmann S, 'The EU Consumer Rights Directive: optimizing, creating alternatives, or a dead end?' (2013) 18(1) Uniform Law Review 98

Guinchard E, 'The Implementation of the Consumer ADR Directive in France' in Cortés P (ed), *The New Regulatory Framework for Consumer Dispute Resolution* (OUP 2016)
Gutman K, *The Constitutional Foundations of European Contract Law: A Comparative Analysis* (OUP 2014)
Häcker B, 'Divergence and Convergence in the Common Law — Lessons from the Ius Commune' (2015) 131 Law Quarterly Review 424
Häcker B, '*La Troisième Jeunesse du Code Civil*: A German Lawyer Looks at the Reform of French Contract Law' in Cartwright J and Whittaker S (eds), *The Code Napoléon Rewritten: French Contract Law after the 2016 Reforms* (Hart Publishing 2017)
Hall E, Howells G, and Watson J, 'The Consumer Rights Directive: An Assessment of Its Contribution to the Development of European Consumer Contract Law' (2012) 8(2) European Review of Contract Law 139
Hall MA and Wright RF, 'Systematic Content Analysis of Judicial Opinions' (2008) 96(1) California Law Review 63
Halson R and Campbell D, 'Harmonisation and its discontents: a transaction costs critique of a European contract law' in Devenney J and Kenny M (eds), *The Transformation of European Private Law: Harmonisation, Consolidation, Codification or Chaos?* (CUP 2013)
Halson R, *Liquidated Damages and Penalty Clauses* (OUP 2018)
Hardt S and Kornet N (eds), *The Maastricht Collection: Selected National, European and International Provisions from Public and Private Law* (4th edn, Europa Law Publishing 2015)
Hartmann M, 'Telemedienrecht' in Wandtke AA (ed), *IT-Recht und Medienstraftrecht* (2nd edn, De Gruyter 2011)
Haythornthwaite R, 'Better Regulation in Europe' in Stephen Weatherill (ed), *Better Regulation* (Hart Publishing 2007)
Hayward B, Zeller B, and Andersen CB, 'The CISG and the United Kingdom—Exploring Coherency and Private International Law' (2018) 67(3) International & Comparative Law Quarterly 607
Helleringer G and Sibony AL, 'European Consumer Protection Through the Behavioral Lense' (2017) 23(3) The Columbia Journal of European Law 607
Hellwege P and Miller L, 'Control of Standard Terms' in Dannemann G and Vogenauer S (eds), *The Common European Sales Law in Context: Interactions with English and German Law* (OUP 2013)
Herbots JH, 'Interpretation of Contracts' in Smits JM (ed), *Elgar Encyclopedia of Comparative Law* (2nd edn, Edward Elgar Publishing 2012)
Hesselink MW, 'Codification and Europeanisation in the Netherlands' in Vogenauer S and Weatherill S (eds), *The Harmonisation of European Contract Law: Implications for European Private Laws, Business and Legal Practice* (Hart Publishing 2006)
Hesselink MW, 'Toward a Sharp Distinction between b2b and b2c? On Consumer, Commercial and General Contract Law after the Consumer Rights Directive' (2010) 18(1) European Review of Private Law 57
Hijma J, 'Validity: Art. 4:110-4:119' in Busch D and others (eds), *The Principles of European Contract Law and Dutch Law: A Commentary* (Kluwer Law 2002)
Hijma J, 'HR 08-02-2013, ECLI:NL:HR:2013:BY4600' (2014) Nederlandse Jurisprudentie 497
Hofmann HCH, Zetzsche DA, and Pflücke F, 'The Changing Nature of "Regulation by Information": Towards Real-time Regulation?' (2023) 28(4–6) European Law Journal 172
Hondius EH, 'De rechtspositie van de consument naar nieuw burgerlijk recht' (1991) 5 Tijdschrift voor Consumentenrecht 325

Hondius EH, 'The Reception of the Directive on Unfair Terms in Consumer Contracts by Member States' (1995) 3(2) European Review of Private Law 241

Hondius EH, 'Non-implementation of the Directive on Unfair Contract Terms: the Dutch case' (1997) 5(2) European Review of Private Law 193

Hondius EH, 'Algemene voorwaarden' in *Monografieën BW: Consumentenrecht* (2nd edn, Kluwer 2013)

Hondius EH, 'Unfair Contract Terms and the Consumer: ECJ Case Law, Foreign Literature, and Their Impact on Dutch Law' (2016) 24(3–4) European Review of Private Law 457

Howells G, 'The Potential and Limits of Consumer Empowerment by Information' (2005) 32(2) Journal of Law and Society 349

Howells G, Marten B, and Wurmnest W, 'Language of Information, Contract, and Communication' in Dannemann G and Vogenauer S (eds), *The Common European Sales Law in Context: Interactions with English and German Law* (OUP 2013)

Howells G, Twigg-Flesner C, and Wilhelmsson T, *Rethinking EU Consumer Law* (Routledge 2017)

Industrie- und Handelskammer (IHK) Schleswig-Holstein, 'Aufbau eines rechtssicheren Online-Shops' (2017) https://www.ihk-schleswig-holstein.de/blob/swhihk24/servicemarken/serviceleistungen/broschueren/1373948/7235c012267d902ad67dd243d271fdac/Broschuere_Aufbau_eines_rechtssicheren_Onlineshops-data.pdf (accessed 9 April 2019)

International Chamber of Commerce, 'What are Incoterms® rules?' (2020) https://iccwbo.org/resources-for-business/incoterms-rules/incoterms-2020/ (accessed 22 May 2021)

Jansen N, 'Unfair Contract Terms' in Jansen N and Zimmermann R (eds), *Commentaries on European Contract Laws* (OUP 2018)

Jaremba U and Mak E, 'Interviewing Judges in the Transnational Context' (2014) 4(2) Law and Method 1

Jarman H, 'Collaboration and Consultation: Functional Representation in EU Stakeholder Dialogues' (2011) 33(4) Journal of European Integration https://doi.org/10.1080/07036337.2011.579748

Joppich TG, *Die Kodifikation des Transparenzgebots in § 307 BGB* (Peter Lang 2008)

Julien J, *Droit de la Consommation* (2nd edn, Librairie générale de droit et de jurisprudence 2017)

Kamer van Koophandel, 'KVK-nummer: alles wat je moet weten' (Kamer van Koophandel, 2020) https://www.kvk.nl/informatiebank/kvk-nummer-alles-wat-je-moet-weten/ (accessed 5 October 2019)

Karimi A, *Les clauses abusives et la théorie de l'abus de droit* (Librairie Generale de Droit et de Jurisprudence 2001)

Karsten J and Sinai AR, 'The Action Plan on European Contract Law: Perspectives for the Future of European Contract Law and EC Consumer Law' (2003) 26(2) Journal of Consumer Policy 159

Kästle-Lamparter D, 'Art 2:403: Information Requirements for Distance and Off-premises Consumer Contracts' in Jansen N and Zimmermann R (eds), *Commentaries on European Contract Laws* (OUP 2018)

Kästle-Lamparter D, 'Art 2:405: Formal and Additional Requirements for Distance Consumer Contracts' in Jansen N and Zimmermann R (eds), *Commentaries on European Contract Laws* (OUP 2018)

Katsh E and Rabinovich-Einy O, *Digital Justice: Technology and the Internet of Disputes* (OUP 2017)

Kippels G, *Die Inhaltskontrolle von allgemeinen Geschäftsbedingungen im kaufmännischen Geschäftsverkehr nach § 9 Abs 2 AGB-Gesetz unter besonderer Berücksichtigung der Klauselverbote der §§ 10 und 11 AGB-Gesetz* (Hundt Verlag 1990)

Klimke D, *Die Vertragsübernahme* (Mohr Siebeck 2010)

Kolb S, *Die Übergangsregelung der Richtlinie über unlautere Geschäftspraktiken* (Mohr Siebeck 2015)

Kötz H, *European Contract Law* (2nd edn, OUP 2017)

Krähmer D and Strausz R, 'Optimal Sales Contracts with Withdrawal Rights' (2015) 82(2) The Review of Economic Studies 762

Krämer L, 'The Origins of Consumer Law and Policy at EU Level' in Hans-Wolfgang Micklitz (ed), *The Making of Consumer Law and Policy in Europe* (Hart Publishing 2021)

Krans BH, Stolker CJJM, and Valk LW (eds), *Tekst & Commentaar Burgerlijk Wetboek: Online Naslagwerk* (30 August 2021 edn, Wolters Kluwer 2021)

Kuczerawy A and Rauchegger C, 'Court of Justice Injunctions to remove illegal online content under the eCommerce Directive: Glawischnig-Piesczek' (2020) 57(5) Common Market Law Review 1495

Lagarde X, 'Qu'est-ce qu'une clause abusive?' (2006) 80(6) Juris-Classeur périodique, édition générale 255

Lando O and Beale H (eds), *Principles of European Contract Law Parts I and II* (Kluwer Law International 2000)

Lando O, Clive E, Prüm A, and Zimmermann R (eds), *Principles of European Contract Law Part III* (Kluwer Law International 2003)

Lazic V, 'Arbitration Law Reform in the Netherlands: Formal and Substantive Validity of an Arbitration Agreement' in van Erp S and van Vliet L (eds) *Netherlands Reports to the Seventeenth International Congress of Comparative Law* (Intersentia 2006)

Leczykiewicz D, 'Regulatory Cost, the Consumer, and the EU Constitutional Framework' in Leczykiewicz D and Weatherill S (eds), *The Images of the Consumer in EU Law: Legislation, Free Movement and Competition Law* (Hart Publishing 2016)

Leczykiewicz D, 'Regulatory Cost and the Consumer' in Leczykiewicz D and Weatherill S (eds), *Images of Consumers* (Hart Publishing 2016)

Leczykiewicz D, 'Private regulation, compliance and reviewability of contracts' in Roger Brownsword, van Gestel RAJ, and Micklitz HW (eds), *Contract and Regulation: A Handbook on New Methods of Law Making in Private Law* (Edward Elgar Publishing 2017)

Leeuw F, 'Empirical Legal Research: The Gap between Facts and Values and Legal Academic Training' (2015) 11(2) Utrecht Law Review 19

Lehmann M and Busch D, 'Make It Stringent: A Plea for an Unfair Terms Regulation' (2023) 31(6) European Review of Private Law 1175

Lehmann M and Ungerer J, 'Save the "Mittelstand": How German Courts Protect Small and Medium-Sized Enterprises from Unfair Terms' (2017) 25(2) European Review of Private Law 313

Listorti G, Basyte-Ferrari E, Acs S, and Smits P, 'Towards an Evidence-Based and Integrated Policy Cycle in the EU: A Review of the Debate on the Better Regulation Agenda' (2020) 58(6) Journal of Common Market Studies 1558

Lodder AR, Egeler MGA, and van Kerkvoorden WEL, *Cyber Law in the Netherlands* (Kluwer Law International 2016)

Lodder AR, 'Directive 2000/31/EC on Certain Legal Aspects of Information Society Services, in Particular Electronic Commerce, in the Internal Market' in Lodder AR and Murray A (eds), *EU Regulation of E-Commerce* (Edward Elgar Publishing 2017)

Lofstedt RE, 'The "Plateau-ing" of the European Better Regulation Agenda: An Analysis of Activities Carried out by the Barroso Commission' (2007) 10(4) Journal of Risk Research 423

Loir R, 'Les nouvelles définitions du professionnel, du consommateur et du non-professionnel' (2016) 27 Juris-Classeur périodique, édition Entreprise 1042

Loos M, 'Veroordeling Nederland wegens niet-omzetting Richtlijn oneerlijke bedingen' (2001) 2(9) Nederlands Tijdschrift voor Europees Recht 242

Loos M, 'Consumer Sales in the Netherlands after the Implementation of the Consumer Rights Directive' in de Cristofaro G and de Franceschi A (eds), *Consumer sales in Europe: after the implementation of the Consumer Rights Directive* (Intersentia 2016)

Loos M and de Moor RRM, 'Hoge Raad 13 september 2013, ECLI:NL:HR:2013:691' (2013) 11(6) Tijdschrift voor Consumentenrecht en Handelspraktijken 262

Loos M and Samoy I, 'The Position of Small and Medium-Sized Enterprises in European Contract Law: An Introduction' in Loos M and Samoy I (eds), *The Position of Small and Medium-Sized Enterprises in European Contract Law* (Intersentia 2014)

Loos M and Luzak JA, 'Wanted: a Bigger Stick. On Unfair Terms in Consumer Contracts with Online Service Providers' (2016) 39(1) Journal of Consumer Policy 63

Looschelders D, Olzen D, and Schiemann G, *Staudinger BGB - Buch 2: Recht der Schuldverhältnisse: §§ 241-243* (Sellier/de Gruyter 2019)

Lopez-Tarruella A, 'A European Community Regulatory Framework for Electronic Commerce' (2001) 38(6) Common Market Law Review 1356

Lubasz D and Namysłowska M, 'Directive 2000/31/EC: Article 5 General information to be provided' in Schulze R and Staudenmayer D (eds), *EU Digital Law: Article-by-Article Commentary* (Bloomsbury 2020)

Lutzi T, *Private International Law Online: Internet Regulation and Civil Liability in the EU* (OUP 2020)

Luzak JA, 'To Withdraw or Not to Withdraw? Evaluation of the Mandatory Right of Withdrawal in Consumer Distance Selling Contracts Taking into Account Its Behavioural Effects on Consumers' (2011) 37(1) Journal of Consumer Policy 91

Luzak JA and Mak V, 'Implementation of the Consumer Rights Directive: The Netherlands' (2014) 3(2) Journal of European Consumer and Market Law 127

Luzak JA and Mak V, 'The Consumer Rights Directive' in Hartkamp AS and others (eds), *De invloed van het Europese recht op het Nederlandse privaatrecht* (Kluwer 2014)

MacDonald E, 'Exclusion Clauses: the Ambit of s 13(1) of the Unfair Contract Terms Act 1977' (1992) 12 Legal Studies 277

MacDonald E, 'Mapping the Unfair Contract Terms Act 1977 and the Directive on Unfair Terms in Consumer Contracts' [1994] Journal of Business Law 441

MacDonald E, 'The Emperor's Old Clauses: Unincorporated Clauses, Misleading terms and the Unfair Terms in Consumer Contracts Regulations' (1999) 58(2) Cambridge Law Journal 413

MacDonald E, 'Unifying Unfair Terms Legislation' (2004) 67(1) The Modern Law Review 69

MacDonald E, 'UCTA Thirty Years On' in Burrows A and Peel E (eds), *Contract Terms* (OUP 2007)

Mackenrodt MO, *Technologie statt Vertrag? Sachmangelbegriff, negative Beschaffenheitsvereinbarungen und AGB beim Kauf digitaler Güter* (Mohr Siebeck 2015)

Maier-Reimer G, 'AGB-Recht im unternehmerischen Rechtsverkehr: Der BGH überdreht die Schraube' (2017) 70(1) Neue Juristische Wochenschrift 1

Mak C, 'Artikel 6:233 BW: Hoe de doorwerking van Europees consumentenrecht tornt aan het systeem van het Nederlandse privaatrecht' in van de Pol F and others (eds), *Vijftig weeffouten in het BW: Een ode aan het Burgerlijk Wetboek, ter ere van zijn 25-jarig bestaan* (Ars Aequi Libri 2017)

Mak V, 'Full Harmonization in European Private Law: A Two-Track Concept' (2012) 20(1) European Review of Private Law 213
Mak V, 'Two levels, one standard? The multi-level regulation of consumer protection in Europe' in Devenny J and Kenny M (eds), *European Consumer Protection: Theory and Practice* (CUP 2012)
Mak V, 'Enforcement and Effectiveness of Consumer Law: The Netherlands' in Micklitz HW and Saumier G (eds), *Enforcement and Effectiveness of Consumer Law* (Springer Publishing 2018)
Mak V, *Legal Pluralism in European Contract Law* (OUP 2020)
Markou C, 'Directive 2011/83/EU on Consumer Rights' in Lodder AR and Murray A (eds), *EU Regulation of E-Commerce* (Edward Elgar Publishing 2017)
Marotta-Wurgler F, 'Competition and the Quality of Standard Form Contracts: The Case of Software License Agreements' (2008) 5(3) Journal of Empirical Legal Studies 447
Marotta-Wurgler F, 'Are "Pay Now, Terms Later" Contracts Worse for Buyers? Evidence from Software License Agreements' (2009) 38(2) The Journal of Legal Studies 309
Marxsen C, 'Open Stakeholder Consultations at the European Level: Voice of the Citizens?' (2015) 21(2) European Law Journal 257
Mateusz Grochowski, 'European Consumer Law after the New Deal: A Tryptich' (2020) 39(1) Yearbook of European Law 1
McKendrick E, *Contract Law* (8th edn, OUP 2018)
McMeel G and Grigoleit HC, 'Interpretation of Contracts' in Dannemann G and Vogenauer S (eds), *The Common European Sales Law in Context: Interactions with English and German Law* (OUP 2013)
Mekki M, 'France: The French Reform of Contract Law: The Art of Redoing Without Undoing' (2017) 10(1) Journal of Civil Law Studies 223
Messinger M, *Rechtsunsicherheiten bei internationalen elektronischen Handelsgeschäften* (Mohr Siebeck 2014)
Mestre J, 'Clause de modification unilateral' in Buy F and others (eds), *Les principales clauses des contrats d'affaires* (2nd edn, Librairie générale de droit et de jurisprudence 2018)
Meuwese ACM, 'Inter-institutionalising EU Impact Assessment' in Weatherill S (ed), *Better Regulation* (Hart Publishing 2007)
Micklitz HW, 'The Targeted Full Harmonisation Approach: Looking behind the Curtain' in Howells G and Schulze R (eds), *Modernising and Harmonising Consumer Contract Law* (Sellier European Law Publisher 2009)
Micklitz HW, 'Reforming European Unfair Terms Legislation in Consumer Contracts' (2010) 6(4) European Review of Contract Law 347
Micklitz HW, 'The Measuring of the Law Through EU politics' in Bartl M and Lawrence J C (eds), *The Politics of European Legal Research* (Edward Elgar Publishing 2022)
Micklitz HW and Reich N, 'Crónica de una muerte anunciada: The Commission proposal for a "Directive on consumer rights"' (2009) 46(2) Common Market Law Review 471
Micklitz HW, and Reich N, 'The Court and Sleeping Beauty: The Revival of the Unfair Contract Terms Directive (UCTD)' (2014) 51(3) Common Market Law Review 771
Micklitz HW and Villanueva AA, 'REFIT or Rethink: The Politics of EU Research: A Grand Misunderstanding?' in van Schagen E and Weatherill S (eds), *Better Regulation in EU Contract Law: The Fitness Check and the New Deal for Consumers* (Hart Publishing 2019)
Micklitz HW, Palka P, and Panagis Y, 'The Empire Strike Back: Digital Control of Unfair Terms of Online Services' (2017) 40 (3) Journal of Consumer Policy 367
Micklitz HW, Palka P, and Panagis Y, *The Politics of Justice in European Private Law: Social Justice, Access Justice, Societal Justice* (CUP 2018)

Miquel R, 'The Implementation of the Consumer ADR Directive in Germany' in Cortés P (ed), *The New Regulatory Framework for Consumer Dispute Resolution* (OUP 2016)
Möllers TMJ, 'European Directives on Civil Law The German Approach: Towards the Re-codification and New Foundation of Civil Law Principles' (2002) 10(6) European Review of Private Law 777
Morgan J, 'The Penalty Clause Doctrine: Unlovable but Untouchable' (2016) 75(1) The Cambridge Law Journal 11
Müller-Broich J, *Telemediengesetz* (Nomos 2012)
Nebbia P, *Unfair Contract Terms in European Law: A Study in Comparative and EC Law* (Hart Publishing 2007)
Nebbia P, 'Unfair Contract Terms' in Twigg-Flesner C (ed), *The Cambridge Companion to European Union Private Law* (CUP 2010)
Neumann-Wedekindt J, *Inhaltskontrolle allgemeiner Geschäftsbedingungen, dargestellt an Vertragsabschlussklauseln* (Dissertation at the Faculty of Law at the University of Münster 1968)
Nobis S, *Missbräuchliche Vertragsklauseln in Deutschland und Frankreich: Zur Umsetzung der Klauselrichtlinie 93/13/EWG des Rates* (Nomos 2005)
Nolan D, 'Offer and Acceptance in the Digital Age' in Burrows A and Peel E (eds), *Contract Formation and Parties* (OUP 2010)
Nowag J and Groussot X, 'From Better Regulation to Better Adjudication? Impact Assessment and the Court of Justice's Review' in Garben S and Govaere I (eds), *The EU Better Regulation Agenda: A Critical Assessment* (Hart Publishing 2018)
Nürnberg M, *Die Durchsetzung von Verbraucherrechten: Eine rechtsvergleichende Analyse der Verbraucherrechtsdurchsetzung in Frankreich, den Niederlanden und Deutschland* (Nomos 2020)
Nutley S and Webb J, 'Evidence and the Policy Process' in Sandra Nutley, Huw TO Davies, and Peter Smith (eds), *What Works? Evidence-based Policy and Practice in Public Services* (Policy Press 2000)
Organisation for Economic Co-operation and Development (OECD), 'Better Regulation Practices across the European Union' (19 March 2019) https://www.oecd-ilibrary.org/sites/dd9b13ad-en/index.html?itemId=/content/component/dd9b13ad-en (accessed 16 April 2023)
Organisation for Economic Co-operation and Development (OECD), 'Better Regulation Practices across the European Union: Executive Summary' (19 March 2019) https://www.oecd-ilibrary.org/governance/better-regulation-practices-across-the-european-union_582c4ee9-en (accessed 16 April 2023)
Palmer N and Yates D, 'The Future of the Unfair Contract Terms Act 1977' (1981) 40 Cambridge Law Journal 108
Parkhurst J, *The Politics of Evidence: From evidence-based policy to the good governance of evidence* (Routledge 2016)
Pavillon C, 'Beter consumentenrecht: naar een scherpere consumentvriendelijke onredelijk bezwarend-norm' (2011) 63(8) Nederlands Tijdschrift voor Burgerlijk Recht 439
Pearson G, 'Further Challenges for Australian Consumer Law' in Marques CL and Wei D (eds), *Consumer Law and Socioeconomic Development: National and International Dimensions* (Springer Publishing 2017)
Péglion-Zika CM, *La notion de clause abusive* (Librairie générale de droit et de jurisprudence 2018)
Pellier JD, 'L'ordonnance portant réforme du droit des contrats, du régime général et de la preuve des obligations enfin ratifiée!' *Dalloz actualité* (30 April 2018)
Pellier JD, *Droit de la consommation* (2nd edn, Dalloz 2018)

Pellier JD, 'Retour sur les clauses noires' *Dalloz actualité* (24 December 2019)
Pflücke F, 'The Implementation of the EU Directives 2019/770 and 2019/771 in Luxembourg' (2022) 11(3) Journal of European Consumer and Market Law 114
Pflücke F, 'The Limits of Consumer Law in Pursuing Sustainability' in Julian Nowag (ed), *Research Handbook on Sustainability and Competition Law* (Edward Elgar Publishing 2024)
Piazzon T, 'L'information et la désinformation des consommateurs: Rapport français' in Straetmans G (ed), *Information Obligations and Disinformation of Consumers* (Springer Publishing 2019)
Podszun R, Busch C, and Henning-Bodewig F, 'Behördliche Durchsetzung des Verbraucherrechts? Darstellung und Systematisierung von Möglichkeiten und Defiziten der privaten Durchsetzung des Verbraucherschutzes sowie Einbeziehung der Kartellbehörden zu dessen Durchsetzung' Bundesministeriums für Wirtschaft und Energie (February 2018) https://www.bmwk.de/Redaktion/DE/Publikationen/Studien/behoerdliche-durchsetzung-des-verbraucherrechts.pdf?blob=publicationFile%20%20&v=13 (accessed 28 March 2024)
Podszun R, Busch C, and Henning-Bodewig F, 'Consumer Law in Germany: A Shift to Public Enforcement?' (2019) 8(2) Journal of European Consumer and Market Law 75
Pohlman J and Leitner D, 'A Comparison of Ordinary Least Squares and Logistic Regression' (2003) 103(5) Ohio Journal of Science 118
Poillot E, *Droit européen de la consommation et uniformisation du droit des contrats* (Librairie Generale de Droit et de Jurisprudence 2006)
Porat A, 'The Law and Economics of Mistake in European Sales Law' (2013) 50(Special Issue) Common Market Law Review 127
Portal of the Justice Authorities of the Federal and State Governments, 'Gemeinsames Registerportal der Länder' (2019) https://www.handelsregister.de/rp_web/mask.do (accessed 4 October 2019)
Prince S, 'Access to Court? "Encouraging" Consumers to Use Court-Connected Mediation in Small Claims and Other Cases' in Cortés P (ed), *The New Regulatory Framework for Consumer Dispute Resolution* (OUP 2016)
Purnhagen KP and Feindt PH, 'Better Regulatory Impact Assessment: Making Behavioural Insights Work for the Commission's New Better Regulation Strategy' (2015) 6(3) European Journal of Risk Regulation 361
Ramsay I, *Consumer Law and Policy: Text and Materials on Regulating Consumer Markets* (Hart Publishing 2012)
Ranchordás S, *Consultations, Citizen Narratives and Evidence-Based Regulation: The Strange Case of the Consultation on the Collaborative Economy* (2017) 19(1) European Journal of Law Reform 52
Reich N, 'The implementation of Directive 93/13/EEC on unfair terms in consumer contracts in Germany' (1997) 5(2) European Review of Private Law 165
Reich N, Micklitz HW, Rott P, and Tonner K, *European Consumer Law* (2nd edn, Intersentia 2014)
Riefa C, 'The REFIT Process in the Area of Consumer Protection: Odds Stacked Against Consumers' in van Schagen E and Weatherill S (eds), *Better Regulation in EU Contract Law: The Fitness Check and the New Deal for Consumers* (Hart Publishing 2019)
Riefa C and Willett C, 'Enforcement and Effectiveness of Consumer Law in the UK' in Micklitz HW and Saumier G (eds), *Enforcement and Effectiveness of Consumer Law* (Springer Publishing 2018)
Rogers H and Clarke M, *The Unfair contract terms act 1977* (Sweet & Maxwell 1978)
Rott P, 'Unfair Contract Terms' in Twigg-Flesner C (ed), *Research Handbook on EU Consumer and Contract Law* (Edward Elgar Publishing 2016)
Rüfner T, 'Art 18:307: Passing of Risk in a Consumer Sales Contract' in Jansen N and Zimmermann R (eds), *Commentaries on European Contract Laws* (OUP 2018)

Rutgers JW, 'Unfair Terms in Consumer Contracts' in Gullifer L and Vogenauer S (eds), *English and European Perspectives on Contract and Commercial Law: Essays in Honour of Hugh Beale* (Hart Publishing 2014)
Sadl U and Palmer H, 'Can Quantitative Methods Complement Doctrinal Legal Studies? Using Citation Network and Corpus Linguistic Analysis to Understand International Courts' (2017) 30(2) Leiden Journal of International Law 327
Salehijam M, 'The Value of Systematic Content Analysis in Legal Research' (2018) 23(1) Tilburg Law Review 34
Salkind NJ in 'Reliability of Scores' in Salkind NJ (ed), *Encyclopedia of Research Design* (SAGE 2010)
Sarpi F, 'Better for Whom?' (2015) 6(3) European Journal of Risk Regulation 372
Savin A, *EU Internet Law* (2nd edn, Edward Elgar Publishing 2017)
Schillig M, 'Inequality of Bargaining Power Versus Market for Lemons: Legal Paradigm Change and the Court of Justice's Jurisprudence on Directive 93/13 on Unfair Contract Terms' (2009) 33(3) European Law Journal 336
Schinkels B, 'Der Kommissionsentwurf einer Verbraucherrechte-Richtlinie und seine Sprengkraft für § 355 BGB' (2009) 64(15–16) Juristen Zeitung 774
Schmidt-Kessel M, 'Consumer Sales in Germany after the Implementation of the Consumer Rights Directive' in de Cristofaro G and de Franceschi A (eds), *Consumer sales in Europe: after the implementation of the Consumer Rights Directive* (Intersentia 2016)
Schulte-Nölke H and Börger A, 'Distance Selling Directive (97/7)' in Schulte-Nölke H, Twigg-Flesner C, and Ebers M (eds), *EC Consumer Law Compendium: The Consumer Acquis and Its Transposition in the Member States* (Sellier European Law Publishers 2009)
Schulze R and Schulte-Nölke H (eds), *Die Schuldrechtsreform vor dem Hintergrund des Gemeinschaftsrechts* (Mohr Siebeck 2001)
Sealy LS, 'Unfair Contract Terms Act 1977' (1978) 37(1) The Cambridge Law Journal 15
Sefton-Green R, 'Case Studies' in Sefton-Green R (ed), *Mistake, Fraud and Duties to Inform in European Contract Law* (CUP 2009)
Seidman Diamond S and Mueller P, 'Empirical Legal Scholarship in Law Reviews' (2010) 6 Annual Review of Law and Social Science 581
Sibony AL, 'Data and arguments: empirical research in consumer law' in Micklitz HW, Sibony AL, and Esposito F (eds), *Research Methods in Consumer Law: A Handbook* (Edward Elgar Publishing 2018)
Sieburgh CH, *Asser 6-III Algemeen overeenkomstenrecht* (15th edn, Wolters Kluwer 2018)
Smits JM, 'A European Private Law as a Mixed Legal System: Towards a Ius Commune through the Free Movement of Legal Rules' (1998) 5(4) Maastricht Journal of European and Comparative Law 328
Smits JM, 'Nogmaals de richtlijn oneerlijke bedingen: Nederland veroordeeld wegens gebrekkige implementatie' (2001) Weekblad voor Privaatrecht, Notariaat en Registratie 853
Smits JM, 'Non-Performance and Remedies in General' in Busch D and others (eds), *The Principles of European Contract Law and Dutch Law: A Commentary* (Kluwer Law 2002)
Smits JM, 'The Action Plan on a More Coherent European Contract Law' (2003) 10(2) Maastricht Journal of European and Comparative Law 111
Smits JM, 'Epistemology and Methodology of Comparative Law' in van Hoecke M (ed), *Epistemology and Methodology of Comparative Law* (Hart Publishing 2004)
Smits JM, 'Party choice and the Common European Sales Law, or: How to prevent the CESL from becoming a lemon on the law market' (2013) 50(Special Issue) Common Market Law Review 51

Srivastava A, 'The New EU Consumer Rights Directive: An Empirical Study on Compliance Issues by E-Tailers' (2017) 32(4) Journal of Business Law 282

Stein G, *Zum Spannungsverhältnis der Kontrollverfahren aufgrund des AGB-Gesetzes und § 242 BGB* (Duncker & Humblot 1982)

Stichting Webshop Keurmerk, 'Algemene Voorwaarden voor Webshops' (1 June 2014) https://www.keurmerk.info/nl/home/gratis-algemene-voorwaarden/ (accessed 22 May 2021)

Stoffel-Munck P, 'The Revolution in Unfair Terms' in Cartwright J and Whittaker S (eds), *The Code Napoléon Rewritten: French Contract Law after the 2016 Reforms* (Hart Publishing 2017)

Stürner M, Inchausti FG, and Caponi R (eds), *The Role of Consumer ADR in the Administration of Justice: New Trends in Access to Justice under EU Directive 2013/11* (Sellier European Law Publishers 2015)

Susskind R, *Online Courts and the Future of Justice* (OUP 2019)

Tanti-Dougall R, 'Implementation of the Consumer Rights Directive: Malta' (2014) 3(3) Journal of European Consumer and Market Law 187

Tenreiro M, 'The Community Directive on Unfair Terms and National Legal Systems: The Principle of Good Faith and Remedies for Unfair Terms' (1995) 3(2) European Review of Private Law 273

Terryn E and Vandenbulcke J, 'Directive 2011/81/EU: Article 6 Information requirements for distance or off-premises contracts' in Schulze R and Staudenmayer D (eds), *EU Digital Law: Article-by-Article Commentary* (Bloomsbury 2020)

Testud M, 'La transposition en droit interne de la directive communautaire sur les clauses abusives' (1996) 13 Dalloz Affaires 372

Teubel JP, *Rücktrittsrecht und AGB-Kontrolle nach der Schuldrechtsreform* (Duncker & Humblot 2018)

Teubner G, 'Legal Irritants: Good Faith in British Law or How Unifying Law Ends Up in New Divergences' (1998) 61(1) Modern Law Review 11

Thompson P, *Unfair Contract Terms Act 1977* (Butterworths 1978)

Thuiswinkel Organisatie, 'Algemene Voorwaarden Thuiswinkel' (1 June 2014) https://www.thuiswinkel.org/veilig-online-shoppen/wat-is-thuiswinkel-waarborg/algemene-voorwaarden-thuiswinkel/ (accessed 22 May 2021)

Thuiswinkel Organisatie, 'Algemene Voorwaarden Thuiswinkel' (2017) https://www.thuiswinkel.org/consumenten/wat-is-thuiswinkel-waarborg/algemene-voorwaarden-thuiswinkel (accessed 9 April 2019)

Tilmann I, *Die Klauselrichtlinie 93/13/EWG auf der Schnittstelle zwischen Privatrecht und öffentlichem Recht* (CH Beck 2003)

Tjeerd GG Raijmakers, 'Art. 233: Burgerlijk Wetboek Boek 6' in Sjoerd P Bakker and others (eds), *Sdu Commentaar Vermogensrecht: Online Naslagwerk* (1 June 2021 edn, Sdu 2021)

Tjeerd GG Raijmakers, 'Art. 236: Burgerlijk Wetboek Boek 6' in Sjoerd P Bakker and others (eds), *Sdu Commentaar Vermogensrecht: Online Naslagwerk* (1 June 2021 edn, Sdu 2021)

Tjeerd GG Raijmakers, 'Art. 237: Burgerlijk Wetboek Boek 6' in Sjoerd P Bakker and others (eds), *Sdu Commentaar Vermogensrecht: Online Naslagwerk* (1 June 2021 edn, Sdu 2021)

Tonner K, 'From the Kennedy Message to Full Harmonising Consumer Law Directives: A Retrospect' in Purnhagen K and Rott P(eds), *Varieties of European Economic Law and Regulation: Liber Amicorum for Hans Micklitz* (Springer Publishing 2014)

Tonner K, 'The Consumer Rights Directive and Its Impact on Internet and other Distance Consumer Contracts' in Reich N and others (eds), *European Consumer Law* (2nd edn, Intersentia 2014)

Trochu M, 'Les clauses abusives dans les contrats conclus avec les consommateurs' (1993) Recueil Dalloz 316
Turner M, Traynor M, and Smith H, 'E-Commerce Directive: UK Implementation' (2002) 18(6) Computer Law & Security Report 396
Twigg-Flesner C, *A Cross-Border-Only Regulation for Consumer Transactions in the EU: A Fresh Approach to EU Consumer Law* (Springer Publishing 2011)
Twigg-Flesner C, 'Consumer Sales in the United Kingdom after the Implementation of the Consumer Rights Directive' in de Cristofaro G and de Franceschi A (eds), *Consumer sales in Europe: after the implementation of the Consumer Rights Directive* (Intersentia 2016)
Twigg-Flesner C, Schulze R, and Watson J, 'Protecting rational choice: information and the right of withdrawal' in Howells G, Ramsay I, and Wilhelmsson T (eds), *Handbook of Research on International Consumer Law* (2nd edn, Edward Elgar Publishing 2018)
Twigg-Flesner C, 'Consolidation rather than codification: or just complication? The UK's Consumer Rights Act 2015' (2019) 27(1) Zeitschrift für Europäisches Privatrecht 170
Ulmer P, Brandner HE, and Hensen HD (eds), *Kommentar zum Gesetz zur Regelung des Rechts der allgemeinen Geschäftsbedingungen* (Verlag Dr. Otto Schmidt KG 1982)
ULYS consortium, 'Study on Liability of Internet Intermediaries' (2007), : Commission, 'Studies: 2007' (European Commission, 24 March 2017) https://ec.europa.eu/digital-single-market/en/news/archive-e-commerce-directive-what-happened-and-its-adoption (accessed 5 October 2019)
Ungerer J, 'No Sunset of Retained EU Conflict of Laws in the UK, but Increased Risk of Sunburn' Conflict of Laws (26 July 2023) https://conflictoflaws.net/2023/no-sunset-of-retained-eu-conflict-of-laws-in-the-uk-but-increased-risk-of-sunburn/ (accessed 11 August 2023)
United Nations, 'Status: United Nations Convention on Contracts for the International Sale of Goods (Vienna, 1980) (CISG)' United Nations Commission on International Trade Law (20 April 2021) https://uncitral.un.org/en/texts/salegoods/conventions/sale_of_goods/cisg/status (accessed 20 April 2021)
van Bochove LM, 'Overriding Mandatory Rules as a Vehicle for Weaker Party Protection in European Private International Law' (2014) 7(3) Erasmus Law Review 147
van den Abeele E, '"Better Regulation": a bureaucratic simplification with a political agenda', Working paper 2015.4 (Etui)
van Dijck G, 'The Ordered Apology' (2016) 37(3) Oxford Journal of Legal Studies 562
van Dijck G, 'Victim-Oriented Tort Law in Action: An Empirical Examination of Catholic Church Sexual Abuse Cases' (2018) 15(1) Journal of Empirical Legal Studies 142
van Dijck G, Sverdlov S, and Buck G, 'Empirical Legal Research in Europe: Prevalence, Obstacles, and Interventions' (2018) 12(2) Erasmus Law Review 105
van Gerven W, 'The Case-law of the European Court of Justice and National Courts as a Contribution to the Europeanisationof Private Law' (1995) 3(2) European Review of Private Law 367
van Schagen E, 'The Draft Common Frame of Reference and Multilevel Governance' (2010) 1(3) Edinburgh Student Law Review 74
van Schagen E, 'The Hidden Potential of Regulatory Impact Assessments (RIAs) in the Private Law Acquis' (2014) 22(1) European Review of Private Law 69
van Schagen E, '"Better" Enforcement of EU Consumer Law: Exploring Responsive Enforcement' in van Schagen E and Weatherill S (eds), *Better Regulation in EU Contract Law: The Fitness Check and the New Deal for Consumers* (Hart Publishing 2019)

van Schagen E, 'The Fitness Check of EU Consumer Law and the Impact Assessment for the New Deal for Consumer' in van Schagen E and Weatherill S (eds), *Better Regulation in EU Contract Law: The Fitness Check and the New Deal for Consumers* (Hart Publishing 2019)

van Schagen E and Weatherill S (eds), *Better Regulation in EU Contract Law: The Fitness Check and the New Deal for Consumers* (Hart Publishing 2019)

van Schagen E and Weatherill S, 'Impact Assessments in EU Contract Law' in van Schagen E and Weatherill S (eds), *Better Regulation in EU Contract Law: The Fitness Check and the New Deal for Consumers* (Hart Publishing 2019)

van Schaick AC, 'Contents and Effects' in Busch D and others (eds), *The Principles of European Contract Law and Dutch Law: A Commentary* (Kluwer Law 2002)

Vasquez-Sosas R, 'The Language of Agreement: A Content Analysis of Employment Contracts' (2017) 12(2) Journal of Humanities and Social Science 2279

Verhage E, 'The Implementation of the Consumer ADR Directive in the Netherlands' in Cortés P (ed), *The New Regulatory Framework for Consumer Dispute Resolution* (OUP 2016)

Viney G, 'Un pas vers l'assainissement des pratiques contractuelles: la loi du 5 janvier 1988 relative aux actions en justice des associations agréées de consommateurs' (1988) Juris-Classeur périodique, édition Entreprise 3355

Vogenauer S, 'Interpretation' in Jansen N and Zimmermann R (eds), *Commentaries on European Contract Laws* (OUP 2018)

Vogenauer S and Weatherill S, 'The European Community's Competence to Pursue the Harmonisation of Contract Law—an Empirical Contribution to the Debate' in Vogenauer S and Weatherill S (eds), *The Harmonisation of European Contract Law: Implications for European Private Laws, Business and Legal Practice* (Hart Publishing 2006)

Wagner SV, *Verbraucherschutz bei Vertragsschluss im Internet: ein Vergleich zwischen englischem und deutschem Recht* (De Gruyter 2010)

Weatherill S, 'Prospects for the Development of European Private Law through Europeanisation in the Court of Justice' (1995) 3(2) European Review of Private Law 307

Weatherill S, 'The Regulation of E-Commerce under EC Law: The Distribution of Competence between Home States and Host States as a Basis for Managing the Internal Market' in Snijders H and Weatherill S (eds), *E-commerce Law: National and Transnational Topics and Perspectives* (Kluwer Law International 2003)

Weatherill S (ed), *Better Regulation* (Hart Publishing 2007)

Weatherill S, 'Competence and European Private Law' in Twigg-Flesner C (ed), *The Cambridge Companion to European Union Private Law* (CUP 2010)

Weatherill S, 'Consumer Policy' in de Búrca G and Craig P (eds), *Evolution of EU Law* (OUP 2011)

Weatherill S, 'Maximum versus Minimum Harmonization: Choosing between Unity and Diversity in the Search for the Soul of the Internal Market' in Shuibhne NN and Gormley LW (eds), *From Single Market to Economic Union: Essays in Memory of John A. Usher* (OUP 2012)

Weatherill S, 'The Consumer Rights Directive: How and why a quest for "coherence" has (largely) failed' (2012) 49(4) Common Market Law Review 1279

Weatherill S, *EU Consumer Law and Policy* (2nd edn, Edward Elgar Publishing 2013)

Weatherill S, 'Article 38 Consumer Protection' in Peers S and others (eds), *The EU Charter of Fundamental Rights: A Commentary* (Hart Publishing 2014)

Weatherill S, 'Empowerment is not the only fruit' in Leczykiewicz D and Weatherill S (eds), *The Images of the Consumer in EU Law: Legislation, Free Movement and Competition Law* (Hart Publishing 2016)

Weatherill S, *Contract Law of the Internal Market* (Intersentia 2016)
Weatherill S, *Law and Values in the European Union* (OUP 2016)
Weatherill S, *The Internal Market as a Legal Concept* (OUP 2017)
Weatherill S, 'The Challenge of Better Regulation' in van Schagen E and Weatherill S (eds), *Better Regulation in EU Contract Law: The Fitness Check and the New Deal for Consumers* (Hart Publishing 2019)
Weatherill S, 'The Court as a Jack-in-the-box: An Old Story in a New Context' in van Schagen E and Weatherill S (eds), *Better Regulation in EU Contract Law: The Fitness Check and the New Deal for Consumers* (Hart Publishing 2019)
Weatherill S, 'Is maximum harmonisation a myth? The story of Directive 2019/771 on contracts for the sale of goods' (2021) 16(2) Revue européenne de droit de la consommation 217
Weber F and Hodges C, 'The Netherlands' in Hodges C, Benöhr I, and Creutzfeldt-Banda N (eds), *Consumer ADR in Europe* (Hart Publishing 2012)
Webley L, 'Qualitative Approaches to Empirical Legal Research' in Cane P and Kritzer H (eds), *The Oxford Handbook of Empirical Legal Research* (OUP 2010)
Wendehorst C, '§ 312i Allgemeine Pflichten im elektronischen Geschäftsverkehr' in Säcker FJ and others (eds), *Münchener Kommentar zum Bürgerlichen Gesetzbuch* (8th edn, CH Beck 2019)
Wendland M, 'Vorbemerkung zu §§ 307-309' in Mäsch G and others (eds), *Staudinger BGB - Buch 2: Recht der Schuldverhältnisse: §§ 305-310; UKlaG (AGB-Recht 1 und Unterlassungsklagengesetz)* (18th edn, Sellier / de Gruyter 2019)
Whittaker S, 'The Language or Languages of Consumer Contracts' (2006) 8 Cambridge Yearbook of European Law 229
Whittaker S, 'Clauses abusives et garanties des consommateurs: la proposition de directive relative aux droits des consommateurs et la portée de l'"harmonisation complète"' (2009) Recueil Dalloz 1152
Whittaker S, 'Unfair Contract Terms and Consumer Guarantees: the Proposal for a Directive on Consumer Rights and the Significance of "Full Harmonisation"' (2009) 5(3) European Review of Contract Law 223
Whittaker S, 'Distinctive Features of the New Consumer Contract Law' (2017) 133 Law Quarterly Review 47
Whittaker S and Zimmermann R, 'Good faith in European contract law: surveying the legal landscape' in Zimmermann R and Whittaker S (eds), *Good Faith in European Contract Law* (CUP 2000)
Willett C, 'The Directive on Unfair Terms in Consumer Contracts and its implementation in the United Kingdom' (1997) 2 European Review of Private Law 223
Willett C, 'General Clauses and the Competing Ethics of European Consumer Law in the UK' (2012) 71(2) The Cambridge Law Journal 412
Willett C and Morgan-Taylor M, 'Recognising the limits of transparency in EU consumer law' in Devenney J (ed), *European Consumer Protection: Theory and Practice* (CUP 2012)
Wissink M, 'Nederland veroordeeld wegens onvolledige omzetting van de richtlijn oneerlijke bedingen: Noot bij HvJ EG 10 mei 2001, C-144-99, Commissie/Nederland' (2002) 16(4) Nederlands Tijdschrift voor Burgerlijk Recht 152
Witte PJ, *Inhaltskontrolle und deren Rechtsfolgen im System der Überprüfung allgemeiner Geschäftsbedingungen* (Dissertation at the Faculty of Law at the University of Münster 1983)
Wolf M, Horn N, and Lindacher W (eds), *AGB-Gesetz* (CH Beck 1984)

Wolters PTJ, 'Regels over de werking van de redelijkheid en billijkheid? Een analyse van de rechtspraak van de Hoge Raad' (2013) 8(9) Maandblad voor Vermogensrecht 249

World Trade Press, Incoterms 2010: A Comprehensive Guide to the INCOTERMS 2010 (World Trade Press 2010)

World Bank, 'The Worldwide Governance Indicators (WGI) project' (World Bank, 2023) http://info.worldbank.org/governance/wgi/#doc (accessed 23 April 2023)

Wrbka S, *European Consumer Access to Justice Revisited* (CUP 2015)

Wulf AJ, *Institutional Competition between Optional Codes in European Contract Law: A Theoretical and Empirical Analysis* (Springer Publishing 2014)

Wurmnest W, '§§ 307-309' in Krüger W (ed), *Münchner Kommentar zum Bürgerlichen Gesetzbuch Band 2: Schuldrecht Allgemeiner Teil 1 §§ 241-310* (8th edn, CH Beck 2019)

Wüstenberg D, 'Immer wieder Online-Impressum: Die Rechtsprechung seit der UGP-Richtlinie bis und die Rechtslage insbesondere ab Juni 2013' (2013) 9(11) Verbraucher und Recht 407

Xanthaki H, 'Improving the Quality of EU Legislation: Limits and Opportunities?' in Garben S and Govaere I (eds), *The EU Better Regulation Agenda: A Critical Assessment* (Hart Publishing 2018)

Zglinski J, *Europe's Passive Virtues: Deference to National Authorities in EU Free Movement Law* (OUP 2020)

Zimmermann R, *The New German Law of Obligations: Historical and Comparative Perspectives* (OUP 2005)

Zimmermann R and Whittaker S (eds), *Good Faith in European Contract Law* (CUP 2000)

Index

For the benefit of digital users, indexed terms that span two pages (e.g., 52–53) may, on occasion, appear on only one of those pages.

Tables are indicated by *t* following the page number

The manufacturer's authorised representative in the EU for product safety is Oxford University Press España S.A. of el Parque Empresarial San Fernando de Henares, Avenida de Castilla, 2 – 28830 Madrid (www.oup.es/en or product.safety@oup.com). OUP España S.A. also acts as importer into Spain of products made by the manufacturer.

www.ingramcontent.com/pod-product-compliance
Ingram Content Group UK Ltd.
Pitfield, Milton Keynes, MK11 3LW, UK
UKHW021818230926
475773UK00024B/80

9780198906384